P9-CFK-346

Narrative, Authority, and Law

Law, Meaning, and Violence

The scope of Law, Meaning, and Violence is defined by the wide-ranging scholarly debates signaled by each of the words in the title. Those debates have taken place among and between lawyers, anthropologists, political theorists, sociologists, and historians, as well as literary and cultural critics. This series is intended to recognize the importance of such ongoing conversations about law, meaning, and violence as well as to encourage and further them.

Series Editors:

Martha Minow, Harvard Law School
Michael Ryan, Northeastern University
Austin Sarat, Amherst College

Narrative, Violence, and the Law: The Essays of Robert Cover, edited by Martha Minow, Michael Ryan, and Austin Sarat

Narrative, Authority, and Law, by Robin West

Narrative, Authority, and Law

Robin West

Ann Arbor

THE UNIVERSITY OF MICHIGAN PRESS

Published in the United States of America by
The University of Michigan Press
Manufactured in the United States of America

1996 1995 1994 1993 4 3 2 1

Library of Congress Cataloging-in-Publication Data

West, Robin, 1954–
Narrative, authority, and law / Robin West.
p. cm. — (Law, meaning, and violence)
Includes bibliographical references and index.
ISBN 0-472-10365-2 (alk. paper)
1. Law—Philosophy. 2. Critical legal studies. 3. Law in literature. 4. Authority I. Title. II. Series.
K235.W47 1993
340'.1—dc20 93-29846
CIP

A CIP catalogue record for this book is available from the British Library.

Acknowledgments

Grateful acknowledgment is made to the following publishers and journals for permission to reprint previously published material.

The Harvard Law Review Association for "Authority, Autonomy and Choice: The Role of Consent in the Jurisprudence of Franz Kafka and Richard Posner," in 99 *Harvard Law Review* 384, copyright © 1985 by the Harvard Law Review Association; and for "Submission, Choice and Ethics: A Reply to Judge Posner," in 99 *Harvard Law Review* 1449, copyright © 1986 by the Harvard Law Review Association.

Mercer Law Review for "Economic Man and Literary Woman: One Contrast," 39 *Mercer Law Review* 867.

New York University Law Review for "Jurisprudence as Narrative: An Aesthetic Interpretation of Modern Legal Theory," 60 *New York University Law Review* 145. Copyright © 1985.

Tennessee Law Review Association for "Adjudication is Not Interpretation: Some Reservations about the Law-as-Literature Movement." This article originally appeared at 54 *Tennessee Law Review* 203 (1987) and this version is used by permission of the Tennessee Law Review Association, Inc.

Tulane Law Review for "Taking Preferences Seriously," 64 *Tulane Law Review* 659 (1989).

University of Michigan Press for "Disciplines, Politics, and Law," from *The Fate of Law,* edited by Austin Sarat and Thomas R. Kearns (Ann Arbor: University of Michigan Press, 1991). Copyright © 1991 by the University of Michigan.

Wisconsin Women's Law Journal for "The Difference in Women's

Hedonic Lives: A Phenomenological Critique of Feminist Legal Theory," 3 *Wisconsin Women's Law Journal* 81.

Every effort has been made to trace the ownership of all copyrighted material in this book and to obtain permission for its use.

Contents

Abbreviations ix

Introduction: Reclaiming Meaning 1

Part 1. Jurisprudence in Literature

Chapter 1. Authority, Autonomy, and Choice 27

Chapter 2. A Rejoinder to Judge Posner 79

Chapter 3. Adjudication Is Not Interpretation 89

Part 2. Legal Criticism and the Narrative Voice

Chapter 4. Women's Hedonic Lives 179

Chapter 5. Economic Man and Literary Woman: One Contrast 251

Chapter 6. Disciplines, Subjectivity, and Law 265

Chapter 7. Taking Preferences Seriously 299

Part 3. The Narrative Voice in Law and Jurisprudence

Chapter 8. Jurisprudence as Narrative: An Aesthetic Analysis of Modern Legal Theory 345

Chapter 9. Narrative, Responsibility, and Death 419

Abbreviations

AC Northrop Frye. *Anatomy of Criticism: Four Essays.* Princeton, N.J.: Princeton University Press, 1957.

AP Stanley Fish. "Anti-Professionalism." *Cardoza Law Review* 7 (1986): 645–77.

CS Franz Kafka. *The Complete Stories and Parables.* Ed. Nahum N. Glatzer. New York: Quality Paperback Books, 1983.

EA Richard A. Posner. *The Economic Analysis of Law.* 2d ed. Boston: Little, Brown, 1977.

EJ Richard A. Posner. *The Economics of Justice.* Cambridge: Harvard University Press, 1981.

ES Richard A. Posner. "The Ethical Significance of Free Choice: A Reply to Professor West." *Harvard Law Review* 99 (1986): 1431–48.

FO John Barth. *The Floating Opera.* Garden City, N.Y.: Doubleday, 1967.

OI Owen Fiss. "Objectivity and Interpretation." *Stanford Law Review* 34 (1982): 739–63.

PW *Pudd'nhead Wilson.* In Samuel Langhorn Clemens, *Pudd'nhead Wilson and Those Extraordinary Twins,* ed. Sidney E. Berger. New York: Norton, 1980.

T Franz Kafka. *The Trial.* Trans. Willa Muir and Edwin Muir. New York: Knopf, 1937.

TP Maria Marcus. *A Taste for Pain: On Masochism and Feminine Sexuality.* New York: St. Martin's, 1981.

WA Dusty Rhodes and Sandra McNeill, eds., *Women against Violence against Women.* London: Onlywomen Press, 1985.

Introduction: Reclaiming Meaning

It is a shared premise of many, perhaps most, American legal scholars that the authority of law in liberal societies—the law's power to influence our behavior and lives—consists not only of the obvious "powers of the sword" but also of the more subtle powers of the moralist as well. According to these scholars, law somehow communicates to the governed the message that the law's commands not only must be obeyed, but that they are also for the most part just, and that legal institutions and procedures—the courts, magistrates, legislators, and police and the rules under which they operate—are also in some fundamental sense morally unproblematic. The law's authority over our lives is thus doubly enhanced: we are inclined to obey the law's commands not only for fear of the sanction if we do otherwise, but also because we tend to find its precepts, institutions, and structures morally salutary. One straightforward consequence, as a number of scholars have argued,[1] is that any argument for civil disobedience on moral grounds faces tremendous psychological as well as political obstacles. We are inclined to obey the law and to resist moral appeals to disobey it not only because we wish to avoid its punitive powers, but also because we have come to view its precepts and procedures as just, and ourselves as accordingly bound by moral duty, as well as by prudence, to respect it.

Although not as widely noted or studied, it seems clear that one further, and perhaps more serious, consequence of the law's moral authority is that not just our assessment of the morality of law, but also the content of our moral beliefs themselves—the ordinary beliefs

1. See, e.g., Tom R. Tyler, *Why People Obey the Law* (New Haven: Yale University Press, 1990); Lynne N. Henderson, "Authoritarianism and the Rule of Law," *Indiana Law Journal* 66 (1991): 379–456.

of most citizens regarding what is right and wrong, just and unjust, or good and evil—may be heavily influenced by the particular legal system under which we live. And if that is right, then the dual nature of the authority of law constitutes not just an obstacle to morally grounded civil disobedience, but more generally, an obstacle to morally grounded legal *criticism.* For if the authority of law is not only political but moral as well—if law profoundly affects not only our behavior but also our moral beliefs—then it is hard to understand how fundamental moral criticism of law can hope to be effective. How could we possibly generate a moral point of view that is external to, independent of, or simply different from the point of view created by legalism, from which we can criticize law? The moral point of view that unproblematically guides criticism of the private conduct of a friend, neighbor, child, or politician may well turn out to be impotent in the face of the law, at least to whatever extent the law informs our moral sense of what we ought to strive for in the creation and administration of our legal institutions, as well as our prudential sense of how we ought behave, if we are to avoid its punitive sanction.

This political, conceptual, and psychological problem—how to criticize the law from a moral point of view, if the law itself so heavily determines so much of our moral sense—might be put in terms of spheres of influence over our moral consciousness: the perspective that informs the moral point of view that will be potent against the authority of law must stem from some part of our consciousness, or perhaps some aspect of our experience, that is more or less untouched by the moral authority of law itself. Yet, given the pervasiveness and permeation of the legal voice in our culture and in our hearts and minds, it is hard to imagine what or where that aspect of our consciousness might be. It is hard, then, to resist the conclusion that because of the degree to which law effects, tutors, and influences, if not entirely determines, our sense of morality, any attempt to criticize law on moral grounds is at best highly problematic and compromised and at worst incoherent or impossible. We might call this problem the "critical dilemma."

How should we respond to this critical dilemma? How should we criticize law from a moral point of view, given the influence of law itself over our moral beliefs? I will briefly argue in this introduction that the traditional methods of the humanities—writing, reading, and responding to narrative texts—constitute at least a partial answer to the critical dilemma. Indeed, one historically central function of humanistic study has always been to provide just such a basis for legal, as well as political and societal, self-criticism. The chapters in this book will examine, employ, and in places defend the various competing conceptions of what I will at times call "humanistic legal criticism": very generally, the use of the humanities as a method (or set of methods) of criticizing law's authority.

Before turning to that argument, however, let me first quickly review how the critical dilemma came to be identified in Anglo-American jurisprudence. It was first recognized in traditional jurisprudence in the late eighteenth and mid-nineteenth century by the English legal positivists. Jeremy Bentham and his utilitarian, positivist followers urged, in direct contrast to their "natural law" colleagues, that in order to facilitate legal criticism, legal critics and reformers should, as a conceptual or definitional act of will, separate law from morality. If we clearheadedly *define* legal authority as extensive only with its political authority—the authority over our actions that law wields by virtue of its use of force—then and only then can we criticize the use of legal power from a moral point of view. Twentieth-century legal positivists for the most part have held fast to this historically defining and still central tenet of legal positivism. Thus, we should rigorously "separate law and morality"[2] in our conceptual scheme of things; we should "wash the law in cynical acid,"[3] so as to rid ourselves of the illusions of moral legitimacy that it seeks to claim for itself; we should force ourselves to see that the legality of a command is one thing, but the rightness or wrongness of that command—its justice or injustice—quite another thing entirely.[4] Through a sheer act of conceptual will, if need be, the positivists insist, we should define and then understand law as that which rests on political authority; we should define law, in the words of John Austin, as the "command of the sovereign" and leave to conscience the demands and commands of morality. To see law solely and exclusively

2. H. L. A. Hart, "Positivism and the Separation of Law and Morals," *Harvard Law Review* 71 (1958): 593–629.

3. Oliver Wendell Holmes, "The Path of the Law," *Harvard Law Review* 10 (1897): 457–78.

4. Jeremy Bentham, *A Comment on the Commentaries: A Criticism of William Blackstone's Commentaries on the Law of England* (Oxford: Clarendon, 1928); David Kairys, ed. *The Politics of Law: A Progressive Critique*, rev. ed. (New York: Pantheon Books, 1990).

as expressive of political power, as a part of that which *is* rather than of that which ought to be, is simply the first step toward a clearer appreciation of the degree to which law fails to live up to our moral ideal. The conceptual separation of law and morality, positivists argue, is hence the first and necessary step toward both legal criticism and morally progressive legal reform.

Legal positivism, however, has proven to be only a limited response to the critical dilemma, as has been the burden of the critical legal studies movement of the last two decades to show. The reason is simple enough. Even if we analytically separate law from morality, and even if we do so for the express purpose of facilitating the moral criticism of law, our shared moral beliefs—the moral standards, beliefs, or norms we use as the baseline for legal criticism—may nevertheless be heavily influenced by legal authority. Legal positivism, for the most part, simply ignores this problem, and as a result the criticism of law that positivism facilitates is fairly tepid. The separation of law and morality may facilitate criticism of existing law against criteria established by our existing moral beliefs, but it will not facilitate—indeed it does not even aim to facilitate—criticism of the content of the moral beliefs against which these particular legal commands are measured. If those beliefs are themselves influenced by the deepest and hence least visible authoritative mandates of the legal system itself, then a tremendously influential and important aspect of legalism is immunized against moral critique. The positivist separation of law and morality, in other words, does not address the way in which we might criticize the moral beliefs against which law is to be judged or criticized. If it is true that the moral norms we use to judge law are themselves at least in part a product of law, then the moral justice of legal authority remains obscured, rather than unmasked, by the positivist's analytically sensible but counterfactual insistence on the separation of law and morality.

The second major philosophical breakthrough in understanding the nature of the critical dilemma came from the critical legal studies movement, and particularly some of the early theoretical efforts (mid-1970s to 1980s) of that movement's founders. Indeed what may prove to be the most significant accomplishment of that period of American jurisprudential thought was the insistence of the early critical legal scholars that we problematize what I am here calling the law's moral, as opposed to simply its political, authority. The critics accepted and built on the positivist's definitional prescription that we separate law and morality so as to facilitate the moral criticism of law. But they then went well beyond traditional positivism by insisting that the moral norms thereby separated *also* be subjected to radical critique, and that they be so subjected because they too, no less than statutes and cases, are at least to some extent a product of legal hierarchy. Our moral beliefs and intuitions must themselves be challenged and not just separated if we are to subject law to meaningful critique. They cannot unproblematically serve as the standards against which we judge extant law, for they are themselves a product of it.

The critics have put forth this challenge in a number of ways, but their clearest statement of the problem is borrowed from Gramscian legitimation theory.[5] Following Gramsci, the critics urge that the authority of the legal system extends well beyond its power to influence our behavior through the threat of force, its capacity to imprison, fine, execute, and otherwise deter undesirable conduct. The critics argue that like other aspects of dominant culture, such as television or advertising, the legal system also—through its symbols, language, arguments, and general control over the means of normative legal discourse—creates in the citizenry what the critics sometimes call "clusters of beliefs"[6] in the overriding legitimacy of the social structures of empowerment and disempowerment that constitute the larger society of which the legal system is only a part. One part of those clusters of beliefs is the moral perspective, or moral point of view, from which particular laws are criticized or celebrated. For example, while we may feel free to criticize a particular legal rule as inefficient, or a proposed bill as nonrepresentative of the public will, or a criminal statute as overintrusive into our privacy, we find it much harder to criticize our moral commitment to efficiency, or representation, or privacy against which these laws are evaluated. Our convictions that law should be efficient, or representative, or respectful of privacy are such a deep part of our social psyche that they feel natural, or inevitable, or necessary, or simply beyond serious criticism.[7] The result is that

5. See generally, Kairys, *Politics of Law*.

6. Robert W. Gordon, "New Developments in Legal Theory," in Kairys, *Politics of Law*, 413.

7. See Roberto Mangabeira Unger, *False Necessity: Anti-Necessitarian Social Theory in the Service of Radical Democracy* (New York: Cambridge University Press, 1987).

the vast bulk of the particular rules and the processes of the extant system that govern our behavior are seen as morally legitimate—as in accord with our moral beliefs. Meaningful criticism of law against truly independent moral standards is thereby frustrated.

The critical legal studies movement has succeeded magnificently in first identifying and then describing this process of legitimation, both as a general phenomenon and in particular areas of law, legal culture, and legal education. The critical scholars have shown, in a number of ways, how our capacity for moral criticism of law and legal culture is blunted by the degree to which our moral beliefs are themselves a product of that legal culture, and hence how the legal system tends to legitimate itself at very fundamental levels, even in the minds of its critics and in the eyes of those who are most harmed by its shortcomings. But it has become increasingly clear over the last few years that the critics, like the legal positivists before them, have reached a conceptual dead end. The movement as a whole has offered very little to explain how we might criticize the law's moral authority in light of the problem of legitimation they have successfully uncovered. Thus, while they have painstakingly and on occasion brilliantly uncovered the basis in extant political, social, and legal hierarchies for many of the common moral intuitions with which we criticize law, they have not articulated (nor for the most part have they attempted to articulate) a credible basis for the moral criticism of law that would be other than complicit in the legitimation of the law's fundamental authority. They have not shown how to develop a moral sensibility truly independent of the legal structure itself and capable of rendering criticism of extant law.

The problem the critics uncovered, then, remains: How might we develop a moral sensibility with which to criticize law that is itself independent of the influence of law? As noted above, the short answer to the question is that we should employ a method of criticism that is both naturalist and humanist: we should criticize not only law, this book will argue, but also the commonly shared moral beliefs with which we typically criticize law (partly themselves a product of law), by reference to some set of criteria culled from a description of our shared human nature; we should derive that description of our nature, in turn, from what is loosely called the humanities: the careful, systematic study of the narratives and critiques of narratives that we tell each other about the substance of our lives. Thus, we might conceivably criticize not only law but also our unreflective moral sense of what law should be—that it should be efficient, participatory, dialogic, punitive, or whatever—by asking whether those goals and the laws we enact that reflect them well serve our best understanding of our true human needs, our true human aspirations, or our true social and individual potential, as gleaned from the stories we tell about ourselves and each other. This mode of naturalist and teleological criticism, grounded loosely in Aristotelean philosophy and humanistic inquiry, if rigorously and objectively pursued, might yield moral criteria that would be independent of the authority, including the moral authority, of the legal system that is the object of criticism. Naturalist and humanist legal criticism—criticism of our ideals, including our legal ideals by reference to our shared human nature—might then constitute a partial resolution of the critical dilemma, or so this book will argue.

More specifically, this book defends both substantive and methodological claims. The unifying substantive thesis is that, contrary to the skeptical claims of both contemporary liberals and their postmodern critics, we can and should rely on universal descriptions of human nature as a grounds for criticism of law, as well as for social and cultural criticism. The methodological claim is that the traditional and not-so-traditional critical methods of the humanities, including the reading and interpretation of literature, the telling and hearing of stories, and the development of a capacity for empathizing with the experiences of others, might constitute one means of pursuing a rich understanding of human nature and, therefore, a partial means of developing criticism of law from a genuine moral perspective. Thus, the human capacities to which study of the humanities gives rise might constitute a set of moral capacities, and hence a sphere of consciousness, sufficiently removed from the influence of law to serve as a vehicle for moral criticism of it.[8] Correspondingly, the knowledge gained from that sphere of consciousness—a knowledge consisting of tentative conceptions of our nature, our needs and

8. The most persuasive argument for this position is put forward by the liberal humanist James Boyd White, *Justice as Translation: An Essay in Cultural and Legal Criticism* (Chicago: University of Chicago Press, 1990). For a quite different argument but for much the same position, see Richard Delgado, "Storytelling for Oppositionists and Others: A Plea for Narrative," *Michigan Law Review* 87 (1989): 2411–41. For an early argument to this effect from a moral conservative, see John Gardner, *On Moral Fiction* (New York: Basic Books, 1978).

aspirations, based in turn on particular narratives of experiences—might prove sufficiently independent of the moral beliefs, to say nothing of the laws themselves, inculcated by legalism to constitute a basis for the formation of legal ideals against which we might criticize existing law. My goal is not to prove any of these propositions. Rather, I hope to show by example only that they are plausible, and that they suggest the viability of a larger project—the criticism of law, based on an understanding of human nature that is in turn drawn, very generally, from the methods of the humanities. My aim is simply to suggest the viability of this project, and to put forward the hope that others might wish to pursue it.

The methods of the humanities might facilitate moral criticism of law in roughly three ways, which correspond with the three major divisions of this book. First, as I will try to demonstrate in the chapters in part 1, a great deal of classical or canonical narrative literature provides, through plots, characterizations, and the conceptions of human nature on which those characterizations rest, telling criticisms of the moral beliefs, or, to use the critical phrase, the belief clusters, held by dominant sectors of society, and that in some way legitimate and celebrate legalism, thus blocking its meaningful critique. Much of this literature remains largely untapped for its critical insights into the nature of law, and the mechanics of its legitimation. In part 1, I therefore identify and criticize a range of such sets of beliefs, and then use the depictions of human nature and of social life conveyed in literary works as a basis for criticizing those arguments.

Thus, the first couple of essays in this volume examine the moral belief, explicitly relied upon by the law-and-economics movement, but more generally a mainstay of liberal legal thought, that particular laws and legal systems, as well as the transactions they facilitate, are morally just so long as they are consensual: so long as they rest on either the actual or implied consent of those persons they affect. Because we only consent to changes in the world that will improve our welfare, the argument goes, legal rules, regimes, or transactions that are fully consensual must accordingly improve our well-being and are therefore morally just. Using Kafka's short stories and novellas, I argue that this argument ignores the extremely problematic moral nature of even fully voluntary acts of consent and hence fails to establish the moral justice of consensual legal regimes, because it ignores the felt, subjective experience of the act of consent itself. If experience is any guide, then we often consent to transactions, punishments, and legal regimes out of a submissive or masochistic urge to obey, rather than out of an egoistic and rationalist urge to improve our own welfare. If so, then even fully consensual transactions, laws, or regimes will not necessarily improve our welfare, or even our felt and exercised autonomy. It was Franz Kafka's modernist genius to explore the felt reality of that "freedom to submit," a felt reality that the liberal and economic argument for the morality of consensual legal regimes ignores. Further, it is that felt reality which the liberal legalist *must* ignore if the argument for the justice of consensual regimes is to be sustained. Conversely, acknowledging the perversity, or at least the complexity, of our urge to "consent" to authoritatively profferred transactions and bargains severely undercuts the argument for the justice of liberal legalism grounded in the ethics of consent. Kafka's stories, read as a commentary on our nature, virtually forces that acknowledgment.

The third chapter in part 1 identifies and criticizes a second argument commonly used to bolster the law's moral authority and the belief clusters about human nature on which it rests: that the law is just because its precepts and procedures reflect the moral commitments and ideals of the community. Again, I use the relatively concrete depictions of human experience conveyed in works of literature, Mark Twain's *Pudd'nHead Wilson* and John Barth's *The Floating Opera,* to examine the largely unargued and universalist assumptions about human nature on which this argument rests.

It is primarily these two arguments that comprise the major tenets of modern law's moral authority in liberal, democratic societies, and it is very largely these two arguments that limit challenges to the justice of particular legal rules or fundamental legal institutions. The belief that we "can't complain" if we've consented to some contractual arrangement, for example, goes a long way toward immunizing the laws of contract and property, and the perpetuation of hierarchies of wealth that those laws facilitate, from fundamental criticism. The belief that law is just, or as just as can be reasonably be expected, so long as it mirrors the dominant moral beliefs of the community similarly truncates criticism of criminal and constitutional law. The chapters in the first part of this book use descriptions of human nature and of social life culled from great works of literature to criticize those beliefs, and hence the legal institutions and regimes that those beliefs insulate against criticism.

In part 2, I explore the role of the narrative voice—telling, listening to, and responding to stories—in moral argument, and therefore in legal criticism and its reform. The chapters in this part all argue in different ways and in different contexts that the empathic knowledge of others that narrative practices facilitate may provide a point of shared reference for moral criticism and growth, including moral criticism of law and its progressive reform. Although narrativity can, and perhaps should, be a part of any sort of moral argument I will argue in part 2 the more limited point that it is a necessary part of moral claims for change made on behalf of those who have traditionally been excluded from the processes of law.[9] If our moral convictions are grounded in conceptions of our shared nature that are in turn informed by our own experiences and the experiences of others, and if some experiences are routinely silenced by empowered groups and our moral convictions consequently skewed, then the imbalance must be corrected by the telling in narrative form of the heretofore silenced experiences. The essays in the second part therefore explore the relevance of storytelling (and story listening) to the larger project of changing law so as to make a more just and humane social world for liberalism's traditional outsiders: women, poor people, and racial, sexual, or ethnic minorities. What has now come to be called narrative jurisprudence—a method uncoincidentally identified with feminist legal theory and critical race theory (those being the two movements consciously concerned with the needs of outsiders)—is described and defended in these chapters as the use of narrative to affect our moral beliefs, including the beliefs with which we criticize or celebrate law.

Finally, the last section of the book explores the role of literature and narrativity in traditional jurisprudence and in law itself. Our inclination to variously celebrate or criticize the values intrinsic in law and legalism is rooted not only in our differing analyses and experience of law, but also in our different imaginings for it. These imaginings are perhaps best captured in the stories we tell about it within conventional jurisprudential and legal writing. Thus, reading

9. For a general analysis of the narrative jurisprudence generated by outsiders, see Kathryn Abrams, "Hearing the Call of Stories," *California Law Review* 79 (1991): 971–1054.

the narrative ministories told in conventional jurisprudence and legal opinions *as literature*—as aesthetic objects—no less than reading literature as legal criticism, might enrich our sense of who we are and what might be our relationship to the law and legal system that we make and that makes us. That enriched sense may in turn improve our understanding of the law we have, and hence our understanding of what we must do to bring it in line with the ideal law we envision.

To summarize, the humanistic approach to legal criticism this book seeks to propound rests on three claims: that moral criticism of law must be grounded in conceptions of human nature and that literature can be and should be used as a basis for formulating such a conception; that the narrative voice can convey the subjective feel of experiences in a way that triggers understanding of others and an empathic response to their plight, thereby changing our moral beliefs and our moral assessment of law; and that the stories told within jurisprudential and legal argument can be read as literature, and as therefore rooted in our dreams and nightmares regarding the role of authority in our lives, as well as in our analytic assessments of law's legitimacy.

This humanistic approach to law and legal criticism is by no means new and the claims for the humanities on which it rests are not new claims. Nor are they idiosyncratic. On the contrary, they have been voiced by a growing number of legal scholars over the last few years (although often for very different reasons and in different ways) and are in various ways associated with the developing law-and-humanities or law-and-literature movement presently gaining momentum and adherents in legal academia. And, perhaps most tellingly, they have already attracted a fair amount of criticism. In the remainder of this introduction I will address four such criticisms, although I expand upon this discussion in a number of the chapters that follow.

The first criticism comes from the legal academic Right, and has been put forward with tremendous energy and at great length by Richard Posner in his book *Law and Literature: A Misunderstood Connection.*[10] Posner argues that works among the canon of great literature that seem to be in some sense about law are rarely if ever *critical* of law in any deep or important sense. Rather, great literature

10. Richard A. Posner, *Law and Literature: A Misunderstood Relation* (Cambridge: Harvard University Press, 1988).

that is truly about law is almost invariably *celebratory*, rather than critical, of legal authority. Literature that appears on its face to be critical of law is simply using law metaphorically as a symbol for something toward which the work truly is critical (such as the authority of the church, of God, of fathers), or, where the literature really is critical toward law itself, the literature is just not very good. Therefore, literature should never be used to mount criticism of law or of legal institutions. Such use is invariably a bald (and banal) misappropriation of high literature for base political ends. The law-and-literature movement, accordingly, is simply engaged in misguided political criticism. The literature is a smokescreen.

There is no short answer to such an argument; an adequate response requires a survey of the literature.[11] It might be noted, however, that Posner's argument on its face is very peculiar: there simply is no good prima facie reason for thinking that of all the aspects of social life explored in great literature, law would either be regarded as too uninteresting or too unproblematic for literary exploration. In the face of the extraordinary amount of canonical literature that is both about law and at least appears to be critical of it, from Sophocles' *Antigone* to Shakespeare's *Measure for Measure*, Melville's *Billy Budd, Sailor,* and Twain's *Pudd'n head Wilson*, to name just a few of hundreds, quite the contrary is almost noncontrovertible: that there is a tremendous amount of legal criticism in the traditional literary canon, to say nothing of the nontraditional, which is for the most part still untapped for its critical jurisprudential insights. The chapters in this book that center on interpretations of literature are collected in part in the hope that they will prompt others to further that larger critical project.

The remaining objections to a humanist approach to legal criticism come from the critical legal studies movement itself, or, more generally, the contemporary legal academic Left. The first such objection unintentionally echoes Posner. According to this objection, what is regarded as great literature in this culture, as well as the depictions

11. For critical reviews that argue as much, see Richard H. Weisberg, "Entering with a Vengeance: Posner on Law and Literature," *Stanford Law Review* 41 (1989): 1597–1626; and Robin West, "Law, Literature and the Celebration of Authority," *Northwestern Law Review* 83 (1989): 977–1011. For a more general criticism of Posner's style of reading, see James Boyd White, "What Can a Lawyer Learn from Literature?" *Harvard Law Review* 102 (1989): 2014–47.

of experience and claims about human nature implied or explicated within it, is invariably determined by a set of self-serving political imperatives that preserve social and cultural hierarchies. Furthermore, those imperatives are not substantially different from those that preserve legal hierarchies and dictate the content of our legal and moral consciousness. Canonical literature, therefore, cannot possibly serve as a basis for criticism of canonical law, because inclusion in either canon is determined by the same political hierarchies and interests that ought to constitute the object of critique.[12]

There are two different meanings of this commonly voiced complaint, one of which has considerable merit. The other, however, does not. If the point of the objection is that we simply should not read Sophocles, Aeschylus, Melville, Shakespeare, Kafka, or Twain for their critical commentaries on the moral authority of law because by virtue of the alignment of those authors with the economically, sexually, or racially dominant societal sectors they could not possibly be making such commentaries, the objection is at heart no different from Posner's and spurious for the same reason: the literature simply belies it. A tremendous amount of canonical literature is highly critical of law, and of the arguments typically put forward to support its moral authority. What is true, though, is that the experiences of law had by this society's traditional outsiders are in fact not well represented in either the literary or the legal canon. It is also true, then, that a focus solely on canonical literature will produce a skewed, even if critical, portrayal of law.[13] For example, (and as I have argued at length elsewhere),[14] although Mark Twain's *Huckleberry Finn* unquestionably puts forward a scathing critique of the institution of slavery and slave law, it does not well communicate either the consciousness or the experiences of slaves, escaped slaves, or free blacks. By contrast, the importance of Toni Morrison's modern novel *Beloved* is in part that it does just that. It does not, however, follow that the greatness of *Huckleberry Finn* is diminished or that we should not read it for its critical insights on the institution of slavery. What does

12. A recent article putting forward this complaint in the legal literature alone is Carolyn Heilbrun and Judith Resnick, "Convergences: Law, Literature and Feminism," *Yale Law Journal* 99 (1990): 1913–56.

13. See Susan Mann, "The Universe and the Library: A Critique of James Boyd White as Writer and Reader," *Stanford Law Review* 41 (1989): 959–1020.

14. Robin West, "Communities, Text, and Law: Reflections of the Law and Literature Movement," *Yale Journal of Law and Humanities* 1 (1988): 129–56.

follow is, simply, that we should also read *Beloved*. A complete and critical understanding of the effect of slavery and slave law requires careful attention to the narratives of, by, and about those outsiders who were the "objects" of slave law and neither the producers nor the intended beneficiaries of either the celebratory texts that legitimated the system or the canonical critical texts that sought to undermine it.

The second objection from the legal academic Left against humanistic legal criticism is that it naively assumes a determinable meaning of both literary and legal texts and therefore ignores the most salient lesson that has emerged from the interdisciplinary law-and-literature movement to date: that texts of any nature—legal, literary or cultural—have no determinable meaning. The meaning they *seem* to have, the objection proceeds, is a function neither of author's intent nor of the text itself, but rather of some set of political, social, or cultural preconceptions of the interpretive community in which the reader is situated.[15] The degree of determinacy or indeterminacy of a text's apparent meaning is thus a function of the stability of those cultural, social, or political preconceptions. A literary text, then, does not itself mean anything about the nature of law, either critical or celebratory, because *it* does not mean anything at all, nor does the legal text that is its purported object of criticism. The meaning of both the literary and legal text is entirely a function of the reader's inclusion and participation in what *is* generative of meaning: communities of interpretation, which in turn competitively vie to generate socially constructed world conceptions, which themselves, in turn, limit and define the culture's received texts.

Here as well, there is one way in which this objection can be construed that seems both true and important but that by no means undercuts the necessity of humanistic criticism: there is no question but that our understanding of the meaning of *Huckleberry Finn*, or of the equal protection clause of the Fourteenth Amendment of the United States Constitution, or of a contract for the sale of a residential home, is heavily influenced by the mores, preconceptions, prejudices, shared common sense, and limited understanding of our cultural time

15. See generally Stanley Fish, *Is There a Text in this Class?: The Authority of Interpretive Communities* (Cambridge: Harvard University Press, 1980); and *Doing What Comes Naturally: Change, Rhetoric, and the Practice of Theory in Literary and Legal Studies* (Durham, N.C.: Duke University Press, 1989).

and place. This is true and important but hardly undercuts the relevance of literature to meaningful legal critique. It is only if the objection is taken to assert the total dependence of a text's meaning on the shared worldview and interests of the interpretive community, that the objection, if valid, undercuts the humanistic critical project. For if this is an accurate portrayal of the nature of reading, of meaning, and of texts, then there is simply no point in reading literature for its critical commentary on law, or for its critical commentary on anything else: what we find in both the literary and legal text is entirely a function of who we already are, influenced, or constituted, as we may be, by the very texts we seek to criticize. We are never doing anything when interpreting texts but the narcissistic act of further elucidating our own social world, and even our own place, and specifically our own hierarchic and political place, within it. We may, if we wish, criticize law from the perspective of that place, but there is no reason to employ literature to do so, in fact, to do so is redundant. Because the meaning of a literary text is a function of our own social constitution and the political power we possess by virtue of it, so the moral and critical authority of literature is simply a mirror of our own, unadorned by arguments from literature. We may as well voice our complaints directly, and spend the saved energy doing the political organizing necessary to garner the power that would make those complaints compelling.

Although I take up the merits of this reader-response understanding of interpretation in chapter 3, it is worth noting here that the view of texts on which that understanding rests—what is generally called the indeterminacy thesis—perversely hinders rather than facilitates meaningful criticism of law. Simply put, a legal text of indeterminate meaning is neither sufficiently stable nor consequential to be a meaningful object of criticism. If the legal text has no meaning, neither it nor its authors can be blamed or praised for the good or ill they do. Radical indeterminacy, in other words, curiously insulates *law itself* from criticism: if the indeterminacy thesis is right, then the *law* is never the problem; the problem is rather the community that dictates or constructs (in some fashion) its meaning and its claim to have meaning. The law *means* what we read it as *meaning*, and therefore *is* what we read it as *being*, where "we" are the culturally, socially, or legally dominant forces in some empowered interpretive community. Whatever might be the moral status of those dominant interpretive communities, the law itself—the legal text—emerges as utterly innocent because utterly impotent. Therefore, while purportedly exposing the societal forces in the interpreter's community that are in some way responsible for the construction of the text's meaning, and hence exposing those forces to criticism, the indeterminacy thesis when applied to law has the bizarre consequence of insulating the legal text—as well as the text's author or authors—from meaningful moral and critical attack.

Furthermore, the indeterminacy thesis undercuts not only the possibility and need for legal criticism, but it also undercuts the possibility of cultural or social criticism of any sort. For if our critical perspective on our social worlds, no less than our interpretive understanding of our cultural texts, is a function of the interpretive communities of which we are a part and of our hierarchical place within them, then criticism is itself grounded in nothing but the disguised interests of the relatively empowered social critic. While criticism moved solely by interest, rather than perception or moral vision, may facilitate reform or change, there is no reason to think that the change thereby facilitated will be change *for the better*. It will only be change so as to accommodate a different, but now dominant, set of interests. And, those interests (like legal texts) are perversely insulated by the indeterminancy thesis from criticism—again, interests are what *generate* criticism, they cannot themselves be criticized. But this insulation of our felt interests against critique defeats the possibility of cultural criticism. Surely, our felt and purported interests must be the *subject*, and not the vehicle, of social criticism, if social criticism is to be at all meaningful, for the simple reason that those interests, more than any aspect of our being, are most directly influenced by societal structures and hierarchies. The related claims that textual interpretation, as well as legal criticism, reflect and rest on the interests, needs, preconceptions, or worldviews of whatever part of the interpretive community has achieved some requisite level of dominance only superficially refocuses attention on those hierarchical structures that determine who is dominant and who is not. It has the ultimate effect, both logically and in practice, of either acquiescing in or indeed exalting the extant structures that determine the felt interests of the dominant critic. The indeterminacy thesis, accordingly, ultimately has the regressive effect of reiterating the empowered position of the already relatively powerful.

The third objection to humanistic criticism from the legal Left draws on contemporary postmodern skepticism regarding human nature: humanistic legal criticism, the argument proceeds, naively and falsely posits an objective and objectively ascertainable view of human nature when no such nature exists. In fact, not just the conceptions of human nature propounded by particular humanist philosophers, but indeed *any* conception of human nature, whether drawn from the humanities, social science, philosophy, literature, or any other conceivable source, is nothing but the unjustified prioritization of one conception and one set of interests—typically the nature and hence the interests of the critic propounding it—over others.[16] Such conceptions of our nature, according to this postmodern view, stand on precisely the same footing as our untutored moral sense or moral intuitions—they too are the product of power, politics, and hierarchies of domination. They have no greater claim to independence from power and from the legal norms that are undebatably the product of power than the unreflective moral beliefs of the citizenry. Just as our untutored moral sense is a product, in large part, of the power of legalism, so the conceptions of our nature on which our more reflective critical traditions depend—including traditional Marxist criticism—are also products of hierarchic, political powers. Consequently, there simply is no principled, objective perspective from which the will of the powerful might be brought under scrutiny, much less under reasoned critique. The humanist project of reasoned moral criticism by reference to some universal conception of our nature, no less than the commonsensical positivist project of moral criticism of law by reference to the society's shared moral beliefs, is compromised by the fact that the standard of criticism grounded in a conception of human nature is itself as much a product of power as the positive law being criticized. All such humanist criticism, whatever it purports to be, is simply a reflection of the interests and perspectives of the particular critic, and more specifically of the subcommunity, defined by power and interest, to which the critic belongs.[17]

16. For a passionate explication of this position, and a defense of the relativism it implies, see Barbara Herrnstein-Smith, *Contingencies of Value: Alternative Perspectives for Critical Theory* (Cambridge: Harvard University Press, 1988). For a critical review, see Robin West, "Contingency, Objectivity and Law," *Yale Law Journal* 99 (1990): 1473–1502.

17. See Herrnstein-Smith, *Contingencies of Value*.

I will examine the merits of this fashionable postmodern skepticism at various points in the text. What I want to stress here is that whatever its merits, the infusion of a postmodern skepticism regarding universal accounts of our nature has led to a debilitating impasse in critical legal thought. While the critics can effectively describe how our moral and critical capacities have been blunted, they cannot, given their recent embrace of postmodern premises, engage in direct moral criticism itself. For, according to those premises, the insights, moral beliefs, and aspirations of those who purport to criticize law, are determined by their interests, and their interests are determined in turn by the political needs and ambitions of the communities and subcommunities, generally defined by race, gender, class, ethnicity, or nationality, from which they come. Those interests and needs, unquestionably themselves partly created by law, cannot themselves be subjected to criticism without inviting an endless regress. As a result, an important dimension of legalism is effectively immunized against critique—that dimension of legalism which constructs the interests that in turn constitute the often disguised foundation of the moral beliefs with which we claim to criticize law. The bottom line is simply that any purported legal criticism is nothing but disguised politics, as is law itself: criticism, no less than law, cannot possibly attain the disinterested universalism or objectivity toward which criticism aspires.

Ironically, this critical impasse implied by postmodern skepticism ought to feel familiar: it almost eerily echoes a similar impasse faced by an earlier generation of liberal legal theorists. Mainstream liberal legal theorists, as the critical scholars themselves have repeatedly argued, have also embraced a relativist account of moral truth and a skeptical account of human nature that immunizes the deeper reaches of legalism from critique: the moral preferences of the individual, according to the liberal legalist, constitute the baseline against which law must be judged, just as the interests of subcommunities do so for the postmodern critic. And, just as the legal structures that determine interests are insulated against postmodern criticism by the logic of postmodernism, so the legal structures that determine individual moral preferences are insulated against liberal criticism by the logic of liberalism. For both groups, then, embrace of a relativist account of truth and a skeptical account of human nature ultimately forestalls meaningful legal criticism: for the postmodernist, all the critic is doing when she advances criticism of law based on a stated view of human nature is advancing the not very well disguised interests of the groups of which she is a member, just as, for the liberal, all the critic is doing when voicing moral criticism of law is expressing her own individual preferences. For both the liberal and the postmodern critic, there is really *nothing but* these individual preferences, group interests, and resulting political strategies. For both groups, genuine, non-self-interested moral criticism is impossible, and ultimately for the same reason: both the liberal and the postmodern critic, while claiming to eschew reliance on accounts of our nature, have implicitly embraced an egoistic account of human nature according to which we are incapable of genuine sympathy for and empathic knowledge or concern for others, and hence incapable of generating universal accounts of our nature that could sustain both social understanding and moral judgment.

The last and perhaps most serious objection to humanistic criticism from the legal academic Left goes not to the use of literature and literary interpretations as a means of articulating legal criticism, but rather to the use of the narrative voice as a way to communicate experience, to touch a sympathetic chord in the listener, and to thereby expand the listener's moral sensibility. The objection to this practice, which has recently come to be called "narrative jurisprudence," is that just as the use of literature for critical purposes rests on a naive conception of textual meaning, so the use of narrativity for reconstruction and reform rests on a naive conception of the nature of experience and, ultimately, of the nature of the experiencing self.[18] The argument is that our understanding of our own experience, to say nothing of the experiences of others, like our interpretations of literature and our critical conceptions of our social world, is itself socially constructed: we do not have a pure experience of pain, pleasure, injury, or insult that is not itself constituted by the construction of that experience placed upon it by the society, or at least those subcommunities within it from which we come. Indeed, the sense of self-possession on which the use of narrativity rests—that my experience is my own, that it ought count as my own, that for reasons of both compassion and justice it should matter whether the

18. I address this postmodern objection at greater length in Robin West, "Feminism, Critical Social Theory, and Law," *University of Chicago Legal Forum* 1989 (1989): 59–97.

quality of that experience is good or bad—is socially constructed: its felt force depends not on the authenticity of the experience, or the degree of self-delusion or enlightenment of the subject, but rather on a liberal conception of the self. This liberal conception denies the force of community in the construction of a conception that emanates from a particular time and place and accordingly reflects the interests of the empowered sectors of the interpretive communities of that time and place. Self-understanding does not reflect the purely subjective experience of the self, for there simply is no such experiencing thing.

The denial of the meaningfulness of subjective experience, like the denial of the possibility of genuine critique or textual meaning, although typically put forward by theorists at least nominally committed to a progressive political agenda, also undercuts the coherence of social and legal criticism, and hence the possibility of moral progress. Indeed, it was a fundamental assumption of pre-postmodern progressive political thought (and action) that a world in which we lead good lives, determined by the quality of our very subjective experience, is a morally better world than one in which we are miserable. One would think that progressive theorists and activists would claim that a world in which we are subjectively and intersubjectively enriched by the pleasures of safe intimacy, education, and culture; challenged and engaged by meaningful and compensated work; nurtured by caring, compassionate community; and mutually respected through the lens of a strong and autonomous regard for individuality and individual differences, is a *good* world; and claim that one in which our experience of intimacy is threatened by violence and the fear of violence; in which education and culture is available only to a few; in which work is repetitive, alienating, unappreciated, nonexistent, or undercompensated; in which each member of the community is uninterested in the fates of others; and in which individuality is routinely denied, squelched, or flattened is not a good world. And surely, if the quality of our lives, on these measures or any others, is the measure of our moral progress, then our subjective experiences must be not just relevant but central to our critical appraisal of the degree to which we have created a society—through law and otherwise—that respects and nurtures those lives. If we want to create a better world, we must be able to communicate the quality of those lives and to empathically respond to others who attempt to do so. We must be able to say, to quote my two-year-old, "Don't do that—you're hurting me," and we must be able to hear that utterance as an ethical mandate to change course.

The coherence of just such a statement and mandate is denied by the postmodern attack on the subjective self. If we do not hear in accounts of suffering a mandate to change course but rather determine that the sufferer is hurting because of arbitrary constructions of his experience imposed by the dominant sectors of society, then we face an endless regression of socially constructed criticism: the experience is felt to be painful not because of any actual experience of the subjective self, but because of social constructs themselves driven by interests, criticism of which can again only be grounded in experiences of the world felt to be injurious or not because of the interests that dictate the social constructs that determine the quality of the experience—and so on. The experience of pain itself, no less than its narrative expression, is flattened and becomes, rather than a mandate for change, simply another manifestation of various constellations of interests: an essentially arbitrary side effect of the empowered interests that dictate the terms by which we experience the world. The result is that moral progress, like interpretation and like cultural criticism quite generally, becomes either meaningless, complicitous, or arbitrary.

There is one final reason to be suspicious of the cluster of quintessentially postmodern claims that our subjective experience and hence understanding of the world is socially constructed, that the experiencing self is itself a construct only of modern liberal society, that claims of authenticity and inauthenticity are disingenuous or meaningless, and that criticism of that which uncontestably *is* societally constructed, such as law, by reference to that which is subjective and experiential is simply impossible because of the lack of non-socially constructed experience. The denial of the self, of subjectivity, of authenticity, and of experience central to postmodernism sounds alarmingly like the *destruction* of self, subjectivity, and authenticity so central to the experience of oppression, domination, terror, and torture.[19] The destruction of the self's authenticity, the denial of subjectivity, the dismissal of experience, and the reduction of the self to a vessel for the interests and ends of others is a familiar experience of the profoundly disempowered—be she slave, rape victim, abused

19. See Elaine Scarry, *The Body in Pain: The Making and Unmaking of the World* (New York: Oxford University Press, 1985).

spouse, abused child, or exploited worker. The intellectual assault on selfhood may indeed be pursued by some postmodernists as a part of a progressive-intellectual agenda designed to decenter the falsely universal claims of liberalism and rationalism. Nevertheless the very concrete assault on the self that has become so central to the postmodern worldview is almost invariably used *in politics* as an incredibly effective strategy of disempowerment and domination.

Correlatively, the capacity to hear and trust one's self, and specifically one's pain, as true testimony to one's injury and hence to a societal injustice is a central and effective strategy of consciousness-raising and eventual empowerment of traditionally disempowered peoples. Similarly, reclamation of the self from ownership of and use by others is a central aspect of the experience of liberation. Construction, discovery, and reclamation of selfhood *is*, for many persons, the subjective experience of the great journey from oppression to liberation. Progressives and leftists in particular should be wary of a conceptual apparatus, postmodern or otherwise, that denies the significance and authenticity of those experiences, particularly if we are genuinely committed to the egalitarian politics and fundamentally liberal value of dignity that those experiences so richly inform.

This book is accordingly put forward not as an attack on traditional or enlightenment understandings of meaning, but quite the contrary, as an attempted reclamation of meaning from contemporary and postmodern critics of both the political Right and Left: the meaning and meaningfulness not only of literary and legal texts, but also of social criticism, of moral change, and of subjectivity, experience, and selfhood. As the critical legal scholars have shown, social criticism and the possibility of moral change are routinely viewed with suspicion by mainstream liberal legalists, who tend to acquiesce in patterns of legal and cultural legitimation. Mainstream liberal legalists, as critical scholars rightly insist, do indeed tend to be willfully blind to processes of legitimation, and hence willfully acquiescent in the conservative undertow that is their obvious consequence. The meaningfulness of legal criticism and the possibility of moral progress are also viewed with suspicion by the conservative Right in legal academia, a suspicion grounded not only in their long-felt loyalty to the law as it is presently constituted, but also in a somewhat more modern loyalty to a conception of the literary canon as inevitably supportive of the "Rule of Law," and celebratory of its virtues. Neither the current liberal legalist nor the conservative legalist's resistance to radical legal criticism, however, should be regarded as surprising. What *is* surprising, and even alarming, about contemporary legal theory is the attack on the possibility of radical legal criticism and the meaningfulness of moral progress by the postmodern *Left*. By denying first the meaningfulness of legal and literary texts, and then the authenticity of experience, and lastly the coherence, integrity, and existence of the subjective self, and asserting instead the contingency of meaning, experience, and selfhood on social constructs themselves dictated by empowered interests, postmodern leftist critics in law and in literature have undermined the coherence of social, cultural, and legal criticism, and hence the possibility of moral progress. Against that quintessentially postmodern spirit of resignation to the politics of group interest, and against that denial of the possibility of utopian vision and social reconstruction, we must, I believe, reclaim our cultural texts, the project of criticism, our moral sense, the authenticity of our subjectivity, and the moral importance of our experiences. And we must reengage our ever-vulnerable, whether or not socially constructed, selves, with the families, lovers, neighbors, and cocitizens that constitute our local, national, and global communities. That reclamation and reengagement is ultimately what I mean by the "method of the humanities." These essays are written and collected in the conviction that that reclamation of meaning and moral purpose in the methods of the humanities is not only enriching, but may well be necessary to our spiritual, intellectual, and perhaps even our physical survival.

Part 1
Jurisprudence in Literature

Chapter 1

Authority, Autonomy, and Choice

Modern legal and political theorists strongly disapprove of authority and just as strongly approve of autonomy. These moral attitudes underlie a vast array of current liberal political and jurisprudential doctrines. Modern arguments for the moral grounds of democracy, for the legitimacy and moral worth of the free market, for the justification of criminal punishment, for limitations upon paternalistic applications of state power, for the priority of individual rights over collective welfare, and even for the legitimacy of law itself all rest on a commitment to the virtues of individual autonomy and an antipathy toward authority.[1] Criticism of these institutions and policies often

1. See, e.g., Bruce A. Ackerman, *Social Justice in the Liberal State* (New Haven: Yale University Press, 1980), discussing autonomy as a justification for the liberal principle of neutrality; R. M. Dworkin, *Taking Rights Seriously* (Cambridge: Harvard University Press, 1977), arguing that respect for autonomy underlies the liberal conception of a right to equal concern and respect and stating that "[g]overnment must treat those to whom it governs with concern, that is, as human beings who are capable of suffering and frustration, and with respect, that is, as human beings who are capable of forming and acting on intelligent conceptions of how their lives should be lived" (272); Charles Fried, *Right and Wrong* (Cambridge: Harvard University Press, 1978), ("[R]ight and wrong have . . . overriding status because they establish our basic position as freely choosing entities. That is why nothing we choose can be more important than the ground—right and wrong—for our choosing. Right and wrong are expressions of respect for persons—respect for others and self-respect"); Richard A. Posner, *The Economics of Justice* (Cambridge: Harvard University Press, 1981), chaps. 3–4 (subsequent references abbreviated *EJ*, are given in the text) contending that autonomy and respect for choice and consent justify the free market and wealth maximization as goals of legal decision making; Hugh Gibbons, "Justifying Law: An Explanation of the Deep Structure of American Law," *Law and Philosophy* 3 (1984): 165–279, arguing that respect for individual autonomy underlies the American system and legal entitlements. See generally W. Nelson, *On Justifying Democracy* (London: Routledge and Kegan Paul, 1980), surveying autonomy-based arguments for democracy.

reflects the same moral attitudes; critics charge that, appearances notwithstanding, the modern liberal state—indeed perhaps any state—is "hierarchical" or "authoritarian."[2] *Choice* and *autonomy* are becoming synonyms for "right" and "good," while *submission, obedience, authority*, and *authoritarian* conjure up the good German, the Nazi soldier, the Stalinist, and the intolerant Falwellian social leader.

In "The Ethical and Political Basis of Wealth Maximization" and two related articles, Professor (now Judge) Richard Posner argues that these widely shared pro-autonomy moral values are furthered by the wealth-maximizing market transfers, judicial decisions, and legal institutions advocated by members of the "law and economics" school of legal theory.[3] Such transactions, decisions, and institutions are morally attractive, Posner argues, because they support autonomy; wealth-maximizing transfers are those to which all affected parties have given their consent. Posner justifies not only classic two-party market transactions on this ground, but also wealth-maximizing market transactions that allocate risk instead of commodities, and wealth-maximizing transfers effected by legal imperatives that operate independently of markets; according to Posner, even the apparent losers in wealth-maximizing transactions have consented to them in a significant moral sense. Wealth-maximizing transfers therefore rest not only on utilitarian considerations for their moral legitimacy, but also on the independent ground that they promote autonomy. Posner finds the latter, Kantian moral tradition more appealing than the economists' traditional utilitarian heritage. He consequently regards his discovery of the compatibility of wealth maximization and our pro-autonomy moral commitments as important evidence of the moral attractiveness of wealth maximization as a rule of judicial decision making.

This chapter argues that Posner's attempt to defend wealth max-

2. See, e.g., Robert Paul Wolff, *In Defense of Anarchism* (New York: Harper and Row, 1970), 16–19.

3. "The Ethical and Political Basis of Wealth Maximization" first appeared as Richard A. Posner, "The Ethical and Political Basis of the Efficiency Norm in Common Law Adjudication," *Hofstra Law Review* 8 (1980): 487–507. It reappears, with some revisions and retitled, in *EJ*. "The Value of Wealth: A Comment on Dworkin and Kronman, *Journal of Legal Studies* 9 (1980): 243–52, reappears in *EJ*, chap. 3, retitled "Utilitarianism, Economics, and Social Theory," References will be made to the versions in *EJ*. See also Richard A. Posner, "Utilitarianism, Economics, and Legal Theory," *Journal of Legal Studies* 8 (1979): 103–40.

imization on principles of consent rests on a simplistic and false psychological theory of human motivation. Posner's argument depends both on an explicit assumption that the presence of consent, without more, satisfies the requirements of an ideal of autonomy and on an implicit assumption that people consent to changes in their worlds in order to improve their well-being. Posner infers from these assumptions that the more "acts of consent" or "opportunities for choice" that the legal system allows, encourages, or mimics," the better off and more autonomous we will all be, and consequently, the more moral our world will be. (*EJ*, 65–73, 92–99). Posner concludes that the legal world should be governed by one overarching normative principle: the legal system ought to give people exactly what they think they want or, when that is not possible, what the legal system thinks they think they want. By doing so, Posner argues, the legal system will promote a more autonomous and wealthy world.

Through a series of contrasts, I will argue that Franz Kafka's fictional works on the nature of law dramatize a dark underside of Posner's argument that the fact of consent morally legitimates our legal, social, and personal worlds.[4] Kafka's fictional characters typically consent to market transactions, employers' imperatives, and legal and familial authority, and thereby get exactly what they think they want. In Kafka's fictional and horrific world, as in Posner's

4. Kafka wrote a great deal about the nature of law and legal authority. This chapter will draw upon Kafka's novel, *The Trial*, the stories "The Judgment," "The Refusal," and "A Hunger Artist," and the parables "The Problem of Our Laws," "The Imperial Colonel," and "The Emperor," in Franz Kafka, *The Complete Stories and Parables* (New York: Quality Paperbacks Books, 1983) (subsequent references, abbreviated *CS*, will be given in the text). These works do not, however, constitute an exhaustive list of Kafka's writings on the nature of law and legal authority. The parables "The New Advocate" and "Advocates," and the story "In the Penal Colony" (all in *CS*) and the novel *The Castle*, trans. Willa Muir and Edwin Muir (New York: Knopf, 193) also deal with the nature of law and the motivations for obedience to political authority.

Kafka's training in law and his work in the law-related field of industrial safety for most of his adult life account for part of his deep understanding of the psychological mechanisms of consent and obedience to legal authority. Kafka's decision to go to law school was largely a submissive one: he could not build a passion for the hard sciences, and he did not feel capable of studying philosophy. His legal education, which he found boring and detestable, focused on the dry study of the Germanic Code. See Ernst Pawel, *The Nightmare of Reason: A Life of Franz Kafka* (New York: Farrar, Straus, Giroux, 1984), 117–22. Pawel reports that, according to Kafka, the study of law had the intellectual excitement of chewing sawdust that "had been prechewed by thousands of other mouths."

theoretical and ideal one, victim, aggressor, and community all regard this consent as validating otherwise unappealing states of affairs. Consent insulates these situations from moral criticism and renders them, without more, morally attractive. In both worlds, consent is a moral trump. Kafka's fictional world thus provides a dramatic enactment of Posner's normative claim: Posner argues that consent morally legitimates all; Kafka illustrates what a world so legitimated might look and feel like. In both worlds, good and evil, and right and wrong, lose all meaning when all that matters is whether and to what extent people get exactly what they think they want.

Yet Kafka's world is tragic and ironic, while Posner's theoretical world is a satisfied and apparently happy one. Even if Posner's ideal world strikes the reader as a sad one, his hypothetical legal actors experience it as a wealthy and satisfactory place. By contrast, even when Kafka's world strikes the reader as funny, his characters experience it as nightmarish. I will argue that this fundamental difference between the two worlds results from Posner's and Kafka's divergent depictions of human nature. Posner's world is populated by characters who are relentlessly egoistic and as psychologically simplistic as the moral rule they live by. In Posner's stories, criminals, contractors, law-abiding citizens, legislators, and judges enter into transactions, both with others and with the state, for only one reason—to maximize their own welfare. As long as they are reasonably well informed of the choices and the nature of the risks presented to them, they are for the most part pleased with the outcomes of their decisions. Kafka's world, by contrast, is peopled by excessively authoritarian personalities. Kafka's characters usually do what they do—go to work in the morning, become lovers, commit crimes, obey laws, or whatever—not because they believe that by doing so they will improve their own well-being, but because they have been told to do so and crave being told to do so. Whereas Posner's characters relentlessly pursue autonomy and personal well-being, Kafka's characters just as relentlessly desire, need, and ultimately seek out authority.

The disjunction between a system that formally and outwardly insists upon the legitimating function of consent and a human personality that inwardly and persistently seeks the security of authority accounts for much of the alienation in the lives of Kafka's characters. That disjunction between the outward descriptions imposed upon the transactions in which Kafka's characters are engaged and the radically different inward experience of those transactions by the parties involved is, I believe, deeply familiar to the modern reader.[5] Kafka's characters, despite the bizarre situations in which they find themselves, are strikingly recognizable: although their outer worlds are bizarre, we have no trouble seeing ourselves and our neighbors in the inner worlds of George of "The Judgement" or Joseph K. of *The Trial*. By contrast, the lack of any disjunction between Posner's simple legal and moral system and his characters' simple welfare-maximizing inner worlds render those characters unfamiliar to the same audience. Posner's actors, despite the ordinariness of the situations in which they find themselves, are not recognizable as ourselves or our neighbors. His wealth-maximizing, racially discriminating employer (*EJ*, 359–63), his wealth-maximizing criminal who decides how best to use his opportunity time and his burglar's tools,[6] and his wealth-maximizing tort victim who is compensated ex ante for an accident uncompensated ex post (*EJ*, 95–97) do not resemble the bigoted bosses, the petty thieves, or the impoverished and paraplegic accident victims we may work with, know, or be. The inner lives and motivations of Posner's characters, are strikingly unrecognizable. They are not we, and their stark inner lives are not ours.

The Role of Consent in Normative Justifications of the Market, Risk, and the State

In "The Ethical and Political Basis of Wealth Maximization," Posner sets out to demonstrate that all wealth-maximizing transfers are consensual in order to provide moral grounding for his claim that judges ought to adopt wealth maximization as the primary normative goal of

---

5. Joyce Carol Oates makes the point in this way:

> Though the words "Kafkan" and "Kafkaesque" invariably point to paradox and human frustration, and suggest childhood memories of terrifying disproportion, it is the case nonetheless that Franz Kafka's stories and parables are not at all difficult to read and to understand. . . . His unique yet powerfully familiar world can be entered by any reader and comprehended *feelingly* at once, regardless of background or literary training. (In fact, unsophisticated—which is to say unprejudiced—readers respond to Kafka most directly, as he would have wished. Perceptive teenagers love him not because he is "one of the great moderns" but because he speaks their private language by speaking so boldly in his own.) (Joyce Carol Oates, *Kafka as Storyteller*, in *CS*, ix, xi).

6. See Richard A. Posner, *The Economic Analysis of Law* (Boston: Little, Brown, 1977), 164–67. Subsequent references, abbreviated *EA*, will be given in the text.

judicial decision making (*EJ*, 88–89). Posner treats wealth-maximizing transfers in three discrete classes: market transactions without third-party effects, market transactions with adverse third-party effects where the third-party losers have at an earlier point consented to the risk of loss, and transfers effected by operation of nonmarket legal institutions. Each of these types of transactions or transfers, Posner argues, are consensual in an important moral sense (*EJ*, 92–99). States of affairs reached through such consensual transactions or transfers are thus morally attractive (*EJ*, 90).

As Posner concedes, however, each class of transfers involves a different kind of consent. First, he notes, wealth-maximizing market transactions with no third-party effects elicit the express consent of all parties affected by the exchange (*EJ*, 88–89). Second, Posner argues, wealth-maximizing market transfers with adverse third-party effects elicit the implied consent of those third parties who have at some earlier time voluntarily assumed the risk of the loss (*EJ*, 94–99). Third, Posner argues, wealth-maximizing institutions that operate outside the market altogether, such as the negligence system of tort law, command the hypothetical consent of even the system's eventual losers, who, being rational, if asked, would consent to the imposition upon them of the nonmarket imperatives (*EJ*, 95–97).[7] Such hypothetical consent can be imputed to parties whenever the nonmarket imperative in question is wealth maximizing. Even nonmarket wealth-maximizing institutions, then, are morally justified because they are grounded on the consent—albeit on an attenuated, hypothetical consent—of even their eventual victims.

Thus, in all three types of wealth-maximizing transfers, winners and losers either expressly, impliedly, or hypothetically consent to the gains or losses they ultimately sustain. Even wealth-maximizing transactions or institutions that ultimately hurt a class of people are morally desirable both because they increase the collective wealth and because they command some sort of consent from all parties affected by the exchange. Posner concedes that a wealth-maximizing transfer

7. Posner sometimes speaks in terms of a single category of nonexpress consent, variously described as "implied" or "hypothetical." In this chapter, I use the phrase "implied consent" to designate the type of consent involved in transfers imposing losses on third parties who earlier consented to the risk of the ultimate loss, and "hypothetical consent" to designate the type of consent involved in nonmarket transfers imposing losses or gains on parties who would consent, if asked, to the legal imperatives in question.

does not necessarily increase the collective well-being, as opposed to the wealth, of the affected parties. Because one person's subjective happiness cannot be quantifiably compared with another's subjective pain, the quantity of overall well-being or subjective utility is simply unknowable (*EJ*, 54). As a class, then, wealth-maximizing transactions cannot be justified on pure utilitarian grounds. Nor, Posner argues, does every wealth-maximizing transfer command the express consent of all affected parties. Wealth-maximizing transfers therefore cannot be justified as a class on the ground of pure consensual autonomy. Posner argues that, contrary to conventional wisdom, neither a showing of utility maximization nor a showing of Pareto superiority is necessary to the moral justification of wealth-maximizing transactions.[8] All wealth-maximizing transfers elicit from all affected parties some form of consent—either express, implied, or hypothetical—any species of which is sufficient to legitimate the resulting state of affairs. Therefore, in Posner's view, wealth maximization rests neither on pure utilitarian grounds nor on the pure Kantian ground of achieving autonomy through express consent; it rests instead upon the virtues of an attenuated vision of consent for its moral foundation. Because they are consensual, wealth-maximizing transfers both leave people wealthier and foster their sense of autonomy. And, because all wealth-maximizing transfers are consensual, they are morally justified as well.

Posner's critics, most notably Ronald Dworkin and Jules Coleman, argue that Posner has not convincingly shown that meaningful consent can be found in all three types of transactions that Posner would like to justify; he has not, the criticism goes, shown that implied and hypothetical consent are meaningful moral concepts.[9] Posner unquestionably strains language and distorts reality in order to find consent in seemingly nonconsensual transactions. I will not, however, pursue that line of criticism here. Instead, I will argue that each of Posner's arguments for the morality of wealth-maximizing transfers fails for a different reason. Even assuming that meaningful

8. "A change is said to be Pareto superior if it makes at least one person better off and no one worse off" (*EJ*, 54). Only expressly consensual transactions can be confidently characterized as Pareto superior.

9. See Jules L. Coleman, "Efficiency, Utility, and Wealth Maximization," *Hofstra Law Review* 8 (1980): 509–51; R. M. Dworkin, "Is Wealth a Value?" *Journal of Legal Studies* 9 (1980): 191–226.

consent can be found in the transactions Posner wishes to justify, Posner has not shown that the presence of consent either entails an increase in well-being or fosters one's sense of autonomy. Although Posner has successfully distinguished his consent-based system of morality from the utilitarian and Kantian moral traditions, he has not shown that his system captures the virtues of either. In short, he has not shown that consent is an attractive value worth encouraging in human affairs.

Franz Kafka's fictional world resembles Richard Posner's ideal world in one remarkable respect: most of what happens to Kafka's fictional characters is fully consensual, as is most of what happens to Posner's actors. Kafka's characters, like Posner's actors, consent to a wide range of legal, personal, and market transactions. First, Kafka's characters expressly consent to all sorts of humiliating and degrading commercial, employment-related, and sexual transactions. Second, like Posner's actors, Kafka's characters voluntarily assume risks of future losses and thereby impliedly consent to losses caused by wealth-maximizing transactions. Third, Kafka's characters, like Posner's, hypothetically consent to the authority of a wide range of nonmarket legal norms, from the norms of criminal law and procedure to the rule of law itself. As a consequence of the ever-present consent of the actors, in both worlds the distinctions between fate and choice, freedom and bondage, and power and servitude are blurred and nonexistent. Prisoners, guards, masters, slaves, criminals, and law-abiding citizens all consent to fates over which they have no control: the powerful put themselves in servitude, and slaves consent to their own bondage. For both writers, the consequence of this central paradox is that their protagonists live in a world of their own creation, but the world is, by their own choice, one that they are powerless to change.

And yet Kafka, more than any modern writer, tells stories about victims, and Posner, more consistently than any modern theorist, defines the problem of victimization out of existence. The two writers depict the same transactions from radically divergent points of view. Kafka supplies descriptions of the internal, subjective experience of the formal transactions that Posner schematizes from his external point of view. In the internal world of Kafka's fiction, the experience of the Posnerian, rational, wealth-maximizing exchange is consistently depicted as the nightmare that follows from doing what one has consented to do.

In the three parts below, I contrast Posner's depiction of the morally legitimizing function of consent—in express consent to market transactions, in implied consent to risk, and in hypothetical consent to legal institutions—with Kafka's dramatic descriptions of the internal experiences of persons tendering each type of consent. To the extent that Kafka's descriptions ring true, they undermine Posner's normative premise that consent is morally valuable. Indeed, the power of Kafka's fiction suggests that Posner's argument rests on a severely inadequate picture of human nature and human motivation. Posner has not shown that any of the types of consent he attributes to wealth-maximizing transactions either strengthen our sense of autonomy or increase our subjective well-being. Consequently, even if wealth-maximizing transactions do meaningfully elicit consent, their moral justification has yet to be shown.

The Morality of Expressly Consensual Transactions: The Thirst for Pain, Surrender, and Humiliation

Posner's central ethical claim is that the state of affairs resulting from an expressly consensual transaction is a moral one (*EJ*, 48–115). He offers two reasons. First, Posner argues, the giving of our express consent fosters our sense of autonomy (*EJ*, 89). Second, expressly consensual transactions, Posner argues, by definition increase the well-being of those who have consented.[10] Relying on two notoriously ambiguous

10. The argument is spread over several chapters of *The Economics of Justice*. In chap. 3, Posner states that, under a Pareto-superior approach, a voluntary transaction with no externalities by definition increases the total amount of happiness in the world by making both parties better off than they were prior to the transaction (54–55). In chap. 4, Posner adds that, in the absence of "serious problems of monopoly and externality," such transactions also, again by definition, increase society's wealth (79). These two claims, if true, suggest a utilitarian basis for the claim that voluntary, expressly consensual exchanges ought to be encouraged. At the end of chap. 4, however, Posner promises more:

> If one views wealth maximization as constrained utilitarianism (the constraint being that society seeks to maximize the satisfaction only of those whose preferences are backed up by a willingness to pay), one can defend it by whatever arguments are available to defend utilitarianism; but one can do better than

passages from Bentham's *Introduction to the Principles of Morals and Legislation*,[11] Posner asserts that individuals act so as to maximize their own pleasure and minimize their own pain.[12] That, Posner explains, is what it means to "act rationally," and that is what people do. People are generally "rational maximizers of their own utility." Thus, when a purchaser pays two dollars for a tomato, he does so because he envisions greater pleasure to be had from the tomato than from other uses he might have made of the two dollars. By giving up the two dollars and gaining the tomato, he has maximized his own pleasure. The seller, conversely, envisions greater pleasure from the two dollars than from the tomato. Both buyer and seller are made happier by the exchange. They both are uniquely capable of deciding which they prefer—the two dollars or the tomato—and they both are similarly motivated to allocate resources between them in such a way

---

that, as the next chapter shows (87).

In the next chapter, Posner tries to shows that one can do better by demonstrating that wealth maximization can be derived from the moral value of consensual relations (89–96). However, the departure from consequentialist argumentation is apparent rather than real: although Posner shows that wealth maximization can be viewed as consensual, he offers nothing beyond the consequentialist argument summarized above to support the moral value of consent. A truly nonconsequentialist defense of wealth would have to demonstrate the moral value of expressly consensual states of affairs independent of the consequential "well-offness" of the parties giving their consent; thus, the act of consenting itself must be shown to have moral value independent of the effect of the transaction on wealth or well-being.

11. "NATURE has placed mankind under the governance of two sovereign masters, pain and pleasure. . . . They govern us in all we do, in all we say, in all we think." Jeremy Bentham, *Introduction to the Principles of Morals and Legislation*, in *The Works of Jeremy Bentham*, ed. Sir John Bowring (1843; rpt., New York: Russell and Russell, 1962), 1:1. "Men calculate, some with less exactness, indeed, some with more: but all men calculate. I would not say, that even a madman does not calculate." Ibid., 90. Posner quotes these passages (*EJ*, 42).

12. "Particularly important to the approach of this book is Bentham's insistence that human beings act as rational maximizers of their satisfactions in all spheres of life, not just the narrowly economic" (*EJ*, 41–42). Bentham does not say, however, that all men calculate to maximize their own pleasure; he says only that all men calculate to maximize pleasure. There is strong evidence that Bentham believed that men often, if not typically, calculate so as to maximize the pleasure of their community, not just their own pleasure. See Bentham, *Introduction*, 143–44. He clearly believed them capable of it. He did not envision the "rational calculator" that Posner ascribes to him. See David Lyons, *In the Interest of the Governed: A Study in Bentham's Philosophy of Utility and Law* (Oxford: Clarendon 1973), 11–18, 64–78. For a discussion of the modern positions regarding the interpretations of these passages, see Robin West, "In the Interest of the Governed: A Utilitarian Argument for Substantive Judicial Review," *Georgia Law Review* 18 (1984): 495 n. 52.

as to possess the resource they will most enjoy (*EJ*, 83). Posner applies the motivations described in this narrow commercial setting to embrace all human interactions and decisions. People act so as to maximize their own utility not only when buying tomatoes on the market, but when committing crimes, (*EJ*, 41; *EA*, 164–72) breaching or performing contractual obligations (*EA*, 65–69), choosing a spouse (*EA*, 104–8, selecting a vocation, deciding to get up and go to work in the morning, or consenting to a sexual affair (*EJ*, 237). There is no reason, Posner suggests, to suppose that people do not act rationally in all phases of their lives (*EJ*, 237).

Many of Franz Kafka's stories depict voluntary market transactions between expressly consenting adults. Kafka's short story "A Hunger Artist," for example, is about just such a perfectly consensual commercial transaction. Kafka's hunger artist is the ultimate Posnerian entrepreneur, and the artist's audience consists of Posnerian consumers. The hunger artist is a professional faster who presents himself at carnivals in various stages of voluntary starvation for the public's amusement, curiosity, or disgust. In this freely chosen line of work, he eventually starves himself to death:

> They poked into the straw with sticks and found him in it. "Are you still fasting?" asked the overseer, "when on earth do you mean to stop?" "Forgive me, everybody," whispered the hunger artist; only the overseer, who had his ears to the bars, understood him. "Of course," said the overseer, and tapped his forehead with a finger to let the attendants know what state the man was in, "we forgive you." "I always wanted you to admire my fasting," said the hunger artist. "We do admire it," said the overseer, affably. "But you shouldn't admire it," said the hunger artist. "Well then we don't admire it," said the overseer, "but why shouldn't we admire it?" "Because I have to fast, I can't help it," said the hunger artist. "What a fellow you are," said the overseer, "and why can't you help it?" "Because . . . I couldn't find the food I liked. If I had found it, believe me, I should have made no fuss and stuffed myself like you or anyone else." These were his last words, but in his dimming eyes remained the firm though no longer proud persuasion that he was still continuing to fast. (*CS*, 27–77)

The carnival exhibitor consensually provides the artist with space and by so doing earns profits from the consenting and amused public, who in turn reap more pleasure from the spectacle than they surrender from the price of admission. Everyone expressly consents to the transactions and as a consequence, on Posner's assumptions, is better off and more autonomous. When the hunger artist finally wills himself—voluntarily—to death by starvation, his actions are still consensual and wealth maximizing. Because the public has grown bored with the spectacle by the time of the hunger artist's death, neither the exhibitor nor the public is made worse off by his decision. And the hunger artist continues to get exactly what he thinks he wants. "A Hunger Artist" depicts a perfectly functioning Posnerian commercial market that leaves all preferences satiated at every moment of autonomous choice.

Nevertheless, unlike the happy stories Posner tells of theoretical markets, "A Hunger Artist" is a tragic story. Unlike Posner, Kafka provides histories beyond mere "moments of choice" for our evaluation. At all times other than the moments of choice, the hunger artist is not only not better off; he is sickly, malnourished, starving, or dead. And, at all times other than the moment of decision, the hunger artist's consent does not strengthen his sense of autonomy; instead, he becomes increasingly enslaved by his obsession. The expanded time frame allows for a more complete depiction of both the hunger artist's sense of autonomy and the way in which the world has changed because of his decisions. Kafka shows the reader that, viewed over the long run, the hunger artist's consent is not "congenial" to autonomy; in a quintessentially Kafkaesque paradox, he becomes enslaved by his thirst for autonomy at the moment of choice. He is a consensual slave to his moment-to-moment passion for self-control, and he eventually allows that passion to destroy him.

In addition, Kafka provides his characters with motives beyond the definitionally tautological motive of wealth maximization. Like the modern anorexic, the hunger artist regards each decision not to eat as a perfectly voluntary act of self-empowerment. But also like the anorexic, the hunger artist exercises power that is followed—necessarily—by the inability to free himself from the deadly consequence of that empty freedom. The hunger artist's control over his life depends upon his absolute denial of the needs and ultimately the existence of his future self; his refusal to compromise the sovereignty of his present desire for pure self-control ultimately denies the welfare—indeed the existence—of his future self. In short, he satiates his present self's preference for perfect autonomy by killing his future self. This paradigmatic Kafkaesque protagonist achieves a pure, momentary Posnerian power, but only by enslaving himself to his decision slowly to starve.

Kafka's depiction of the Posnerian reasoning behind the hunger artist's choice and the community's reaction to that choice is tragic. The community Kafka describes behaves in accordance with Posner's ideal world: the artist's subjective and actual reasons for fasting affect neither the perceived rationality of his decision nor the moral legitimacy of the community's failure to intervene. All that matters to the community's sense of fair play is the outward depiction: he fasted consensually. Motives are as irrelevant as the actual consequence of the choice. In Kafka's story, we find the community's failure to intervene morally repugnant. What in Posner's world is an expression of respect for the individual becomes in Kafka's story an instance of the community's moral failure.

Kafka's novels and stories contain other dramatic depictions of expressly consensual private transactions. Indeed, Kafka provides descriptions of the internal experience of many of the same expressly consensual transactions that Posner describes from an external, formal perspective. Both Posner and Kafka, for example, describe a consenting employee, but the images reflect drastically divergent points of view. In Posner's world, the consenting employee's sale of labor to the employer, like the consenting buyer's purchase of goods off the shelf, is wealth maximizing, conducive to autonomy, and moral because it is consensual. Even consensual enslavement, Posner insists, constitutes such a wealth-maximizing, voluntary, and thus moral sale of labor:

> Suppose A, perhaps to provide money for his family (but the reason is unimportant), sells himself into slavery to B. . . . From a wealth-maximization standpoint there is no economic basis for refusing to enforce [the] contract unless some element of fraud or duress is present. Nor would the economist think [the] contract so irrational as to create an irrebuttable presumption that it was procured by fraud or duress or is vitiated by insanity or other incapacity. (*EJ*, 86)

Kafka depicts a world of expressly consensual employment that is not so unproblematic. In Kafka's writings, expressly consensual employment not only lacks positive moral value, it is generally portrayed as humiliating, repulsive, tragic, or fatal. In the novel *The Trial*, for example, the protagonist, Joseph K., discovers his warders—the men whose job it is to effect his arrest—being whipped by their superior, who is himself at the mercy of a yet higher employing authority. The consensual employment of these characters is hardly cause for moral approbation. Although the employees articulate the same reason for employment that Posner attributes to his hypothetical voluntary slave—to provide money for the family—their deeper motives reflect an urge to accept obedience and authority, not to foster their autonomy, wealth maximization, or self-improvement. The resulting world is not primarily a place in which prior preferences have been satiated—although it is that. It is not the wealthy, autonomous employment Posner depicts; instead, it is primarily a world of powerful, hierarchical relationships that are humiliating, stifling, torturous, and painful:

> One of the men, who was clearly in authority over the other two and took the eye first, was sheathed in a sort of dark leather garment which left his throat and a good deal of his chest and the whole of his arms bare. He made no answer. But the other two cried: "Sir! . . . [A]ll is lost now . . . our careers are done for . . . and, besides that, we're in for a whipping, and that's horribly painful." "Can that birchrod cause such terrible pain?" asked K., examining the switch. . . . "Well [*sic*] have to take off all our clothes first," said Willem. "Ah I see," said K. . . . "Is there no way of getting these two off their whipping?" K. asked him. "No," said the man, smilingly shaking his head. "Strip," he ordered the warders. . . . The warder Franz, who . . . had thus far kept as much as possible in the background, now came forward to the door clad only in his trousers, fell on his knees, and clinging to K's arm whispered: "If you can't get him to spare both of us, try to get me off at least. Willem is older than I am, and far less sensitive too, besides he's had a small whipping already . . . but I've never been in disgrace yet, and I was only following Willem's lead in what I did, he's my teacher, for better or worse. . . . I'm so ashamed and miserable." . . . "I can't wait any longer," said the Whipper, grasping the rod with both hands and

> making a cut at Franz. . . . Then the shriek rose from Franz's throat, single and irrevocable, it did not seem to come from a human being but from some martyred instrument. . . . [T]he birchrod found [Franz] where he was lying, its point swished up and down regularly as he writhed on the floor. (*T*, 95–99)

K.'s own consensual employment is less brutal, but it is no less authoritarian. Although K. suffers no physical abuse on the job, he is humiliated and dehumanized, not enriched, by his white-collar employment as chief clerk in a bank:

> It was eleven o'clock, he had wasted two hours in dreaming, a long stretch of precious time, and he was, of course, still wearier than he had been before. . . . The attendants brought in several letters and two cards from gentlemen who had been waiting a considerable time. . . . Weary of what had gone before and wearily awaiting what was to come, K. got up to receive the first of his clients.
>
> [As his boss, the Assistant Manager, and his client, the manufacturer,] leaned against his desk . . . it seemed to K. as though two giants of enormous size were negotiating above his head about himself. Slowly, lifting his eyes as far as he dared, he peered up to see what they were about, then picked one of the documents from the desk at random . . . and gradually raised it, rising himself with it, to their level. In doing so, he had no definite purpose. . . . The Assistant Manager . . . merely glanced at the paper without even reading what was on it, for anything that seemed important to the Chief Clerk was unimportant to him, took it from K.'s hand, said: "Thanks, I know all that already," and quietly laid it back on the desk again. K. darted a bitter look at him, but the Assistant Manager did not notice that, or, if he did, was only amused, he laughed loudly several times. (*T*, 144–47)

Kafka's depictions of consensual sex provide a similar contrast to Posner's world. In Posner's world, consensual sex, like any other consensual transaction, should strengthen the parties' sense of autonomy, increase well-being, and render the world more moral. Yet in Kafka's fiction, consensual sexual relinquishment of control over one's sexuality rarely promotes autonomy or well-being. Instead, sexual actors are often driven by an urge to obey a person of the opposite sex who is perceived as powerful. In *The Trial*, for example, Joseph K. happens upon a woman who works in the court in which he is being tried. The woman allows herself to be sexually used by her husband, by a "student of the Law Court," and by the examining magistrate in charge of investigating Joseph K.'s case. She explains to K.:

> The man you saw embracing me has been persecuting me for a long time. I may not be a temptation to most men, but I am to him. There's no way of keeping him off, even my husband has grown reconciled to it now; if he isn't to lose his job he must put up with it for that man you saw is one of the students and will probably rise to great power yet. He's always after me, he was here today, just before you came. (*T*, 60–61)

Later, K. watches the student carry the woman to the examining magistrate, at the latter's command:

> K. ran a few steps after [the student,] ready to seize and if necessary to throttle him, when the woman said: "It's no use, the Examining Magistrate has sent for me, I daren't go with you; this little monster," she patted the student's face, "this little monster won't let me go." "And you don't want to be set free," cried K., laying his hand on the shoulder of the student, who snapped at it with his teeth. "No," cried the woman, pushing K. away with both hands. "No, no, you mustn't do that, what are you thinking of? It would be the ruin of me. Let him alone, oh, please, let him alone! He's only obeying the orders of the Examining Magistrate and carrying me to him."
>
> . . . The woman waved her hand to K. as he stood below, and shrugged her shoulders to suggest that she was not to blame for this abduction, but very little regret could be read into that dumb show. (*T*, 69–70)

The woman herself expresses the motivational ambiguity latent in her submission to the magistrate. She may, as she tells Joseph K. in the preceding passage, tolerate the magistrate's attentions for the welfare-maximizing reason that she needs to maintain her husband's job security. In another passage, however, she explains her attraction to this hierarchical, authoritarian relationship in very different terms:

> "I didn't know that he was only a petty official, but as you say so it must naturally be true. All the same, I fancy that the reports he sends up to the higher officials have some influence. And he writes out so many reports. You say that the officials are lazy, but that certainly doesn't apply to all of them, particularly to the Examining Magistrate, he's always writing. Last Sunday, for instance, the session lasted till late in the evening. All the others left, but the Examining Magistrate stayed on in the courtroom, I had to bring a lamp for him, I had only a small kitchen lamp, but that was all he needed and he began to write straight away. . . . Suddenly, in the middle of the night . . . I woke up, the Examining Magistrate was standing beside our bed shielding a lamp with his hand to keep the light from falling on my husband. . . . I was so startled that I almost cried out, but the Examining Magistrate was very kind, warned me to be careful, whispered to me that he had been writing till then, that he had come to return the lamp, and that he would never forget the picture I had made lying asleep in bed. I only tell you this to show that the Examining Magistrate is kept really busy writing reports. . . . Such long reports as that surely can't be quite unimportant. . . . And by this time I have other proofs that he is anxious to win my favor. Yesterday he sent me a pair of silk stockings. . . . They're beautiful stockings, look"—she stretched out her legs, pulling her skirt above her knees, and herself contemplated the stockings—"they're beautiful stockings, but too fine, all the same, and not suitable for a woman like me." (*T*, 64–66)

In Posner's world, reasons for consent are strictly irrelevant: expressly consensual transactions by definition promote both autonomy and well-being. In Kafka's sexual world, reasons are not irrelevant, but they are maddeningly ambiguous: for every sexual transfer that Kafka describes, he provides a conventional, welfare-maximizing motive (often spoken by the victim) for the consent, along with overwhelming evidence that the truer motive is submission to the power of male authority. The woman in the law court says that she grants access to her body for welfare-maximizing reasons: either in exchange for her husband's job security or for sexual pleasures of her own. Alternatively, however, she may consent to the transactions because she is attracted to the examining magistrate's power and authority. For her, as for Kafka's characters generally, the sexual act is consensual and in some sense satisfying. In no case, however, is the resulting transaction portrayed as conducive to autonomy or individual well-being, and in no case is the resulting state of affairs portrayed as moral. The sexual transfers, like the consensual enslavements, are repulsive and perceived as such by the reader, if not by the participant themselves.

In all of these market transactions—commercial, employment-related, and sexual—Kafka portrays one party consenting to a transfer of power over that party's body, and in each instance the transfer, although consensual, is horrifying. In none of Kafka's depictions does consent entail an increase in well-being. The hunger artist's welfare is not improved by his decision; he starves. The warders' welfare is not increased by their endurance of whippings; they are humiliated and pained. The woman in the law court is not enlivened by her multiple sexual encounters; she is dehumanized. Nor do these consensual transactions leave the parties more autonomous: each consensual act was motivated by a desire to submit to authority, not to enhance autonomy, and in each case, the authoritarian relationship they create proves to be a damaging one. The hunger artist's bondage to his own tyrannical whim destroys him; the warders' acquiescence to the whipper's sadism further enslaves them; and the woman's sexual submission to the magistrate weakens her. Each of these expressly consensual transactions strengthens a belittling, humiliating, and sometimes fatal relationship.

Kafka's depictions of commercial, employment-related, and sexual transactions illustrate a simple truth: the consensual bargain that underlies commerce, labor, and sex may save those transactions from being theft, slavery, or rape, but it hardly accords them positive moral value. Consensual acts of commerce, labor, or sexual intercourse are not morally good simply because they are not coerced: a bad trade is still bad, even if it is not theft; a bad job is still bad, even if it is not slavery; and bad sex is still bad even if it is not rape. The morality of any of these consensual transactions depends upon the value of the worlds they create, which in turn depends in part upon the worth of the relationships they contain. A sexual transaction between an authoritarian employer and a submissive woman does not typically create a morally good relationship, even if it is not rape. The consensual contract between a sadistic employer and a submissive employee is not a morally good relationship, even if the employee would have worked for less. Relationships such as these are harmful for both the submissive and the dominant party. It is immoral to participate in such consensual transactions and immoral for the community to tolerate them.

If Kafka's descriptions of consensual transactions reveal a truth about the complexity of human motivations, Posner's claim that express consent reinforces one's sense of autonomy and by definition maximizes one's well-being is simply untenable. It does not follow from the definition of consent that people consent to what they think will make them better off, or what will in fact make them better off. To whatever degree consensual transactions maximize well-being or autonomy, they do so by virtue of our human motivations and capabilities. At best, then, it is only contingently and not analytically true that expressly consensual states of affairs are congenial to autonomy or that they maximize the well-being of those who consent.

Posner's definitional claims that consent both promotes autonomy and triggers an increase in well-being hide the need for an empirical argument. The latter definitional claim depends upon two distinct empirical premises. The claim that we choose what maximizes our well-being depends, first, on our being capable of preferring and choosing that which leaves us best off and, second, on our being motivated to prefer and choose that which will leave us better off. Both of these claims are contestable. As other critics of the law-and-economics tradition have shown, we have good reasons (such as ignorance, duress, or addiction) for distrusting our ability to maximize our own well-being through choice.[13] We ought also be skeptical of our motivation to increase our well-being through choice. Even an actor fully capable of improving his well-being may choose a state of affairs that leaves him worse off because he is disinclined to improve his well-being through consensual transactions. If our reasons for consenting to changes in our worlds are varied, then the automatic

13. See, e.g., Mark Kelman, "Choice and Utility," *Wisconsin Law Review* (1979): 769–97.

equation of consent to change and either an attempted or an actual increase in well-being is specious.

Posner's other definitional claim—that consensual transactions promote autonomy—fails for a similar reason. We may consent to a transaction not to foster our autonomy, but rather solely to please or defer to a perceived authority. Whether or not the resulting transaction promotes autonomy depends on the authoritarian relationship thereby created. Some such relationships promote autonomy. Many, however, do not.

Moral assessment of a change in resource allocation depends on a rich, full description of the changed world. If the transaction to which we have consented involves only an increase in our own well-being, then the assessment of the moral value of the posttransaction world can focus solely on that increase. The trade may indeed both promote autonomy and increase well-being. But if the trade is for one or both parties not an act of welfare betterment, but an act of submission to an authority, then the posttransaction world includes a newly created or strengthened hierarchical relationship. If so, the moral value of the resource reallocation also depends upon the moral value of that change in the world. The theorist must evaluate the consequences of that change—whether, by obeying, we have submitted to a valuable authoritarian relationship that will foster our autonomy and help us grow, or whether we have succumbed to an exploitative relationship that will damage or destroy us.

An accurate identification of our motives for acting is a necessary, but not sufficient, component of a moral evaluation of the worlds that our consensual acts create. Just as there is no automatic equivalency between consent and egoistic motivation, there is no definitional correlation between any particular motivation or set of motivations and good or evil. If a purchaser buys a tomato for two dollars in order to increase her own well-being, she may or may not create a better world in the process. If she likes tomatoes and uses them as part of a nutrious diet, she very likely has increased her well-being by the purchase. If, on a daily basis, she buys twelve tomatoes, eats five plates of spaghetti, and regurgitates it all, thus destroying her digestive tract as surely as an alcoholic destroys his liver, then the purchase of the tomatoes has not maximized her well-being, regardless of what she would have paid for them and regardless of the resultant consumer surplus.

Alternatively, if the purchaser buys the tomato not to increase her own welfare, but because she has been told to do so, again, she may or may not have thereby created a morally better world. The hierarchical relationship she has furthered may be either good or bad for the parties involved. Hierarchical relationships can strengthen our autonomy and leave us better off if they help us grow, develop talents, or improve our mental health, physical health, store of knowledge, or wisdom. They weaken us and leave us worse off if they render us dependent on an unreliable or untrustworthy source of information, if they divest us of the power to engage in essential human activities, or if they deprive us of self-respect or the ability to make independent moral judgments. In the case of the tomato purchase, it is not hard to imagine a desirable world in which we reasonably rely upon the benign and informed authoritative guidance of others on questions of health and diet—perhaps we live in such a world. Our diet is improved if the authority we trust has superior competence, our time is freed to be spent on other concerns, and our faith in good intentions and competence of other members of our community is strengthened by their successful regulation of this aspect of our lives. Yet one can also easily envision an overregulated, authoritarian nightmare in which our health, as well as other aspects of our private lives, is strictly controlled by others. We might find ourselves eating plastic-textured tomatoes, estranged from the natural process of planting, harvesting, and managing vegetables, ignorant of our biological and nutritional needs, and ultimately enslaved by our dependence on the dubious authority of unknown others. Women suffering from bulimia, anorexia, and related dietary disorders may be living in just such an excessively authoritarian and nightmarish world. Whether the world, including our own world, is better or worse because of our decisions to buy tomatoes because we have been told to purchase them, and whether our autonomy is strengthened or depleted, depends upon the nature and moral quality of this authoritarian relationship.

Our natural inclination to follow the advice or command of perceived and actual authorities is no more intrinsically bad than our self-interested and autonomous inclinations, lauded by the law-and-economics school, are intrinsically good.[14] Inclinations toward

14. Posner's insistence that the wealth-maximizing decision is the morally correct

obedience and submission to authority unquestionably have good effects—one of which is that they make possible the development of the egoistic, autonomous self that is of such concern to the law-and-economics school. It would be difficult or impossible to become meaningfully autonomous if we were not inclined to subordinate our own will to the dominant will of someone we trust or respect. For example, it would be hard to learn to play the piano if we had to reassess on our own the merit of playing scales with every practice session, and it would be hard to achieve personal intimacy if we derived no pleasure or satisfaction from the voluntary act of submission. Growth itself, whether psychological, cognitive, artistic, or emotional, depends upon our ability to submerge our spontaneous will at least as much as it depends upon our ability to assert it. It would be impossible for the present self to give way to a future, happier, more productive self if it were not motivationally inclined on occasion to deny itself or submit to the will of others.

There are, then, good prudential reasons for furthering the greater happiness of a future self over the momentary pleasures of the present self by subordinating the latter to the will of others. But inclinations toward obedience and submission also make possible a wide range of structures, communities, and relationships of social and moral, not just prudential, value. Religious callings clearly depend upon the human urge to submit to and serve higher authority.

---

decision is manifest throughout *The Economics of Justice*. Thus, Posner not only views the wealthy thief as morally superior to the impoverished thief, (*EJ*, 62 n. 1), and the wealthy purchaser as more moral than the impoverished thief (*EJ*, 66), but he also views the wealth-maximizing producer as morally superior to the wealthy philanthropist:

> Most of the conventional pieties—keeping promises, telling the truth, and the like—can also be derived from the wealth-maximization principle. Adherence to these virtues facilitates transactions and so promotes trade and hence wealth by reducing the costs of policing markets through self-protection, detailed contracts, litigation, and so on. Even altruism (benevolence) is an economizing principle, because it can be a substitute for costly market and legal processes. And yet even the altruist might decide to sell his services to the highest bidder [rather] than donate them to the neediest supplicant. Because of the costs of determining need other than through willingness to pay, allocation by price may confer greater net benefits on the rest of society than allocation by "need" or "desert." Allocation by price will also result in a greater accumulation of wealth. This wealth can be given away in whole or in part—though again the altruist will not want to spend so much time screening applicants for charity that he greatly reduces his productive work and the benefits it confers on other people. (*EJ*, 67–68; footnotes omitted)

Our major moral traditions also rely upon authoritarian urges: to behave morally is, centrally, to submit to the authority of higher rules of moral conduct—either the duties imposed upon us by force of traditionally conceived moral rules, Kant's formulation of the "categorical imperative," or the utilitarian mandate to contribute to the community's happiness. Furthermore, we often regard a morally submissive attitude as exemplary of virtue: the obedience of the foot soldier in a just war or of a monk in a Benedictine monastery is regarded by some, at least, as morally exemplary. The soldier who dies in battle while unflinchingly obeying a superior does not exhibit the same virtue as the soldier who hurls himself on the live grenade of his own accord, but he certainly makes the same sacrifice. The ability to submit to a duty or to a moral rule is as necessary a part of moral conduct and of religious life as the ability to determine individually, independently, and rationally the rule one ought follow.[15]

On the other hand, our authoritarian instincts have tremendously destructive potential. When we willingly relinquish too much control over ourselves or our environment, we risk losing our selves altogether to the wills of others. When we regularly submit to rules and directive of others, we become less practiced at assessing the moral, social, or prudential aspects of a particular situation—our own or any other. A learned habit of impotence can be as addictive, as attractive, and ultimately as dangerous as a learned preference for heroin, or, for that matter, as the thirst for power. The easy freedom from responsibility that follows from the misperception that one is not able to change one's situation can imprison us in destructive work environments, careers, marriages, home lives, and sexual relationships. It can seduce us into the comfortable belief that the ruler we have submitted to, whether retailer, employer, or lover, is omniscient, when he is in fact ignorant or misinformed; that he is moral when he is in fact corrupt; that he is acting in our interest when he is in fact acting in his own; or that he is leading us toward the shining City on the Hill when he is leading us toward disaster. The dangers latent in our need for obedience and submission should not be understated: when the authoritarian relationship is a bad one, at best we lose a measure of self-respect and the pleasures that come from true autonomy; at worst

15. See generally William Henry Werkmeister, "The Function and Limits of Moral Authority," in *Authority: A Philosophical Analysis*, ed. Harris R. Baine (Tuscaloosa: University of Alabama Press, 1976), 94.

we become dehumanized automatons hypersensitive to authoritarian suggestion and a danger to ourselves and others. But we do not avert these dangers by denying the human motivation within us that renders these phenomena possible. Nor, for that matter, do we avert them by denying the valuable social relations the same motivation facilitates.

The Morality of Impliedly Consensual Transactions: The Attraction of the Risk of Loneliness and Death

Although the Pareto morality of expressly consensual transactions constitutes Posner's ethical ideal (*EJ*, 88–90), he willingly concedes that only a small subset of the wealth-maximizing transfers he wishes to justify have been expressly consented to by all affected parties (*EJ*, 88–89, 94–97). Most wealth-maximizing transactions have both intentional and unintentional effects on third parties who have not expressly consented to the transaction. Such transactions cannot be justified by reference to express consent and the automatic increase in well-being that such consent definitionally entails (*EJ*, 88–90). Nor can they be justified with a utilitarian calculus if we insist, as Posner does, upon the incomparability of subjective utility values. Society is, of course, collectively wealthier if the transaction is wealth maximizing, but there may nevertheless be a loser; therefore, we cannot infer that the transaction has increased the collective well-being, as opposed to the wealth, of the community. The loss as felt by the loser may outweigh the gains experienced by the winners.

Nevertheless, Posner argues, in many of these cases, the losing parties have impliedly consented to the wealth-maximizing transaction. "The version of consent used here," Posner writes, "is ex ante compensation" (*EJ*, 94). By ex ante compensation Posner does not mean that the losing parties received beforehand a benefit equal to the full value of the loss subsequently suffered. Instead, in an earlier transaction, the eventual loser received some benefit in exchange for the voluntary decision to assume the risk of the subsequent loss.

Posner gives two examples to demonstrate the operation of ex ante compensation. In the first, a plant relocates from one town to another, causing a loss for surrounding landowners. The move is by hypothesis wealth maximizing: "The plant owners are better off, and the pecuniary externalities cancel out" (*EJ*, 91). In the second example, an entrepreneur suffers losses as a result of the entrance of a more successful product into the market. In both cases, "the wealth-maximization criterion . . . would allow the move," yet in neither case have the losers expressly consented to the event that causes their loss. In neither case, Posner states, is there any way of knowing whether "the utility to the winners . . . exceeds the disutility to the losers" (*EJ*, 91).

According to Posner, however, in both cases the losing parties assumed the risk of the loss that eventually befell them. Both losers impliedly consented to the loss, and the wealth-maximizing transaction is accordingly justified:

> Since the entrepreneur's expected return includes a premium to cover the risk of losses due to competition, he was compensated for the loss ex ante. . . . [T]he landowners [were compensated in this manner] at the time they bought the land: the probability that the plant would move was discounted in the purchase price they paid. (*EJ*, 94)

Posner employs a metaphor to illustrate the manner in which the ex ante compensation of the landowner and of the entrepreneur can be viewed as a proxy for their implied consent. The consent, Posner suggests, is similar to the consent of the loser of a lottery to the loss of the cost of the ticket:

> It is my contention that a person who buys a lottery ticket and then loses the lottery has "consented" to the loss so long as there is no question of fraud or duress; at least he has waived any objection to the outcome, assuming there was no fraud in the lottery. (*EJ*, 94)

The landowner and the entrepreneur similarly buy a "lottery ticket" in buying land or going into business. Because the parties bargain for a "bundle" of benefit-plus-risk, by definition it leaves them better off than would alternative uses of resources to which they could have consented. In exchange for shouldering the particular risks involved in their purchases, they receive a value greater than the cost of all of the possible results discounted by the probability of their occurrence. That one of those assumed risks eventually comes to pass does not change the result. Therefore, according to Posner, even an eventual loser in the wealth-maximizing transaction is made wealthier by the consensual assumption of the risk, because he voluntarily bargains for the risk of the loss he eventually sustains. And of course, even eventual losers strengthen their sense of autonomy; they choose to enter the risk-allocation lottery.

Kafka provides several examples of failed entrepreneurs who have consented ex ante to the loss they suffer ex post in just the manner Posner describes. Kafka's entrepreneurs, like Posner's, are compensated during their early successful days for the risk of the losses that subsequently befall them. Like Posner's actors, these businessmen voluntarily assume the risk of the failure they ultimately suffer. Again, "A Hunger Artist" is the classic text. Kafka's hunger artist voluntarily chooses his profession and therefore voluntarily assumes the risks the path entailed. He is compensated, ex ante, for the risk that events beyond his control would someday render his art out of vogue—that someday he would fail to inspire or even draw an audience:

> During these decades the interest in professional fasting has markedly diminished. It used to pay very well to stage such great performances under one's own management, but today that is quite impossible. We live in a different world now. At one time the whole town took a lively interest in the hunger artist; from day to day of his fast the excitement mounted; everybody wanted to see him at least once a day; there were people who bought season tickets for the last few days and sat from morning till night in front of his small barred cage. . . .
>
> A few years later when the witnesses of such scenes called them to mind, they often failed to understand themselves at all. For meanwhile the aforementioned change in public interest had set in; it seemed to happen almost overnight; there may have been profound causes for it, but who was going to bother about that; at any rate the pampered hunger artist suddenly found himself deserted one fine day by the amusement-seekers, who went streaming past him to other more-favored attractions. (*CS*, 268–73)

The hunger artist reacts to his situation as Posner would expect: he moves to a new position.

> Fasting would surely come into fashion again at some future date, yet that was no comfort for those living in the present. What, then, was the hunger artist to do? He had been applauded by thousands in his time and could hardly come down to showing himself in a street booth at village fairs, and as for adopting another profession, he was not only too old for that but too fanatically devoted to fasting. So he . . . hired himself to a large circus; in order to spare his own feelings he avoided reading the condition of his contract. (*CS*, 273–74)

The hunger artist again voluntarily assumes risks, including the risk of unread contract terms. The hunger artist is compensated ex ante: his fanatical devotion to fasting compensates for the assumed risk of desertion by his public, while his "spare[d] . . . feelings" compensate for the assumed risk of unknown employment conditions.

In the short story "The Judgment," Kafka contrasts a failed entrepreneur's implied consent to the risk of failure with a successful entrepreneur's more fortunate spin of the wheel. Kafka allows the reader to view the failed entrepreneur's situation from the more successful protagonist's point of view:

> He was thinking about his friend, who had actually run away to Russia some years before, being dissatisfied with his prospects which had flourished to begin with but had long been going downhill, as he always complained on his increasingly rare visits. So he was wearing himself out to no purpose in a foreign country, the unfamiliar full beard he wore did not quite conceal the face George had known so well since childhood, and his skin was growing so yellow as to indicate some latent disease. By his own account he had no regular connection with the colony of his fellow countrymen out there and almost no social intercourse with Russian families, so that he was resigning himself to becoming a permanent bachelor. (*CS*, 77)

The reader next learns of the protagonist's contrasting fate:

> But during these three years George's own position in life had changed a lot. Two years ago his mother had died, since when he and his father had shared the household together. . . . Since

> that time, however, George had applied himself with greater determination to the business as well as to everything else.
>
> Perhaps during his mother's lifetime his father's insistence on having everything his own way in the business had hindered him from developing any real activity of his own, perhaps since her death his father had become less aggressive, although he was still active in the business, perhaps it was mostly due to an accidental run of good fortune—which was very probable indeed—but at any rate during those two years the business had developed in a most unexpected way, the staff had had to be doubled, the turnover was five times as great; no doubt about it, further progress lay just ahead. (*CS*, 78–79)

Kafka's failed businessmen, unlike Posner's, neither gain in well-being nor enhance their sense of autonomy by deciding to enter the market. The hunger artist's professional choice confines him to a cage, where he depends upon the fickle interest of the consuming public and ultimately is enslaved and killed by his own passions. The consensual decision of George's friend places him in the "vastness of Russia," alienated from friendship and community, and expatriated from native soil. Both entrepreneurs become trapped by their business ventures, not freed. By choosing to starve or by choosing to run away to a foreign land, these entrepreneurs consensually alienate their autonomy to the authority of fate. Their choices reflect despair, not triumph. Kafka's depictions of unsuccessful entrepreneurs, formally so similar to Posner's risk-taking entrepreneurs and landowners, dramatize the failure of community, not the victory of the autonomous individual.

Nor is the well-being of the hunger artist or George's friend in any meaningful sense increased by the chance for success or the premium of gain received during their early success. Their subsequent loss, discounted by the risk of its occurrence, is simply not compensated ex post by their early success or the chance for success initially purchased. The hunger artist himself expresses the point; he knows that he has been abandoned by his fickle public and not compensated either ex post or ex ante for his eventual failure:

> [T]he artist simply fasted on and on, as he had once dreamed of doing, and it was no trouble to him, just as he had always

> foretold, but no one counted the days, no one . . . knew what records he was already breaking, and his heart grew heavy. And when once in a while some leisurely passer-by stopped, made merry over the old figure on the board, and spoke of swindling, that was in its way the stupidest lie ever invented by indifference and inborn malice, since it was not the hunger artist who was cheating, he was working honestly, but the world was cheating him of his reward. (*CS*, 276)

The failure of George's friend is similarly uncompensated, either ex post or ex ante. In a moment of pained self-enlightenment, George perceives this truth clearly:

> His friend in St. Petersburg . . . touched his imagination as never before. Lost in the vastness of Russia he saw him. At the door of an empty, plundered warehouse he saw him. Among the wreckage of his showcases, the slashed remnants of his wares, the falling gas brackets, he was just standing up. Why did he have to go so far away! (*CS*, 85)

If the entrepreneurial opportunities our market system provides are truly like lottery tickets, as Posner's example suggests, then the fact that the system produces wealth-maximizing winners who increase the size of the pie does indeed entail that there will be losers as well and that those losers will suffer. Posner teaches us that when the risk of a loss is voluntarily assumed, the ultimate suffering of that loss is consensual and we consequently need concern ourselves no more with losers in the market than with those in a lottery. Kafka's stories tell a different tale. In Kafka's stories, the community's refusal to intervene and come to the aid of the market's losers is revealed as a breakdown of community and brotherhood, not a legitimate response to a morally satisfactory state of affairs. The human attraction to winners and revulsion toward losers do not serve as reliable guides to moral conduct, but instead carry the seeds of tragedy.

Thus, in "A Hunger Artist," the cage left empty by the artist's death is filled by a young panther, to the community's immense relief and satisfaction. The community much prefers the panther's strength, his successful conquest of life, to the hunger artist's failed attempt to stay alive while starving. The attraction to the panther's success is depicted to be as inhuman and immoral as the community's earlier distaste for the hunger artist's self-imposed death. Indeed, the community is as incapable of recognizing the panther's bondage as it was earlier incapable of responding to the hunger artist's despair:

> "Well, clear this out now!" said the overseer, and they buried the hunger artist, straw and all. Into the cage they put a young panther. Even the most insensitive felt it refreshing to see this wild creature leaping around the cage that had so long been dreary. The panther was all right. The food he liked was brought him without hesitation by the attendants; he seemed not even to miss his freedom; his noble body . . . seemed to carry freedom around with it too; . . . and the joy of life streamed with such ardent passion from his throat that for the onlookers it was not easy to stand the shock of it. But they braced themselves, crowded around the cage, and did not want ever to move away. (*CS*, 277)

Similarly, in "The Judgment," Kafka portrays George's failure to come to the aid of his failed friend not as a legitimate response to a morally satisfactory state of affairs, but as a thinly rationalized, self-serving abandonment of friendship:

> What could one write to such a man, who had obviously run off the rails, a man one could be sorry for but could not help. Should one advise him to come home, to transplant himself and take up his old friendship again—there was nothing to hinder him—and in general to rely on the help of his friend? But that was as good as telling him, and the more kindly the more offensively, that all his efforts hitherto had miscarried, that he should finally give up, come back home, and be gaped at by everyone as a returned prodigal, that only his friends knew what was what and that he himself was just a big child who should do what his successful and home-keeping friends prescribed. And was it certain, besides, that all the pain one would have to inflict on him would achieve its object? Perhaps it would not even be possible to get him to come home at all—he said himself that he was now out of touch with commerce in his native country—and then he would still be left an alien in a foreign land embittered

> by his friend's advice and more than ever estranged from them. But if he did follow their advice and then didn't fit in at home—not out of malice, of course, but through force of circumstances—couldn't get on with his friends or without them, felt humiliated, couldn't be said to have either friends or a country of his own any longer, wouldn't it have been better for him to stay abroad just as he was? Taking all this into account, how could one be sure that he would make a success of life at home? (*CS*, 77–78)

There is ultimately no way, George concludes, to tender aid and comfort to his failed friend. Consequently, he reasons, he should refrain from pointing out to his friend the difference between his own extraordinarily lucky roll of the dice—both in business and in romance—and the less fortunate experience of his friend. On the contrary, those differences should be minimized, trivialized, or ignored. George thereby renders himself incapable not only of caring for a friend in need, but also of the intimacy of friendship:

> For such reasons, supposing one wanted to keep up correspondence with him, one could not send him any real news such as could frankly be told to the most distant acquaintance. It was more than three years since his last visit, and for this he offered the lame excuse that the political situation in Russia was too uncertain. . . .
>
> So George confined himself to giving his friend unimportant items of gossip such as rise at random in the memory when one is idly thinking things over on a quiet Sunday. (*CS*, 78–79)

Again, Kafka's stories illustrate a simple truth: to say that the risk of a loss is consensually assumed is not to imply that the subsequent "ownership" of a set of risks promotes either one's well-being or one's sense of autonomy. Nor does the loser's consent insulate community and friends from a moral obligation to relieve the impact of personal tragedy or to ease suffering. It may be natural to love winners and strong panthers, but it is morally inexcusable to dismiss losers on the basis of a facile judgment that they consented to play the game. When George faces the true magnitude of his friend's suffering and his own self-imposed alienation from that suffering, he is driven to such guilt and despair that he ultimately feels compelled to carry out his own death sentence. The cost of George's self-knowledge—guilt, a death sentence, a suicide—is grotesque, but the lesson itself is not. Excusing one's own inhumanity by protecting the freedom of the loser to suffer is revealed as a type of sin.

If we grant Posner's normative assumption that any consensual state of affairs is moral because of the fact of consent, then his conclusion that consensually assumed risk is moral readily follows.[16] If consensual transactions necessarily promote one's sense of autonomy and increase well-being—thus leaving the world a morally superior place—then there is no reason to believe that the world is not improved just as much by consensual allocations of risk as by consensual allocations of tangible resources. The problem with Posner's argument is that even if these losses have been impliedly consented to, he has not shown that anything of moral significance follows from that fact. Posner has not shown that implied consent to a risk of loss morally validates our failure to compensate losers. Nor has he shown that consent to a risk of loss renders the world containing the risked loss morally superior to the world that preceded the allocation of risk.

Posner's lottery analogy demonstrates the poverty of his argument. Nothing illustrates more dramatically the moral insufficiency of consent to risk taking than a lottery. Because Posner assumes that any consensual market transaction by definition strengthens autonomy and increases the well-being of the consenting party, he never asks whether the purchase of risks and chances strengthens autonomy or increases the well-being of contingent, particular risk buyers. Yet it seems clear that whereas such purchases improve the world for some people, they do not for others. As with the expressly consenting tomato buyer, a risk buyer may fail to increase his well-being for any number of reasons. The preference for the risks and chances associated with the purchase of a lottery ticket may reflect misinformation or a lack of information; it may, for example, register an

---

16. This argument about assumed risk serves only, of course, to justify transactions to which eventual losers have at some earlier point given their implied consent. In a footnote, Posner indicates his willingness to extend the conclusion beyond these parameters:

> [The argument] . . . resemble[s] a position taken by many welfare economists: that the Kaldor-Hicks criterion for deciding whether to undertake a public project satisfies the Pareto-superiority criterion provided there is a sufficient probability that an individual will benefit in the long run from such projects, though he may be a loser from a particular one. (*EJ*, 94 n. 18)

exaggerated belief in the buyer's control over fate. But more fundamentally, it also seems clear that for vast numbers of people, the purchase of risk and chance results not in a reenforcement of personal autonomy, but in a disastrous deterioration of that important human value.

In fact, Posner's lottery example highlights the gross disjunction between consensual acceptance of risk and the autonomous values that consent purportedly promotes. Even assuming that the bettor is fully informed of the risk and fully cognizant of alternative uses of his money, the purchase of a particular bundle of risks may result from a compelling or compulsive urge to relinquish control over his future. Regardless of one's definition of well-being, assumption of risk is the very antithesis of autonomy when it entails abandonment, not enrichment, of personal responsibility. The frequenter of a homosexual bathhouse who engages in indiscriminate and dangerous sex, for example, may be consciously assuming the risk of contracting AIDS, but that risk preference may register the depth of that consumer's compulsive attraction to the risk of death, not the height of his risk-taking lust for life. Assumption of that risk neither leaves the bathhouse customer better off nor furthers his autonomy, no matter what price he would have paid for admission, and no matter what the consumer surplus.[17] The European libertines who accepted bundles of consensual sex and high risks of death during the outbreak of syphilis in the sixteenth century may have been similarly motivated. The bathhouse customer, like the sixteenth-century libertine, may experience his preference not as a rational response to his own level of risk affinity and desire for consensual sex, but as an intense relinquishment of responsibility for his own life and well-being.

The innocuous purchase of a lottery ticket might also reflect not the buyer's attraction to risk, but instead the buyer's preference that fate govern his fortune over alternative uses of resources that would enhance his ability to control his own future. Although the purchase is consensual, what the purchaser may be buying is not a reallocated

17. The San Francisco bathhouses—defined by one authority as "sex establishments where men engage in . . . high-volume, high-frequency sex"—were closed by the San Francisco Director of Public Health in October 1984. See Katie Leishman, "San Francisco: A Crisis in Public Health," *Atlantic*, October 1985, 18, 28. As of October 1985, San Francisco was the only city to close its bathhouses. The San Francisco gay community was and remains divided over the closing of the baths.

bundle of risks of loss and chances for fortune, but instead his own submission to a postbet world governed by the authority of luck. No matter what the odds, and no matter how well informed a buyer so motivated, the purchase is an act of submission, not an act that enhances autonomy. Indeed, the pleasure of submitting one's fate to the spin of the wheel, the authority of luck, is often precisely what the casual and occasional bettor buys. When we bet we give full reign to our impulse to abandon the pursuit of autonomy and submit instead to forces outside of our control. No authority is as absolute, or as blind to individuating circumstance, as luck. Like the urge to submit to the dictates of personal authority, the inclination to submit to the authority of fate may manifest a relinquishment, not an enrichment, of autonomy.

When an individual is motivated by the inclination to submit to the authority of fate, the purchase of risk constitutes consensual control over one's future in only the most superficial of ways. In a narrow sense, the bettor—like the hunger artist—is in complete control of his future; he consciously decides whether or not to consent to proffered odds. But that total control is manifested in a decision to relinquish control over one's own creation of future selves. In the most literal sense the bettor puts his faith in a higher authority—random fate—and abandons his own attempt to create a meaningful future for himself. No single consensual act stands in more striking contrast to the rich meaning of personal autonomy—the phenomenon of personal empowerment, the ability to change one's own world and social world for the better, and the possession of faith in one's powers—advocated by John Stuart Mill and Adam Smith.

An assessment of the moral value of a postbet world, then, must begin with an accurate description of the world and the transaction that brought it into being. If the purchase of the risk was a consensual relinquishment of personal autonomy to the authority of luck, then the value of the postbet world must include a valuation of that changed relationship, and not simply an examination of changed odds. It is not inevitably damaging to oneself to assume risks, buy chances, or gamble. An occasional bet makes for a happier world. Betting is probably more fun when it is a relinquishment of responsibility for consequences, once the purchase is made, then when it is simply the purchase of preferred risks. The experience of submission in a controlled and limited context is exhilarating and entertaining.

But the relationship between the authority of luck and a submissive bettor is often destructive. The danger of addictive gambling lies in the very fact that it is such an easy release for our impulse to abandon control over the future. When the consensual relationship between authoritarian fate and a bettor is a bad one, the consequences are devastating. The human tragedies caused by compulsive gambling testify to the danger inherent in our natural propensity to submit. We are right to be wary of our enjoyment of gambling and to urge restraint of the inclination to buy risks of loss and chances for fortune.

In the entrepreneurial context as well, risk taking may or may not be antithetical to the ideal of personal autonomy. When the entrepreneur goes into business for herself, she may be doing so because, unlike either the compulsive or casual bettor, she has faith in her ability to carve her own future and her own contribution. She may also, like the bettor, be attracted to the prospect of the gamble that entrepreneurship represents. But our admiration of the courage or pluck of the individual entrepreneur stems from our belief that most entrepreneurs are drawn to their projects by the urge to be masters of their own fate. Entrepreneurship is at best creative and self-affirming. The entrepreneur we admire unquestionably takes risks, but she takes them because of her faith in her own ability to overcome them, not because the odds are more attractive than her own creative powers. The landowner that we admire buys land to use it productively in a manner that will afford him a degree of control over his fate and his contribution. The speculating landowner, by contrast, is only tolerated, not admired; he does not represent our moral ideal of the social value gained from the individual ownership of property.

Posner's lottery metaphor, far from explaining why consensually assumed risks of loss definitionally entail a morally superior world, illustrates the radical contingency of that implication. The assumption of risk and the purchase of chance can, but often do not, manifest motivations that we rightly admire: self-control, faith in one's own abilities, productive and creative use of one's environment. At other times, assumption of risks manifests an urge to relinquish control over one's future. At worst, it manifests total lack of control over oneself and the world. The preference revealed by such a purchase expresses the belief that luck will deal a better hand than we can create for ourselves. As such, it reveals the measure of our self-contempt, not the measure of our individual greatness, and in every way conceivable contradicts the ideal of self-respect and autonomy that Posner purports to celebrate in consent.

If one can morally justify our refusal to compensate the losses suffered by Posner's failed entrepreneur, the disappointed landowner, the bathhouse frequenter who contracts AIDS, the sixteenth-century libertine who contracts syphilis, the hunger artist, or George's expatriated friend, the reason must be other than the resemblance of any of these individuals to the consensual gambler. There may be no good reason to compensate unsuccessful gamblers beyond what they receive ex ante, but that is not because we find the postbet world morally superior to the prebet world. The purchase of a lottery ticket is not an example of a consensual transaction that necessarily creates a morally superior world. The purchase of a lottery ticket, like any voluntary, consensual assumption of risk, often manifests a self-destructive, not a creative, human potential. If Posner's lottery metaphor, which he believes speaks for itself, illustrates anything at all, it illustrates only the poverty of a moral system that rests exclusively on one human ability, one metaphor, and one deeply ambiguous human act.

The Morality of Hypothetically Consensual Transactions: Authoritarian Masochism and the Will to Submit to Legal Imperatives

The final element of Posner's argument is that even nonmarket wealth-maximizing institutions can be justified by reference to the principle of consent. The sort of consent such institutions command, however, is neither express nor implied: affected parties neither expressly bargain for the reallocation the transfer entails, nor do they impliedly assume the risks of that reallocation. Rather, nonmarket wealth-maximizing institutions, if they are truly wealth maximizing, command the hypothetical consent of affected parties, including potential losers (*EJ*, 94–97). If a citizen were to be asked, counterfactually, whether she would prefer to accept the bundle presented by the wealth-maximizing institution—for example, the high benefits in savings, combined with the low probability of devastating losses, inherent in the negligence system—rather than the bundle of benefits and risks entailed by systems that are not wealth maximizing, she would prefer, and hence consent to, the bundle presented by the wealth-maximizing institution:

> If a driver is injured by another in an accident in which neither was at fault, in what sense has the injured driver consented . . . to not being compensated for his injury, which is the result under the negligence system?
>
> To answer this question, we must consider the effect on the costs of driving of insisting on ex post compensation, as under a system of strict liability. By hypothesis the costs would be higher. . . . Would drivers be willing to incur higher costs in order to preserve the principle of ex post compensation? Presumably not. Any driver who wanted to be assured of compensation in the event of an accident, regardless of whether the injurer was at fault, need only buy first-party, or accident, insurance—by hypothesis at lower cost than he could obtain compensation ex post through a system of strict liability. (*EJ*, 95)

Posner concludes that the cheaper system will command the hypothetical consent of all affected parties. Therefore, even nonmarket wealth-maximizing institutions are consensual and justifiable according to ethics of personal autonomy:

> I have used the example of negligence versus strict liability because it has been used to argue that the wealth-maximization approach is inconsistent with an approach based on notions of personal autonomy. If a requirement of consent in the sense in which I am using the term is deemed an adequate safeguard of the autonomy interest, this argument must fail unless it is shown that a strict liability system would be cheaper than a negligence system. (*EJ*, 96)

Thus, although we might obey a wide array of nonmarket legal imperatives, we would consent only to those nonmarket imperatives that are wealth maximizing. It is only this subset of nonmarket legal imperatives—those that are wealth maximizing—that command not just our obedience but also our hypothetical consent. Therefore, only wealth-maximizing nonmarket imperatives are morally justifiable.

Posner's argument depends on the psychological claim that if we were asked, counterfactually, whether we would consent to the nonmarket imperatives imposed upon us, we would consent to those nonmarket legal institutions, and only to those legal institutions, that are cheaper. If asked, we would give our consent to cheap, rather than expensive, legal imperatives, because we are psychologically constituted in such a way as to prefer that which maximizes our wealth. Wealth-maximizing legal institutions that satisfy the "cheapness criterion" are thus morally desirable not only because they are cheaper, but also because they are consensual and support autonomy. Given this assumption, the "autonomy interest," as Posner calls it, turns out to be coextensive with the "cheapness interest."

Kafka is also convinced that people would give their consent, were they asked, to many of the nonmarket legal imperatives that they obey. Kafka's descriptions of obedient citizens leave little doubt that, if asked, those citizens would consent to at least many, if not all, of the imperatives imposed upon them. The vast bulk of Kafka's citizens obey legal imperatives not because they fear the consequences of noncompliance, but because they generally concur in the norms and judgments those imperatives entail. Their obedience is not typically coerced; Kafka makes clear that, if asked, these citizens would consent to the norms they obey. They have tendered, in Posnerian language, their hypothetical consent to the wide array of legal (and parental) imperatives that unquestionably command their obedience.

The reasons for which Kafka's citizens would give their consent, however, differ markedly from the considerations that Posner supposes would be decisive. Whereas Posner's citizens would consent, if asked, to those legal imperatives that are wealth maximizing, Kafka's citizens are governed by a different internal psychology. Kafka's characters would consent to legal imperatives that satisfy a very different and well-specified set of cravings. Kafka's characters, if asked, would consent to impersonal state imperatives in order to satisfy an unquenchable thirst, not for wealth, but for judgment and ultimately for punishment. The legal imperatives of a state, Kafka suggests, hold out an offer we cannot refuse: an opportunity for pronouncement and hence acknowledgment of our guilt, for judgment, and for punishment.

Because of this dramatically non-Posnerian psychological assumption, the legal imperatives to which Kafka's characters would hypothetically consent, and which they do in fact emphatically obey, promote neither their well-being nor their autonomy. The legal imperatives that command the actual obedience and the hypothetical consent of Kafka's characters promote instead their feelings of guilt, inadequacy, and punitive self-doubt. In Kafka's psychologically complex world, unlike Posner's, nothing of moral significance follows from the bare fact that a citizen would, if asked, consent to the imposition upon him of any of the many legal imperatives that he dutifully obeys.

Kafka's earliest and most powerful dramatization of his psychological claim portrays a son's acquiescence to the punitive and judgmental imperative of his father. In "The Judgment," George's father finds George guilty of insensitivity, selfishness, and devilishness, and sentences him to death by drowning:

> "How long a time you've taken to grow up! Your mother had to die, she couldn't see the happy day, your friend is going to pieces in Russia, even three years ago he was yellow enough to be thrown away, and as for me, you see what condition I'm in. You have eyes in your head for that!"
>
> "So you've been lying in wait for me!" cried George.
>
> His father said pityingly, in an offhand manner: "I suppose you wanted to say that sooner. But now it doesn't matter." And in a louder voice: "So now you know what else there was in the world besides yourself, till now you've known only about yourself! An innocent child, yes, that you were, truly, but still more truly have you been a devilish human being!—And therefore take note: I sentence you now to death by drowning!" (*CS*, 87)

Upon hearing the verdict, George is driven by internal need—not an external sanction—to acquiesce voluntarily to his father's judgment. George carries out the sentence of death not because he is forced to, but because he concurs in the correctness of his father's law as applied against him. In Posnerian language, George gives his hypothetical consent to the norm imposed upon him—if asked, he would agree that his crime of being devilish warrants the punishment of death. His obedience is not coerced by force or sanction, but is instead a product of his implicit concurrence in the accuracy of the judgment and the appropriateness of the sentence. George's hypothetical consent to this harsh and bizarre sentence—the death penalty for devilishness—is surely not prompted by the belief that in the long haul such a norm maximizes his wealth. Kafka makes vividly clear that, if asked, George would consent to such a norm because it satisfies his need for recognition of his own guilt and for punishment:

> George felt himself urged from the room, the crash with which his father fell on the bed behind him was still in his ears as he fled. On the staircase, which he rushed down as if its steps were an inclined plane, he ran into his charwoman on her way up to do the morning cleaning of the room. "Jesus!" she cried, and covered her face with her apron, but he was already gone, Out of the front door he rushed, across the roadway, driven toward the water. Already he was grasping at the railings as a starving man clutches food. He swung himself over, like the distinguished gymnast he had once been in his youth, to his parents' pride. With weakening grip he was still holding on when he spied between the railings a motor-bus coming which would easily cover the noise of his fall, called in a low voice: "Dear parents, I have always loved you, all the same," and let himself drop. (*CS*, 87–88)

Kafka's later parables, short stories, and novels, including of course *The Trial*, extend the example presented in "The Judgment" to the submission of citizens to legal and state authorities. In "The Imperial Colonel," Kafka poses, without resolving, the question of why the obedient are inclined to obey. Kafka's short parable constitutes a sharp rebuke to Posner's insistent psychological claim that we would consent to the imperatives of a state when and only when those imperatives will maximize our wealth. To the contrary, Kafka's story implies that behind such hypothetical consent to the impersonal imperatives of the state lies not an urge to increase one's own well-being, but the urge to submit:

> One is ashamed to say by what means the imperial colonel governs our little town in the mountains. His few soldiers could be disarmed immediately, if we so wished, and help for him, even supposing he could summon it—but how could he do that?—would not come for days, indeed for weeks. And so he is utterly dependent on our obedience, but he does not try either

> to enforce it by tyrannical means or to wheedle it out of us by cordiality. And so why do we tolerate his hated rule? There is no doubt about it: only because of his gaze. . . . (*CS*, 475–76)

In the parable "The Emperor," Kafka shifts his attention away from the ruler and focuses on the mechanism of consent itself. Why would we, if asked, consent to legal imperatives? We would consent because it is psychologically satisfying, or perhaps necessary, to believe in the divine authority or the natural superiority of those with power. It is this psychological compulsion, not any state force, that ultimately quiets doubts as to the law's transcendent authority:

> A man doubted that the emperor was descended from the gods; he asserted that the emperor was our rightful sovereign, he did not doubt the emperor's divine mission (that was evident to him), it was only the divine descent that he doubted. This, naturally, did not cause much of a stir; when the surf flings a drop of water on to the land, that does not interfere with the eternal rolling of the sea, on the contrary, it is caused by it. (*CS*, 476)

In the short story "The Refusal," Kafka provides a psychological account of the legitimating urge for divine or supernatural authority upon which successful rule depends. Kafka's protagonist describes his own perception of the psychological process through which the governed come to perceive estate authority and state judgments as legitimate, which in turn leads them to tender their hypothetical consent to the state's imperatives:

> Now it is remarkable and I am continually being surprised by the way we in our town humbly submit to all orders issued in the capital. For centuries no political change has been brought about by the citizens themselves. In the capital great rulers have superseded each other—indeed, even dynasties have been deposed or annihilated, and new ones have started . . . yet none of this had any influence on our little town. . . . The highest official is the chief tax-collector, he has the rank of colonel, and is known as such. . . .
>
> This colonel, then, commands the town. I don't think he has ever produced a document entitling him to this position; very

> likely he does not possess such a thing. Maybe he really is chief tax-collector. But is that all? Does that entitle him to rule over all the other departments in the administration as well? . . . One is almost under the impression that the people here say: "Now that you've taken all we possess, please take us as well." In reality, of course, it was not he who seized the power, nor is he a tyrant. It has just come about over the years that the chief tax-collector is automatically the top official, and the colonel accepts the tradition just as we do. (*CS*, 263–64)

It has also "just come about" that the colonel regularly and ceremonially denies petitions from members of the community. Those denials are not simply tolerated; they are met by the "undeniable relief" of the community. Thus, the citizens' obedient compliance with the colonel's denials reflects not only the coercive influence of force, but the citizens' hypothetical consent to the impersonal imperatives of the government. Force is not needed because, if asked, the citizens would consent to the denials arbitrarily imposed upon them. That hypothetical consent is in turn motivated, Kafka suggests, by the seductive appeal of punitive hierarchy. If the citizens were asked, they would give their consent to these denials not because the denials maximize their wealth, but because they satisfy their need for self-denial and adverse judgment. The citizens are inclined to legitimate the state with their hypothetical consent to its imperatives because it feels good to be ruled and to be denied, not because those imperatives serve their well-being:

> "The petition has been refused," he announced. "You may go." An undeniable sense of relief passed through the crowd, everyone surged out. . . .
>
> In all important matters, however, the citizens can always count on a refusal. And now the strange fact is that without this refusal one simply cannot get along, yet at the same time these official occasions designed to receive the refusal are by no means a formality. Time after time one goes there full of expectation and in all seriousness and then one returns, if not exactly strengthened or happy, nevertheless not disappointed or tired. About these things I do not have to ask the opinion of anyone else, I feel them

> in myself, as everyone does; nor do I have any great desire to find out how these things are connected. (*CS*, 267)

Kafka's masterpiece *The Trial* explores the ramifications of our masochistic submission to authority when the state is considerably more malignant than the states that appear in the parables. At the outset of the novel, Joseph K is arrested "without having done anything wrong" (*T*, 7). Joseph never learns the nature of the charges brought against him. The state and its officials are unpredictable and sadistic. Yet Joseph is never physically forced to do anything: he is arrested but not imprisoned; he is interrogated but never forced to reappear; he is tried but never held against his will. Instead, he comes to accept the jurisdiction and legality of the court, its authority, its legitimacy, and ultimately its omnipotence and omniscience. Thus, Joseph does not simply obey the state's imperatives; his acquiescence is far more complete. By the end of the year, Joseph acknowledges the court's and the law's authority, concurs in the verdict against him, and complies in his own death sentence.

The horror and the familiarity of *The Trial* stem only superficially from the lawlessness of the legal system and the state's exercise of power. More fundamentally, the horror stems from Joseph's willing acquiescence to this corrupt authority—his hypothetical consent to, or legitimation of, the mindless, sadistic force being applied against him. In the last paragraphs, as Joseph is being led to the spot of his execution, his acquiescence is total, his identification with his warders complete. The sole comfort he allows himself is contemplation of the lesson that acquiescence has taught him:

> [H]e suddenly realized the futility of resistance. There would be nothing heroic in it were he to resist, to make difficulties for his companions, to snatch at the last appearance of life by struggling. He set himself in motion, and the relief his warders felt was transmitted to some extent even to himself. They suffered him now to lead the way. . . . "The only thing I can do now," he told himself [,"]is to keep my intelligence calm and analytical to the end. I always wanted to snatch at the world with twenty hands, and not for a very laudable motive, either. That was wrong, and am I to show now that not even a year's trial has taught me

> anything? Am I to leave this world as a man who has no common sense? . . . I don't want that to be said." (*T*, 251–52)

Only at the moment of execution does Joseph refuse to lend his affirmative assistance in what is happening to him. He experiences even this refusal, however, as an inability, rather than as an affirmative act of resistance:

> Once more the odious courtesies began, the first handed the knife across K. to the second, who handed it across K. back again to the first. K. now perceived clearly that he was supposed to seize the knife himself, as it traveled from hand to hand above him, and plunge it into his own breast. But he did not do so, he merely turned his head which was still free to move, and gazed around him. He could not completely rise to the occasion, he could not relieve the officials of all their tasks; the responsibility for this last failure of his lay with him who had not left him the remnant of strength necessary for the deed. . . . .
>
> But the hands of one of the partners were already at K.'s throat, while the other thrust the knife deep into his heart and turned it there twice. . . . "Like a dog!" he said; it was as if the shame of it must outlive him. (*T*, 254–55)

What motivates Joseph K.'s compliance? As in so much of Kafka's legal fiction, it is neither fear nor the threat of force; Joseph's obedience is not coerced from him. Instead Joseph K. complies with his trial and execution because, like George of "The Judgment," he concurs in the verdict against him and in the appropriateness of the punishment. In Posnerian terms, Joseph K. would consent, if asked, to the verdict of guilt and would agree that death is the appropriate sanction for his unspecified crime. As with the depiction of George, Kafka leaves little doubt about what would motivate such hypothetical consent: Joseph K. would consent to the punitive norms imposed upon him not because those norms in the long run maximize his wealth, but because they acknowledge his sense of guilt and satisfy his craving for punishment.

Finally, in a short parable entitled "The Problem of Our Laws," Kafka straightforwardly describes his vision of the nature of law and legal authority, and the mechanism of legitimation upon which it depends. The authority of law, Kafka tells us, is ultimately sustained not by force, but by the craving of the governed for judgment by lawful, "noble" authority. It is this human craving, even more than the urge of the powerful to dominate, that sustains the illusion of certainty, fairness, generality, and justice. We would consent to the imperatives of our laws and of the nobility that controls them, not because it would be in our interest to do so, but because we desire to see nobility in those who judge us and because we desire to be judged by those we see as noble. It is that craving that motivates our hypothetical consent to the imposition of laws whose substance we do not even know:

> Our laws are not generally known; they are kept secret by the small group of nobles who rule us. . . .
>
> The very existence of these laws, however, is at most a matter of presumption. There is a tradition that they exist and that they are a mystery confided to the nobility, but it is not and cannot be more than a mere tradition sanctioned by age, for the essence of a secret code is that it should remain a mystery. . . . There is a small party who . . . try to show that, if any law exists, it can only be this: The Law is whatever the nobles do. This party see everywhere only the arbitrary acts of the nobility and reject the popular tradition, . . . for it gives the people a false, deceptive, and overconfident security in confronting coming events. . . .
>
> . . . Any party that would repudiate not only all belief in the laws, but the nobility as well, would have the whole people behind it; yet no such party can come into existence for nobody would dare to repudiate the nobility. . . . The sole visible and indubitable law that is imposed upon us is the nobility, and must we ourselves deprive ourselves of that one law? (*CS*, 437–38)

If Kafka's descriptions ring true—if we would consent when asked, not to those legal imperatives that promote our wealth or self-interest, but to those that satisfy our cravings for judgment and punishment by noble authority—then nothing of moral consequence can follow from the fact of our hypothetical consent. It does not follow that the imperative to which we would hypothetically consent is one that will serve either our enlightened or our perceived self-interest. It does not follow that the hierarchical relationship between us and the state to which we hypothetically consent, and which we thereby hypothetically legitimate, is a good one. It does not follow that the institutions to which we hypothetically consent are just or that the hypothetical choices we make are choices that reflect, much less foster, autonomy. If, as Kafka suggests, we are motivationally inclined to submit to authority, we must examine the value of the hierarchical relationships that the act of submission creates. The fact of submission, like the fact of consent, in itself implies nothing.

Thus, even if nonmarket legal institutions would command our consent, nothing normative follows from that assumption. Posner has not shown that we would consent, if asked, only to those legal imperatives that leave us better off, or that reinforce autonomous virtues, or that are morally superior, or even that are cheaper. He simply assumes that we would give our consent to all legal imperatives that are wealth maximizing, and to none that are not. A nonmarket legal imperative indeed may be morally preferable if it is cheaper. But the argument supporting such a proposition can draw nothing from the consent that we may be inclined to give it.

Why might we give our consent to particular nonmarket legal institutions if we were asked to do so? We might consent, as Posner suggests we invariably would, because of the high odds that the nonmarket institution will leave us wealthier than some other alternative (*EJ*, 97). We might, however, give our consent to such nonmarket legal institutions because of their authoritarian and punitive structure. Nonmarket legal institutions embody legal imperatives: "Don't fix prices." "Don't kill another human being." "Don't drive negligently." Obedience to the legal imperatives of the impersonal state and our willingness to legitimate that authority may be as ingrained as an instinct for self-preservation. Thus, if asked, we might be inclined to consent to wealth-maximizing legal imperatives of the state not because they are wealth maximizing, but simply because we are attracted to the authoritarian structure of law, just as we may be inclined to buy a lottery ticket not because the bundle of risks it presents will maximize our welfare, but simply because we are attracted to the authoritarian structure of fate.

An assessment of the moral value of that to which we would hypothetically consent must include an assessment of the relationship flowing from the transaction. Hypothetically consensual submission to legal authority does not necessarily imply a change for the better.

As with our expressly consensual submission to personal authority, and impliedly consensual submission to risk, our willingness to legitimate—through our hypothetical consent—the relinquishment of a measure of our autonomy to legal imperatives has obvious prudential, moral, and social value. When we hypothetically consent to the imposition upon us of a state imperative, we are freed from the burden of resolving on our own course of action. When we hypothetically consent to the imposition of legal imperatives ordering us not to kill, fix prices, steal, or commit adultery, we have at the same time freed ourselves from the burden of reaching those decisions independently. Obedience to legal rules to which we would have consented relieves us of the task of evaluating the morality and prudence of our own actions, a task that would be time consuming and perhaps beyond our powers.[18] If we want to lead moral lives, both for the sake of virtue and for the sake of others, the best way to do so may be simply to obey, whether we choose to obey God's commandments, Kant's categorical imperative, the utilitarian's command to maximize the community's happiness, or the state's criminal code. The impulse to legitimate those imperatives by tendering our hypothetical consent facilitates that obedience. The impulse to legitimate our submission to imperative authority also has within it, however, the seeds of tragedy. That impulse is the means by which we allow ourselves to become tools that enable those who use us to destroy others.

Thus, hypothetically consensual submission to legal authority and the loss of power and responsibility that follows may have morally desirable or morally abhorrent consequences. The hypothetical consent of the judge, citizen, and lawyer to the nonmarket imperatives of the Nazi state, although arguably excusable, was certainly not morally good. Similarly, the hypothetical consent of a citizen to the legal imperatives of a participatory democracy, although not exemplary of autonomous virtue, is certainly not evil. Our tendency to legitimate lawful authority—to give our hypothetical consent—may have good or evil consequences, depending upon the moral value of the legal system to which we have submitted and the moral quality of the relationship between state and citizen that our consent nurtures. If we are attracted to the power and punitive authority of the state, and if this attraction accounts for our tendency to consent to its

18. See, e.g., Joseph Raz, "Authority and Justification," *Philosophy and Public Affairs* 14 (1985): 3–29.

imperatives, a good deal of harm may come from our persistent denial of the potential for both evil and virtue inherent in this central aspect of our nature.

Conclusion

Posner's normative defense of wealth maximization rests on an inadequate picture of human nature. Although Posner has not expressly addressed the relevance of truth or falsity to moral theory, he justifies his admittedly oversimplified picture of our nature on the ground of scientific theory. It is not realism, but predictive value, Posner claims, that is the test of positive theory:

> [A]n economic theory of law . . . will not capture the full complexity, richness, and confusion of the phenomena. . . . But its lack of realism, far from invalidating the theory, is the essential precondition of theory. . . . The true test of a theory is its utility in predicting or explaining reality. Judged by this criterion, economic theory, despite (because of?) the unrealism of its assumptions, may be judged a success. (*EA*, 13)

In a famous passage of Kafka's *The Trial* reminiscent of Posner's claim, a priest explains that necessity, not truth, is that on which the powerful rely: "No," said the priest, "it is not necessary to accept everything as true, one must only accept it as necessary." Joseph's response to this lesson sounds like a warning: "A melancholy conclusion," said K. "It turns lying into a universal principle" (*T*, 246–47).

False or unrealistic premises may not defeat a scientific theory, but when we allow such premises to ground a moral theory—to dictate what we should do, as well as what we will do—we indeed run the risk of elevating lying to the level of principle. It does matter, for purposes of moral truth and moral theory, what we are like. Posner and Kafka both examine worlds in which citizens typically consent to an array of authorities—family, state, employer. Their characters, however, evince drastically different human personalities, and the moral attractiveness of the worlds they inhabit varies accordingly. Posner's hypothetical legal actors expressly, impliedly, and hypothetically consent to changes in their circumstances with a view toward the improvement of their own welfare, whereas Kafka's protagonists expressly, impliedly, and hypothetically consent because of a felt compulsion to legitimate the will of an authority. Perhaps both portraits are caricatures; Kafka's protagonists may be as unrealistically masochistic as Posner's are unrealistically egoistic. But although the masochism of Kafka's characters is exaggerated, we can nevertheless recognize glimpses of ourselves in these characters. Kafka's characters help us to see that Posner's actors are also exaggerations. It may be true, as Bentham thought, that "all men calculate."[19] It is not true, as Posner blithely assumes, that all men calculate all of the time. Sometimes we calculate. Other times, we simply obey, acquiesce, or submit.

If we are motivationally complex, then we cannot delegate to any ambiguously motivated human act such as consent the task of moral legitimation. We cannot infer that a consensual world leaves every individual better off (and is therefore morally superior) simply because all affected parties have consented to it, unless everyone was trying to improve his individual welfare when consenting to change—and succeeding. The traditional moral or legal theorist can accommodate our psychological complexity in one of two ways. First, if the theorist retains welfare as the criterion of moral decision making, then that welfare must be ascertained by reference to indicia other than consent. Alternatively, if consent is the criterion of moral decision making, then the moral theorist must establish the value of consent by some means other than the automatic implication of an increase in individual well-being. She must similarly establish the fact of autonomy by some means other than its automatic implication from an "opportunity for choice." Posner's attempted merger of consequentialist and deontological moral reasoning through the operational mechanism of consent fails if we sometimes consent for reasons unrelated to our own well-being.

A consequentialist's moral evaluation of a particular consensual transaction must address all changes actually brought on by a transaction, not just those that are presumed to have been intended. I have argued that if we are creatures predisposed to accept authority and hierarchy, we will consent to many transactions in order to

19. Bentham, *Introduction*, 90.

submit to power, not to increase our own well-being. The new hierarchical societies we thereby create may be damaging, as are many of the relationships Kafka hypothesizes and explores.[20]

If the deontological theorist retains consent as the only legitimating moral criterion despite our motivationally complex reasons for giving consent, she must account for this preference. People expressly, impliedly, and hypothetically consent to a wide range of changes in our world. Many of those acts of consent seem to be morally unattractive human decisions that leave the world a morally unattractive place. Our express consent may be driven by a rational assessment of our choices, or it may spring from fear, hysteria, feelings of inadequacy, or masochistic compulsion. It is not obvious why consent driven by any of the latter should be regarded as a morally appealing human act. Similarly, we impliedly consent to assume a wide range of risks, and we do so for a wide range of reasons. Sometimes assuming these risks is a rational, justified, or otherwise morally appealing act, but at other times it is not. The entrepreneur may be taking a worthy risk when he enters his own business. The customer of the San Francisco bathhouse, however, may not be taking a risk worth respecting when he purchases a bundle of consensual sex and high risk of AIDS, just as the sixteenth-century libertine may not have been taking a risk worth respecting when he purchased from a prostitute a bundle of consensual sex plus a high risk of syphilis-induced death. Respect for the courage of the entrepreneur should not compel respect for the destructive inclinations of the others. Finally, if asked, we would also consent to the authority of nonmarket institutions for many reasons: because we recognize the virtue of the values the institution reflects, because we think of the institution as operating for the most part in our self-interest, or because consenting to authority confirms our feeling of guilt and meets our need for punishment. It is not obvious why consent motivated by the latter two reasons should compel the same respect as does consent to a morally defensible authority motivated by rational desires.

20. Alternatively, we may occasionally consent to transactions neither to increase our individual well-being nor to create a hierarchy, but instead to create an equal community of some sort. Noncommercial consensual transactions, such as the equalizing bonds of marriage, friendship, love, and family, are not motivated exclusively by either hierarchy or self-interest, but by an inclination to create a shared point of view or equality of outlook. If so, a consequentialist account of such a transaction must evaluate the moral quality of the community thereby created.

People consent to changes in the world that involve a wide range of market choices, risk pools, and apparent authorities. Wives submit to abusive husbands; employees consent to exploitative and humiliating work environments; consumers consent to sales of defective, dangerous, and overpriced merchandise; women consent to sexual harassment on the street and on the job; religious converts submit to directives compelling consensual suicide; subjects in an experiment consent to the dehumanizing, authoritative instruction to electrically shock other human beings; monks consensually abide by vows of poverty; Zen students consensually endure assaults by their teachers; patients in therapy abide the directives of their therapists; soldiers follow the orders of their superiors; and citizens generally obey, without need of coercion, the legal injunctions of their governments. Many of those consensual changes leave both individual and community not just worse off, but miserable. It is not obvious why we should assume that all of these consensual changes in the world are moral changes on the ground that they promote autonomy. It does not follow from the fact that coerced states are immoral by virtue of their coercive element that voluntary world states are of positive moral value by virtue of their voluntariness.

Finally, a moral theorist may coherently and perhaps sensibly insist that for some purposes we ought to forgo concern for both utility and consent and justify actual or proposed institutions by reference to the moral value of the human personality they engender. But in order to do so and remain true to that human personality, we need to develop rich and true descriptions of the subjective experience of our institutions. We live the subjective experience of our lives, not their formal, conventional, outward descriptions. Our subjective experiences of the consensual transactions we enter do not accord with Posner's external descriptions of those transactions. From the external point of view, we consensually choose to move from state A to state B. But from an interior perspective, we experience that act in any number of complex ways—as a submission to a perceived or actual authority suggesting or mandating a change, as the imposition of a change upon a resisting party, as an agreement to a change with a newly discovered equal partner. Submission, imposition, and agreement imply a conscious will to create a new community through human interaction at the same time that they evidence a will to effect a reallocation of resources. That implication is lacking in the starkly solitary act of choice. Submission and imposition also imply a will to create a hierarchical community through human interaction. That further implication is lacking in the equalizing act of reaching agreement. The act of consent is a broad description that only outwardly, and only transparently, embraces all of these radically different subjective experiences.

In only one respect are these widely disparate consensual decisions subjectively alike: no one of them by itself constitutes the essence of the experience of being human. No one of these consensual acts, and certainly not the act of consent itself, should define the essential experience of morality. Moral theory, if not scientific theory, must be about truth, not necessity. Our assessment of the moral significance of our legal institutions cannot be based upon necessary depictions of human nature. We must attain a true depiction, indeed we must attain many true depictions, of the joys and sufferings to which we give our consent. Only then can we assess the wisdom of imposing those experiences upon others.

Chapter 2

A Rejoinder to Judge Posner

Judge Posner's response to the preceding chapter, which appeared originally in the *Harvard Law Review* and again in his book *Law and Literature*, ends with a true insight; that he and I live in different worlds. I am sorry, though, that Posner did not choose to defend in that response the vision of personality that he so passionately holds and that so clearly motivates his unique claims about law and ethics. And I am disappointed that he left unchallenged the very different vision of personality that underlies my own ethical positions: the belief that we as people are more authoritarian and submissive than the depictions of our nature relied upon by mainstream liberal theorists. It is clear, at least to me, that these divergent phenomenological depictions of our inner lives lie at the root of Posner's and my divergent conclusions about the ethical significance of choice. Perhaps the reason Posner chose not to respond to my essentially descriptive and psychological claim—other than to note that I made it—is simply because it struck him as so bizarre that he did not recognize it as the only claim in my article requiring a response.

I am also simply surprised that in his closing sentence Posner claims the reader's world as his own. I had thought that Posner took pleasure in the oddity and the counterintuitiveness of his own theory of human nature and his conclusions about the ethics of choice that are grounded in that theory. In that limited respect, I had viewed him as a fellow traveler. For Posner's ethical world is, I suspect, quite far from that of the *Harvard Law Review* reader. I don't know, but I doubt that the reader shares Posner's belief that we should be allowed to sell our babies for profit.[1] I doubt that the reader believes, as Posner apparently does, that we should be allowed to sell ourselves

1. See Richard A. Posner, *Economic Analysis of Law,* 2d ed. (Boston: Little, Brown, 1977), sec. 5.4; Elisabeth M. Landes and Richard A. Posner, "The Economics of the Baby Shortage," *Journal of Legal Studies* 7 (1978): 323–48.

into slavery.[2] I would guess that the average reader, unlike Posner, views rape and prostitution as manifestations of what is wrong with sexual relations in this society and would not view the legal availability of prostitution (along with sex markets such as dating and marriage) as a reason for the wrongness of rape.[3] I think that most of the *Harvard Law Review*'s readers, unlike Posner, believe that there are certain things we simply *should not sell* and that our laws should reflect this ethical prohibition: we should not sell our babies; we should not sell our bodies; we should not sell our sexuality; we should not sell our freedom; and we should not sell our mortal lives. Surely some readers, perhaps most, also believe there are things we should not buy: we should not buy lottery tickets instead of food, no matter how much we thrill to the gamble; we should not buy alcohol instead of shelter, no matter how much we love the bottle; we should not buy the services of prostitutes, no matter how much we lust for sex; and we should not buy slaves, no matter how much we pay their families and no matter how free their consent. At least some readers, I hope, know that we have good reason to sympathize with anorexics, bulimics, compulsive gamblers, bankrupt farmers, and AIDS victims. Surely some readers, perhaps most, know that when and if we reach the point where we decide not to hear people cry, whether out of concern for "privacy and freedom" or out of a reluctance to indulge the "bellyaching" of those in pain,[4] we will have given up a central part of our humanity. We will have alienated our moral lives.

Posner's sterile and idiosyncratic vision of human nature skews his approach to fiction and ethics alike. The first section of this rejoinder briefly comments on the relation I see between Posner's view of human nature and his interpretation of Kafka's fiction. The second examines the new argument for the ethical significance of choice that emerges from Posner's response and contrasts it with the argument put forth in *The Economics of Justice*. Finally, I argue that the new argument, like the old, rests on unsupported empirical assumptions.

2. See *EJ*, 86; Anthony T. Kronman and Richard A. Posner, *The Economics of Contract Law* (Boston: Little, Brown, 1979), 256–60.

3. See Richard A. Posner, "An Economic Theory of Criminal Law," *Columbia Law Review* 85 (1985): 1193–1231.

4. Richard A. Posner, "The Ethical Significance of Free Choice: A Reply to Professor West," *Harvard Law Review* 99 (1986): 1440. Subsequent references, abbreviated *ES*, are given in the text.

Posner on Kafka

Like virtually every other reader or critic of Kafka, Posner understands Kafka's stories to be about relationships of authority and submission. The question, of course, is *what* authority the stories depict. There are many authorities in our lives, and Kafka's rich stories and symbolic imagery can be read to depict many of them. Posner's reading of Kafka simply places three authorities off limits: the state, the law, and the employer. Whatever Kafka's odd stories are about, they are not, in Posner's view, about governmental authority, law, markets, workplaces, or business. I believe that Posner's idiosyncratic view of human nature fully determines this idiosyncratic interpretation of Kafka's fiction. Two examples will illustrate the general point, which applies to all of Posner's chosen interpretations.

First, Posner argues, the law depicted in Kafka's fiction is not really true law at all. True law, Posner claims, is "a system of rules." The law that Kafka describes in, for example, his parable "Before the Law" is "malevolent whimsy" (*ES*, 1433 n. 8). Therefore, what Kafka calls law is not really law at all. Posner's premises are correct: Kafka does depict something well described as "malevolent whimsy," and malevolent whimsy is surely not what we think of when we think of law as a "system of rules." But Posner's conclusion—that what Kafka depicts as malevolent whimsy is not *really* law—completely begs the question of the nature of real law. *Is* law a system of rules, or *is* law malevolent whimsy?

It is Posner's view of our nature that compels his answer to this question and thus his reading of Kafka's parable. We can give rational consent to a system of rules. We cannot give rational consent to malevolent whimsy, for by definition, any consent given to malevolent whimsy will not be rational. And we *do* consent, given Posner's expanded definition of consent (with which I have no quarrel), to much of the law that governs us. And, given Posner's vision of our personality, the consent we give must be rational, because that's just the kind of people we are: rational. Therefore, because we do consent to law, law must be a system of rules, and because what Kafka describes is surely not that, Kafka is not really talking about law at all.

Likewise, Posner argues, the work environments described in Kafka's fiction are not *really* about work (1433 n. 8). The whipping scene in *The Trial*, for example, is not really about low-level warders getting whipped by their boss. The scene is not about work at all, Posner explains, because it "reeks of sadomasochism" (*ES*, 1441 n. 28), and the relationship between cop and sergeant, *as we know it*, just isn't sadomasochistic. Again Posner's reading of Kafka begs the question, for the nature of work relationships is precisely the question at issue. If work generally, and life in your local precinct in particular, is a bit on the sadomasochistic side, then Kafka's whipper scene might *really* be about work after all, and not about kinky sex. The question is whether the real employer-employee relationship is sadomasochistic.

Again, it is Posner's vision of human nature that determines his answer and hence his reading of the scene. Workers generally consent to their jobs. That consent must be rational, given Posner's view of human nature, because that's the way people are. Because one does not give *rational* consent to sadomasochism, work, to which people consent, just cannot be sadomasochistic. Because Kafka's scene is surely sadomasochistic, it isn't really about work.

Thus, Posner's passionate commitment to his view of our nature prejudges his reading of Kafka. These stories just *can't* be telling us something about *law*, because law is a system of rules, and what Kafka describes is more like malevolent whimsy; they can't *really* be about work because work is welfare maximizing, and what Kafka describes is sadomasochism. This is reading by political fiat. Posner reads Kafka as a chronicler of our inner turmoil but refuses to read him as a chronicler of the choices and of the social institutions in which that turmoil is so strikingly reflected. One does not have to be a literalist to think that "The Judgment" really is about judgment or that *The Trial* really is about a man's trial, whether inner or outer. Both works are unquestionably about our sense of guilt, but more than that, they are about the choices made under the influence of that guilt. The choices that Kafka's guilt-ridden characters make—to go to work, to have sex, to submit to law—are as masochistic and irrational as the motivations that drive them; they are *not* welfare maximizing or autonomy promoting, nor are the institutions those choices legitimate. Kafka, of all modern writers, understands and portrays the unity between our tumultuous inner lives, the outer world, and the role of choice in mediating the two.

And finally, both Posner's description of the historical Kafka, and the argument from authorial intent derived from it, are skewed by Posner's own commitment to the invariable rationality of choice. As Posner insists, Kafka unquestionably hated his father; the question is *why*. Posner's endorsement of a Freudian response reduces Kafka to every man; Kafka hated his father because his father made love to his mother (*ES*, 1433). Ronald Hayman gives a much richer account of Kafka's relationship with his father—an account that calls into question Posner's facile suggestion that Kafka's psychological torment left him apolitical and apathetic toward market capitalism. If anything, Hayman suggests, quite the reverse was true:

> Early on, . . . Franz's attitude (toward his father's) business changed. At first it was a pleasure to be in the shop, . . . to help occasionally, to look admiringly while his big father sold things, [and] gave orders. But before long Franz was constantly ill at ease, and especially upset to see how his father would shout, rage and swear at the Czech staff—"paid enemies" he called them. . . . Why be nasty to people who were nice? . . . [I]n the shop it was obvious that his father was often unjust. The staff, unable to answer back, must be "in a terrible state of indignation," which made the child nervous and anxious to placate them. What he felt was an extreme form of what most Prague Jews felt, knowing themselves to be aliens among the Czechs both as Jews and Germans, and to be better off, financially, socially and culturally.[5]

In fact, Kafka's "experience in handling disability and death claims on behalf of workers maimed or killed on the job," Ernst Pawel writes in his biography of Kafka, "served to reinforce the instinctive identification with the underdog that defined his manifest political orientation."[6] As reported by Pawel, Kafka's understanding of and identification with the underdog's situation was most assuredly not sentimental. It was radical—it went to the root of the nature of submission. Kafka's description of the mangled and injured workmen, whose accidents it was his responsibility to minimize, reflects the

5. Ronald Hayman, *Kafka: A Biography* (New York: Oxford University Press, 1982), 13.

6. Ernst Pawell, *The Nightmare of Reason: A Life of Franz Kafka* (New York: Farrar, Straus, Giroux, 1984), 187.

same observation that appears and reappears in Kafka's fictional depiction of the arational submissions of workers: "How modest these people are. Instead of storming the institute and smashing the place to bits, they come and plead."[7]

Ultimately, Posner's refusal to read Kafka's fiction as capable of telling him something about law or business is just silly. Sometimes, as the great man said, a cigar really is just a cigar. *The Trial*, "The Judgment," "The Problem with Our Laws," "The New Advocate," "The Emperor," "The Advocate," and "Before the Laws" are unquestionably, as Posner tells us over and over, "about" religious authority, familial authority, Oedipal complexes, the overbrooding conscience, the neurosis of the sensitive soul's inner life. But that is no reason *not* to read them for their tremendous and multiple insights into the nature of law. Quite the contrary: we need to understand how guilt-ridden souls react to the authority of law, just as we need to understand how such souls react to the authority of gods and fathers—particularly because those guilt-ridden souls may be our own.

Posner's New Argument for Freedom and Consent

The philosophical argument for freedom and choice that Posner makes in his response is far more modest than the one advanced in *The Economics of Justice*, the target of my article. Most strikingly, the new argument is explicitly—even aggressively—independent of all descriptive claims about the rationality of our motivational nature. The new argument does not pursue Posner's earlier suggestion that people behave as rationally in marriage, friendship, procreation, and crime as they do in traditional economic markets (*EJ*, 237). Indeed, Posner now tells us that such a claim about the nature of our motivation could not be justified within the terms of the discipline: "Economics does not seek to depict states of mind; it is concerned with what people . . . do, not what they feel or think" (*ES*, 1439).

Posner's newfound motivational agnosticism, it should be noted, is not entirely consistent: even while denying the need to do so, Posner implicitly reaffirms his earlier descriptive claims about the rational motivation behind choice. He tells us, for example, that

7. Max Brod, *Franz Kafka: A Biography*, trans. G. Humphreys Roberts (New York: Schocken Books, 1960), 76.

lottery ticket buyers are risk preferrers, pure and simple; that a person would not decide to be an employee rather than an independent contractor unless the expected payoff was worth it;[8] and that the homosexual bathhouse frequenter—assuming no mental illness—is simply put to an unhappy choice, unproblematic for the economist: "life-style or life expectancy" (*ES*, 1444, 1446, 1442). But for the most part, Posner's response does not pursue the claims that such rational, consensual transactions by definition leave people better off and more autonomous and that they thus satisfy both utilitarian and Kantian notions of value. Instead, and far more modestly, he argues that the ethical significance of the Pareto-superior transaction is merely a "principle of political philosophy [that] delimit[s] the proper role of the state" (*ES*, 1432). Simply put, the state should not interfere in voluntary transactions that impose no uncompensated costs on nonparties. Thus, Posner's new argument reduces to the claim that if we deny the ethical significance of Pareto-superior transactions, coercive and unpalatable state action will inexorably follow.

Where do these two theories—the new political-philosophy approach and the old descriptive-economics approach—leave the ethical significance of choice? Reflect again on the abused wife who, Posner reminds us, in "our" society is always free to leave (*ES*, 1444). We now have two Posnerian arguments against intervening in these private domestic tragedies. The old descriptive economics argument is this: the wife is a rational creature who will choose the best course open to her; she has chosen to stay with her assaultive husband; she is therefore best off doing so, and we ought not to interfere with that wealth-maximizing decision. The argument rests on an unsupported empirical assumption about the wife's motivational nature: that she chooses rationally. That assumption was the target of my article.

The new political-philosophy approach advanced in Posner's response is, however, agnostic on motivation. It allows no inference of rationality from the wife's behavior and thus no inference about the comparative value of her decision to stay home. Instead, the argument for nonintervention that emerges from the new political-philosophy approach is this: by definition, the only possible intervention in the wife's action is state intervention; by definition, state intervention is horrible. Regardless of the rationality of her motivation, therefore,

8. See ibid., 1446.

and regardless of the comparative value of her alternative courses of action, the wife is better off enduring brutal domestic assaults than enduring *any* state interference with her choice. But this new fiction is just cruel: there are obviously no such definitions. Both the truth of the political claim that the only alternative to individual freedom is unpalatable state oppression, and the merit of the political judgment that choice must therefore be protected against all intervention, depend on the nature of the state, the nature of the individual, and the nature of our collective political life. Posner fails to provide the necessary empirical support for his new definitional claims; indeed, he gives *no* reason beyond red-baiting and jingoistic appeals to patriotism to concur in his denunciation of state power. His new argument is consequently as weak as the old: the old one rests on an unsupported empirical assumption about our motivational nature; the new one rests on equally unsupported assumptions about the nature of our collective political life.

Only when we drop *both* sets of assumptions will we be able to ask the truly difficult but only important question, and that is *why* these staggeringly depressing alternatives—an abusive husband, grinding poverty, or an oppressive state—are the only choices we can imagine for an abused wife. If these are in fact her only choices, it is because we have failed to act. And we will not create or even envision better alternatives until we cease to believe what is surely false: that we are all inexorably rational individuals, that we can never assess the misery of a victimized woman's life better than can the victim herself, or that we cannot do so without bringing down the oppressive iron fist of the state. Until we truly understand that a marriage of terror, no less than a state of terror, is *bad*—even when consensual—we will not be moved to create better alternatives. Posner's insistence that consent is *the* absolute moral trump simply traps us in our present lives. His Panglossian satisfaction notwithstanding, our present community is not as happy a place as we can make it.

Posner insists, and I agree, that he and I live in different worlds. In his world, because abused wives are free to leave, their chosen worlds must be wealth maximizing (*ES*, 1444); in my world, their evident misery demands community intervention. In his world, we do not and should not indulge the "bellyaching" of others (*ES*, 1444); in my world, we can and should pay close heed to the pains and pleasures of others; we are a community, and their pains and pleasures are ours. In his world, "our" political decision to affirm each other's choices is better than "their" political decision to brand them insane (*ES*, 1440); in my world, this is a false dilemma—these are surely not our only political options. In his world, in short, the state is by definition evil and the individual is by definition rational; in my world, the state has the potential for good and the individual for submissive, as opposed to rational, free choice. Posner's world strikes me as flat and radically counterexperiential; it misdescribes our external social life and our internal motivational nature. My world, I suppose, strikes Posner as too bizarre to reckon with. There must be a way to cure our mutual ignorance—there must be a way to talk across the descriptive and normative divide. I thought literature might provide the bridge. That hope may have been naive: literature, like politics, may be endlessly contested. The use of literature may have merely shifted the battleground. And yet Posner obviously shares my passion for Kafka. That alone makes us two a community of sorts.

Chapter 3

Adjudication Is Not Interpretation

Among other achievements, the modern law-as-literature movement has prompted increasing numbers of legal scholars to embrace the claim that adjudication is interpretation, and more specifically, that constitutional adjudication is interpretation of the Constitution.[1] That adjudication is interpretation—that an adjudicative act is an interpretive act—more than any other central commitment, unifies the otherwise diverse strands of the legal and constitutional theory of the late twentieth century. Owen Fiss, for example, begins his influential article "Objectivity and Interpretation" with the claim that "[a]djudication is interpretation: Adjudication is the process by which a judge

1. The law-as-literature movement is becoming increasingly difficult to define, as it comes of age. It has, I think, at least three strands. First, there is a growing body of scholarship from legal scholars regarding the legal and jurisprudential ideas contained in literature. See, e.g., Judith Schenck Koffler, "Capital in Hell: Dante's Lesson on Usury," *Rutgers Law Review* 32 (1985): 608–60; Richard Weisberg, "How Judges Speak: Some Lessons on Adjudication in *Billy Budd, Sailor* with an Application to Justice Rehnquist," *New York University Law Review* 57 (1982): 1–69. Second, both legal and literary scholars are studying the relationship between literary criticism and legal criticism, and between literary theory and legal theory. In addition to the articles discussed in this piece, see R. M. Dworkin, *A Matter of Principle* (Cambridge: Harvard University Press, 1985), 146; R. M. Dworkin, "Law as Interpretation" *Texas Law Review* 60 (1982), 527–50, "Interpretation Symposium," *Southern California Law Review* 58 (1985): 1–725. See also Robert M. Cover, "Nomos and Narrative," *Harvard Law Review* 97 (1983): 4–68; Frank I. Michelman, "Traces of Self-Government," *Harvard Law Review* 100 (1986): 4–77. Third, there is a growing awareness among legal scholars that both law and legal theory can profitably be read as literature. See, e.g., James Boyd White, *The Legal Imagination: Studies in the Nature of Legal Thought and Expression* (Boston: Little, Brown, 1973) (reading law as literature). For a general bibliography of writings of the law and literature movement through 1979, see Harold Suretsky, "Search for a Theory: An Annotated Bibliography of Writings on the Relation of Law to Literature and the Humanities," *Rutgers Law Review* 32 (1979): 727–39.

comes to understand and express the meaning of an authoritative legal text and the values embodied in that text."[2] Ronald Dworkin begins his article "How Law Is Like Literature" with a remarkably similar declaration:

> I shall argue that legal practice is an exercise in interpretation not only when lawyers interpret particular documents or statutes but generally. . . . [W]e can improve our understanding of law by comparing legal interpretation with interpretation in . . . literature. I also expect that law, when better understood, will provide a better grasp of what interpretation is in general.[3]

Tom Grey summarizes the state of the art in the opening paragraphs of his most recent contribution to the interpretivism literature, *The Constitution as Scripture*, thusly:

> If the current interest in interpretive theory, or hermeneutics, does nothing else, at least it shows that the concept of interpretation is broad enough to encompass any plausible mode of constitutional adjudication. We are all interpretivists; the real arguments are not over whether judges should stick to interpreting, but over what they should interpret and what interpretive attitudes they should adopt.[4]

However, Grey's claim that "we are all interpretivists," while it states an important truth, also misleads. For while it is true, in a sense, that today most constitutional theorists are interpretivists, it is not the case that all constitutional theorists are interpretivists, and it is surely not the case that this has always been so. That adjudication consists primarily of the interpretation of texts is a very old claim; its roots lie in Blackstone's insistence that adjudication is primarily the discovery, not the creation, of law. But in our century as in Blackstone's time, there is a competing, noninterpretivist vision of

2. Owen Fiss, "Objectivity and Interpretation," *Stanford Law Review* 34 (1982): 739–63. Subsequent references, abbreviated *OI*, are given in the text.

3. Dworkin, *Matter of Principle*, 146.

4. Thomas C. Grey, "The Constitution as Scripture," *Stanford Law Review* 37 (1984): 1–25.

what adjudication is, and although no longer dominant, that competing vision is nevertheless still a part of American legal theory. The competing vision is that adjudication, including constitutional adjudication, is an imperative act, not an interpretive act. According to this imperativist tradition, the essence of adjudication, including constitutional adjudication, is the creation of law backed by force, not the interpretation of a preexisting legal text guided by reason. Adjudication is an act of power, not of cognition. It is a branch of politics, not a branch of knowledge.

Grey's claim and state-of-the-art hermeneutic theory notwithstanding, these two conflicting traditions—one united around the claim that adjudication is interpretive, and the other around the opposing claim that adjudication is imperative—are both still with us, and in one form or another have always been with us. In the eighteenth and nineteenth centuries, the imperativist-interpretivist debate could be heard in the competing tenets of the English legal positivists and the natural lawyers.[5] In the early twentieth century, the imperativist-interpretivist divide could be found in the competing theories and pedagogies of the legal formalists and the legal realists.[6]

5. The legal positivist's classic formulation (that law is "the command of the sovereign") is, of course, Austin's. See John Austin, *The Province of Jurisprudence Determined and the Uses of the Study of Jurisprudence* (London: Weidenfeld and Nicolson, 1954), 101-14. The sentiment is echoed in Jeremy Bentham, *Of Laws in General*, ed. H. L. A. Hart (London: University of London, Athlone Press, 1970), 31–33. For the leading positivists' exposition of the interpretive-imperative debate, see Jeremy Bentham, *A Comment on the Commentaries and a Fragment on Government*, ed. James Henderson Burns and H. L. A. Hart (London: University of London, Athlone Press, 1977). For a modern review of the Blackstone-Bentham debate, see H. L. A. Hart, *Essays on Bentham: Studies in Jurisprudence and Political Theory* (Oxford: Clarendon, 1982).

6. For the realists' exposition of the imperative-interpretive debate, see John Chipman Gray, *The Nature and Sources of the Law* (New York: Columbia University Press, 1909); Karl N. Llewellyn, *The Bramble Bush: Some Lectures on Law and Its Study* (New York: Printed for the use of students at Columbia University School of Law, 1930); Joseph W. Bingham, "What Is the Law?" *Michigan Law Review* 11 (1912): 1–25 and 109–21; Jerome Frank, "Mr. Justice Holmes and Non-Euclidean Legal Thinking," *Cornell Law Quarterly* 17 (1931): 568–603; Oliver Wendell Holmes, "The Path of the Law," *Harvard Law Review* 10 (1897): 459–62; Oliver Wendell Holmes, "Ideals and Doubts," *Illinois Law Review* 10 (1915): 1–3; Oliver Wendell Holmes, "Natural Law," *Harvard Law Review* 32 (1918): 40–44; Joseph C. Hutcheson, Jr., "Lawyer's Law and the Little, Small Dice," *Tulane Law Review* 7 (1932): 1–12; Harold D. Lasswell and Myres S. McDougal, "Legal Education and Public Policy: Professional Training in the

In the second half of this century, we feel the same imperativist-interpretivist tension between the contrasting visions of the liberal legalists and at least a few (by no means most) of the critical legal scholars.[7] In this decade, though, and in this country, and in this legal culture (meaning law schools and law reviews), Grey is surely right. Interpretivism dominates in the academy and in the law reviews; and imperativism is declining. Today, it is indeed the case that most modern American legal theorists, and almost all modern constitutional theorists, are interpretivists of one sort or another. This fact alone is significant but not really surprising. As Grant Gilmore observed in a different context,[8] imperativism and interpretivism tend to come and go in waves, with one tradition dominating one generation's jurisprudential fancy, only to be supplanted in the next generation by some revamped version of the out-of-fashion minority view.

What is surprising about our modern theory, I believe, is that the widely shared commitment to interpretivism has not generated a consensus on the nature and justification of adjudication itself. In fact, far from producing consensus, modern interpretivism is today a house badly divided—far more so than in its past. The rift is over the nature of interpretation. On the one hand, "objective interpretivists" claim that interpretation, whether of legal, literary, or, indeed, "behavioral" texts, is a rational and objective enterprise.[9] When applied to legal theory, this turns out to be not just a descriptive claim about the nature of interpretation, but also a prescriptive claim about the morality of adjudication: its interpretive core gives adjudication both its rational persuasive power and its moral justification. "Subjective interpretivists," on the other hand, claim that interpre-

---

Public Interest," *Yale Law Journal* 52 (1943): 203–95; Karl N. Llewellyn, "Some Realism about Realism Responding to Dean Pound," *Harvard Law Review* 44 (1931): 1222–64; Roscoe Pound, "Mechanical Jurisprudence," *Columbia Law Review* 8 (1908): 605–23.

7. See generally Mark Tushnet, "Truth, Justice, and the American Way: An Interpretation of Public Law Scholarship in the Seventies," *Texas Law Review* 57 (1979): 1307–59; Mark Tushnet, "Anti-Formalism in Recent Constitutional Theory," *Michigan Law Review* 83 (1985): 1502–44; Roberto Mangabeira Unger, "The Critical Legal Studies Movement," *Harvard Law Review* 96 (1983): 561–675.

8. Grant Gilmore, *The Ages of American Law* (New Haven: Yale University Press, 1977).

9. See, e.g., *OI*, 739; Dworkin, *Matter of Principle*, 119–81; R. M. Dworkin, *Law's Empire* (Cambridge: Harvard University Press, Belknap Press, 1986).

tation of texts, whether of legal, literary, or behavioral texts, is subjective and contextual, rather than bounded and objective.[10] When applied to legal theory, this turns out, again, to be not just a descriptive claim about the nature of interpretation, but also a debunking claim about the purported morality of adjudication claimed by objectivists. Because interpretation is subjective, legal interpretation, including adjudication, is also subjective. If the morality of adjudication depends on its objectivity, then while adjudication is indeed interpretive, as the objectivists correctly insist, this fact gains nothing: if morality requires objectivity, then adjudication cannot rely on its interpretive core for either its claim to rationality or for its moral justification.

Thus, the distinctive feature of modern constitutional and legal theory is that the loudest debate is not between interpretivists and imperativists, but is instead between contending schools who agree that adjudication is an interpretive enterprise and disagree over the nature and consequences of interpretation. According to the first school, adjudication is objective and rational, and therefore morally defensible, because it is an interpretive enterprise and interpretation is objective and rational; according to the second school, adjudication is subjective and contextual, and therefore morally arbitrary, because adjudication is an interpretive enterprise and interpretation itself is subjective and contextual.

I will argue in this chapter against both modern forms of interpretivism. The analogy of law to literature, on which much of modern interpretivism is based, although fruitful, has carried legal theorists too far. Despite a superficial resemblance to literary interpretation, adjudication is not primarily an interpretive act of either a subjective or objective nature; adjudication, including constitutional adjudication, is an imperative act. Adjudication is in form interpretive, but in substance it is an exercise of power in a way that truly interpretive acts, such as literary interpretation, are not. Adjudication has far more in common with legislation, executive orders, administrative decrees, and the whimsical commands of princes, kings, and tyrants

10. See, e.g., Stanley Fish, *Is There a Text in This Class?: The Authority of Interpretive Communities* (Cambridge: Harvard University Press, 1980); Stanley Fish, "Fish v. Fiss," *Stanford Law Review* 36 (1984): 1325–47; Stanley Fish, "Anti-Professionalism," *Cardoza Law Review* 7 (1986): 645–77. Subsequent references to the latter, abbreviated *AP,* are given in the text.

than it has with other things we do with words, such as create or interpret novels. Like the commands of kings and the dictates of a majoritarian legislature, adjudication is imperative. It is a command backed by state power. No matter how many similarities adjudication has with literary linguistic activities, this central attribute distinguishes it. If we lose sight of the difference between literary interpretation and adjudication, and if we do not see that the difference between them is the amount of power wielded by the judiciary as compared to the power wielded by the interpreter, then we have either misconceived the nature of interpretation, or the nature of law, or both.

Furthermore, I will argue, the danger posed by interpretivist excesses is not simply conceptual confusion. By insisting that adjudication is interpretation, interpretivists misconceive not only the nature of adjudication, but also the nature, and even the possibility, of legal criticism. As a result, both objective and subjective interpretivists dangerously undercut the viability of radical legal criticism—including radical critique of adjudication. Again, the problem stems from an insistence on identity, where there is at best similarity, between literary and legal enterprises. From literary critics, legal interpretivists have adopted the insight that normative criticism of any practice is necessarily interpretive. Criticism of a piece of literature, for example, is inevitably interpretive—saying how good a novel is inevitably entails declaring what it means—and an interpretation of a piece of literature is at the same time inevitably normative, or critical—when we try to say what a novel means, we aim for the best meaning we can give it according to some aesthetic theory of the nature of art.[11] According to this argument, the boundary between interpretive claims about the meaning of a work of literature and critical claims about the value or merit of a work of literature—how good it is—are inevitably blurred. It is an easy step from this argument to the analogous position that criticism of law is also inevitably interpretive, and that an interpretation of law is therefore inevitably critical. After all, if law is like literature, then whatever is true for literature ought also hold for law: critical claims about the value of a law are inextricably tied with claims about the law's meaning, and interpretive claims about its meaning are inevitably value laden. Finally, when this

11. This argument forms the basis of Dworkin's view of adjudication as interpretation. See Dworkin, *Matter of Principle*, 146.

argument is coupled with the two claims that adjudication is interpretive, and that adjudication is law, they yield this sum: if both adjudication and criticism of adjudication—both the criticism of law as well as the creation of law—are interpretive, then the criticism of law and the creation of law turn out to be one and the same, or at least more similar than dissimilar. The result is that the distinction between the law that is and the moral ideal that law ought to be becomes blurred, just as for the literary theorist, the distinction between literature and literary criticism has become blurred.[12]

It is one thing, though, to blur the divide between the creation and criticism of literature, and quite another to blur the distinction between the creation and criticism of law. Historically, the consequence of the blending of the law and the moral basis from which we criticize law has almost always been a politically regressive insistence upon the morality of existing power;[13] and the present decade's fashionable denial of the difference between fact and value (whether indulged by the political Left or by the political center) has proven to be no exception. The most obvious and compelling implication of the claim that there is no real difference between the law that is and the law that ought to be is that the law that is, is perfect: the law that is, is as it ought to be. The antipositivist blurring of that which is from that which ought to be entails a noncritical, accepting complacency with the status quo.

The routes, of course, by which objectivists and subjectivists arrive

12. Dworkin, of course, regards this feature as the strength of his position:

> There is a better alternative: propositions of law are not merely descriptive of legal history, in a straightforward way, nor are they simply evaluative in some way divorced from legal history. They are interpretive of legal history, which combines elements of both description and evaluation but is different from both. Lawyers would do well to study literary and other forms of artistic interpretation. . . . Not all of the battles within literary criticism are edifying or even comprehensible, but many more theories of interpretation have been defended in literature than in law, and these include theories which challenge the flat distinction between description and evaluation that has enfeebled legal theory. (Ibid., 14–48)

13. Thus Bentham noted that the natural lawyer's identification of law with a higher morality almost always serves the ends of the powerful. See Jeremy Bentham, "A Commentary on Humphrey's Real Property Code," in *The Works of Jeremy Bentham*, ed. Sir John Bowring (1843; rpt., New York: Russell and Russell, 1962), 389. H. L. A. Hart makes the same point in "American Jurisprudence through English Eyes: The Nightmare and the Noble Dream," *Georgia Law Review* 11 (1977): 969–89. See generally Hart, *Essays on Bentham*.

at their shared conservatism, are drastically different from each other. Objectivism, I will argue, entails a conservative vision of the scope of legal criticism because it embraces a relativistic account of morality. Subjectivism, I will argue, entails a limited, regressive vision of the scope of legal criticism because it embraces a nihilistic account of morality (although not for the reasons most often put forward by objectivists). But the difference in the arguments put forward by objective and subjective interpretivists has diverted attention from the incredible amount of ground that they share. They both view adjudication, or law, and criticism of adjudication as interpretive acts. By so doing, they tie the basis of legal criticism to communicative texts written or conceived by the community's collective or not-so-collective past. Accordingly they tie the use of power, as well as its critique, to the norms and ideals generated by the audible voices of our political history. As a consequence they both preclude on their own terms the possibility of a truly radical critique of power: a critique based on the norms and ideals generated not by the audible voices of our political past, but instead by a "self" who has been trampled, not celebrated, by our history, and whose vision has been ignored, not expressed, in the collective communicative texts of our culture's political past.

In order, partly, to demonstrate what I take to be the real value of literature to lawyers, I will argue that two works of literature themselves teach us the irresponsibility of viewing legal analysis as either an objective or subjective interpretive act. I will argue that the exploits of two fictional lawyers, Mark Twain's Pudd'nhead Wilson from the novel of the same name, and John Barth's Todd Andrews from *The Floating Opera,* are illustrative of where, in my view, interpretivism has gone wrong.[14] Thus, it is my contention that Mark Twain and John Barth have done important work for legal theorists: Twain's lawyer protagonist Pudd'nhead Wilson scrupulously follows the objective interpretive strategies of Ronald Dworkin's mythical and interpretive Hercules, yet he is no hero. And John Barth's lawyer protagonist Todd Andrews just as scrupulously lives out the assump-

14. Mark Twain, *Pudd'nhead Wilson,* in Samuel Langhorn Clemens, *Pudd'nhead Wilson and Those Extraordinary Twins,* ed. Sidney E. Berg (New York: Norton, 1980). (Subsequent references, abbreviated *PW,* are given in the text); John Barth, *The Floating Opera* (Garden City, N.Y.: Doubleday, 1967) (subsequent references, abbreviated *FO,* are given in the text).

tions of subjectivist interpretivism in his law practice in a small town on Maryland's Eastern Shore. Todd Andrews, similarly, is no hero; in fact, he constitutes a form of evil. These two works of fiction about lawyers and lawyering reveal important truths about interpretivism: both stories reveal interpretivism to be a justificatory illusion. When we exercise power, through courts or otherwise, we must do better than Wilson and Andrews. We must do better than even the highest ideal of interpretive behavior upon which our modern interpretivists insist.

In part 2 I will argue that objective interpretivism, as defined in Owen Fiss's influential article "Objectivity and Interpretation," should be rejected. Part 3 argues that the danger of relativism posed by objective interpretivism is thematically explored in Mark Twain's legal novel *Pudd'nhead Wilson*. Part 4 argues that subjective interpretivism, as expressed in a recent article by Stanley Fish entitled "Anti-Professionalism," should be rejected because it rests on a nihilistic morality. Part 5 argues that the dangers of subjective interpretivism are dramatized by the exploits of the protagonist Todd Andrews in John Barth's legal novel *The Floating Opera*. In the conclusion, I will argue briefly that only by first focusing on the imperative core of adjudication can we state and clearly apply the moral criteria by which law should be criticized.

Objective Interpretivism

Modern objective interpretivism, what I will call objectivism, is rooted in a fear of power. It is not power, objectivists claim, but wisdom tempered by the dictates of objective texts, that constitutes the essence of the adjudicative act. Adjudication cannot be power, because power is bad—power destroys—and adjudication is good. Adjudication, which is good, restrains power, which is bad. Thus, it is primarily a fear of power and distrust of politics that drives Fiss's modern attack on the deconstructionists:

> A recognition of the interpretive dimensions of adjudication and the dynamic character of all interpretive activity . . . might enable us to come to terms with a new nihilism, one that doubts the legitimacy of adjudication—a nihilism that appears to me to be unwarranted and unsound, but that is gaining respectability and

> claiming an increasing number of important and respected legal scholars, particularly in constitutional law. They have turned their backs on adjudication and have begun a romance with politics. This new nihilism might acknowledge the characterization of adjudication as interpretation, but then would insist that . . . for any text . . . there are any number of possible meanings, . . . and that in the choosing of one of those meanings, . . . the judge will inevitably express his own values. All law is masked power. In this regard the new nihilism is reminiscent of the legal realism of the early twentieth century. It too sought to unmask what was claimed to be the true nature of legal doctrine. . . . It saw law as a projection of the judge's values. (*OI*, 740–41)

This fear of power, both judicial and otherwise, is not new to modern objectivism. It echoes the natural lawyer's eighteenth- and nineteenth-century distrust of legal positivism, and the turn-of-the-century formalistic reaction to the legal realists. Roscoe Pound expressed the same passionate distrust of power in his attack on the legal realists half a century ago:

> I suggest to you that so-called realism in jurisprudence is related to realism in art rather than to philosophical realism. Like realism in art it is a cult of the ugly. . . . An artist commissioned to paint the portrait of one of the outstanding judges of the recent past noted that he had a huge fist and a habit of holding it out before him. Accordingly, as a realist, he painted the fist elaborately in the foreground as the chief feature of the portrait, behind which, if one's gaze can get by the fist, one may discover in the background a thoughtful countenance. The judge did have such a fist and did hold it out in front of him on occasion. But having known him well for years, I doubt if anyone thought about it till the artist seized upon it and made it the main feature of his portrait. The fist existed. But was it the significant feature of the judge? Was reality in the sense of significance in the fist or in the countenance?[15]

For Fiss, no less than for Pound, the judge who simply wields

15. Roscoe Pound, *Justice according to Law* (New Haven: Yale University Press, 1951), 90–91.

power, who effectuates politics through adjudicative decisions, who uses his power to promote his own vision of our social ideal, is acting amorally or immorally: he is acting outside the parameters of the Rule of Law. In Fiss's view, such a creature constitutes an apocalyptic nightmare: he "threatens our social existence and the nature of public life as we know it in America," and he "demeans our lives (*OI*, 763)." To return to Pound's metaphor, for the objectivist the appropriate symbol for power is the fist. Power is destructive. Like the fist, it has no constructive function. Like the fist, it lashes out and destroys. Fiss ends his piece by decrying our social future, should the imperativist implications of the new nihilism, subjectivism, ever come to be widely accepted:

> The great public text of modern America, the Constitution, would be drained of meaning. It would be debased. It would no longer be seen as embodying a public morality to be understood and expressed through rational processes like adjudication; it would be reduced to a mere instrument of political organization—distributing political power and establishing the modes by which that power will be exercised. Public values would be defined only as those held by the current winners in the processes prescribed by the Constitution; beyond that, there would be only individual morality, or even worse, individual interests.
>
> Against the nihilism that scoffs at the idea that the Constitution has any meaning, it is difficult to reason. . . . I believe it imperative to respond, . . . for this nihilism calls into question the very point of constitutional adjudication; it threatens our social existence and the nature of public life as we know it in America; and it demeans our lives. . . . It must be combatted and can be, though perhaps only by affirming the truth of that which is being denied—the idea that the Constitution embodies a public morality and that a public life founded on that morality can be rich and inspiring. (*OI*, 763)

As noted above, this fear of unrestrained power is a familiar feature of the natural law tradition. What distinguishes modern objectivism from the rest of the natural law tradition, and what distinguishes Fiss from Pound, is the solution objectivism proposes to the problem of power. Unlike their natural-law predecessors, modern objectivists insist that obedience to an authoritative legal text is the solution, and the only solution, to the problem of power posed by the "significance in the fist." Judicial obedience to legal text, the modern objectivist insists, will curb, legalize, restrain, and moralize "personal or partisan politics,"[16] the destructive exercise of power, and politically victorious "individual interests" (*OI*, 763).

Obedience to text is everything that power is not. Power is destructive, demeaning, irrational, arbitrary, immoral, and threatening to the community's life; while obedience to text, particularly to constitutional text, is constructive, uplifting, communitarian, moral, and rational. The judge who interprets the objective text and fairly applies it protects our public morality, promotes the community's collective existence, and ensures that our collective existence has meaning and value. Judicial obedience to text transforms power into reason. It converts personal partisan politics into objective, communitarian wisdom. Obedience to an objective text thus purifies as it disciplines subjective power. The morality of obedience to the objective text of the constitution is a fundamental commitment that simply cannot be challenged:

> [W]hy must we respect the Constitution? [To] answer such a question . . . one must transcend the text and the rules of interpretation to justify the authority of the text; to justify the Constitution itself or explain why the Constitution would be obeyed, one must move beyond law to political theory, if not religion. Such questioning can itself become a moment of crisis in the life of a Constitution, and since it is occasioned by a rigid insistence on the principles of positivism and the separation of law and morals, judges have an incentive to temper their commitment to that legal theory and thus to read the moral as well as the legal text. (*OI*, 753–54)

The judge's willingness to obey the mandates of objective texts is both the necessary and sufficient condition for the morality of adjudi-

16. Thus, Dworkin argues that "[l]aw . . . conceived [as interpretation] is deeply and thoroughly political. Lawyers and judges cannot avoid politics in the broad sense of political theory. But law is not a matter of personal or partisan politics. . . ." Dworkin, *Matter of Principle*, 146.

cation itself. It morally justifies the judge's institutional authority. Fiss puts the point this way:

> [A]n individual has a moral duty to obey a judicial interpretation . . . because the judge is part of an authority structure that is good to preserve. This version of the claim of authoritativeness speaks to the individual's conscience and derives from institutional virtue, rather than institutional power. It is the most important version of the claim of authoritativeness, because no society can heavily depend on force to secure compliance. . . . It vitally depends on a recognition of the value of judicial interpretation. Denying the worth of the Constitution, the place of constitutional values in the American system, or the judiciary's capacity to interpret the Constitution dissolves this particular claim to authoritativeness. (*OI*, 756)

The judge who is properly engaged in constitutional adjudication is not exercising power—objective interpretation is the opposite of power. Rather, he is relinquishing power. He is engaging in an act of "civil obedience." But the judge who interprets and obeys texts is no automaton; he is doing truly heroic and profoundly difficult intellectual and moral labor. Objective interpretation is as difficult as it is moral. Dworkin calls his interpretivist judge "Hercules" to underscore the dimensions of the task. Fiss captures the complexity of interpretation in this passage:

> A secure concept of the judicial role, and the priorities within that role, and a proper recognition of the source of legitimacy, may enable the judge to order and perhaps even reconcile tasks that may otherwise tend to conflict. The core of adjudication, objective interpretation, can be protected from the pressures of instrumentalism, as it can be protected from the tensions produced by the claim of authoritativeness. The multiple demands of adjudication often make law an elusive, partly realized ideal, for they mean the judge must manage and synthesize a number of disparate and conflicting roles—literary critic, moral philosopher, religious authority, structural engineer, political strategist; but it would be wrong to abandon the ideal in the face of this

> challenge. The proper response is increased effort, clarity of vision and determination, not surrender. (*OI*, 762)

There are two problems with the modern objectivists' solution to the problem of power. The first might be called the problem of moral contingency: the morality of judicial obedience to an objective text depends entirely upon the morality of the objective text that is obeyed. An obedient, pliant attitude toward text is no more a guarantee against the evils of chaotic power than is fascism a moral alternative to anarchy. To borrow H. L. A. Hart's phrase, the "noble dream"[17] of the objective interpreter can indeed become a nightmare. The second problem is the practical one of possibility: objective interpretation can only guarantee moral decision making if there is some means of ensuring that judges will indeed engage in it. The objectivist must, that is, specify how it is that the text, and not the judge's whim, generates the final judicial outcome.

Objectivists have developed distinctive responses to both problems. First, modern objectivists know that the noble dream can become a nightmare. They know, even if they sometimes repress the knowledge, that the moral efficacy of obedience to legal text as a solution to the problem of power is dependent upon the morality of the legal text. South Africa, Nazi Germany, Stalinist Russia, and the slave-holding South, if nothing else, have taught us that there is no moral guarantee in the idea of law.[18] Yet, objectivists maintain their allegiance to legal text as the solution to the problem of power in the face of this knowledge. The first distinguishing feature of modern objectivism, therefore, has been its elaborate efforts to specify the "legal text" that judges ought to obey in such a way as to make plausible their claim that obedience to law's mandates will ensure the morality of adjudicatory power.

They begin by denying allegiance to older views that bear a strong but misleading resemblance to objectivism. Thus, strict constructionists identify the text narrowly with the intent of the framers while textualists identify the text as the written document itself. But

17. Hart, "American Jurisprudence."

18. Thus, Dworkin makes clear in *Law's Empire* that he rejects the natural lawyer's claim that an "unjust law is not a law," citing both the laws of South African apartheid and those of Nazi Germany as obvious counterexamples. See Dworkin, *Law's Empire*, 102–8.

both of these positions fail, and it has been modern objectivists who have made clear why: the framers, no matter how much we ought respect them, were neither kings nor Gods; there is no good reason for thinking that obedience to their commands will ensure the moral purity of judicial actions. The document itself is just that—a legal document—not a sacred text. There is no good reason to worship it, no matter how understandable may be the impulse to do so.[19]

For these reasons, objectivists have rejected an identification of the text to be obeyed with either original intent or literal meaning, and have carved out instead a third alternative: the text (including the constitutional text) that can morally purify judicial power, and the interpretation of which constitutes the core of adjudication, must embrace society's conventional morality. This position might be called supplementalism. The appeal of supplementalism is obvious. If a legal text includes the community's moral code (as well as the community's statutes, precedents, and constitutions) and if the community's moral code is as close as one can possibly get to moral truth (or even better if it is moral truth), then adjudication conceived as interpretation is moral. Supplementalism is precisely the claim that is needed to transform the rationality that is obedience into a rationality that is noble and virtuous.[20]

---

19. The literature outlining the critical attack by modern interpretivists on strict constructionists and textualists is vast and, I am sure, all too familiar. See Dworkin, *Matter of Principle*, 154–58, 162–64; Paul Brest, "The Misconceived Quest for the Original Understanding," *Boston University Law Review* 60 (1980): 204–38. On Constitution worship in general, and its relation to modern interpretivist movements, see Grey, "Constitution as Scripture," 1, 3 n. 4.

20. Supplementalism, however, spawns problems of its own. One is causal: How did the law come to be supplemented with the community's moral code? The multiplicity and inconsistency of the metaphors used to explain this process of supplementation rather starkly reveal the interpretivists' uncertainty—is public, conventional morality "read into" the Constitution, or does it "emanate from" it? Is it a separate "social text" that the judge is morally but not legally bound to abide by, or is it an addendum incorporated by reference into a contract? For some of the theorists, these are apparently not mutually exclusive alternatives. Fiss, for example, seems to endorse both positions.

> Public morality is a "prism" through which judges read the Constitution, but furthermore, the Constitution itself establishes positivistically, if you will, certain values which are and must be regarded as fundamental. Its fundamental justness cannot be questioned: Positivism tries to separate law from morals, . . . but the separation will . . . never be complete. Two forces modulate the separation. . . . The first derives from the fact that the judge is trying to give meaning and expression to public values (those that are embodied in a legal

It is the second problem, however—the charge that it is not possible to constrain a judge, even a well-meaning judge, to the objective meaning to be gleaned from a text—which has become the modern battleground for objectivism. Objective interpretation of the legal text is made possible, Fiss argues, by the existence of "disciplining rules" that narrow the range of interpretive discretion open to any particular judicial interpreter:

> [T]he freedom of the interpreter is not absolute. The interpreter is not free to assign any meaning he wishes to the text. He is disciplined by a set of rules that specify the relevance and weight to be assigned to the material, . . . as well as by those that define basic concepts and that established the procedural circumstances under which the interpretation must occur. [Disciplining rules] constrain the interpreter, thus transforming the interpretive process from a subjective to an objective one, and they furnish the standards by which the correctness of the interpretation can be judged. These rules are not simply standards or principles held by individual judges, but instead constitute the institution . . . in which judges find themselves and through which they act. The disciplining rules operate similarly to the rules of language, which constrain the users of the language, furnish the standards for judging the uses of language, and constitute the language. (*OI*, 744)

Acquiescence in the disciplining rules is a necessary condition to participation in the interpretive practice that constitutes adjudication:

> text) and that his understanding of such values—equality, liberty, property, due process, cruel and unusual punishment—is necessarily shaped by the prevailing morality. The moral text is a prism through which he understands the legal text. The second force relates to an intellectual dilemma of positivism: A too rigid insistence on positivism will inevitably bring into question the ultimate moral authority of the legal text—the justness of the Constitution. (*OI*, 753)

However it is that the Constitution becomes permeated with moral values, Fiss, like Dworkin, is clear that it is indeed so permeated. He is also clear that it is by virtue of the incorporation of public morality, or values, into the legal text that obedience to that text is a moral act: "The idea of adjudication requires that there exist constitutional values to interpret, just as much as it requires that there be constraints on the interpretive process. Lacking such a belief, adjudication is not possible, only power" (*OI*, 763).

> Rules are not rules unless they are authoritative, and that authority can only be conferred by a community. Accordingly, the disciplining rules that govern an interpretive activity must be seen as defining or demarcating an interpretive community consisting of those who recognize the rules as authoritative. . . . [I]n law the interpretive community is a reality. It has authority to confer because membership does not depend on agreement. Judges do not belong to an interpretive community as a result of shared views about particular issues or interpretations, but belong by virtue of a commitment to uphold and advance the rule of law itself. They belong by virtue of their office. There can be many schools of literary interpretation but . . . in legal interpretation there is only one school and attendance is mandatory. All judges define themselves as members of this school and must do so in order to exercise the prerogatives of their office. Even if their personal commitment to the rule of law wavers, the rule continues to act on judges; even if the rule of law fails to persuade, it can coerce. Judges know that if they relinquish their membership in the interpretive community, or deny its authority, they love their right to speak with the authority of the law. (*OI*, 745)

Thus, substantive supplementation of the text with the community's values solves the problem of moral contingency, while the existence and operation of disciplining rules solve the problem of possibility. Disciplining rules facilitate interpretation of the legal text, while supplementation of the text with values moralizes the act. By virtue of the disciplining rules that constrain discretion, adjudication is an interpretive act of reason rather than an act of power, and by virtue of the values that supplement the text to be interpreted, it is an act of morality rather than politics. The objectivist thesis, then, is this: properly understood, adjudication is the disciplined interpretation of a supplemented legal text. It is by virtue of its substantive supplementation and its procedural discipline that it is a morally justified practice.

However, even assuming its coherence, objectivism thus defined—the view that adjudication consists of the disciplined interpretation of a supplemented, objective legal text—does not do what Fiss hopes: it does not transform acts of amoral power into acts of moral reason.

It may indeed transform an act of power into an act of reason, but this does not necessarily translate into a gain in morality. For the conventional morality, or the public morality, with which the supplementalists gloss the legal text is not the same as true morality: there is no guarantee that the conventional code of virtue to which a community subscribes is a moral one. It might be felt as moral and in fact be horrific. The same is true of a disciplining rule. Supplementing the text of the Constitution with the conventional morality of the community does not confer upon the Constitution any mantle of moral wisdom, and constraining the act of interpretation with disciplining rules may transform an adjudicative act into an interpretive act, but it does not transform an interpretive act into a moral act. Substantive supplementation confers upon the court only the wisdom of the community, which may be no wisdom at all; and obedience to rules of discipline derived from community practice imposes upon the judge obligations commensurate with the community's practices, which may or may not be just. Objective interpretivism does indeed guarantee the interpreter a modicum of popularity, or success, in the community. It ensures that Dworkin's Hercules will be loved, in spite of the fact that he was not elected. But it does not guarantee that his decisions will be just, or that his actions will be good.

Fiss has anticipated at least part of this objection. He knows, and even insists, that the degree of "objectivity" he is describing is relative:

> [T]he objective quality of interpretation is bounded, limited, or relative. It is bounded by the existence of a community that recognizes and adheres to the disciplining rules used by the interpreter and that is defined by its recognition of those rules. The objectivity of the physical world may be more transcendent, less relativistic, . . . but as revealed by the reference to language and the disciplining rules of interpretation, the physical does not exhaust the claim of objectivity, nor does it make this bounded objectivity of interpretation a secondary or parasitic kind of objectivity. Bounded objectivity is the only kind of objectivity to which the law—or any interpretive activity—ever aspires and the only one about which we care. To insist on more, to search

for the brooding omnipresence in the sky, is to create a false issue. (*OI*, 745–46)

But unfortunately, Fiss fails to address the obvious implication of his concession, which is just this: if the source of adjudicative morality is its objectivity, and if objectivity is relative, then the morality of adjudication is relative as well. Thus what Fiss concedes of objectivity must also be conceded of morality, and Fiss's crucial penultimate sentence so amended becomes this—"Bounded morality is the only kind of morality to which the law . . . aspires and the only one about which we care." But this is just wrong: bounded morality is not the only kind of morality to which the law ever aspires, and bounded morality is not the only one about which we care. Moral relativism is no alternative to the moral nihilism Fiss fears in subjectivism. The claim that it is, I think, rests upon an optimism regarding community, and more specifically our own historical community, which is simply unwarranted. Surely, from the perspective of those *most in need of the law's protection*—slaves, women, workers, children, the poor, the illiterate, the uneducated, dissidents, and other members of that vast and silenced majority whom the community in its relative moral wisdom has at one time or another cast off—a relativism that ties justice to community norms and practices is as odious and even frightening as the nihilism Fiss imagines he sees in the deconstructive instincts of his opponents.

My claim, then, is simply that the supplemental strategy of modern objectivism is marred by an undue optimism regarding community (as well as an undue pessimism regarding power). Objectivism indeed gives us a somewhat counterpositivist means by which to criticize adjudicative outcomes. According to objectivism's current supplementalist strategies, we can and should test substantive legal outcomes against the community's moral code. We can criticize its procedures against the community's interpretive practices, and if we discover that an act of adjudication does not accord with the community's moral sense or that the process breaks a disciplining rule, we can, if objectivism is right, infer from either fact that the decision is legally as well as morally wrong. If the Constitution incorporates the community's conventional morality and its interpretive practices by reference, then the adjudicative decision that incorrectly reads the conventional morality or the conventional rules will be as wrong, legally, as the decision that incorrectly reads the statute book. As progressive strategy, this enrichment of legal norms might be helpful and then again it might backfire, and badly. It might be progressive or regressive—explicitly depending upon the community's present moral mood. But whichever it is, we should be clear that legal enrichment of legal norms is all that supplementalism entails. The decision that is out of kilter with the community's moral sense (and therefore an "illegal" decision) is not necessarily an immoral decision, and a decision that is in accord with the community's conventional morality and conventional rules of reasoning is not necessarily morally righteous. Supplementing the legal text with the conventional morality of the community, and insisting upon judicial acceptance of such a supplemented text, might ensure judicial popularity; it might, that is, ensure judicial stability. It does not, however, ensure judicial virtue. Relativism is not a moral alternative to what Fiss perceives, either rightly or wrongly, to be the specter of nihilism, regardless of whether or not it is politic.

Interpretation, Popularity, and Folly: Conventional Morality and Pudd'nhead Wilson

Mark Twain's legalistic novel *Pudd'nhead Wilson* takes place in an interpretive community and as such it has a lot to teach about the relative virtues of interpretive practices. The interpretive community in this novel is a small town, "the town of Dawson's Landing, on the Missouri side of the Mississippi." The business district is just one street, six blocks long, where "three brick stores three stories high towered above interjected bunches of little frame shops" (*PW*, 3). It is, Twain tells us, a "slave-holding town, with a rich slave-worked grain and pork country back of it." The "chief citizen" of the town is a judge of the county court: York Driscoll, of Virginian ancestry, and a gentleman. The second citizen is a lawyer, Pembroke Howard, another "old Virginian grandee with proved descent from the First Families" (*PW*, 4), also a gentleman and an authority on the "Code." As the identity of its chief citizens reveals, the town respects its judges and lawyers immensely, and takes its law and its legal rights very seriously indeed.

Further, as Dworkin and Fiss would have it, the town's "law," which it holds in such high regard is by no means merely the positivistic legal enactments found in statute books, case reports, and constitutional documents. The law of Dawson's Landing is supplemented by the town's conventional morality. Thus supplemented, it is in constant need of interpretation. That interpretation, in turn, requires disciplining rules. In fact, the positive law of Dawson's Landing is supplemented with at least three social texts and is interpreted in accord with at least three disciplining rules of interpretation. The first supplemental text, and to the reader the most obvious, is the town's code of honor, which governs relations among the town's nobility. According to the code of honor, a man is responsible not for his individual commission of legally proscribed acts, but for the honor of his family name. Where the code of honor conflicts with positive law, the code of honor prevails. Twain spells out the disciplining rule that governs the interpretive practices of the nobility, and hence the interpretation of the code of honor, explicitly:

> In Missouri a recognized superiority attached to any person who hailed from Old Virginia; and this superiority was exalted to supremacy when a person of such nativity could also prove descent from the First Families of that great commonwealth. The Howards and Driscolls were of this aristocracy. In their eyes it was a nobility. It had its unwritten laws, and they were as clearly defined and as strict as any that could be found among the printed statutes of the land. The F.F.V. was born a gentleman; his highest duty in life was to watch over that great inheritance and keep it unsmirched. He must keep his honor spotless. Those laws were his chart. . . . These laws required certain things of him which his religion might forbid: then his religion must yield—the laws could not be relaxed to accommodate religion or anything else. Honor stood first; and the laws defined what it was and wherein it differed, in certain details, from honor as defined by church creeds and by the social laws and customs of some of the minor divisions of the globe that had got crowded out when the sacred boundaries of Virginia were staked out. (*PW*, 58)

Second, and more important to the plot, the community's positive law is supplemented by the racial code, which governs relations between slaves—or, more accurately, "niggers"—and whites. The primary disciplining rule of the racial code (although nowhere explicitly stated) is that "niggers are guilty" and that slavery is their punishment. But unlike the disciplining rule governing the code of honor, Twain does not give us a direct recitation of this rule. Instead, he sets the plot around it. Thus, Twain begins the novel with a series of interpretations of the racial code, all of which are facilitated by its implicit disciplining rule.

First, the novel opens with a white owner's legal interpretation of a behavioral text. A slave owner accuses his slaves of a petty theft. The owner's interpretation of the slave's act and its appropriate sanction is disciplined by the owner's understanding not just of the law of property and the positive prohibition against larceny, but of that law supplemented by the disciplining rule of black guilt and its punishment of slavery:

> Driscoll's patience was exhausted. He was a fairly humane man, toward slaves and other animals; he was an exceedingly humane man toward the erring of his own race. Theft he could not abide, and plainly there was a thief in the house. Necessarily the thief must be one of his Negroes. He called his servants before him. . . . "You have all been warned before. It has done no good. This time I will teach you a lesson. I will sell the thief. Which of you is the guilty one?" . . .
>
> "I give you one minute . . . if at the end of that time you have not confessed, I will not only sell all four of you, *but*—I will sell you DOWN THE RIVER!" (*PW*, 9–10; emphasis added)

Twain next describes the slaves' interpretation of Driscoll's threat—itself, of course, a command backed by sanction, and thus itself a legal text. The slaves' interpretation of the legal text "I will sell you down the river!" no less than Driscoll's interpretation of the slaves' act is disciplined by, and thereby facilitated by, the disciplining rule that governs the racial code; to wit, that "niggers are guilty":

> *It was equivalent to condemning them to hell!* No Missouri negro doubted this. . . . Tears gushed from their eyes, their supplicating hands went up, and three answers came in the one instant:
>
> "I done it!"
>
> "I done it!"

> "I done it!" . . . "Very good," said the master, . . . "I will sell you *here*, though you don't deserve it. You ought to be sold down the river."
>
> The culprits flung themselves prone, in an ecstasy of gratitude, and kissed his feet, declaring that they would never forget his goodness. . . . They were sincere, for like a god he had stretched forth his mighty hand and closed the gates of hell against them. He knew, himself, that he had done a noble and gracious thing, and he was privately well pleased with his magnanimity; and that night he set the incident down in his diary, so that his son might read it after years and be thereby moved to deeds of gentleness and humanity himself. . . . (*PW*, 12; emphasis added)

The one slave of the four who had not committed the theft, and was therefore not sold in retaliation, alone understands Driscoll's words for what they are: an act of power. Only Roxy, who becomes a major character, fully understands and acts upon the imperative import of Driscoll's spoken threat:

> Percy Driscoll slept well the night he saved his house-minions from going down the river, but no wink of sleep visited Roxy's eyes. A profound terror had taken possession of her. Her child could grow up and be sold down the river! The thought crazed her with horror. (*PW*, 12–13)

Roxy responds to Driscoll's threat by switching her own mulatto baby—who is a "nigger," but is to all appearances white—with the master's baby under her care, so as to ensure that her own baby will never be sold down the river. Her moral justification for this act, both to herself and to God, is facilitated by her interpretation of an anecdote related by a preacher, in which a white "nigger"—an English servant girl—had done the same thing. Roxy's interpretation of the preacher's text depends upon the disciplining rule that white people are innocent:

> "'Tain't no sin—white folks has done it! It ain't no sin, glory to goodness it ain't no sin! Dey's done it—yes, en dey was de biggest quality in de whole bilin', too—Kings! . . . De preacher said it was jist like dey done in Englan' one time, long time ago. De

> queen she lef' her baby layin' aroun' one day, en went out callin'; en one o' de niggers roun' 'bout de place dat was mos' white, she come in en see de chile layin' aroun', en tuck en put her own chile's clo'es on de queen's chile, en put de queen's chile's clo'es on her own chile, en den lef' her own chile layin' aroun' en tuck en toted de queen's chile home to de nigger quarter, en nobody ever foun' it out, en her chile was de king, bimeby, en sole de queen's chile down de river one time when dey had to settle up de estate. Dah, now, . . . it ain't no sin, caze white folks done it. Dey done it—yes, dey done it; en not on'y jis' common white folks, nuther, but de biggest quality dey is in de whole bilin'." (*PW*, 15)

And third, the town's law is supplemented (or comes to be supplemented) by the familiar substantive parameters of legal liberalism, and comes to be interpreted in light of the familiar liberal-legalistic disciplining rule of individual responsibility: legal guilt or innocence attaches to an individual person by virtue of his commission of a legally proscribed act. At least at the beginning of the novel, however, this final and to our eyes most familiar disciplining rule is a hostile and foreign element in the town's interpretive practices. It is brought to the community from the outside by the novel's protagonist—an Eastern-trained, Eastern-born lawyer, David Wilson. Over the course of the novel, the community comes to accept Wilson as a lawyer and comes to accept the legalistic individualism he propounds. But the town's initially hostile reaction to Wilson's brand of legalistic individualism is neatly conveyed in the novel's first explicit act of interpretation. Wilson tries to tell a joke, and the community's overly literal interpretation casts Wilson and his legalistic individualism as the outsider:

> In . . . February Dawson's Landing gained a new citizen. This was Mr. David Wilson, a young fellow of Scotch parentage. He had wandered to this remote region from his birth-place in the interior of the State of New York, to seek his fortune. He was twenty-five years old, college bred, and had finished a post-college course in an eastern law school a couple of years before.
>
> He was a homely, freckled, sandy-haired young fellow, with

an intelligent blue eye that had frankness and comradeship in it and a covert twinkle of a pleasant sort. But for an unfortunate remark of his, he would no doubt have entered at once upon a successful career at Dawson's Landing. . . . He had just made the acquaintance of a group of citizens when an invisible dog began to yelp and snarl and howl and make himself very comprehensibly disagreeable, whereupon young Wilson said, much as one who is thinking aloud—

"I wish I owned half of that dog."

"Why?" somebody asked.

"Because I would kill my half."

The group searched his face with curiosity, with anxiety even, but found no light there, no expression that they could read. They fell away from him as from something uncanny, and went into privacy to discuss him. One said—

"'Pears to be a fool."

"'Pears?" said another. "*Is*, I reckon you better say."

"Said he wished he owned *half* of the dog, the idiot," said a third. "What did he reckon would become of the other half if he killed his half? Do you reckon he thought it would live?"

"Why, he must have thought it, unless he is the downrightest fool in the world; because if he hadn't thought that, he would have wanted to own the whole dog, knowing that if he killed his half and the other half died, he would be responsible for that half, just the same as if he had killed that half instead of his own. Don't it look that way to you, gents?". . . .

"In my opinion the man ain't in his right mind."

"In my opinion he hain't *got* any mind. . . ."

"I'm with you gentlemen, . . . it ain't going too far to say he is a pudd'nhead. If he ain't a pudd'nhead, I ain't no judge, that's all."

Mr. Wilson stood elected. . . . Within a week he had lost his first name; Pudd'nhead took its place . . . . That first day's verdict made him a fool, and he was not able to get it set aside, or even modified. The nickname soon ceased to carry any harsh or unfriendly feeling with it, but it held its place, and was to continue to hold its place for twenty long years. . . .

[H]is deadly remark had ruined his chance—at least in the law. No clients came. [He] offered his services now in the humble

> capacities of land surveyor and expert accountant. . . . With Scotch patience and pluck he resolved to live down his reputation and work his way into the legal field yet. (*PW*, 5–6)

As modern interpretivists insist, legal interpretation is only one interpretive practice among many, and Dawson's Landing bears this out. The interplay of its three disciplining rules—(1) that individuals are responsible for their actions, (2) that the nobility are responsible, primarily, for their family's honor, and (3) that "niggers" are collectively guilty—governs the interpretation of a wide range of texts, not just legal texts. Most importantly, these supplementing codes and the disciplining rules that regulate them also govern the interpretation of the various texts by which a person is demarcated. Thus, the primary subtext according to which identity for purposes of the first rule of responsibility—individual responsibility for legally prescribed actions—is established, is the body: continuity of physical identity. In the novel's climactic court scene, Pudd'nhead Wilson describes to the awestruck courtroom audience how the body can be read as a text so as to establish the physically continuous identity across time that is the necessary condition for legal and liberal responsibility:

> "Every human being carries with him from his cradle to his grave certain physical marks which do not change their character, and by which he can always be identified—and that without shade of doubt or question. These marks are his signature, his physiological autograph, so to speak, and this autograph cannot be counterfeited, nor can he disguise it or hide it away, nor can it become illegible by the wear and the mutations of time. This signature is not his face . . . it is not his height, . . . it is not his form, . . .
>
> "This autograph consists of the delicate lines or corrugations with which Nature marks the insides of the hands and the soles of the feet. If you will look at the balls of your fingers . . . you will observe that these dainty, curving lines lie close together, like those that indicate the borders of oceans in maps, and that they form various clearly defined patterns, . . . and that these patterns differ on the different fingers. . . . The patterns on the right hand are not the same as those on the left. One twin's patterns are never the same as his fellow-twin's patterns. . . .

"For more than twenty years I have amused my compulsory leisure with collecting these curious physical signatures in this town. . . . There is hardly a person in this room, white or black, whose natal signature I cannot produce, and not one of them can so disguise himself that I cannot pick him out from a multitude of his fellow creatures and unerringly identify him by his hands. . . .

"I have studied some of these signatures so much that I know them as well as the bank cashier knows the autograph of his oldest customer. While I turn my back, now, I beg that several persons will be so good as to pass their fingers through their hair and then press them upon one of the panes of the window near the jury, and that among them the accused may set *their* finger-marks."

. . . Then, upon call, Wilson went to the window, made his examination, and said—

"This is Count Luigi's right hand. . . . Here is Count Angelo's right.

. . . Am I right?"

A deafening explosion of applause was the answer. The Bench said—

"This certainly approaches the miraculous!" (*PW*, 108–10)

The text for reading noble identity, as opposed to individual identity, is not the body, but title and surname; as it is family membership, not one's individual history for which, according to the code of honor, one is responsible. Thus York Driscoll, the judge and eventual murder victim, was "proud of his old Virginian ancestry, and in his hospitalities and his rather formal and stately manners he kept up its traditions. He was fine, and just, and generous. To be a gentleman—a gentleman without stain or blemish—was his only religion, and to it he was always faithful." Similarly, Twain introduces Pembroke Howard, lawyer and bachelor, "another old Virginian grandee with proved descent from the First Families. He was a fine, brave, majestic creature, a gentleman according to the nicest requirements of the Virginian rule" (*PW*, 4). The Italian twins who play the foil to Tom's villainry (and become Pudd'nhead's clients, wrongly accused of murder), explain their noble identity in the same familial terms: "Our parents were well-to-do, there in Italy, and we were their only child. We were of the old Florentine nobility" (*PW*, 50). In this passage, the community interprets the text of the twins' surname:

> None of these visitors was at ease, but being honest people, they didn't pretend to be. None of them had ever seen a person bearing a title of nobility before, and none had been expecting to see one now, consequently the title came upon them as a kind of pile-driving surprise and caught them unprepared. A few tried to rise to the emergency, and got out an awkward My Lord, or Your Lordship, or something of the sort, but the great majority were overwhelmed by the unaccustomed word and its dim and awful associations with gilded courts and stately ceremony and anointed kingship, so they only fumbled through the handshake, and passed on, speechless. (*PW*, 29)

One's racial identity, by contrast to both liberal and noble identity, is neither a matter of individual continuity (race constitutes a collective, not an individual identity) nor a matter of family name (as the characters in this novel often remark, "niggers" have no surname). Thus, when Roxy tells the grown Tom that he is in fact her son, her message is clear: for purposes of guilt and for purposes of determining who can and who can't be sold down the river, it is blood line and racial heritage—not upbringing, family name, or continuity of physical identity—that constitutes the relevant text by which identity is determined:

> "Yassir, en *dat* ain't all! You is a *nigger*!—*bawn* a nigger en a *slave*!—en you's a nigger en a slave dis minute; en if I opens my mouf, ole Marse Driscoll'll sell you down de river befo' you is two days older den what you is now! . . ."
>
> "It ain't no lie, nuther. It's jes' de truth, en noth'n *but* de truth, so he'p me. Yassir—you's my *son*— . . .
>
> . . . "[E]n dat po' boy dat you's been a kickin' en a cuffin' today is Percy Driscoll's son en yo' *marster*. . . . en *his* name's Tom Driscoll en *yo'* name's Valet de Chambers, en you ain't *got* no fambly name, becaze niggers don't *have* 'em!" (*PW*, 41)

In one of the great interpretive triumphs of the novel, Roxy renders a masterful interpretation of Tom's egregious behavior. Her interpretation takes account of the discipline rules that govern bloodline, racial group, and family name:

> It's de nigger in you, dat's what it is. Thirty-one parts o' you is white, en on'y one part nigger, en dat po' little one part is yo' *soul*. 'Tain't wuth savin'; 'tain't wuth totin' out on a shovel en tho'in' in de gutter. You has disgraced yo' birth. What would yo' pa [a member of the white nobility] think o' you? It's enough to make him turn in his grave. . . ."
>
> "What ever has 'come o' yo' Essex blood? Dat's what I can't understan'. En it ain't only jist Essex blood dat's in you, not by a long sight—'deed it ain't! My great-great-great-gran'father en yo' great-great-great-great-gran'father was ole Cap'n John Smith, de highes' blood dat Ole Virginny ever turned out; en *his* great-great-gran'mother or somers along back dah, was Pocahontas de Injun queen, en her husbun' was a nigger king outen Africa—en yit here you is, a slinkin' outen a duel en disgracin' our whole line like a ornery low-down hound! Yes, it's de nigger in you. . . .
>
> "Ain't nigger enough in him to show in his finger-nails, en dat takes mighty little—yit dey's enough to paint his soul. . . . Yassir, enough to paint a whole thimbleful of 'em." (*PW*, 70)

Twain leaves no doubt as to the relationship between supplemental social text and positivistic legal text. The supplemental texts and the disciplining rules that govern them—of individual responsibility for one's own acts, of black collective guilt, and of noble responsibility for family honor—do indeed constitute the moral prism through which the community's legal texts are interpreted. Pudd'nhead's climactic triumph in the book's final courtroom scene evidences this relationship, and also evidences Pudd'nhead's understanding of this fundamental law of interpretation.

In a narrow sense, the novel celebrates the rule of law: the "guilty" party is convicted and is convicted by virtue of Pudd'nhead's interpretive prowess. However, Pudd'nhead does not achieve his legal triumph by convincing the community to abandon its noxious noble and racial codes in favor of the morally preferable legalistic code of individual responsibility. At no point does he try to move the community to abandon its conceptions of racial guilt and familial nobility. Rather, what Pudd'nhead achieves is a Dworkinian, or Herculean, interpretive triumph: he convinces the town of Tom's guilt by interpreting the legal text prohibiting murder through the prism of the community's disciplining rules of race and family. Pudd'nhead triumphs at the book's conclusion, not by transforming the community's sense of law so as to match the liberal norms with which it has come into conflict, but rather through a masterful, even Herculean, act of interpretation. Pudd'nhead reads the legal text through the prism of the community's norms. He is truly a Dworkinian legal hero. Pudd'nhead begins his case by explaining to the courtroom the means by which the body's text—or fingerprints—can be read so as to discover the historical continuity necessary to the liberal and legalistic notion of responsibility, on which legal liability rests. He then reads—or interprets—a range of fingerprints to demonstrate to the openly admiring spectators that the charged defendants, his clients, did not commit the murder. The fingerprints on the murder weapon, the knife, do not match the twins' fingerprints. After first explaining the phenomenon of fingerprints, the text of continuous physical identity, and demonstrating to the crowd's awestruck satisfaction that his clients are not physically continuous with the murderer who held the knife, Wilson concludes with a flourish: "These men are innocent—I have no further concern with them" (*PW*, 111).

Wilson then turns to the next question: Who did murder the judge? Put aside, for now, the answer; the question is more complex than it appears. The question is complex because it involves conflicting disciplinary rules of the relevant interpretive community. In terms of physical continuity, the human being raised as Tom and known by the community as Tom committed the murder, and Wilson comes to court prepared to prove as much. Thus, the answer to the legal and liberal question of who (where "who" now means what "physically continuous person") committed the murder is clearly Tom, and Wilson comes prepared to prove it by reading the text of the physical body: the fingerprints on the murder weapon are the same as the fingerprints on the person known as Tom.

But he never has to. Wilson begins appropriately enough: he begins by emphasizing the legal-liberal meaning of continuous physical identity, and the legal-liberal meaning of guilt as responsibility for one's deeds that it implicates:

> "May it please the court, the claim given the front place, the claim most persistently urged, the claim most strenuously and

> I may even say, aggressively and defiantly insisted upon by the prosecution, is this—that the person whose hand left the blood-stained finger-prints upon the handle of the Indian knife is the person who committed the murder. . . . *We grant that claim*. . . ."
>
> "Upon this haft stands the assassin's natal autograph, written in the blood of that helpless and unoffending old man who loved you and whom you all loved. There is but one man in the whole earth whose hand can duplicate that crimson sign." (*PW*, 106–9)

But the question "who"—whether who committed the murder or whose hand can duplicate that crimson sign—is simply ambiguous, and it is in response to the ambiguity that Wilson's interpretive prowess emerges. For Wilson must be careful to answer the question not only by reference to disciplining rules of legal liberalism but also in light of the disciplining rules of identity and responsibility that govern the community's supplemental texts: the honor code and the racial code. The murderer is Tom in terms of the legal text, and in terms of the liberal disciplining rule of identity that at least at times governs its interpretation: the person who committed the murder is physically continuous with the person known as Tom. But the murderer is not Tom in terms of the racial or noble meaning of identity and the disciplining rules that govern the interpretive practices by which such identity emerges. Tom was born a slave—and therefore, according to the racial code, is a slave, or more precisely, a "nigger." Tom is Valet de Chambers masquerading as nobility. The apparent Tom lacks the family name that is definitive of the nobility, and possesses instead the racial blood that is sufficient for membership in the collectivity known as "slaves."

To fully answer the question of who killed Judge Driscoll, then, Wilson must not only prove that the physically continuous person known as Tom killed Driscoll, in terms of the legal-liberal code, but must also establish that that person is really Valet de Chambers, and not Tom at all, in terms of the racial and aristocratic code. Interpreting physical, behavioral, and historical facts in accord with the racial, liberal, and noble meanings of identity and responsibility, Wilson achieves his climactic courtroom triumph:

> "We will turn to the infant autographs of A and B. I will ask the jury to take these large pantograph facsimiles of A's, marked five months and seven months. Do they tally?"

The foreman responded—"Perfectly."

"Now examine this pantograph, taken at eight months, and also marked A. Does it tally with the other two?"

The surprised response was—

"No—they differ widely!" . . .

"Do you know how to account for those strange discrepancies? I will tell you. For a purpose unknown to us, but probably a selfish one, somebody changed those children in the cradle.

. . . "Between the ages of seven months and eight months those children were changed in the cradle . . . and the person who did it is in this house!"

"A was put into B's cradle in the nursery; B was transferred to the kitchen, and became a negro and a slave . . . but within a quarter of an hour he will stand before you white and free! . . . From seven months onward until now, A has still been a usurper, and in my finger-records he bears B's name. Here is his pantograph, at the age of twelve. Compare it with the assassin's signature upon the knife handle. Do they tally?"

The foreman answered—

"To the minutest detail!"

Wilson said solemnly—

"The murderer of your friend and mine—York Driscoll, of the generous hand and the kindly spirit—sits among you. Valet de Chambre, negro and slave—falsely called Thomas a Becket Driscoll—make upon the window the finger-prints that will hang you!" Tom turned his ashen face imploringly toward the speaker, made some impotent movements with his white lips, then slid limp and lifeless to the floor. Wilson broke the awed silence with the words—

"There is no need. He has confessed." (*PW*, 111–13)

The Racial Code and the Code of Honor: Disciplining Rules and Supplemental Texts

The three supplemental Codes involved in *Pudd'nhead Wilson*—the liberal code, the code of honor, and the racial code—fulfill in virtually every respect the criteria Ronald Dworkin establishes for supplemental moral texts in *Taking Rights Seriously*. The disciplining rules similarly fulfill in every respect the criteria Owen Fiss establishes for disciplining rules in "Objectivity and Interpretation." First, as Dworkin would insist, the supplemental codes do indeed have legal force: they define the interpretive limits of the community's legal texts. The code of honor limits the jurisdictional reach of the law in a relatively overt manner: gentlemen are responsible for breaches of family honor, not individual breaches of law. In Dworkin's world, the "principle of honor" that "no man can profit from his own wrong," for example, limits the positivistic impact of both wills and the law of testamentary disposition. Similarly, in *Pudd'nhead Wilson* we learn that whatever the written law of homicide, the unwritten code of honor requires that an assault upon one's honor of a certain magnitude be met with death. We also learn that the code of honor demands that a gentleman defend an assault on one's brother, to the death if necessary. And, we learn that upon being assaulted, a gentleman responds on the field of honor, and not in a court of law.

Furthermore, just as we learn of the rule that "no man can profit from his own wrong" from a court, we learn virtually all of the rules of the code of honor operative in Dawson's Landing from the town's legal community: either from the judge, from Pembroke, or from Pudd'nhead himself. Each important member of the legal interpretive community makes explicit his complete endorsement and embrace of the disciplining rules of honor. Indeed, Judge Driscoll is not just surprised to learn of his (purported) nephew's breach of the jurisdictional rule that a victim of an assault must respond on the field of honor, he is horrified:

> "You cur! You scum! you vermin! Do you mean to tell me that blood of my race has suffered a blow and crawled to a court of law about it? Answer me! . . . .
>
> "A coward in my family! A Driscoll a coward! Oh, what have I done to deserve this infamy!" He tottered to his secretary in the corner repeating that lament again and again in heart-breaking tones, and got out of a drawer a paper, which he slowly tore to bits. . . .
>
> "There it is, shreds and fragments once more—my will. Once more you have forced me to disinherit you, you base son of a most noble father! Leave my sight! Go—before I spit on you!" (*PW*, 60)

Pudd'nhead Wilson, retained as counsel for the defendants in the assault case, is equally offended by Tom's breach and makes clear his understanding of the limit on the criminal law of assault and battery imposed by the code of honor:

> "Tom, I am ashamed of you! I don't see how you could treat your good old uncle so. I am a better friend of his than you are; for if I had known the circumstances I would have kept that case out of court until I got word to him and let him have a gentleman's chance. . . .
>
> "You degenerate remnant of an honorable line! I'm thoroughly ashamed of you, Tom!" (*PW*, 62–63)

Judge Driscoll and Pudd'nhead Wilson are not the only characters devastated by Tom's multiple breaches of the code of honor. Roxy (Tom's true biological mother) knows what the rest of the community does not know, and that is Tom's true paternity. For although Tom is not the nephew of Judge Driscoll, as he is pretending, he is indeed the biological son of another descendent of the First Families (in addition to being a slave, by virtue of his mother's identity). In Roxy's eyes, therefore, Tom is as committed to uphold the code of honor by virtue of his paternity as he is collectively guilty by virtue of his "nigger" blood. She too is horrified to hear of the breach:

> "What is you mumblin' 'bout Chambers?"
>
> "The old man tried to get me to fight one [a duel] with Count Luigi, but he didn't succeed; so I reckon he concluded to patch up the family honor himself."
>
> He laughed at the idea, and went rambling on with a detailed account of . . . how shocked and ashamed the Judge was to find that he had a coward in his family. He glanced up at last, and got a shock himself. Roxana's bosom was heaving with suppressed passion, and she was glowering down upon him with measureless contempt written in her face.
>
> "En you refuse' to fight a man dat kicked you, 'stid o'jumpin' at de chance! En you ain't got no mo' feelin' den to come en tell me, dat fetched sich a po' low-down ornery rabbit into de worl'! Pah! It make me sick!" (*PW*, 70)

The racial code similarly limits the jurisdictional and remedial reach of the positive law. "Niggers" are guilty, but they are guilty not by virtue of individual responsibility for breaches of law; they are guilty by virtue of collective identity, and the appropriate punishment for this collective guilt is slavery itself, not legally prescribed sanctions. In the novel's final act of legal interpretation, the newly reconstituted interpretive community—the court, the governor, the community, and the murder victim's creditors—reads the relevant texts—Tom's act, Tom's status, the law of property, and the law of murder—in accord with all of the appropriate disciplining rules. They pose, collectively, a very difficult interpretive problem. Tom committed a murder, for which the legal punishment is imprisonment, but Tom is a slave, for which the racial punishment is slavery. In the book's denouement, they arrive at this highly creative interpretive solution to their legal problem:

> The false heir made a full confession and was sentenced to imprisonment for life. But now a complication came up. The Percy Driscoll estate was in such a crippled shape when its owner died that it could pay only sixty percent of its great indebtedness, and was settled at that rate. But the creditors came forward, now, and complained that inasmuch as through an error for which they were in no way to blame the false heir was not inventoried at that time with the rest of the property, great wrong and loss had thereby been inflicted upon them. They rightly claimed that "Tom" was lawfully their property and had been so for eight years [and that but for the false inventory] they would have sold him and he could not have murdered Judge Driscoll, therefore it was not he that had really committed the murder, the guilt lay with the erroneous inventory. Everybody saw that there was reason in this. Everybody granted that if "Tom" were white and free it would be unquestionably right to punish him—it would be no loss to anybody; but to shut up a valuable slave for life—that was quite another matter.
>
> As soon as the Governor understood the case, he pardoned Tom at once, and the creditors sold him down the river. (*PW*, 114–15)

As Fiss would insist they should, the disciplining rules do indeed discipline: there is only one school, and attendance is mandatory.

The rules of discipline rule out certain interpretations, just as they validate and enable others. Indeed, for each text and textual interpretation facilitated by a disciplining rule, another text and another interpretation is ruled out. Twain gives three examples of this principle of exclusion, one for each of his central disciplining rules.

First, we learn early on that Pudd'nhead Wilson has in fact taken up two hobbies during his extended period of relative underemployment, fingerprinting and palmistry. But Pudd'nhead is clear, even if others are not, that it is fingerprinting, not the palm, that must constitute the text from which individual, continuous identity is read. The disciplinary rule of legalistic individualism is physical continuity with the person who committed the deed, and only the fingerprint can give absolute testimony to that continuity across time. Nevertheless, to those members of the community who do not understand as fully as does Wilson himself the nature of legal liberalism and individualism, the allure of the palm as a text for individual responsibility is great:

> Wilson began to study Luigi's palm, tracing life lines, heart lines, head lines and so on . . . he felt of the fleshy cushion at the base of the thumb, and noted its shape; he felt of the fleshy side of the hand between the wrist and the base of the little . . .
>
> He mapped out Luigi's character and disposition, his tastes, aversions, proclivities, ambitions and eccentricities. . . .
>
> Next, Wilson took up Luigi's history. He proceeded cautiously . . . moving his finger slowly along the great lines of the palm, and now and then halting it at a "star" or some such landmark and examining that neighborhood minutely. He proclaimed one or two past events . . . and the search went on. Presently Wilson glanced up suddenly with a surprised expression—
>
> "Here is a record of an incident which you would perhaps not wish me to—"
>
> "Bring it out," said Luigi, good-naturedly, "I promise you it shan't embarrass me."
>
> *"You have killed some one—but whether man, woman or child, I do not make out."* . . .
>
> "Caesar's ghost!" commented Tom, with astonishment. "It beats anything that was ever heard of! Why, a man's own hand is his deadliest enemy! Just think of that—a man's own hand

> keeps a record of the deepest and fatalest secrets of his life, and is treacherously ready to expose him to any black-magic stranger that comes along." (*PW*, 51; emphasis added)

Similarly, the "sham text" for racial identity is appearance: dress, skin color, and, in general, the perceptions of others. Although you might think you could infer racial identity by these factors, you cannot. The disciplining rule that governs interpretation of the racial code precludes such an interpretation and precludes such a text; it is birth and bloodline, not behavior, that provides the link to collective guilt that is race. Thus, when Roxy switches her baby for the child of her master, she learns the proffered difference that clothes can make. But this text, like palmistry, is a sham and a trap. The interpretation of racial identity from clothes, bearing, perception of others, and skin color is a compelling one, but it is not determinative, for it is precluded by the disciplining rule itself:

> She undressed Thomas a Becket, stripping him of everything, and put the tow-linen shirt on him. She put his coral necklace on her own child's neck. Then she placed the children side by side, and after earnest inspection she muttered—
>
> "Now who would b'lieve clo'es could do de like o' dat? Dog my cats if it ain't all *I* kin do to tell t'other fum which, let alone his pappy."
>
> She put her cub in Tommy's elegant cradle and said—
>
> "You's young Marse *Tom* fum dis out, en I got to practice and git used to 'memberin' to call you dat, honey, or I's gwyne to make a mistake some time en git us bofe into trouble. Dah—now you lay still en don't fret no mo', Marse Tom—oh, thank de good Lord in heaven, you's saved! . . . —dey ain't no man kin ever sell mammy's po' little honey down de river now! . . ."
>
> She got up light-hearted and happy, and went to the cradles and spent what was left of the night "practicing." She would give her own child a light pat and say, humbly, "Lay still, Marse Tom," then give the real Tom a pat and say with severity, "Lay *still*, Chambers! . . .
>
> As she progressed with her practice, she was surprised to see how steadily and surely the awe which had kept her tongue reverent and her manner humble toward her young master was

> transferring itself to her speech and manner toward the usurper, and how similarly handy she was becoming in transferring her motherly curtness of speech and peremptoriness of manner to the unlucky heir of the ancient house of Driscoll. (*PW*, 14–16)

And third, the sham text for nobility is upbringing, and the habits of self-regard they instill. Again, this text is compelling but the interpretations it suggests are bound to be misleading. The disciplining rule itself precludes it:

> [After Tom learned his true identity, for] days he wandered in lonely places thinking, thinking, thinking—trying to get his bearings. It was new work. If he met a friend he found that the habit of a lifetime had in some mysterious way vanished—his arm hung limp instead of involuntarily extending the hand for a shake. It was the nigger in him asserting its humility, and he blushed and was abashed. And the nigger in him was surprised when the white friend put out his hand for a shake with him. He found the nigger in him involuntarily giving the road, on the sidewalk, to the white rowdy and loafer. . . . So strange and uncharacteristic was Tom's conduct that people noticed it and turned to look after him when he passed on; . . . it gave him a sick feeling, and he took himself out of view as quickly as he could. . . .
>
> In several ways his opinions were totally changed, and would never go back to what they were before, but the main structure of his character was not changed, and could not be changed.
>
> . . . Under the influence of a great mental and moral upheaval his character and habits had taken on the appearance of complete change, but after a while with the subsidence of the storm both began to settle toward their former places. He dropped gradually back into his old frivolous and easy-going ways, and conditions of feeling, and manner of speech, and no familiar of his could have detected anything in him that differentiated him from the weak and careless Tom of other days. (*PW*, 44–45)

And, as Fiss also would insist, the disciplinary rules that govern these texts are the definitive parameters of the interpretive community—again, there is only one school, and attendance is indeed mandatory. To be a member of the community of Dawson's Landing is to accept and live by the honor and racial codes—those codes define the members, as much as the members define the codes. This mandatory attendance policy has two consequences. First, while there are other nonmandatory codes subscribed to by parts of this community, they play no role in the community's core interpretive practices, and therefore play no role in the interpretation of law. Religion, for example, constitutes a nonmandatory moral code subscribed to in some form by most members of the community, but not by its "first citizen," the judge—head of the town's agnostic "freethinkers" society. Similarly, the ethic endorsed by the villainous Tom—a lawless, gambling-prone and profit-motivated greed—may be the wave of the future (as Twain foresees) but it is not sanctioned by this conservative community, complete with its debauched democratic politics and its aristocratic bias. Twain makes his own contempt for it equally clear.

Second, the mandatory attendance policy entails that the members of this interpretive community, lawyers and judges, are incapable of transcending the disciplining rules that govern them; to do so would constitute expulsion from the interpretive community that is law. Not once does it occur to the town's freethinkers, Pudd'nhead and Judge Driscoll, to question either the racial code or the code of honor (or the sanctity of property, another major theme of the novel). Indeed these freethinkers have more thoroughly and expertly absorbed these codes than has the rest of the community. They each earn the community's highest accolades of respect through their masterful interpretations of the community's definitive texts. It is the disciplinary rules that define the boundaries of acceptable interpretation, and it is indeed submission to the disciplinary rules that defines membership in the interpretive community responsible for the town's legal order.

Disciplining Rules, Objectivity, and Hidden Imperatives

The objectivity that legal interpretation achieves through reliance on disciplining rules comes with a high cost: it masks the imperative nature of the text being interpreted, and consequently the criteria against which the text and the rules that facilitate interpretation should be judged. Thus, the declaratory grammatical form of the disciplining rule that "niggers are guilty," like the racial code whose interpretation it facilitates, masks its imperative origin and hence masks the criteria against which it should be judged. That "niggers are guilty" in Dawson's Landing is a true proposition, as are the related propositions that "Tom is a slave" and that "Roxy is black" and that both, therefore, can be (and are) sold down the river. But all of these true propositions are true by virtue of white fiat, not natural fact. They are true by virtue of an act of power, not an act of reasoned observation. It is not natural fact, but white dominance over slaves, that is reflected in the rule's proclamation of meaning—to be a "nigger" means to be guilty. It is most assuredly not skin color (for Roxy's skin is white), but white fiat, reflected in the claim that "Roxy is black." And finally, it is not his individual guilt for his individual act of murder, but rather the white collective power over his collective race, that is reflected in the court's conclusion that Tom is guilty, for which his punishment is to be sold down the river.

The cost of objective interpretivism is just this: when we accept a state of the world that derives from an act of power as a part of the natural world, we lose sense of how to evaluate that state of the world; it becomes arbitrary in a perfectly benign sense. Twain gives us a metaphor. In an early passage, Roxy notes the arbitrary power of God to damn and save at whim. So long as the power is unquestioned, the result is viewed as natural. If guilt is a matter of celestial fiat, the arbitrariness of the outcome is no more something to be challenged or questioned than the natural fact that grass is green and the sky blue:

> [A]in't nobody kin save his own self—can't do it by faith, can't do it by works, can't do it no way at all. Free grace is de *on'y* way, en dat don't come fum nobody but jis' de Lord; en *He* kin give it to anybody He please, saint or sinner—*He* don't k'yer. He do jis as He's a mineter. He s'lect out anybody dat suit Him, en put another one in his place, en make de fust one happy forever en leave t'other one to burn wid Satan. (*PW*, 15)

If it is part of God's nature that salvation and damnation are at whim, and if God is omnipotent, then it makes as little sense to question the arbitrariness of his judgment as to object to the sun's daily rising. Similarly, if it is part of being white to have unchecked power over blacks, and if black collective guilt simply is the white judgment, then it will not occur to any member of the interpretive community to question the arbitrariness of this judgment. Thus, the question "what did the 'nigger' *do* that accounts for his guilt" is not just *unanswerable*; more importantly, it is *unaskable*. Like the question "what did the sinner do to deserve salvation," the question is precluded by the disciplining rules that enable the discourse. Black guilt is a function of collective identity, not individual deed; the question "what did he do" is *ruled out*. It is therefore not surprising that the only character in the novel who ever broaches the question is Tom, and he raises it only once, right after he has learned he is a "nigger." When Tom learns his true identity, after twenty-five years of believing himself white, he is suddenly cast out of the interpretive community—he is neither white nor black. Because of his exclusion, and only because of his exclusion, he can ask the very question that the members of the community cannot themselves possibly utter:

> Why were niggers and whites made? What crime did the uncreated first nigger commit that the curse of birth was decreed for him? And why is this awful difference made between white and black? . . . . How hard the nigger's fate seems, this morning!—yet until last night such a thought never entered my head. (*PW*, 44)

In this case, of course, objective interpretation and submission to the disciplining rules that facilitates it, has not only masked the imperative nature of the primary rule of the racial text—that "niggers" are guilty—it has also masked the imperative nature of the rule's constitutive *parts*. For to take Tom's questions in order: "niggers" and whites were not made by God—the division of the species into "niggers" and whites is not a part of the natural order. There are no natural "niggers"; there is no such natural attribute. The "niggers" in *Pudd'nhead Wilson* underscore this truth. Both Roxy and Tom share the skin coloring of *whites*. Roxy is one-sixteenth black, Tom is one thirty-second. The categories "nigger" and "white" were indeed made, but they were made by whites, not by God, as Tom's question falsely implies. When the imperative is exposed, and only when the imperative is exposed, does the "why" become askable and answerable: "niggers" were made by whites to serve the interest of whites.

Thus, the *reader* of the novel, free of the disciplining rules that govern and define the interpretive community of Dawson's Landing, unlike the interpretive community itself, can assess the merits of this imperative. In a parallel fashion, I believe, the careful reader of this novel, unlike the interpretive community itself, can correctly interpret Pudd'nhead Wilson's ill-fated joke, for it is squarely in this macabre joke, I believe, that the central message of this peculiar novel is to be found. As mentioned above, at the outset of the novel Wilson hears an invisible dog barking, and jokes that he wished he owned half of it, for if he did, he would kill his half. The joke never receives an adequate interpretation through the entire novel—in fact it may be the *only* thoroughly misinterpreted text in the book. This suggests, I submit, that the joke is in there for the reader, not the characters, to interpret.

What does the joke mean? First, as several commentators have noted, *dog* is a central metaphor in this book for "nigger." Sometimes *dog* metaphorically connotes "villain" and sometimes "victim," but it is *always* a symbol for "niggers." "Niggers" generally and Tom in particular are referred to as "dogs" no less than half a dozen times. The most telling reference of the first type (dog as metaphor for guilty villain) is made by Pudd'nhead Wilson himself when he finally solves the murder mystery (but before he discovers the switch in identity). Tom is visiting Wilson the night before the twins' trial is to commence, and inadvertently leaves a fingerprint on one of Wilson's glass plates:

> [Tom] took up another strip of glass, and exclaimed—"Why, here's old Roxy's label! Are you going to ornament the royal palaces with nigger paw-marks, too? By the date here, I was seven months old when this was done and she was nursing me and her little nigger cub. There's a line straight across her thumb-print. How comes that?. . ."
>
> "That is common," said the bored man, wearily. "Scar of a cut or a scratch, usually"—and he took the strip of glass indifferently and raised it toward the lamp.
>
> [As Wilson recognized Tom's fingerprints as the same as those on the murder weapon, all the blood sunk suddenly out of his face; his hand quaked, and he gazed at the polished surface before him with the glassy stare of a corpse. . . .
>
> [A]s Tom went out he couldn't deny himself a small parting

> gibe: "Don't take it so hard; a body can't win every time; you'll hang somebody yet."
>
> Wilson muttered to himself, "It is no lie to say I am sorry I have to begin with you, miserable dog though you are!" (*PW*, 103)

The most telling reference of the second sort—dog as a metaphor for victim—is made by Roxy, upon learning that Tom has committed the ultimate betrayal and sold her down the river in order to reap the cash: "Sell a pusson down de river—*down de river*! . . . I wouldn't treat a dog so!" (*PW*, 85). Roxy immediately follows this exclamation with a comparison of Tom with a dog-as-scoundrel:

> "What could you do? You could be Judas to yo' own mother to save yo' wuthless hide! Would anybody b'lieve it? No—a dog couldn't! You is de low-downest orneriest hound dat was ever pup'd into dis worl'—en I's 'sponsible for it!"—and she spat on him. (*PW*, 90)

How, even with this information, should we interpret Pudd'n-head's joke? The reader can interpret the joke in light of the disciplining rules by which the community lives but fails to question: first that *dog* is a metaphor for "slave," and second that a dog, like a slave, is both property and villain, both owned and guilty. Now in a fairly literal sense, both the novel in general and the joke in particular are about the problem white slave-owning communities faced regarding mulattoes. As mentioned above, both of the central "nigger" characters in this novel are of mixed blood: Roxy is one-sixteenth black, and Tom is one thirty-second. Further, both characters have the blood of nobility as well as the blood of the Negro race. One interpretation of the joke then is simply this: enslavement of the Negro race is tantamount to ownership of half a dog—it is just as cruel and just as foolish. You cannot enslave the "nigger" half of Tom and expect the "noble" half to be honorable; you cannot victimize the slave half and expect the noble half to be strong; you cannot damn the slave half and expect the noble half to be virtuous; you most assuredly cannot own the slave half and expect the noble half to breathe free. To *try* to do so—to own the slave and sell him as property and condemn him to hell by selling him down the river—

is to kill him; and as the neighbors rightly insist, you cannot kill half a living creature and expect the other half to live. What they do not see, of course, is that this is as true of human beings as it is of dogs. Nor do they see, therefore, the necessary implication of their own literalistic interpretation of Pudd'nhead's joke: the man that owns and kills half the dog will be equally responsible for the death of the other half. The race that owns, enslaves, kills, and damns half a human being as "slave" will kill the other half as well and some day be held responsible for doing so.

If we turn our backs on the disciplining rule of Dawson's Landing and embrace instead one closer to our own frame of reference, we can generate a related and more powerful interpretation of Wilson's joke. A dog is a living organism, and in a different sense so is a community. We might, then, regard the dog in the joke as a metaphoric reference to the community itself. Owning and killing half a dog, with this disciplining rule of interpretation, is a metaphor for the imperative institution of slavery itself: the owning and killing of a half of the community, with the same consequences. You cannot enslave and kill half the community without killing the whole, any more than you can kill half a dog and keep the whole alive. If you try, you may one day be held responsible for the death of the whole, where the whole is a community no less than where the whole is a dog.

The Morality of the Objective Interpretivist

The most difficult and ambiguous aspect of Twain's novel concerns the character of Pudd'nhead himself. No issue more divides the criticism and interpretations of this novel than whether or not Pudd'nhead, surely the protagonist, is also a hero. The case for his heroism (endorsed by nineteenth-century critics far more consistently than twentieth) is straightforward: Pudd'nhead is smart, even a genius. He is inventive, clever, and legalistic; he is a Dworkinian Hercules. He understands the community and the community's foibles better than do its members. He is shunned for twenty years but perseveres and finally comes into his own. He goes from town fool to town mayor, and he does so through the honorable means of success in the law. He is neither materialistic nor greedy. He is funny. He rises in popularity as he brings Tom, the villain, down. He brings both law and science to a relatively lawless and superstitious community.

He is respectful of the community he seeks to reform. He knows human nature, he is insightful, and finally, of course, he is successful.

All this, though, leaves a bitter taste, and I suspect that the further we move in history from the date of the novel, the stranger the taste becomes. There is something deeply wrong with this fairly standard interpretation of the heroic Pudd'nhead. First, and most simply, there is something wrong with the idea that Mark Twain—who gave us Huckleberry Finn, Jim, the Mississippi River, and the journey *up* the Mississippi River as a powerful symbol of freedom and salvation—would create a hero who sends a slave *down* the river into slavery and damnation, no matter how evil the slave. Second, there is something wrong with the idea that Mark Twain would give us a novel *heralding* the racist and aristocratic values of a small slave-holding town, and trumpeting as a hero an outsider who becomes an insider by embracing those values. Furthermore, Twain himself referred to Wilson's role in the novel as a mere "machine."[21] (Surely, author's intent should count for something.) But considerably more than author's intent must be put aside to accommodate a reading of Wilson as a lawyer-hero. There is no doubt that Wilson is clever, and there is no doubt that he achieves what he's craved: popularity and success in the community. Wilson's virtue, however, depends upon the virtue of the community that has embraced him, and on the virtue of this community not just Twain but the novel itself is anything but ambiguous. The community is evil, plain and simple. The irony of this novel, finally, is that while as reader we condemn the community's values, we want to applaud the protagonist who has won that community's approval, even when he achieves it by advocating the values we wish to condemn.

One plausible interpretation of the meaning of Twain's novel, I believe, is that we should learn to be skeptical (if we aren't naturally so) of the interpretivist means by which Wilson wins his way into the community's embrace—and into the hearts of many readers as well. How we evaluate Wilson's character depends upon how we regard his interpretive legal practices, and thus how we regard the nature of law itself. If we regard law, properly supplemented by community values,

21. This remark is attributed to Twain by Marvin Fisher and Michael Elliott in their interpretive essay, "Pudd'nHead Wilson: A Half a Dog Is Worse than None," in *PW*, 309, following a reference in Henry Nash Smith, *Mark Twain: The Development of the Writer* (Cambridge: Harvard University Press, 1962), 181.

as a set of texts to be interpreted, we will also tend to regard Wilson as a hero. If we regard law as a set of imperative commands, we will tend to regard Wilson as complicit, to some degree commensurate with his power, in the town's evil. The "objectivity" of the supplemental, disciplined interpretation in which Wilson engages, I submit, masks the moral character of this most masterful interpreter, as well as the criteria by which we should evaluate his acts.

For it is undoubtedly true that from a Dworkinian and Fissian perspective, Pudd'nhead is a hero—he achieves the kind of success for which Hercules is the ideal. The story of Pudd'nhead's success is the story of Hercules's success: it is a story of the triumph of legalism. Disputes are resolved in court, advocated by lawyers, decided by neutral judges, according to agreed-upon rules. And furthermore, the triumph of law in the community is not a victory of an invading, foreign, or hostile force. Wilson achieves his triumph by *incorporating* the town's moral values into the legal values he brings with him from back East, not by displacing those values. As Fiss would concede must be the case, and as Dworkin insists should be the case, Wilson learns to read the law through the prism of the town's values. Through that process the town's morality becomes infused in the town's law, and the distinction between moral and legal rules dissolves. The town's legal order becomes circumscribed by the town's moral order—they each define as they facilitate the other. It is by mastering that process that Wilson (like Hercules) achieves success.

More specifically, from what Fiss calls an *internal* perspective (*OI*, 748), Pudd'nhead emerges from Tom's trial a community hero, a widely acclaimed interpretive Hercules. He reads the objective legal text through the prism of the town's moral values, and he interprets the resulting supplemented text in accordance with the disciplining rules that govern the town's interpretive practices. He performs as both a "servant of the law and a servant of the community." He holds the community's values—not his own—paramount in his legal analysis. By interpreting the town's multiple codes, by respecting their interpretive practices, by integrating their moral values with their legal text, he achieves the popularity he had so long craved—he becomes successor to the title "first citizen" previously held by the murdered judge. And, even from what Fiss calls the outsider's external perspective (*OI*, 748), Pudd'nhead is absolved from responsibility. The same objectivity that constitutes his internal heroism shields him from external responsibility. Pudd'nhead *himself* is not responsible for the town's morality—Pudd'nhead is an Eastern-trained outsider. And, it is the town's morality—not the lawyer's—that must supplement the text of the positive law and discipline its interpretation. Consequently Pudd'nhead, no less than Hercules, cannot be held responsible for the results the legal system, supplemented as it must be by the town's morality, generates. More graphically, Pudd'nhead *himself* does not sell Tom down the river. Pudd'nhead simply supplies the most coherent, most correct, and most powerful interpretation of the community's texts. It was those *texts* that sold Tom down the river. The law did it, not the lawyer.

However, if we regard law, including the values that supplement it and the disciplining rules that govern it, as a set of imperatives rather than objective texts, Pudd'nhead's character takes on a different hue. Wilson is a political actor in a political community, and like all the actors in that community he has some power. Not much, but some. With power comes responsibility—not much, perhaps, but some. If we regard law as an imperative, Wilson's incorporation of the community's racial code into the law is an act of power and a choice, not an act of passive interpretation. As such it renders him complicit in the town's corruption; it does not ennoble him. And in fact, Wilson is complicit in the town's evil: Wilson does sell Tom down the river. For it is not by virtue of the "liberal legalism" to which Wilson is purportedly committed that Wilson feels he must expose Tom as a slave in court. All Wilson has to do to show who killed the victim is prove that the fingerprints on the knife are Tom's. Although it has escaped notice of most commentators on this novel, there is no reason either in law or in liberal logic that this heroic lawyer-protagonist *has* to go the extra step and expose Tom as a slave. He chooses to. And it is because he chooses to that Tom is delivered downstream

Wilson exposes Tom as a slave as well as a murderer not because the legal code demands it, but because the community's *racial code* demands it, and Wilson has learned that to be successful—to be popular—in this town, he must interpret the law through the prism of the rules of race. This act of interpretation, however, was neither natural nor necessary: Wilson chose to interpret the law in light of the racial code; he did not have to do so. He could have done otherwise. He could have forfeited popularity and used his small amount of power instead to challenge the racial code. He could have challenged the social construction by which black is delineated from white. But he did not. Instead he embraced, endorsed, absorbed, incorporated, and then used the community's racial code. He mastered it and became the town's first citizen by virtue of that mastery. By doing so, he became an authority on its meaning and responsible for its content. By endorsing the community's code, Wilson perpetuated it; by incorporating the racial code into the legal code, he authored it. He read the objective law through the prism of the community's moralistic embrace of evil, and by doing so he embraced that evil as his own. Wilson got the wish he initially expressed as a joke: he owned and then killed half the dog—he exposed Tom as a slave and sent him down the river. And he should be held responsible for having done so.

Why did he do it? This is not a hard question. Wilson craved what Hercules has: popularity and respect. For twenty years, he craved the town's respect, and through his interpretive prowess he eventually got it. He achieved the popularity he needed through an act of paradigmatic conformity: objective, disciplined interpretation of the community's supplemented legal texts. What Wilson doesn't gain is a more just community, and what Tom doesn't gain, of course, is justice. Pudd'nhead Wilson is no hero, nor is Dworkin's Hercules, and neither are the judges, lawyers, and legal foot soldiers that emulate his aspirations. Pudd'nhead, like Hercules, is the ultimate conformist, and conformity for the sake of popularity is no virtue.

Of course, conformity for the sake of popularity, success, or for that matter survival is no sin, either, at least during the normal run of things. It is natural for us to interpret our community's mores as just if we are to survive in our community; perhaps it is even inevitable. And, it is natural for those of us who are political actors to become expert interpreters, and to turn that skill into political gain. But we should not confuse what is natural, and excusable, and understandable with what is virtue, any more than we should confuse the absence of villainy with heroism. Pudd'nhead may be a popular mayor and Hercules may be a popular judge. Both political triumphs are achieved through interpretive prowess rather than the ballot box. But they are just that: political victories. Whether or not they are moral victories as well is a separate question entirely.

Subjective Interpretivism

Subjective interpretivism, as the name I have given it implies, shares one commitment with objective interpretivism: like their objective counterparts, subjective interpretivists view adjudication as an interpretive act. Thus for subjectivists such as Stanley Fish, no less than for objectivists such as Dworkin and Fiss, adjudication is primarily an act of interpretation. Subjective interpretivists differ from objectivists over the nature of interpretation, and as a result over the *consequences* of adjudication's interpretive core. Subjectivists insist that the malleability of text—its lack of an "objective meaning"—renders interpretation itself inevitably subjective. Therefore, the interpretation of a text is really an act of power rather than an act of understanding. The interpreter chooses the meaning; he does not deduce it. For the subjectivist, the fact that adjudication is interpretation, far from being what constrains the judge, is what *empowers* the judge. The fact that adjudication is interpretation, then, creates rather than cures the problem of power. The interpretive core of adjudication is precisely what renders adjudication an act of power. Interpretation is imperative. Adjudication is imperative. Therefore, adjudication is imperative.

As a consequence of their view of the nature of interpretation, subjective interpretivists *also* share a commitment with the imperativist tradition. Like the imperativists, they hold that adjudication is an act of power, and not an act of discovery. Their argument, however, for the claim that adjudication is an act of power is different from that put forward by the imperativists. For the imperativists, including both the British legal positivists and the American legal realists, that adjudication is power follows from the force distinctively wielded by the judiciary: adjudication is an act of power because it is backed by the command of the state. For subjective interpretivists, by contrast, that adjudication is imperative follows not from the force commanded by the judiciary, but instead from its interpretive core. Adjudication is an act of power *because it is interpretive*, and interpretation is *itself*, inevitably, an act of power. For the subjective interpretivist, it is the *interpretive* core of adjudication that entails its imperative nature, not the force it wields.

Subjective interpretivism is typically criticized today (almost always by objective interpretivists) on the grounds that its claim that interpretation is necessarily subjective (and hence that objective interpretation is impossible) is wrong. What is at stake in this debate between objective and subjective interpretivists is the possibility of objectivity in interpretive adjudication. If the objectivists are right about the nature of interpretation, and if adjudication is primarily an interpretive act, then adjudication is an act of discovery rather than an act of power. If the subjectivists are right about the nature of interpretation and if adjudication is an interpretive act, then adjudication is an act of power rather than an act of discovery. If adjudication is indeed interpretation, the debate between objective and subjective views of the interpretive enterprise is surely an important one. It is not, however, the question I will pursue here.

What I will argue here is that subjectivists are wrong about the nature of interpretation, and more specifically, that they are wrong in their claim that so many of the things we do with words—including both adjudication and criticism of adjudication—constitutes interpretation. In one respect, their incredibly inclusive view of the scope of our interpretive practices is false, but harmlessly so. Adjudication is not primarily interpretation, it is primarily imperative and secondarily interpretation. This mistaken emphasis, however, is relatively harmless. We can reap the benefits of subjectivist analysis of the interpretive aspect of adjudication without having to accept (or reject) their underlying claim that adjudication is *primarily* interpretation. But in another respect the wide net subjectivists have cast in the name of interpretation is dangerously overbroad: it is dangerously overbroad because of its implication that *criticism* of law, no less than adjudication itself, is an interpretive act. I will argue that the view of criticism that emerges from the subjectivist's view of interpretation is not just mistaken, but dangerously so. Contrary to the claim of at least some of its adherents, the view of criticism that follows from subjectivist premises is deeply reactionary, not progressive, in its political implications.

Subjective Interpretivism and Imperativism

Subjective interpretivism (or subjectivism) and imperativism are often confused for good reason: they share a vision of law and adjudication that is more similar than dissimilar. Both traditions view adjudication as imperative, and both traditions differ from objectivism on precisely that point. The proposition "this contract is unconscionable," for example, would be regarded by the objective interpretivist as a statement of legal fact, or a part of legal knowledge. It is either right or wrong; it is either true or false. For both the subjectivist and the imperativist, the same proposition is declaratory in grammatical form only, and that grammatical form is misleading. In fact, when uttered by a judge, the proposition states (or masks) an imperative: this court will refuse to enforce this contract. This shared commitment to the underlying imperative core of adjudication is an important one. It is this shared belief that constitutes the premise, for both traditions, of their central work: the discovery (or the unmasking, or the deconstruction) of the imperative lurking behind all purportedly propositional statements of legal truth.

However, imperativism and subjectivism reach this shared commitment by divergent analyses of the nature of interpretation, which in turn entail divergent views of the nature of legal criticism. For the imperativist the proposition "this contract is unconscionable," uttered by a court, is a masked imperative—it is declaratory in form only. It expresses a command of the court, not a truth about an existing contract. Its truth or falsity, then, depends upon the power of the court, not upon the content of some preexisting legal rule or the nature of the contract. But the imperative nature of *legal* truths is solely a function of judicial power; it does not imply the imperative nature of *all* truths. By contrast, the critical claim, for example, that "unconscionable contracts frustrate real human needs" is a claim about our real human needs, not a hidden imperative. The critical claim is just what it appears to be: a propositional claim about the relation between a political practice and a human need. Whether or not it is true or false depends upon whether or not it is true or false that unconscionable contracts frustrate real human needs. Its truth or falsity depends on the nature of our real human needs, not on the power or lack of power of the critic.

Subjective interpretivists, distinctively, deny this. For the subjectivist, both legal adjudication and legal criticism are interpretive acts, and *all* interpretive acts are imperative in the same way that adjudication is imperative. An interpretive act is a (necessarily subjective) interpretation of a text that is itself socially constructed. Thus, the legal text that constitutes the major premise for the court's conclusion that "this contract is unenforceable" is not a real contract or a real precedent or a real legal doctrine existing in a land of discoverable legal reality but rather is a social construction generated by political processes. Similarly, the subjectivist holds, the social text for the *critical* (rather than adjudicatory) claim that "enforcing unconscionable contracts frustrates real human needs" is not our real human needs. Human beings do not have real human needs any more than the legal world has real contracts or real rules of law. The critical claim that we have a real need—and that a law frustrates it—is but an interpretation, necessarily subjective, of a socially constructed text generated by political processes. The criticism of law, then, because it is no less interpretive, is therefore no less imperative than the adjudication of law. The critical claim that "enforcing unconscionable contracts frustrates real human needs," like the adjudicative claim that "this contract is unconscionable," is not something that is either true or false. Like all acts of interpretation, it is a masked assertion of power. It is a chosen interpretation of a social text that we have created, not a proposition (either true or false) about our human needs. All we can say about the claim that "unconscionable contracts frustrate real human needs" is whether or not the claim has attained political success: if it is something a great number of people have come to live by, it is successful; if not, it is unsuccessful. We cannot determine whether it is true or not for the simple reason that there are no real human needs against which it can be judged, any more than there are contracts prelabeled unconscionable or enforceable. All there is, is the speaker's desire to see certain contracts struck, the speaker's desire to couch that commitment in the language of real human needs, and the speaker's relative power (of persuasion or force) in imposing that preference on others. We should not be fooled by this mystifying claim that there are real needs any more than we should allow ourselves to be fooled by the obfuscating declaratory rhetoric of courts regarding the real existence of contracts.

The central and distinguishing commitment of subjective interpretivism, unshared by imperativism, then, is this: there is no real basis for moral criticism of law any more than there is a real basis for adjudication. There are no real human needs (or real anything else—real rights, real justice, real human potential) by which to criticize law any more than there are real contracts or real neutral principles by which to adjudicate. That there are real needs is an illusion in precisely the way (and for precisely the reason) that it is an illusion that there are real contracts. Both illusions manifest as well as result from the power of some political actor. There are no real needs because there is no ahistorical, noncontingent human nature. There are only conflicting critical subjective interpretations of our contingent social and political history, including the history of our various political imaginings. The human nature we think we see, with its attendant human needs, and perhaps human rights, is but a product of some strand of our contingent social history, which could well have been otherwise. There are no real needs, rights, or justice that transcend our history, or our conventions. There is only political will: felt, perceived, and interpreted in a thousand different ways.

This rift between imperativists (whether they regard themselves as legal realists or legal positivists or critical legal scholars) and subjective interpretivists (whether or not they regard themselves as deconstructionists), typically obscured by their considerable common ground, has recently come to the surface. In a revealing article entitled *Anti-Professionalism*, Stanley Fish, our foremost subjective interpretivist, attacks a range of theorists he calls, generically, "antiprofessionalists," including two prominent legal critics, Bob Gordon and Duncan Kennedy. Fish takes the antiprofessionalists to task for their insistence on the existence of real needs and real ideals and a real human potential, as a basis for criticism of politics, professions, laws, and institutional histories. The article is the clearest exposition to date of the nature of the divide between subjectivists on the one hand and imperativists on the other.

Fish begins his attack on Gordon by laying stake to their common ground. Gordon and Fish agree on the nature of law. They agree that purportedly neutral law is in fact political:

> Gordon [has discovered] that legal reasoning is not "a set of neutral techniques available to everyone" but is everywhere informed by policy, and that judicial decisionmaking, despite claims to objectivity and neutrality, rests on "[s]ocial and political judgments about the substance, parties, and context of a case . . . even when they are not the explicit or conscious basis of decision." [He] has discovered, in short, that rather than being grounded in natural and logical necessity, the legal process always

> reflects the interests and concerns of some political or economic agenda, and [he] moves on to unfreeze the world as it appears to common sense as a bunch of more or less objectively determined social relations and to make it appear as (we believe) it really is: people acting, imagining, rationalizing, justifying. (*AP*, 656)

With Gordon's legal imperativism, Fish is in agreement. But, Fish complains, Gordon next implies that we should criticize these "actings, imaginings, rationalizings and justifyings" of the legal culture by reference to our real nature. This, Fish insists, we cannot do. There is no more of a real human nature than there are real contracts (or neutral principles). From Fish's point of view, Gordon's insistence on the viability of such criticism is not only ill-founded, but illogical. It is illogical, Fish argues, because it is inconsistent with Gordon's insistence on the political underpinnings of purportedly neutral law:

> The full force of this contradiction becomes clear . . . when Gordon declares that the "discovery" that the "belief structures that rule our lives are not found in nature but are historically contingent" is "liberating"; but of course the discovery can only be liberating (in a strong sense) if by some act of magic the insight that one is historically conditioned is itself not historically achieved and enables one . . . to operate outside of history. Gordon's capitulation to the essentialist ideology he opposes is complete when he fully specifies what he means by liberating: "This discovery is . . . liberating . . . because uncovering those [belief] structures makes us see how arbitrary our categories for dividing up experience are." . . . What Gordon wants (although by his own principles he should want no such thing) are categories uninvolved in interest; and it is in the context of that absolutist and essentialist desire, that the ways and categories we have can be termed arbitrary. (*AP*, 658)

Fish next criticizes Duncan Kennedy for the same sin. Having exposed the imperative and political underpinning of the declaratory form of legal ideology, doctrine, and culture, Fish argues, Kennedy cannot then assert the existence of a real natural basis for normative criticism of those unmasked imperatives:

> Exactly the same line of reasoning is displayed by Gordon's colleague Duncan Kennedy when he moves from the observation that legal reasoning is everywhere informed by policy to the conclusion that those who teach legal reasoning teach "nonsense," *only* argumentative techniques, "policy and nothing more." But arguments based on policy can be devalued and declared nonsensical only if one assumes the existence and availability of arguments . . . based on a sense beyond policy, a sense which, because it is apolitical or extrapolitical, can serve as a reference point from which the merely political can be identified and judged. . . . He buys into that vision again when he declares that "the classroom distinction between the unproblematic, legal case and the policy-oriented case is a *mere artifact*." [Artifact] is a "hinge" word, poised between the insight that reality as we know and inhabit it is institutional and therefore "man-made" and the desire (which contradicts the insight) for a reality that has been made by nature. That desire is the content of "mere," a word that marks the passage (already negotiated) from an observation—that the distinction between the unproblematic and the policy-oriented case is conventional—to a judgment—that because it is conventional, it is unreal. . . . Both [Kennedy and Gordon] proceed, in an almost unintelligible sequence, from the insight that the received picture of things is not given but historically contingent to the conclusion that history should be repudiated in favor of a truth that transcends it. Kennedy's specific target, . . . like Gordon's, . . . is to "abolish . . . hierarchies, to take control over the whole of our lives, and to shape them toward the satisfaction of our real human needs." (*AP*, 659–60)

Both Kennedy and Gordon, Fish argues, improperly assume the existence of real human needs as the basis for criticism of exercises of power. This insistence is impermissible. There are no real human needs. There are only more or less politically successful claims to the existence of such:

> The key word in the last sentence—taken from Peter Gabel and Jay Feinman's essay *Contract Law as Ideology*,—is "real." . . . The complaint is that a set of related and finally equivalent realities—real truth, real values, real knowledge, real authority, real

> motives, real need, real merit, the real self—is in continual danger of being overwhelmed or obscured or usurped by artifacts (fictions, fabrications, constructions) that have been created (imposed, manufactured) by forces and agencies that are merely professional or merely institutional or merely conventional or merely rhetorical or merely historical; and the program is simply to sweep away these artifacts—and with them professions, institutions, conventions, rhetorics and history—so that uncorrupted and incorruptible essences can once again be espied and embraced. (*AP*, 661)

According to Fish, *any* critical claim that a professional, empowered group (such as lawyers, judges, doctors, or chairmen of English departments) has used that power in a way that frustrates something real (such as "real human needs") is confused, disingenuous, incoherent, and, worst of all, right wing. Any such criticism violates the fundamental commitment of subjective interpretivism: there are only *interpretations* of right, *interpretations* of needs, or *interpretations* of truth; there are no *real* rights, needs, or truths against which these interpretations can be evaluated:

> What is surprising . . . is to find this the declared program of intellectuals who think of themselves as being on the left, and who therefore begin their considerations with a strong sense of the constitutive power of history and convention, and this leads me to [this] declaration . . . : at the moment that a left-wing intellectual turns anti-professional, he has become a right-wing intellectual in disguise. (*AP*, 661)

What left-wing critics *ought* to be doing, Fish informs us (and them), is not criticizing law on the basis of our "real" human needs or "real" potential, but instead, simply presenting alternative "imaginings, rationalizings, justifications, etc." to those presently espoused by the dominant vision. Just as the judge can't claim truth when he asserts that a contract does or doesn't exist (but can only claim institutional power), similarly a critic can't assert truth when she asserts that a law is frustrating our real needs, or is hurting us more than helping us, or is or isn't morally repugnant. All the critic, like the judge, can assert is institutional power—she either has it or she doesn't. The critic's alternative imagining, then, also cannot be judged on the basis of whether its assumptions are true or false to our real nature, our real needs, or our real potential. It can only be judged on the basis of whether or not the criticism has proven successful—whether it has displaced the dominant vision and become dominant itself. Thus, Fish completes his critique of Kennedy:

> Kennedy is right to say that teachers who persuade students that "legal reasoning is distinct as a *method* . . . from ethical and political discourse in general" have persuaded them to something false; but that is not the same as saying that they teach nonsense; they teach a very interested sense and teach it as if there were no other. The way to counter this is to teach or urge some other interested sense, some other ethical or political vision, by means of alternative arguments which, if successful, will be the new content of legal reasoning. This is in fact what Kennedy is doing in his essay, but it isn't what he thinks he's doing—he thinks he's clearing away the "mystification" of mere argument and therefore replacing nonsense with sense; but he can only think that in relation to a sense that is compelling apart from argument, a sense informed not by policy, but by something more real; and once he begins to think that way he has already bought into the ahistorical vision of his opponents, a vision in which essential truths are always in danger of being obscured by the special . . . pleading of partisan interest. (*AP*, 661)

My sense (although perhaps not shared by either Gordon or Kennedy) is that Fish has exposed neither closet right wingism (Marx, for example, clearly believed there were such things as real human needs) nor confused, self-contradictory Left intellectuals, but rather left-wing imperativism. What Fish objects to in Kennedy and Gordon is not a function of the latters' hidden right-wing politics, but the profound difference, often masked by the ground they share, between Fish's subjective interpretivism and the imperativism of Gordon and Kennedy. For Gordon and Kennedy, whatever their other sins, have never committed the sin of self-contradiction that Fish thinks he has uncovered. Neither Gordon nor Kennedy have ever espoused the subjectivist thesis. Both thinkers, like Fish, are committed to the proposition that law is an act of power—that adjudication is political.

But their reasons for thinking this differ from Fish's, and as a result of the difference, they are simply not bound to the view of the nature of criticism with which Fish wishes to saddle them. For Fish, adjudication is political *because it is interpretive*, and all interpretation—including all critical acts such as legal criticism as well as literary criticism—is political. There are no more real human needs than there are real legal constructs (such as contracts, or rights, or duties). There are only interpretations of needs. For Kennedy and Gordon (as for the legal realists before them), adjudication is imperative because it is backed by force, not because it is interpretive. That adjudication is imperative, then, does not, for Kennedy and Gordon imply the nonexistence of a reality on which criticism of such imperatives can be built. From the imperativist perspective, the nonexistence of real legal categories that preexist adjudication is a function of the power of judges to create those categories. The nonexistence of real legal knowledge does not entail the nonexistence of real anything else, such as human needs. Kennedy and Gordon may be right or wrong to insist on the existence of real human needs (or in their claims regarding what those needs are). But their claim that they exist does not ensnare them in contradiction, or in "right-wing" intellectual thinking.

In fact, Fish's charge is peculiarly inappropriate, for it is his own view, not the view he attacks, that mutes radical criticism of law. For Fish, just as law is contingent on the political, historical will that creates it, *value* as well, whether derived from needs or rights, is contingent on the political will that creates it. We cannot criticize our political acts on the basis of their tendency to promote or frustrate real human needs or create real value: there are no real human needs just as there is no objective value. There are only claims to the existence of real human needs that may or may not prove politically successful. The claim that a particular law frustrates our real needs has no more truth value than the claim that there exists a set of voidable contracts, tainted by objectively discoverable standards of unconscionability. Since value can only be whatever the historically powerful have succeeded in claiming it to be (just as contracts are whatever the courts enforce), and since criticism of law can only proceed by reference to value, we can only criticize law for its failure to comply with the standards generated by the powerful. We can ground our criticisms in our alternative imagining, but we cannot ground that imagining in a vision of our real needs, or nature, or potential. Such a vision is nonsense—we have none. All we really have are varying degrees of power.

Thus, subjective interpretivism is at one and the same time profoundly radical and profoundly conservative. As a mechanism for uncovering the political basis of legal ideology, it is radical: it goes to the root. The root of law is indeed power, and that insight is essential for any radical criticism of law. It shares this radicalism with imperativism, and it is this feature, I believe, that makes subjectivism attractive to critical theorists such as Kennedy and Gordon. But subjective interpretivism, *unlike* imperativism, is also committed to a conservative vision of the potential of criticism. We cannot criticize the world given us by the powers that be on the basis of what ought to be—for there is no realm of the "ought" that is not itself an aspect of that which is. Criticism is interpretive, and interpretations must be based on texts. Texts are things that people—and more particularly, empowered people, such as people in professions—*create*. Criticism, then, can only be based upon interpretations of the positive values created by that branch of the community that has at some time made itself heard. We can use those positive values to criticize political acts that diverge from them. But we cannot criticize the values themselves on the basis of human needs drawn from extraprofessional (or extrapolitical or ahistorical) sources. To do so is to commit the logical error of antiprofessionalism.

Proprofessionalism

Fish insists that his attack on antiprofessionalism—the misguided tendency to criticize the dominant values of a profession (or a society) by reference to real human needs, real human potential, or a real human nature—is dictated by necessity: he is only describing what must be. We cannot coherently attack professionalism itself, or institutionalism itself, or power itself, because professionalism, institutionalism, and contingent power are all there is: they give us the values with which we criticize the part, and there are no independent values to which we can turn to criticize the whole. There is no real need to meet, or true potential to frustrate. There are, at best, alternative imaginings (*AP*, 673–75).

Yet, if the deconstruction movement has taught us anything useful at all, it has taught us to be suspicious of precisely these sorts of claims of necessity. Fish is, after all, engaged in an interpretive act: he is interpreting the nature as well as the content of our social life. All of Fish's interpretations rest on his rock-bottom conviction that there is no ahistoric, noncontingent, natural realm, beyond (or beneath) history, against which history and the products of history (such as judicial decisions) can be judged. From this it follows that there are no natural needs, identities, pleasures, pains, potentials, or values. But surely this dreary view is not the only possible interpretation one can give of our experience of social life. Here's another: we have real needs that may or may not be met by the historical, contingently chosen values of the empowered. To name a few, we need love, food, shelter, meaningful work, nurturance, healing, play, and community. We have a natural need for and attraction to life itself. We have a natural self inside our three-piece suits: it is the self who finds the suit stifling. We have a real potential for growth, creativity, work, community, and meaning in our lives, and that potential may well be frustrated by our current social institutions. We judge those institutions, and we should judge those institutions including the professions and professionalism itself, by reference to how well they meet our very real human needs, whether they foster or stunt our very real potential, and whether they encourage or stifle our very real and natural longing for community. We criticize our professionalism by reference to the natural needs, feelings, and sensitivities of our noncontingent, ahistorical, noninstitutional, and thoroughly nonprofessional selves. If our social history, our professional selves—in short, the society we have created through our contingent choices—frustrates our natural needs, we have good reason to change course. If professionalism stifles our natural and naturally social human life rather than encourages it to flourish, then we have reason to question professionalism. Professionalism, or the institutional history of the empowered, is not, as Fish insists, *all there is*. It is not the only source of value.

Why does Fish go to such lengths to deny the natural self? More importantly, why do so many? Why is *this* dreary interpretation—that we are, essentially, not what we eat, or what we love, or what we read, or what we dream, but what we *profess* in our public, professional lives—such a popular modern interpretation of life? Why has it captured the attention and the imagination of so many Left critical scholars? The reason *Fish* is attracted to this vision is not hard to discern. Underscoring all of Fish's interrelated claims—that we have no real human nature; that our lives are exhaustively political; that we have no real needs or real potential against which to judge the acts or decisions of the powerful, but only conflicting imaginings that from time to time, and for various strategic reasons, assert that we do; that as a result of all of this, criticism, like law, is a series of commands with no real referent; that criticism, like law, can only be judged successful or unsuccessful, not warranted or unwarranted—is an unabashed celebration of power, in its institutional and professional manifestations. All there is, Fish argues again and again, is institutional, professional, and historical power, and therefore the only critical values there are are those generated by institutions and professions. But, Fish reassures us, this turns out to be not cause for alarm, but *cause for content*. Power—and its historical manifestation in professional organizations, hierarchies, law, and elsewhere—is generally benign. Power doesn't crush, Fish reassures us, power *facilitates*. Power enables. Power is energy itself. Power is the life-force (*AP*, 670).

Thus, Fish asserts a proprofessional faith that is at least as relentless as the antiprofessionalism he is attacking. He defends the hierarchies in traditional English departments, is scornful of attacks on the professional roles of lawyers, and even comes to the defense of the gynecological community of the late-nineteenth century (*AP*, 669, 647, 646). Power, Fish concludes, "not only constrains and excludes, but enables, and . . . without some institutionally articulated spaces in which actions become possible and judgments become inevitable there would be nothing to do and no values to support."[22] Thus underlying at least Fish's subjective interpretivism is an unabashed embrace of professional power. The contrast with Fiss is striking. Whereas Fiss solves the problem of power by constraining it with objectivity, Fish solves the problem of power by celebrating it. Fish sees interpretation, and therefore power, everywhere: he sees it not only in the courts (although of course he sees it there), but also in medical diagnoses, literary reviews, and English departments. Of

22. Although Fish would never put the point this way, what we mean by the claim that the power wielded in English departments is generally benign may simply be that English departments, even with their internal wars, further more than they frustrate our "real" human need for culture, diversity, language, and intellectual and linguistic stimulation.

course interpretations of literature are acts of power, Fish explains, of course it is true that they are generated by as well as themselves determine careers, tenure decisions, appointments, and dismissals. But this is not cause for alarm; in fact, all is more or less as it should be. Power enables. The politics of interpretation is necessary. Far from being a necessary evil, it is an affirmative and necessary good.

Noxious and even dangerous as I take the general view to be, there is nevertheless something refreshing about Fish's happy acceptance of the powers that be in English departments: many outsiders have begun to suspect that the critics of literary traditionalism have been protesting too much. Perhaps it is true that the institutional power wielded in English departments enables, or facilitates, more than it crushes, just as Fish suggests. It might be true that English departments, and the hierarchies that define them, promote discourse more than they silence it. They probably do encourage speech, over the long haul, more than they censure. Even the most sadistic, wrong-headed, ill-willed, and ruthless departmental chairperson—of which, I suspect, there are relatively few—has limited reach. He or she can crush careers. But she does not and cannot fine, imprison, or execute. The exercise of power in English departments may well be generally benign. Although Fish would never put the point this way, English departments, even with their internal wars, may further more than they frustrate our real human needs for culture, diversity, language, and intellectual and linguistic stimulation.

It is a mistake though, and an unnecessary one, to view English departments and law courts as part of a seamless, interpretive web. Fish's optimism regarding the use of power in English departments is wildly out of place when applied to the power wielded by courts or legislatures. We can, perhaps, afford to be complacent about the power wielded by the departmental chair and the interpretive discourses that power facilitates. But we cannot afford to be complacent about the power wielded by judges, lawyers, police, the wealthy, the dominant race, or the dominant gender. We cannot afford complacency about the extent of power held by legal professionals any more than we can afford the opposite tendency, evidenced by Fiss, to be blindly fearful of their power. Professionalism may facilitate, as Fish insists, but it also crushes. Power may sometimes enable, but it oftentimes destroys. We must recognize power when we see it, and we cannot afford to trivialize the discovery by insisting that we see it everywhere. We cannot afford to view the critic, whether literary or legal, as simply another center of power, professing simply another imagining, which may or may not prove successful. What the critic does, criticize the law, is profoundly different from what judges do, which is to command. They both use words and they both interpret the words of others. But we allow their shared tools to overshadow the difference between them at great risk. One speaks with the force of the state, and the other speaks, at best, with the force of reason. We should beware of the proprofessional's insistence that they are both cut from the same cloth.

Subjectivism, Politics, and Nature: The Floating Opera

John Barth's nihilistic novel *The Floating Opera* relates the story of a day in the life of a lawyer-protagonist named Todd Andrews on Maryland's Eastern Shore. On this day, Todd decides to commit suicide, then decides to commit mass murder, and finally decides not to do either. The burden of the novel is to explain these decisions. The novel is also a stinging indictment of subjective interpretivism. For Todd Andrews, like Stanley Fish, is a subjective interpretivist. Like Fish, Andrews embraces a subjective theory of interpretation, an imperative theory of law, a nihilistic theory of value, and an acquiescent, proprofessional attitude toward the powers that be and the values they have generated. The novel reveals Andrews's suicidal and murderous urges as attempts to come to grips with the logical derivatives of these premises.

Todd Andrews as a Subjective Interpretivist

Early in the novel, Andrews explains his subjective view of interpretation. Social life, Andrews claims, is a "floating opera." What we see as life, and what we see as law, and what we see as value, are all simply what we have happened to glimpse of the opera from our historical, contingent, and pathetically accidental spot along the shore. What we claim to know is entirely derived from the constructs given us by the creator of the opera, and the creator of the opera is us. We cannot know anything other than the floating opera. As a consequence, the interpretations we place upon the parts of the opera we happen to see are subjective and contingent: they depend upon our place on the shore—our perspective upon what we have made:

> Ah, me. Everything, I'm afraid, is significant, and nothing is finally important. . . .
>
> Why *The Floating Opera*? . . . That's part of the name of a showboat that used to travel around Virginia and Maryland tidewater areas. . . . It always seemed a fine idea to me to build a showboat with just one big flat open deck on it, and to keep a play going continuously. The boat wouldn't be moored, but would drift up and down the river on the tide, and the audience would sit along both banks. They could catch whatever part of the plot happened to unfold as the boat floated past, and then they'd have to wait until the tide ran back again to catch another snatch of it, if they still happened to be sitting there. I needn't explain that that's how much of life works; our friends float past; we become involved with them; they float on, and we must rely on hearsay or lose track of them completely; they float back again, and we either renew our friendship—catch up to date—or find that they and we don't comprehend each other any more. And that's how this book will work, I'm sure. It's a floating opera, friend, fraught with curiosities, melodrama, spectacle, instruction, and entertainment, but it floats willy-nilly on the tide of my vagrant prose. (*FO*, 6–7)

For Andrews as for Fish, this subjective theory of interpretation entails an imperative theory of law:

> That will-o'-the-wisp, the law: where shall I begin to speak of it? Is the law the legal rules, or their interpretations by judges, or by juries? Is it the precedent or the present fact? The norm or the practice? I think I'm not interested in what the law is.
>
> Surely, though, I am curious about things that the law can be made to do, but this disinterestedly, without involvement. A child encounters a toy tractor, winds it up, and sets it climbing over a book. The tractor climbs well. The child puts another book here, so, and angles the first. The tractor surmounts them, with difficulty. The child opens the pages of the first book, leans the second obliquely against it, and places his shoe behind the

> two. The tractor tries, strains, spins, whirrs, and falls like a turtle on its back, treads racing uselessly. The child moves on to his crayons and picture puzzles, no expression on his face. I don't know what you mean, sir, when you speak of justice. . . .
>
> All right. I have no general opinions about the law, or about justice, and if I sometimes set little obstacles, books and slants, in the path of the courts, it is because I'm curious, merely, to see what will happen. On those occasions when the engine of the law falls impotently sprawling, I make a mental note of it, and without a change of expression, go on to my boat or my *Inquiry*. (*FO*, 84–85)

Furthermore, adjudication is imperative, Andrews shows, not by virtue of the judge's institutional power (as imperativists would have it)—it is not that adjudicative judgments are backed by force—but because judges use words. Words, through their multiple meanings, give their users, including judges, interpretive power. A court's interpretation of a will, for example, is "subjective" (and therefore chosen, not mandated) because it must be: there is no objective meaning of the will's provision to be discovered, whether or not the court makes a pretense of looking for one.

Andrews demonstrates the point with a case. The issue in the case was whether Andrews's client, Harrison Mack, had breached a will condition that Harrison not engage in activities that show sympathy for communist causes. The lawyers' conflicting interpretations of the relevant social facts underscored the subjectivity of legal interpretation:

> Froebel . . . announced that he had such evidence [of communist sympathies] . . . enough to warrant the reversal of bequests provided for by our will. . . .
>
> "For Heaven's sake!" Harrison whispered. "You don't think he means my Spanish donations!"
>
> "If you were silly enough to make any, then I daresay he does," I replied, appalled anew at Harrison's innocence.
>
> And indeed, the "Spanish donations" were precisely what Froebel had in mind. . . .
>
> "May I point out," Froebel continued blandly, "that not only is a gift to the Loyalists in essence a gift to Moscow, but this

> particular subscription agency is a Party organization under FBI surveillance. A man . . . doesn't send checks to this subscription outfit unless one is sympathetic with the Comintern. Young Mr. Mack, like too many of our idle aristocrats is, I fear, a blue blood with a Red heart."
>
> I believe it was this final metaphor that won Froebel the judgment. . . . Men, I think, are ever attracted to the *bon mot* rather than the *mot juste*, and judges, no less than other men, are often moved by considerations more aesthetic than judicial. Even I was not a little impressed, and regretted only that we had no jury to be overwhelmed by such a purple plum from the groves of advocacy. *A blue blood with a red heart*! How brandish reasonableness against music? Should I hope to tip the scales with puny logic, when Froebel had Parnassus in his pan?
>
> "My client, a lover of freedom, and human dignity," I declared, "made his contributions to the oppressed Loyalists as a moral obligation, proper to every good American. . . ."
>
> And on I went for some minutes, trying to make capital out of the Spanish confusion, wherein the radicals were the *status quo* and the reactionaries the rebels. It was an admirable bit of casuistry, but I knew my cause was lost . . . [The room was filled with the sound of] *blue bloods with Red hearts*.
>
> And Judge Lasker, as I think I mentioned, was famously conservative. Though by no means a fascist himself . . . he epitomized the unthinking antagonism of his class toward anything pinker than the blue end of the spectrum: a familiar antagonism that used to infuriate me when . . . I was interested in such things as social justice. (*FO*, 93–95)

The judge, of course, must render an opinion consistent with law, not with poetry. The issue for the judge was whether or not Harrison's checks to the subscription agency representing the Spanish Loyalist government constituted, within the meaning of the phrase in the will, an act manifesting communist sympathies, thus precluding Mack's inheritance under the will. The judge reasoned that it did:

> It does not matter whether there is a difference between the Moscow and Madrid varieties of communism, . . . or whether the Court or anyone else approves or disapproves of the defendant's

> gifts or the cause for which they were intended. The fact is that the subscription agency involved is a communist organization under government surveillance, and a gift to that agency is a gift to communism. There can be no question of the donor's sympathy with what the agency represented, and what it represented was communism. The will before me provides that should such sympathy be demonstrated, . . . the terms of the document are to be reversed. The Court here orders such a reversal. Well, we were poor again. Harrison went weak, and when I offered him a cigar he came near to vomiting. (*FO*, 95–96)

Andrews, of course, like Fish, sees a multiplicity of meaning in the will's phrase. Andrews is as good as Fish at spotting linguistic and behavioral ambiguities. The ambiguity Andrews spots in the judge's reasoning turns on the meaning of "sympathy." The judge had given sympathy a nonintentional meaning. Andrews points out, correctly, that such a meaning is by no means mandated by the will's language. Just as plausibly, the will could be read as requiring an intent to foster communism, which in this case, given Andrews' interpretation of Harrison's behavior, was absent:

> "Do you give up?" I asked him. "Or shall I appeal?"
>
> . . . He clutched at the hope. "Can we appeal?"
>
> "Sure," I said. "Don't you see how unlogical Lasker's reasoning is? . . . He said the subscription agency was sympathetic to communism. You give money to the agency; therefore you're sympathetic to communism. It's like saying that if you give money to a Salvation Army girl who happens to be a vegetarian you're sympathetic to vegetarians. The communists support the Loyalists; you support the Loyalists; therefore you're a communist."
>
> Harrison was tremendously relieved, but so weak he could scarcely stand. . . . "Well! That puts us back in the race, doesn't it? . . . Damned judge! We've got it now, boy!" (*FO*, 96)

The answer to Mack's question, of course, is "not necessarily." Andrews, like Fish, knows that judges decide cases by any number of factors, and that the disciplining rule that is deductive logic is not one of them. Unlike Fish, however, Andrews has the unpleasant task of explaining this to his client:

> "I'll appeal," I said, "but we'll lose again, I guess."
>
> "How's that? Lose again!" He laughed, and sucked in his breath.
>
> "Forget about the logic," I said. "Nobody really cares about the logic. They make up their minds by their prejudices about Spain. I think you'd have lost here even without Froebel's metaphor. I'd have to talk Lasker into liberalism to win the case."
>
> I went on to explain that of the seven judges on the Court of Appeals . . . three were Republicans with a pronounced antiliberal bias, two were fairly liberal Democrats, one was a reactionary "Southern Democrat," . . . and the seventh, an unenthusiastic Democrat, was relatively unbiased.
>
> "I know them all," I said. "Abrams, Moore, and Stevens, the Republicans, will vote against you. Forrester, the Southern Democrat, would vote for you if it were a party issue, but it's not; he'll go along with the Republicans. Stedman and Barnes, the liberals, will go along with you, and I think Haddaway will too, because he likes me and because he dislikes Lasker's bad logic.
>
> "But hell, that's four to three!" Harrison cried. "That means I lose!"
>
> "As I said." . . . Harrison was crushed. "It's unjust!" (*FO*, 96–97)

Finally, like Fish, Andrews subscribes to the distinguishing commitment of subjectivism: the denial of the existence of objective values. Like Fish, Andrews derives from his imperative vision of law and his subjective theory of meaning the nonexistence of such things as justice or fairness. This too must be explained to the client. Just as there are no real needs, or truths, or rights, or testator's intents, Mack is going to have to come to grips with the fact that there is no real justice either:

> I smiled. "You know how these things are." "Aw, but what the hell!" He shook his head, tapped his feet impatiently, pursed his lips, sighed in spasms. I expected him to faint, but he held on tightly, though he could scarcely talk. The truth was, of course, that it is one thing—an easy thing—to give what Cardinal Newman calls "notional" assent to a proposition such as "There is no justice"; quite another and more difficult matter to give it

"real" assent, to learn it stingingly, to the heart, through involvement. I remember hoping that Harrison was strong enough at least to be educated by his expensive loss.

I appealed the judgment of the Court.

"Just to leave the door open," I explained. "I might think of something." (*FO*, 97–98)

Thus, for Andrews as for Fish, there are no more objective values than there are objective laws. All values are socially constructed, or subjective:

What was on my mind, as I walked, was the grand proposition that had occurred to me while I was licking my cigar: that absolutely nothing has intrinsic value. Now that the idea was articulated in my head, it seemed to me ridiculous that I hadn't seen it years ago. All my life I'd been deciding that specific things had no intrinsic value—that things like money, honesty, strength, love, information, wisdom, even life, are not valuable in themselves, but only with reference to certain ends—and yet I'd never considered generalizing from those specific instances. But one instance was added to another, and another to that, and suddenly the total realization was effected—*nothing* is intrinsically valuable; the value of everything is attributed to it, assigned to it, from outside, by people.

I must confess to feeling in my tranquil way some real excitement at the idea. . . . Doubtless (as I later learned) this idea was not original with me, but it was completely new to me, and I delighted in it like a child turned loose in the endless out-of-doors, full of scornful pity for those inside. *Nothing is valuable in itself*. Not even truth; not even this truth. I am not a philosopher, except after the fact; but I am a mean rationalizer, and once the world has forced me into a new position, I can philosophize (or rationalize) like two Kants, like seven Philadelphia lawyers. Beginning with my new conclusions, I can work out first-rate premises.

On this morning, for example, I had opened my eyes with the knowledge that I would this day destroy myself. . . ; here the day was but half spent, and already premises were springing to my mind, to justify on philosophical grounds what had been a

> purely personal decision. The argument was staggering. Enough now to establish this first premise: nothing is intrinsically valuable. (*FO,* 170–71)

The consequences of Andrews's moral nihilism, however, are far more devastating for Andrews than for his client. Andrews's adamant denial of the existence of objective value leads him to contemplate suicide:

> On this particular evening, to be sure, their progress would cease, for the notes I took then I intended to be my last.
>
> I. *Nothing has intrinsic value.*
>
> II. *The reasons for which people attribute value to things are always ultimately irrational.*
>
> III. *There is, therefore, no ultimate "reason" for valuing anything.*
>
> IV. *Living is action. There's no final reason for action.*
>
> V. *There's no final reason for living.* (*FO,* 222–28)

Andrews's argument against objective value tracks Fish's. The source of value, Andrews argues, is social history—the floating opera. Our social history is the floating opera, and the floating opera is all there is. All we know about life is the sum total of our interpretations of the opera. The floating opera is the sole text from which subtexts are generated, so any values we adopt or employ are but interpretations of some subscript from the text of the floating opera. We can indeed criticize parts of the opera, but we can only criticize parts of the opera by reference to parts of the script we have heard or witnessed elsewhere. To translate from the metaphor: there are no objective interpretations of values by which we can criticize law (or politics, or professionalism, or the values of the dominant) just as there are no objective laws by which we adjudicate cases. We cannot evaluate institutionalism or professionalism objectively for the same reason that we cannot interpret law objectively: we are institutional and professional creatures, our values are institutional and professional values, and the criticisms we make will reflect our institutional and professional situation; indeed they will be dependent upon it. Value, like law, is a product of history: it is all a part of the opera. Our critical inclinations, like all our interpretive choices, are functions of our historical contingency. Values, far from being the bases for criticism of the powerful acts of others, are themselves nothing but disguised or not so disguised grabs at power and influence.

Todd Andrews as a Proprofessional

Like Fish, Andrews emerges from his subjectivism as a card-carrying proprofessional. Andrews also harbors an acquiescent and even celebratory attitude toward the professions that generate dominant values. Like Fish, Andrews has moved beyond critique (and like Fish, he repeatedly reminds the reader of that fact). Andrews has seen the subjectivist's light. Life is the floating opera, and life is only the floating opera. Thoughts, perceptions, and most importantly critical values are all dependent upon communicative texts generated by whatever snippets the opera provides the audience on the shore. The values that emerge from the opera exhaust the evaluative options open to us, and the values that emerge are, unsurprisingly, those of professions. Thus, Andrews explains his attitude toward his law practice:

> Winning or losing litigations is of no concern to me, and I think I've never made a secret of that fact to my clients. They come to me, as they come before the law, because they think they have a case. The law and I are uncommitted.
>
> One more thing, . . . if you have followed this chapter so far, you might sensibly ask, "Doesn't your attitude—which is, after all, irresponsible—allow for the defeat, even the punishment, of the innocent, and at times the victory of the guilty? And does this not concern you?" It does indeed allow for the persecution of innocence—though perhaps not so frequently as you might imagine. And this persecution concerns me, in the sense that it holds my attention, but not especially in the sense that it bothers me. Under certain circumstances, to be explained later, I am not averse to pillorying the innocent, to throwing my stone, with the crowd, at some poor martyr. Irresponsibility, yes: I affirm, I insist upon my basic and ultimate irresponsibility. Yes indeed.
>
> It did not deeply concern me, as I said before, whether Harrison received his inheritance or not, though I stood to profit by some fifty thousand dollars or more if he did. (*FO*, 85)

And also like Fish, Andrews is utterly scornful of critical claims that lawyerly professionalism can sometimes frustrate real justice, real needs, or real individuals.[23] In the Mack will case, the testator's own mercurial and imperative attitude toward will making had resulted in a multiplicity of wills, and it had remained to his legatees and their lawyers (including Harrison and Andrews) to fight over which was binding. This prompted a thoroughly professional lawyer's brawl. Andrews thoroughly approved:

> Of the seventeen wills . . . only the first two were composed during the time when the old man's sanity was pretty much indis-

23. Andrews's proprofessionalism extends to the use of power facilitated by all political and hierarchical institutions, not just the legal profession. Thus, for example, the testator in the Mack case, like Andrews himself, harbors a proprofessional attitude toward the power that testamentary capacity and wealth bestows. Andrews thoroughly approves:

> Old man Mack . . . died in 1935, after years of declining physical and mental health. He left a large estate. . . . It was, undeniably, an estate that many people would consider worth going to court about.
>
> Now of the several characteristics of Harrison pere, three were important to the case: he was in the habit of using his wealth as a club to keep his kin in line—he was, apparently, addicted to the drawing up of wills; and, especially in his last years, he was obsessively jealous of the products of his mind and body, and permitted none to be destroyed. . . .
>
> It seems that disinheritance, or the threat of it, was the old man's favorite disciplinary measure, not only for his son, but also for his wife. When young Harrison [Andrews's eventual client] attended Dartmouth rather than Johns Hopkins; when he studied journalism rather than business; when he became a communist rather than a Republican; he was disinherited until such time as he mended his ways. When Mother Mack went to Europe rather than to West Palm Beach; when she chose sparkling Burgundy over highballs, Dulaney Valley over Ruxton, Roosevelt and Garner over Hoover and Curtis, she was disinherited until such time as she recanted her heresies.
>
> All these falls from the reinstatements to grace, of course, required emanations of Father Mack's will. . . . After the old man's death, when his safe was opened, a total of seventeen complete and distinct testamentary instruments was found, chronologically arranged, each beginning with a revocation of the preceding one. . . . Now this situation, though certainly unusual, would in itself have presented no particular problem . . . because the law provides that where there are several wills, the last shall be considered representative of the testator's real intentions, other things being equal. . . . But alas, with Mr. Mack all other things weren't equal. Not only did his physical well-being deteriorate in his last years, . . . his sanity deteriorated also. . . . In the first stages he merely inherited and disinherited his relatives and his society; in the second he no longer went to work, . . . and he allowed nothing of his creation including hair and nail clippings, urine, feces, and wills to be thrown away; in the last stages he could scarcely move or talk. . . . To be sure, the stages were not dramatically marked, but blended into one another imperceptibly. (*FO*, 85–87)

> putable; that is, prior to 1933. The first left about half the estate to Harrison Jr. and the other half to Mother Mack, provided it could not be demonstrated to the court that she had drunk any sparkling burgundy since 1920. . . . The other . . . left about half the estate to Mrs. Mack unconditionally and the rest to Harrison, provided it could not be demonstrated to the court that during a five year probationary period, 1932–37, Harrison had done, written, or said anything that could reasonably be construed as evidence of communist sympathies. . . .
>
> Of the other fifteen documents, ten were composed in 1933 and 1934, years when the testator's sanity was open to debate. The last five . . . could be established without much difficulty . . . as being the whims of a lunatic: one left everything to Johns Hopkins University on condition that the University's name be changed to Hoover College (the University politely declined). . . .
>
> Luckily for the majesty of Maryland's law, there were only two primary and four secondary contestants for the estate. . . . [T]he testator's widow was interested in having Will #6 . . . adjudged the last testament: it bequeathed her virtually the entire estate, on the sparkling-burgundy condition described above. Harrison Jr., preferred #8, . . . [I]t bequeathed him virtually the whole works, on the clean skirts condition also described above. [Three] registered nurses . . . liked Wills #3, 9, and 12, . . . [t]herein, . . . their late employer provided them remuneration for services beyond the line of duty. The final contestant was the pastor of the Macks' neighborhood church; in Will #13 the bulk of the estate was to pass to that church, with the express hope that the richer and more influential organized religion became, the sooner it would be cast off by the people. (*FO*, 87–89)

Andrews's argument is Fish's: the dependency of inheritance entitlements on the outcome of a lawsuit rather than the intent of the testators—and hence on the vagaries of professionalism rather than the disinterested application of objective norms—is entirely necessary, thus obviating the issue of whether it is justifiable. If the text that is the judicial system is the only text we have by which to determine inheritance entitlements, then obviously, an inheritance entitlement means the sum total of whatever courts might be persuaded to rule. The antiprofessional complaint that the court's ruling might be wrong because the entitlement was really otherwise rests upon the false claim that there exists ideal legal entities that transcend the history and politics that is adjudication—such as entitlements, or intents or testamentary capacities. Thus the Mack case, Andrews explains, was ultimately decided not through the disciplined application of objective standards of testamentary capacity, but rather, through a "welter of legal nonsense, threats and counterthreats":

> Each of [the three contestants] must attempt to prove two things: that Father Mack was still legally sane when the will of their choice was written, and that by the time the subsequent wills were written, he no longer could comprehend what he was about. On this basis, Miss Kosko (the nurse) had the strongest case, since her will . . . was the earliest of the three. But love was her undoing: she retained as her attorney her boy friend, a lad fresh out of law school, none too bright. After our initial out-of-court sparring, I was fairly confident that he was no match for either Froebel or myself, and when, late in 1936, he refused on ethical grounds a really magnanimous bribe from Froebel, I was certain.
>
> And sure enough, when the first swords clashed in Baltimore Probate Court, . . . Froebel was able, with little trouble, to insinuate that the young lawyer was an ass; that the nurse Miss Kosko was a hussy out to defraud poor widows of their honest legacies by seducing old men in their dotage; that Mrs. Mack . . . had already offered the trollop a gratuity more munificent than she deserved . . . and that even to listen tolerantly to such ill-concealed avariciousness was a tribute to the patience and indulgence of long-suffering judges. In addition, Froebel must have offered some cogent arguments, for surrogate courts, even in Baltimore, are notoriously competent, and the judge ruled in his favor. (*FO*, 89–90)

With the field narrowed, the case became a dispute between mother and son. That the lawsuit was hostage to the lawyers' overriding adversarial interest—whether for money or for the thrill of the game, was entirely appropriate. Andrews insists on the proprofessional prerogative:

> There was not much difference between Mack's mental state in late 1933 and his mental state in early 1934. . . . I got the impres-

> sion that the judge—a staid fellow—believed Mack had been insane from the beginning. The newspapers, too, expressed the opinion that there was no particular evidence on either side, and that, besides, it was a disgraceful thing for a mother and her son to squabble so selfishly. All the pressure was for out-of-court settlement on a fifty-fifty basis, but both Harrison and his mother—who had never especially liked each other—refused, on the advice of their attorneys. Froebel thought he could win, and wanted the money; I thought I could win, and wanted to see. (*FO*, 90–91)

The Floating Opera and Proprofessionalism

Like Fish's, Andrews's proprofessional attitude proves hard to contain to the professions. Andrews acquiesces not only in the professional mores of his own field, but in all dominant mores. If the legal text is "the only text there is" for testamentary entitlements, then there is no way to criticize the legal outcome as untrue to the real entitlement. In a perfectly parallel fashion, if the floating opera, our social history, provides the only text of moral value, then there is no way to criticize the opera itself as untrue to the real text of value. We cannot evaluate the opera by reference to values derived from the opera's text. Our reaction to the floating opera can only be a reaction to the part of the opera we happen to see, and the part we happen to see is a function of our place on the shore. We can criticize parts of the opera on the basis of other parts of the opera, but we cannot criticize the opera itself.

Andrews, however, carries this argument one step further than Fish, and that step is both logical and murderous. The lack of a real basis for criticism of the opera directly implies the lack of a real basis for its justification. The floating opera cannot provide a basis for justification of its own existence any more than it can provide a basis for critique. There is no ultimate reason why the floating opera should not be destroyed. And if that's so, Andrews asks, why not blow it up? Andrews can see no reason to either blow it up or not blow it up. In a moment of mercurial and imperative proprofessional whimsy, Andrews resolves to destroy the opera, with himself as a member of the audience:

> It was, of course, entirely dark outside except for the *Opera's* lights. I found myself, as I'd planned, on the outboard side of the theatre. . . . I walked swiftly down the starboard rail . . . and let myself into the dining room, under the stage. . . . I struck a match and lit three kerosene lanterns mounted along the dining-room walls.
>
> . . . Finally I entered the galley, a few feet away, put a match to one burner, and turned the others . . . full on, unlighted. A strong odor of bottled illuminating gas filled the little room at once.
>
> . . . Then I slipped out as I'd entered and took my place again in the audience, now wonderfully agitated, . . . My heart, to be sure, pounded violently, but my mind was calm. Calmly I regarded my companion Captain Osborn. . . . Calmly I thought of Harrison and Jane: of perfect breasts and thighs scorched and charred; of certain soft, sun-smelling hair crisped to ash. Calmly too I heard somewhere the squeal of an overexcited child, . . . I considered a small body, formed perhaps from my own and flawless Jane's, black, cracked, smoking. Col. Morton, Bill Butler, old Mr. and Mrs. Bishop—it made no difference, absolutely. (*FO*, 42–43)

For unexplained reasons, however, the boat does not explode. The opera does not burn. Andrews, true to form, doesn't particularly care. The unexpected turn of events does, though, prompt a new answer to his question "why not blow up the floating opera?" The answer: "Why bother?"

> I rather suspected that either some hidden source of ventilation . . . or wandering member of the crew had foiled my plan. Need I tell you that I felt no sense either of relief or disappointment? As when the engine of the law falls sprawling against my obstacles, I merely took note of the fact that despite my intentions six hundred ninety-nine of my townspeople and myself were still alive.
>
> Why did I not, failing my initial attempt, simply step off the gangplank into the Choptank, where no fluke could spoil my plan? Because, I began to realize, a subtle corner had been turned. I asked myself, knowing there was no ultimate answer,

> "Why not step into the river?" as I had asked myself in the afternoon, "Why not blow up the Floating Opera?" But now, at once, a new voice replied casually, "On the other hand, why bother?" There was a corner for you! Negotiated unawares, . . . this corner confronted me with a new and unsuspected prospect—at which, for the moment, I could only blink. (*FO*, 246–47)

There is a better answer to Andrews's question than "why bother." Of course it is true, as both Andrews and Fish correctly insist, that the answer to the question "why not blow up the floating opera," or "why preserve the floating opera," or "why not make the floating opera better," cannot be found in the floating opera itself; it is the floating opera whose value is in question, including any values the opera establishes. We cannot turn to the values generated by professionalism, or the legal system, or institutional histories, if we wish to determine the value of professionalism, the legal system, or institutionalism. If we look only to the opera, we will not find there values by which we can judge the opera. The values created by a profession cannot be used to judge the profession. The values created by the system of law cannot be used to judge it. The values held by a community cannot be the referent against which the community is judged. But that doesn't mean the question is unanswerable. If we want to judge the opera, if we want an answer to the question "why not blow up the floating opera," we must look to a different text.

Andrews's question is only unanswerable if the floating opera is the only text there is. But it isn't. As Andrews reminds us at the beginning, the floating opera is *social life*, not life itself. It is a metaphor for our socially created, contingent, constructed history. If we want to judge the social life we have politically created, we must look not to our held social values (for those are part of our creation), but to the needs and values of the unconstructed, ahistorical animal self within. The natural self and its needs—for fulfillment, nurturance, intimacy, productivity, security, and variety—provide the stable text against which to judge the value of the floating social self we have created.

The Animalistic Self and the Rejection of Nature

Andrews, like Fish, rejects the natural self as a moral text for criticism of social life, but for entirely different reasons. Fish, as argued above, denies the existence of the natural, ahistorical self and accordingly denies the reality of natural human needs. Andrews does not. In fact, Andrews insists upon the reality of a natural, ahistorical, noncontingent, animalistic self, complete with natural, ahistorical, noncontingent, and real human needs, defined by nature instead of social history. Andrews does not *deny* the animal within (as does Fish); he *suppresses* the animal within. Andrews's proprofessionalism is not an attitude masked as logical necessity. Rather, it is an openly acknowledged *preference*. Andrews simply *prefers* the floating opera to the stable, instinctual, universal, and natural experiences of animalism. Andrews's suppression of his natural self and the values he might generate from it is based almost entirely upon his memory of a war experience. The war story is worth retelling—for Andrews's interpretation of it, I will argue, is wrong, as is the antinaturalism lesson he learned.

The story, as Andrews relates it "apropros of nothing," is as follows. During World War II, in the middle of the Battle of the Argonne, in the middle of vast confusion and in the middle of the night, Andrews experienced for the first and only time in his life real fear. The fear was animalistic. It was not socially constructed. It was not a part of the floating opera. It was not the product of professionalism, power, choice, or social construct. The feeling originated in his natural, not his social, self:

> The next thing that happened . . . happened in the dark. Suddenly it had been nighttime for a while. This time it was I who was in a hollow, on all fours in a shell hole half full of muddy water. I still had my rifle, but it was empty, and if I owned any more ammunition, I didn't remember how to put it in the rifle. . . . And now there came real fear, quickly but not suddenly, a purely physical sensation. It swept over me in shuddering waves from my thighs and buttocks to my shoulders and jaws and back again, one shock after another, exactly as though rolls of flesh were undulating. There was no cowardice involved; in fact, my mind wasn't engaged at all. . . . Cowardice involves choice, but fear is independent of choice. When the waves reached my hips and thighs I opened my sphincters; when they crossed my stomach and chest I retched and gasped; when they struck my face my jaw hung slack, my saliva ran, my eyes watered. Then back they'd go again, and then return. I've no way of knowing how

> long this lasted: perhaps only a minute. But it was the purest and strongest emotion I've ever experienced. I could . . . regard myself objectively: a shocked, drooling animal in a mudhole. It is one thing to agree intellectually to the proposition that man is a species of animal; quite another to realize, thoroughly and for good, your personal animality, to the extent that you are actually never able to oppose the terms man and animal, even in casual speech. (*FO*, 62–63)

Next, Andrews continues, he experienced real loneliness—a real need for intimacy and companionship. Furthermore, when the feeling came upon him it was in sharp conflict with the demands of his professional role of soldier:

> The other part of the incident followed immediately. Both armies returned from wherever they'd been hiding, and I was aware for the first time that a battle was really in progress. A great deal of machine-gun fire rattled across the hollow from both sides; . . . and there was much shooting, shouting, screaming and cursing. . . . With a part of my mind I was perfectly willing to join in the fighting, though I was confused; if someone had shouted orders at me, I'm certain I'd have obeyed them. But I was left entirely alone, and alone my body couldn't move. . . .
>
> Finally the artillery opened up again, apparently laying their fire exactly in the hollow, where the hand-to-hand fighting was in progress. Perhaps both sides had resolved to clean up that untidy squabble with high-explosive shells and begin again. Most of the explosions seemed to be within a few hundred feet of my hole, and the fear returned. There was no question in my mind but that I'd be killed; what I feared was the knowledge that my dying could very well be protracted and painful, and that it must be suffered alone. The only thing I was able to wish for was someone to keep me company while I went through it.
>
> Sentimental? It certainly is, and I've thought so ever since. But that's what the feeling was, and it was tremendously strong, and I'd not be honest if I didn't speak of it. (*FO*, 63–64)

His natural need for companionship, however, overcame his professional duty as soldier. Thus, when an enemy soldier jumped unexpectedly into Andrews's hole, instead of attacking him, Andrews attempted to embrace him:

> It was such a strong feeling that when from nowhere a man jumped into the mudhole beside me, I fell on him instantly and embraced him as hard as I could. Very sensibly he assumed I was attacking him, and with some cry of alarm he wrenched away. I fell on him again, before he could raise his rifle, . . . I shouted in his ear that I didn't want to fight with him; that I loved him; and at the same time—since I was larger and apparently stronger than he—I got behind him and pinioned his arms and legs. He struggled for a long time, and in German, so that I knew him to be an enemy soldier. How could I make everything clear to him? . . . [H]e would certainly think me either a coward or a lunatic, and kill me anyway. He had to understand everything at once. (*FO*, 64)

Andrews next wrestled with an internal as well as external struggle between need and power, loneliness and conquest, natural life and professional role:

> Of course, I could have killed him, and I'm sure he understood that fact; he was helpless. What I did, finally, was work my rifle over to me with one hand, after rolling my companion onto his stomach in the muddy water, and then put the point of my bayonet on the back of his neck, until it just barely broke the skin and drew a drop of blood. My friend went weak—collapsed in fact—and what he cried in German I took to be either a surrender, a plea for mercy, or both. Not wanting to leave any doubts about the matter, I held him there for several minutes more, . . . until he broke down, lost control of all his bodily functions, as I had done earlier, and wept. He had, I believe, the same fear; certainly he was a shocked animal.
>
> Where was the rest of the U.S. Army? Reader, I've never learned where the armies spent their time in this battle! (*FO*, 64–65)

Finally, these two "shocked animals," shed of their professional roles, fulfilled what Fish denies exists: their natural, human needs.

They acted on the basis of natural need, rather than on the basis of professional role. To judge the acts of two shocked animals by reference to the values derived from the contingencies of professionalism, history, and power, Andrews insists, would simply be "stupid":

> Now read this paragraph with an open mind; I can't warn you too often not to make the quickest, easiest judgments of me, if you're interested in being accurate. The thing I did was lay aside my rifle, bayonet and all, lie in the mud beside this animal whom I'd reduced to paralysis, and embrace him as fiercely as any man ever embraced his mistress. I covered his dirty stubbled face with kisses: his staring eyes, his shuddering neck. Incredibly, now that I look back on it, he responded in kind! The fear left him, as it had left me, and for an hour, I'm sure, we clung to each other.
>
> If the notion of homosexuality enters your head, you're normal, I think. If you judge either the German sergeant or myself to have been homosexual, you're stupid. (*FO*, 65)

As the professional power of the two men subsided, the fear diminished as well, and in its place arose feelings of pleasure and intimacy that accompany the satiation of need. Andrews's experience, I believe, stands as a sharp rebuke to Fish's claim that there are no natural needs, and that the satiation of those needs cannot constitute a natural text for the derivation of ethical values against which to judge our historical and professional exercises of power. For one night for these two soldiers, the battle had moved elsewhere, and the deprofessionalized soldiers enjoyed animalistic pleasure of intimacy:

> After our embrace the trembling of both of us subsided, and we released each other. There was a complete and, to my knowledge, unique understanding between us. . . . A great many shells were whistling overhead, but none were bursting very near us, and the hand-to-hand fighting had apparently moved elsewhere.
>
> The German and I sat on opposite sides of the shell hole, perhaps five feet apart, smiling at each other in complete understanding. Occasionally we attempted to communicate by gestures, but for the most part communication was unnecessary. I had dry cigarettes; he had none. He had rations; I had none. Neither had ammunition. Both had bandages and iodine. Both

> had bayonets. We shared the cigarettes and rations; I bandaged the wound in his neck, and he the wound in my leg. He indicated the seat of his trousers and held his nose. I indicated the seat of my trousers and did likewise. We both laughed until we cried, and fell into each other's arms again—though only for an instant this time: our fear had gone, and normal embarrassment had taken its place. We regarded each other warmly. Perhaps we slept.
>
> Never in my life had I enjoyed such intense intimacy, such clear communication with a fellow human being, male or female, as I enjoyed with that German sergeant. . . . While he slept I felt as jealous and protective—I think exactly as jealous and protective—as a lion over her cub. If any American, even my father, had jumped into the shell hole at that moment, I'd have killed him unhesitatingly before he could kill my friend. What validity could the artifices of family and nation claim beside a bond like ours? I asked myself. . . . He and I had a private armistice. . . . For the space of some hours we had been one man, had understood each other beyond friendship, beyond love, as a wise man understands himself. (*FO*, 65–66)

As light returned, however, Andrews's sense of professionalism returned, and with that sense came power, suspicion, role morality, professional duty, and fear:

> Let me end my story . . . [A]fter a while [there arose] a germ of a doubt in my mind. . . . How could I be certain that our incredible sympathy did not actually exist only in my imagination, and that he was not all the while smiling to himself, taking me for a lunatic or a homosexual crank, biding his time . . . until he was good and ready to kill me? Only a hardened professional could sleep so soundly and contentedly in a mudhole during a battle. There was even a trace of a smile on his lips. . . . Was it not something of a sneer? . . .
>
> I grew increasingly nervous, and peered out of my hole. Not a living soul was visible, though a number of bodies lay in various positions and degrees of completeness on the ground. . . . The air was full of smoke and dust and atmospheric haze. . . . I sat back in the hold and stared nervously at the Ger-

> man sergeant, waiting for some sign of his awakening. I even took up my rifle . . . just to be safe. I was getting jumpier all the time. (*FO*, 66–67)

Next ensued—again—the familiar struggle between natural need and professional power, between intimacy and fear, between mutual trust and destruction, and finally, between life and death. This time, professional suspicion overtook natural need. Andrews killed his friend and enemy:

> Finally I decided to sneak quietly out of the hole and make my way to the Americans, . . . leaving the German asleep. A perfect solution! I rose to my feet, holding my rifle and not taking my eye from the German soldier's face. At once he opened his eyes, and although his head didn't move, a look of terrible alarm flashed across his face. In an instant I lunged at him and struck him in the chest with my bayonet. The blow stunned him, . . . but the blade lodged in his breastbone and refused to enter.
>
> *My God*! I thought frantically. *Can't I kill him*? He grasped the muzzle of my rifle in both hands, trying to force it away from him, but I had better leverage. . . . We strained silently for a second. My eyes were on the bayonet; his, I fear, on my face. At last the point slipped up off the bone, from our combined straining—our last correspondence!—and with a tiny horrible puncturing sound, slid into and through his neck, and he began to die. I dropped the rifle . . . and fled, trembling, across the shattered hollow. By merest luck, the first soldiers I encountered were American, and the battle was over for me. (*FO*, 67–68)

It is on the basis of this experience that Andrews decided to reject naturalism and limit his moral universe to the conventionalism that emerged from the floating opera:

> That's my war story . . . [I]t cured me of several things. . . . I never expect very much from myself or my fellow animals. I almost never characterize people in a word or phrase, and rarely pass judgment on them at all. I no longer look for the esteem or approbation of my acquaintances. . . . To be sure, I don't call that one incident, traumatic as it proved to be, the single cause of

> all these alterations in me. . . . But when I think of the alterations, I immediately think of the incident (specifically, I confess, of that infinitesimal puncturing noise), and that fact seems significant to me. (*FO*, 68)

But Andrews has misinterpreted his own war story. It was not animalism, but professionalism, that prompted him to kill the German sergeant. The two "animals" in the hole in the battle of the Argonne met each other's needs—for sustenance, for intimacy, for companionship, for love, for "merging" (Barth's word), for union, for healing, and for nurturance. When stripped of their professional identities and roles, these two animals fed each other, embraced each other, protected each other, healed each other, and loved each other. It was only as their culturally created, socially constructed, professionally defined roles returned, that the two men came, once again, to see themselves as in opposition to each other. As Andrews became more of a professional and less of an animal, he viewed his friend as less of a friend and more a professional sergeant, less a companion and more a German enemy, less a source of nurturance and more a threat. It was the reawakened professional, not the animal, that killed the German soldier. It was Andrews's participation in the floating opera, not his participation in nature, that dictated his final act of power. It was professionalism, not animalism, that Andrews should have learned to mistrust.

Furthermore, because Andrews has wrongly interpreted these acts, he has also wrongly judged them. If our evaluative and critical strategies are constrained by professional imperatives, then Andrews's act in the Argonne—his unnecessary killing of the German soldier—surely cannot be criticized. If, as Fish would insist, the professional text Andrews was given—the professional duty to kill or capture enemy soldiers, and the enemy status of the German sergeant—was all that was critically available to him, then he could not *help* but employ those texts. He killed within a professional context that rendered that behavior both right and inevitable. To kill was the imperative of the professional context in which he found himself. If it is true that our professional context provides the only basis on which we can ground the critical moment, then Andrews's action is beyond criticism: he literally had no choice. It was what the professionalism of his place and time demanded.

However, the professional text is not the only text, and it was not the only text available to Andrews. If, as opposed to Fish's view, the professional script that dictated Andrews's act was one of (at least) two possible scripts, one professional and the other natural, then Andrews's act was a choice, not a historical necessity, and should be judged as such. Andrews did have a choice: he chose to kill. He chose to act professionally when he could have acted naturally. He chose to reject need, nature, life, and intimacy and act instead with the full destructive power of the professional. He chose to oppose rather than embrace. He could have acted on the basis of natural need, and instead he acted on the basis of professional power. He could have fled, and instead he fought. The professional imperatives within which Andrews acted help the reader forgive the act. But professional imperatives do not, as Fish suggests, exhaust our critical capacities.

We can indeed criticize our professional acts and professional roles from the point of view of our real human needs. The natural, intimate, needy, and animalistic self can criticize the contingent, historical, powerful, and professional killer. The animalistic self alongside the professional self generates value that transcends historical values, and a knowledge beyond and beneath that which history provides. The knowledge and value of the animalistic self provide what Fish insists does not exist: an ahistorical referent from which we can critique the product of history; an ahistoric point of view from which to critique the floating opera. The animalistic self is a way of being that is not contingent on the happenstance of history, and provides us a source of value that is tied to nature rather than culture. From the vantage of the natural self, we critique the floating opera, just as, from our position in the floating opera, we critique the animal within us. The relationship must be reciprocal: professionalism gives us a referent from which to critique our natural self and our natural setting, just as our natural self gives us a position from which to critique the products of history, culture, and professionalism. From the natural text, we evaluate the communicative text. It is the natural self to which we must return, if we are to question the value of our professional roles.

Conclusion

I do not mean to insist by this critique that lawyers and legal scholars have nothing to learn from the many conflicting views on the nature of literary interpretation and criticism presently being debated by hermeneutic thinkers. Law is surely like literature in some important ways, and legal criticism, whether done by judges as a part of the adjudicative enterprise, or by legal theorists as part of the critical enterprise, is surely like literary criticism in important ways. Literature and law, literary criticism and legal criticism, and literary interpretation and legal interpretation all deal in verbal texts. But insights drawn from literary theory can mislead as well as inform, if applied to law too unthinkingly. There are important differences between literature and law, between literary criticism and legal criticism, and between literary interpretation and legal interpretation. The most important difference is the most obvious: law, including adjudicative law, is imperative, and literature is expressive. People who create law use words to express commands backed by sanctions; novelists do not. The legal text is a command; the literary text is a work of art. This difference implies others. Legal criticism, criticism of law, is criticism of acts of power; literary criticism, criticism of literature, is the criticism of acts of expression. Legal interpretation is the attempt to ascertain the meaning behind a command; literary interpretation is the attempt to ascertain the meaning behind an artistic expression. Law is a product of power. Literature, when it is good, is not. Participants in the law-as-literature movement go to great lengths to deny these differences. For all interpretivists, power does not distinguish adjudication from other uses to which we put our language.

The arguments of objectivists and subjectivists for the law-literature parallel, and the consequences they draw from that parallel, radically diverge, and it is to these internal divisions that the energies of subjectivists and objectivists have been devoted. Objective interpretivists insist that it follows from the interpretive core of adjudication that law is not an act of power but is instead an act of cognition, while the subjective interpretivist insists that it follows from the interpretive core of adjudication that law is indeed an act of power, as are all interpretive acts. But both groups deny the central claim of imperativism: to wit, that adjudication, of all interpretive acts, is *distinctively* an act of power—that adjudication, *even though* it is interpretive, has more in common with legislation than it has with either literary creativity or literary criticism. As a consequence of their shared ground, both views have stultifying consequences for the criticism of law. To the objective interpretivist, our basis for legal criticism is limited to standards of consistency, coherence, or, in Dworkin's telling phrase, "integrity" with the community's moral codes: we should ask for consistency with the community's positivistic morality, but we can't ask for much more. For the subjective interpretivist, legal criticism is even more constrained: like law itself, criticism is a product of power, and like law itself, there is no non-political realm against which its value or truth can be measured. Legal criticism is limited to standards of consistency, not with the community's moral code, but with the professional's.

By focusing on the distinctively imperative core of adjudication, instead of its interpretive gloss, we free up meaningful criticism of law. Adjudication, like all of law, is imperative; it is a part of politics. Politics, like all of history, is contingent—it is part of that which is—and interpretation of law is and should be grounded in this historical, contingent, and positive text. The criticism of law, by contrast, must be grounded in a different text. It cannot be grounded in yet another interpretation of that which is. It must rest on a claim regarding that which ought to be, not a claim regarding that which is, or how power has been used to date. It must be grounded in the text we didn't write—the text of our natural needs, our true potential, our utopian ideals. Criticism of law must be grounded in the natural and ideal text, not the contingent text, if it is to be truly critical.

How do we, or should we, criticize an act of power? In public life, no less than in private life, I believe we should criticize acts of power not by reference to their rationality, or their coherency, or their integrity, but by reference to their motivation and their effects. An act of power in public life as well as in private life that is praiseworthy is an act of power that, in short, is loving: it is the act that originates in the heart and is prompted by our sympathy for the needs of others, and empathy for their situation. I see no reason not to hold adjudicatory acts of power to this standard. *Brown v. Board of Education*,[24] for example, is a good opinion, because it is a sympathetic rather than cynical response to a cry of pain, not because it renders consistent conflicting strands of constitutional jurisprudence. Indeed, the strength of the opinion lies more in its willingness to ignore the community's texts rather than its willingness to read them: the opinion speaks to our real need for fraternity rather than

24. 347 U.S. 483 (1954).

our expressed xenophobia; and it taps our real potential for an enlarged community and an enlarged conception of self rather than our expressed fear of differences. The test of the morality of power in public life as in private life may be neither compliance with community mores, as objectivists insist, nor political success, as subjectivists claim, but love. Imperativism, distinctively, frees the critic for this possibility.

Part 2
Legal Criticism and the Narrative Voice

Chapter 4

Women's Hedonic Lives

Women's subjective, hedonic lives are different from men's. The quality of our suffering is different from that of men's, as is the nature of our joy. Furthermore, and of more direct concern to feminist lawyers, the quantity of pain and pleasure enjoyed or suffered by the two genders is different: women suffer more than men. The two points are related. One reason that women suffer more than men is that women often find painful the same objective event or condition that men find pleasurable. The introduction of oxymorons in our vocabulary, wrought by feminist victories, evidences this difference in women's and men's hedonic lives. The phrases "date rape," for example and "sexual harassment," capture these different subjective experiences of shared social realities: for the man, the office pass was sex (and pleasurable), for the woman, it was harassment (and painful); for the man the evening was a date—perhaps not pleasant, but certainly not frightening—for the woman it was a rape and very scary indeed. Similarly, a man may experience as at worst offensive, and at best stimulating, that which a woman finds delimiting, dehumanizing, or even life threatening. Pornographic depictions of women that facilitate by legitimating the violent brutalization of our bodies are obvious examples. Finally, many men are simply oblivious to—they do not experience at all—external conditions that for women are painful, frightening, stunting, torturous, and pervasive—including domestic violence in the home, sexual assault on the street, and sexual harassment in the workplace and school.

Feminists generally agree—it should go without saying—that women suffer in ways that men do not, and that the gender-specific suffering that women endure is routinely ignored or trivialized in the larger (male) legal culture. Just as women's work is not recognized or compensated by the market culture,[1] women's injuries are often

1. See generally Margaret Benston, "The Political Economy of Women's Lib-

not recognized or compensated as injuries by the legal culture. The dismissal of women's gender-specific suffering comes in various forms, but the outcome is always the same: women's suffering for one reason or another is outside the scope of legal redress. Thus, women's distinctive, gender-specific injuries are now or have in the recent past been variously dismissed as trivial (sexual harassment on the street); consensual (sexual harassment on the job); humorous (nonviolent marital rape); participatory, subconsciously wanted, or self-induced (father/daughter incest); natural or biological, and therefore inevitable (childbirth); sporadic, and conceptually continuous with gender-neutral pain (rape, viewed as a crime of violence); deserved or private (domestic violence); nonexistent (pornography); incomprehensible (unpleasant and unwanted consensual sex); or legally predetermined (material rape, in states with the marital exemption).[2]

eration," in *From Feminism to Liberation*, ed. Edith Hoshino Altbach (Cambridge, Mass: Schenkman Publishing, 1971), 199–210. Jean Gardiner, "Women's Domestic Labor," *New Left Review* 89 (1975): 47–58, and Joan Landes, "Wages for Housework: Subsidizing Capitalism," *Quest: A Feminist Quarterly* 2, no. 2 (1975): 17–30.

2. The trivialization of the harm women sustain by sexual abuse on the street is reflected in the lack of writing on the topic. It is now law, of course, that consent is not a defense to a discrimination action for sexual harassment. As every woman who has ever complained of harassment knows, however, the presumption that the harassment was in fact consensual is as difficult to dislodge, as is the belief that by virtue of that consent, it is permissible. See generally Catharine A. MacKinnon, *Sexual Harassment of Working Women: A Case of Sex Discrimination* (New Haven: Yale University Press, 1979). Also see Billie Wright Dziech and Linda Weiner, *The Lecherous Professor: Sexual Harassment on Campus* (Boston: Beacon Press, 1984), for a description of sexual harassment in schools, and the various ways in which universities and male professors characterize the harm as nonharm.

The dismissal of the harm women sustain through unwanted marital sex as comical is clearly reflected in our pop culture: think of the number of stand-up routines that explore the ridiculousness of the frigid or unwilling wife. Domestic violence as well is apparently regarded by many "decent folks" as humorous. *Time* reports: "'As a society,' says Sociologist Gelles of private violence, 'we laugh at this behavior.' . . . But indeed, such behavior is not so completely unthinkable that decent folks do not chuckle when Jackie Gleason's Ralph Kramden angrily threatens to sock his ever-loving wife" (Kurt Anderson, "Cover Story: Private Violence," *Time*, 5 September 1983, 18–19).

Freud, of course, has done more than any other individual to popularize the notion that incest is desired by the child rather than the parent. His reasons for insisting that this is so are the subject of popular debate. See Jeffrey Moussaieff Masson, *The Assault on Truth: Freud's Suppression of the Seduction Theory* (New York: Farrar, Straus, Giroux, 1984); and Janet Malcolm, *In the Freud Archives* (New York: Knopf, 1984); and Alice Miller, *Thou Shalt Not Be Aware: Society's Betrayal of the Child*, trans. Hildegarde Hannun and Hunter Hannun (New York: Farrar,

It is not so clear, though, why women's suffering is so pervasively dismissed or trivialized by legal culture, or more importantly what to do about it. As I will argue in a moment, feminist legal theorists do not typically frame the problem in the way I have just posed it. Nevertheless, it is not hard to construct two characteristic feminist explanations of the phenomenon, and the strategies they entail. The liberal feminist would characterize the legal culture's discriminatory treatment of women's suffering as the reflection of a perceptual error committed by that culture. Women are in fact the same as—and therefore equal to—men, in the only sense that should matter to liberal legal theory. Women, like men, are autonomous individuals who, if free to do so, will choose among proffered alternatives so as to fashion their own "good life" and thereby create social value. However, the legal culture fails to see or acknowledge this central sameness—and hence equality—of women and men. Because we are not perceived as identical to men in this way, we are not treated as such. Our choices are differentially restricted, and as a result we

---

Straus, Giroux, 1984). For a summary of more recent "experts" who have praised incest as desirable, liberating, consensual, and beneficial for all, and an account of the more subtle ways in which we all condone and encourage the sexual use of children, particularly girls, see Ellen Bass, "In the Truth Itself There Is Healing," included as introduction to Ellen Bass and Louise Thornton, *I Never Told Anyone: Writings by Women Survivors of Child Sexual Abuse* (New York: Harper and Row, 1983). See generally Florence Rush, *The Best Kept Secret: Sexual Abuse of Children* (New York: McGraw-Hill, 1980).

On the presumed inevitability of the pain of childbirth, see Shulamith Firestone, *The Dialectic of Sex: The Case for Feminist Revolution* (New York: Morrow, 1970).

The privatization of domestic violence is eloquently expressed as well as documented in Erin Prizzey's classic treatment, *Scream Quietly or the Neighbors Will Hear* (Short Hills, N.J.: R. Enslow Publishers, 1977). The explosion of derisive, dismissive, and derogatory treatments of the Meese Commission report on pornography makes clear that the literate and concerned public still does not understand, and perhaps does not want to understand, that pornography causes physical injury. For just one example of hundreds, see Carole S. Vance, "Porn in the U.S.A.: The Meese Commission on the Road," *Nation* 2 and 9 August 1986, 6–82.

Finally, the invisibility and incomprehensibility of marital rape is dramatically reflected in *Time*'s 1983 report, "Private Violence: Child Abuse, Wife Beating, and Rape." The only mention of marital rape occurs in the following passage:

> Most cases of private violence are closer calls. What to do about a man who rapes his wife? What about the fight between spouses that are not pat, villain-and-victim episodes? . . . One problem is that reasonable, well-intentioned people disagree. (Maureen Dowd, "Rape: The Survival Weapon," *Time*, 5 September 1983, 27–29)

On marital rape generally, see Diana E. H. Russell, *Rape in Marriage* (Bloomington: Indiana University Press, 1990).

disproportionately suffer. The liberal feminist's strategy is directly implied by her diagnosis: what we must do is prove that we are what we are—individualists and egoists, as are men—and then fight for the equal rights and respect that sameness demands. Equal respect will in turn ensure, through the logic of formal justice and the equal protection clause of the Fourteenth Amendment, that our suffering will be alleviated by law—just as is men's suffering—through a liberating expansion of our opportunities for choice.[3]

The radical feminist's explanation of this phenomenon is also not hard to construct. The blanket dismissal of women's suffering by the male legal culture is not a reflection of a misperception. Indeed the larger culture's perception is accurate: women are not as autonomous or individualistic as men. The liberal is wrong to insist that women and men are equal in this way. The reason the legal culture tends to dismiss women's gender-specific sufferings is that women don't matter. Those in power ignore women's suffering because they don't care about the suffering of the disempowered. Hierarchical power imbalances do that to people—they make the disempowered less than human, and they make the empowered ruthless. The radical feminist's strategy follows directly from her diagnosis: what we must do is dismantle the hierarchy. The equal protection clause—at least if we can interpret it (and use it) as an "Equality Promotion Clause"—might help.[4]

---

3. See, e.g., Wendy W. Williams, "Equality's Riddle: Pregnancy and the Equal Treatment/Special Treatment Debate," *New York University Review of Law and Social Change* 13 (1984): 325–80; and Wendy W. Williams, "The Equality Crisis: Some Reflections on Culture, Courts, and Feminism," *Women's Rights Law Reporter* 7 (1982): 175–200.

The pornography debate has triggered a rebirth of liberal-legal feminism, or at least, a feminism that draws on, rather than distinguishes itself from, traditional liberal-legal commitments to individualism, freedom, and autonomy. See, e.g., Varda Burstyn, ed., *Women against Censorship* (Vancouver: Douglas and McIntyre, 1985); Rubin, "Sexual Politics, the New Right, and the Sexual Fringe," in *What Color Is Your Handkerchief: A Lesbian S/M Sexuality Reader* (1979); Ann Barr Snitow, Christine Stansell, and Sharon Thompson, *Powers of Desire: The Politics of Sexuality* (New York: Monthly Review Press, 1983); and Carole Vance, ed., *Pleasure and Danger: Exploring Female Sexuality* (Boston: Routledge and Kegan Paul, 1984).

4. See, e.g., Nadine Taub and Elizabeth M. Schneider, "Women's Subordination and the Role of Law, "in *The Politics of Law: A Progressive Critique*, rev. ed., ed. David Kairys (New York: Pantheon Books, 1990), 151–76; Catharine A. MacKinnon, "Feminism, Marxism, Method, and the State: An Agenda for Theory," in *Feminist Theory: A Critique of Ideology*, ed. Nannerl O. Keohane, Michelle Z. Rosaldo, and

The recent explosion of feminist writings on the multitude of problems generated by women's "difference"[5] prompts me to suggest a third explanation of this blanket dismissal by the legal culture of women's pain, and thus a third strategy. This dismissal may reflect the extent to which the pain women feel is not understood. It may not be understood because it is itself different from men's pain; that is, misunderstanding is not just a product of our social or linguistic difference. The pain we feel is *itself* different and thus it may be that women suffer more because we suffer differently. (Is there anything quite like the pain of childbirth?) If this is right, then the legal culture has committed a perceptual error, but the error is not, as the liberal feminist believes, in perceiving us as different where we in fact are the same. The perceptual error is in failing to understand the difference—not the sameness—of our subjective, hedonic lives. If the pain women feel is in fact discontinuous from—different than—what is experienced by men, then it is not really surprising that the injuries we sustain are trivialized or dismissed by the larger male culture. It is hard to empathize with the pain of another when the nature of that pain is not understood. If the pain women feel is different—not shared by men—then it is not surprising that men cannot readily empathize with women who suffer, much less share in the effort to resist the source of their injuries. The strategic inference I draw is this: if we want to enlist the aid of the larger legal culture, the feel of our gender-specific pain must be described before we can ever hope to communicate its magnitude.

Focus on the difference of our hedonic lives also suggests a different way to address the related problem of false consciousness. As feminists know all too well, it is not just the legal culture that trivializes women's suffering, women do so also. Again, if we focus on the distinctiveness of our pain, this becomes less surprising. An injury

---

Barbara C. Gelpi (Chicago: University of Chicago Press, 1982) (hereinafter MacKinnon, "Agenda"); Catharine A. MacKinnon, "Feminism, Marxism, Method, and the State: Toward Feminist Jurisprudence," *Signs* 8 (1983): 635–58.

5. See, e.g., Hester Eisenstein and Alice Jardin, eds., *The Future of Difference* (Boston: G. K. Hall, 1980). The classic works are Carol Gilligan, *In a Different Voice: Psychological Theory and Women's Development* (Cambridge: Harvard University Press, 1982); and Nancy Chodorow, *The Reproduction of Mothering: Psychoanalysis and the Sociology of Gender* (Berkeley and Los Angeles: University of California Press, 1978).

uniquely sustained by a disempowered group will lack a name, a history, and in general a linguistic reality. Consequently, the victim as well as the perpetrator will transform the pain into something else, such as, for example, punishment, or flattery, or transcendence, or unconscious pleasure. A victim's response to an injury that is perceived by the victim as deservedly punitive, consensual, natural, subconsciously desired, legally inevitable, or trivial will be very different from a response to an injury that is perceived as simply painful. We change our behavior in response to the threat of what we perceive as punishment; we diminish ourselves in response to injuries we perceive as trivial; we reconstruct our pasts in response to injuries we perceive as subconsciously desired; we negate our inner selves in response to injuries we perceive as consensual; and we constrain our potentiality in response to injuries we perceive as inevitable.

We respond to pain, on the other hand, by resisting the source of the pain. The strategic inference should be clear: we must give voice to the hurting self, even when that hurting self sounds like a child rather than an adult; even when the hurting self voices "trivial" complaints; even when the hurting self is ambivalent toward the harm; and even when (especially when) the hurting self is talking a language not heard in public discourse. Only by so doing will we ourselves become aware of the meaning of the suffering in our lives, and its contingency in our history. Only when we understand the contingency of that pain will we be free to address it and through legal tools to change the conditions that cause it.

If my argument is correct, then it would seem that feminist legal theorists should be hard at work providing rich descriptions of women's subjective, hedonic lives, particularly the pain in those lives, and more particularly the pain in our lives that is different. And yet we aren't. I can think of four possible reasons for this neglect. The first three are problems that plague discussion of all aspects of our difference. The fourth reason is philosophical and is the subject of this essay.

The first reason is linguistic. It is hard to talk about our pain and pleasure, and it is hard to talk about our pain and pleasure because they are different. Our language is inadequate to the task. As women become more powerful, this linguistic barrier is eased: we now possess, for example, the legal and social labels that at least identify some of our experiences as injurious, such as *sexual harass-*

ment and *date rape*. But we still lack the descriptive vocabulary necessary to convey the quality of the pain we sustain by virtue of these experiences. The second reason is psychological. Before we can convince others of the seriousness of the injuries we sustain, we must first convince ourselves, and so long as others are unconvinced, to some extent, we will be as well. This is a circle that must be broken, not inhabited. The third and underlying problem is political. The inadequacy of language and the problem of false consciousness are but reflections of what is surely the core obstacle to the development of feminist discourse on the nature of gender-specific pain, which is an unwilling and resisting audience. When we struggle to find the words to describe the pain (or pleasure) in our lives, and the effort is rewarded with dismissal and trivialization, the fully human response is to silence ourselves.

However, at least one reason, and perhaps the main reason, that feminist legal theorists have neglected the hedonic dimension of our difference is not the difference problem, but the emerging logic of feminist legal theory itself. By virtue of the models of legal criticism that feminist legal theorists have embraced, we've literally defined the subjective, hedonic aspect of our differences out of existence. That is, feminist legal theorists have adopted nonfeminist normative models of legal criticism and then applied those models to women's problems. The two major normative models of legal criticism that feminist theorists have thus far embraced, liberal legalism and radical legalism, themselves deny the normative significance of the subjective pleasure and suffering of our lives. Because of the normative models employed by modern feminists, the internal, phenomenological reality of women's hedonic lives, and its difference from men's, has become virtually irrelevant to feminist legal theory.

Thus, I will argue that liberal feminists, true to their liberalism, want women to have more choices, and that radical feminists, true to their radicalism, want women to have more power. Both models direct our critical attention outward—liberalism to the number of choices we have, radicalism to the amount of power. Neither model of legal criticism and therefore, derivatively, of feminist legal criticism posits subjective happiness as the direct goal of legal reform, or subjective suffering as the direct evil to be eradicated. Neither model directs our critical attention inward. Consequently, and unsurprisingly, neither liberal nor radical feminist legal critics have committed themselves to the task of determining the measure of women's happiness or suffering.

Which is not to say that liberal and radical feminists are unconcerned about women's subjective well-being. Rather, each group dismisses the normative significance of women's pain and suffering because of the essentially strategic choices made by the underlying (nonfeminist) politics embraced by that group, and the depictions of human nature those choices entail. That is, radicals, liberals, and feminists all have great concern for people's subjective happiness. But neither radical nor liberal legalism nor their feminist derivatives aim for happiness or well-being directly. Instead, they both assert a definition of the human being that in turn assumes a correlation between some condition of the objective world and a subjective state of well-being and then aim to maximize that objective, external condition. Thus, definitionally, liberal legalism assumes that, if free to do so, people will choose what will make them happy, and that therefore there exists a correlation between the objective act of consent and a subjective gain in happiness. On this assumption, liberal legalists seek to maximize not our subjective happiness, but our objective opportunities for choice.[6] Radical legalism assumes that there exists a correlation between people's objective equality and subjective happiness, or well-being. On this assumption, radicals seek to maximize not our subjective happiness, but our objective equality.[7] In each case, the correlation between objective, external condition and subjective, internal, hedonic state is a function of the definition of the human to which each tradition is committed. Both models share a refusal to inquire into whether their assumed correlation between objective condition and subjective well-being is true or false of contingent, embodied human beings. Therefore, both models methodologically

6. The commitment to personal choice reappears in different forms all over the political spectrum that falls under liberal legalism's umbrella. See as an example from the liberal Left, R. M. Dworkin, "Liberalism," in *A Matter of Principle* (Cambridge: Harvard University Press, 1985), 181–204, and for an example from the Right, see *EJ*.

7. Whatever else they may be, and whatever inconsistencies divide them, radical legalists are antihierarchical, seemingly regardless of the hierarchy in question. The best statement, I believe, of this commitment is found in Roberto Unger's much-maligned but well-reasoned exposition of the critical legal studies movement. Roberto Mangabeira Unger, "The Critical Legal Studies Movement," *Harvard Law Review* 96 (1983): 563.

preclude, on their own terms, feminist inquiry into whether the account of the human being that the model assumes is a true account of women. And finally, they both direct the feminists that embrace them away from an investigation of the differences of women's internal, hedonic lives.

The cost to women of feminist theorists' endorsement of the antiphenomenological methodology and antihedonic norms of the models they endorse is very high.[8] It renders liberal and radical feminists peculiarly uncritical—as feminists—of the visions of the human and thus of the normative assumptions of the models for legal criticism that they have respectively embraced. The antiphenomenological methodology of radicalism and liberalism rule out the only inquiry that could conceivably determine the value to women of the model itself, and that is whether the description of the human that each model embraces is true of women. Thus, liberal feminists fail to ask—by virtue of the intrinsic commitments of liberals—whether the liberal conception of the phenomenology of choice is true of women's experience. As a result liberal feminist theorists cannot even ask the question that as feminists they should start with, whether the liberalism they embrace will be of any value *to women*. Radical feminists fail to ask—by virtue of the intrinsic commitments of radicalism—whether the radical commitment to the ideal of equality resonates with women's felt desires. As a result, radical feminist theorists cannot even ask the question that as feminists they should start with, and that is whether the radical ideal of equality is desirable *for women*. It is only by focusing directly on what both models definitionally exclude—our phenomenological, hedonic experience—that we will be able to ask these questions. Only by asking these questions we will determine the limits of liberal and radical models of legal criticism

8. Although feminist legalists have apparently embraced the mainstream twentieth-century resistance to ethical hedonism, the ethical theory that asserts pleasure as the good toward which we ought aim, and pain as the evil we should eradicate, some feminists, notably Marilyn French, are leaning toward an explicit endorsement of hedonism. See Marilyn French, *Beyond Power: On Women, Men, and Morals* (New York: Summit Books, 1985). The "female voice" that Gilligan describes in *In a Different Voice* also bears strong resemblance to the classical hedonist's voice. A small number of feminists have noted the hostility of the deontological tradition to feminist concerns and have for that reason endorsed hedonism, its traditional contender. See, e.g., Randall Lake, "The Metaethical Framework of Anti-Abortion Rhetoric," *Signs* 11 (1986): 478–99.

and reform, and only by understanding those limits we will understand where a truly feminist model of legal criticism must begin.

Part 1 of this chapter provides a phenomenological and hedonic critique of the conception of the human, and thus the female, that underlies liberal feminism. Part 2 presents a phenomenological critique of the conception of the human, and thus the female, that underlies radical feminism. Again, I will argue that in both cases the theory does not pay enough attention to feminism: liberal feminism owes more to liberalism than to feminism, radical feminism more to radicalism than to feminism. Both models accept a depiction of human nature that is simply untrue of women. Thus, both accept uncritically a claimed correlation between objective condition and subjective reality that, I will argue, is untrue to women. As a result, both groups fail to address the distinctive quality of women's subjective, hedonic lives, and the theories they have generated therefore have the potential to backfire—badly—against women's true interests.

In the concluding section I will suggest an alternative normative model for feminist legal criticism that aims neither for choice nor equality, but directly for women's happiness, and a feminist legal theory that has as its critical focus the felt experience of women's subjective, hedonic lives. My substantive claim is that women's happiness or pleasure, as opposed to women's freedom or equality, should be the ideal toward which feminist legal criticism and reform should press, and that women's misery, suffering, and pain, as opposed to women's oppression or subordination, is the evil we should resist. I will argue that feminist theorists, in short, have paid too much attention to the ideals of equality and autonomy and not enough attention to the hedonistic ideals of happiness and pleasure, and that correlatively we have paid too much attention to the evils of subordination and oppression, and not enough attention to the hedonistic evils of suffering and pain. My methodological assumption is that the key to moral decision making lies in our capacity to empathize with the pain of others, and thereby resist the source of it, and not in our capacity for abstraction, generalization, or reason. My strategic claim is directly entailed: the major obstacle to achieving the empathic understanding that is the key to significant moral commitment, including the commitment of the legal system to address the causes of women's suffering, is the striking difference between women's and men's internal lives, and more specifically, the different quality of our joys and sorrows. This obstacle can only be overcome through rich description of our internal hedonic lives.

Liberal Feminism: Consent, Autonomy, and the Giving Self

Perhaps the most widely held normative commitment of mainstream liberal theorists is that individuals should be free to choose their own style of life, and to exercise that freedom of choice in as many spheres as possible—economic, political, and personal.[9] The conception of the human and the relation between the individual and the state that implicitly motivates this commitment is relatively straightforward. According to the liberal vision, value is produced in our social world through satiation of the subjective desires and preferences of the individual. That satiation is in turn manifested and facilitated through the individual's voluntary choices. The individual's choice will reflect that individual's judgment of what will best satisfy that individual's own desires. It follows that whatever is freely consented to by an individual is what is good for that individual, and, if free of adverse effects on others, is good for society. The way to maximize value in the social world is therefore to maximize the opportunities for the exercise of choice through voluntary transactions between individuals. A law that either facilitates or mimics consensual transactions between freely choosing individuals is a good law on this model, while a law that frustrates such transactions is a bad law. Individual freedom is the ideal toward which law and legal reform ought press, and coercion or restraint on freedom is the evil.[10]

The contribution of feminist liberalism has been to extend the umbrella of this normative vision to women as well as men. The

9. See, e.g., Dworkin, "Liberalism"; *EJ*, and Bruce A. Ackerman, *Social Justice in the Liberal State* (New Haven: Yale University Press, 1980).

10. For an excellent discussion of liberal feminism, see Alison M. Jagger, *Feminist Politics and Human Nature* (Totowa, N.J.: Rowman and Allanheld, 1983), 27–49. By "feminist liberal legalism," I have in mind a characteristic way of thinking about the relation of women to legal theory, not a particular individual. In fact, to my knowledge, no liberal feminist thinker conversant with legal theory has spelled out sympathetically what the tenets of feminist liberal legalism would be. In spite of this gap, though, feminist liberal legalism, as I have characterized it in the text, dominates the way most legalists—feminist, nonfeminists, and even perhaps some antifeminists—think about women and law.

liberal feminist insists that the depiction of the human embraced by liberalism, which I will sometimes refer to as the *liberal self,* is also true of women, and that therefore the relationship of the state to the individual must be the same for both women and men. What it means for women to be equal to men in the liberal feminist vision is basically that women and men are the same in the only sense that matters to the liberal: women as well as men create value by satiating their subjective desires through consensual choices. Because women and men are equal in this way, because they share the same definitive human attribute, women should be equally free to choose their own life plans, and women should be equally entitled to the respect from the state that freedom requires.

The liberal feminist's legal strategy for dealing with women's suffering is directly entailed by her liberalism. Women, like men, consent to that which will minimize their own suffering and maximize their own felt happiness. Therefore, the way to deal with women's suffering is to increase women's sphere of consensual freedom. What we should do with law, then, is ensure that women's sphere of consensual freedom is as large as possible, or at least as large as men's. Thus, the liberal feminist's central jurisprudential commitment tracks the liberal's: a law is a good law if it increases the freedom of women to enter into consensual transactions or if it equalizes that freedom with that enjoyed by men. A law is a bad law if it decreases that freedom.

Liberal feminist legal theory carries with it the same problems that now plague liberal legalism, but multiplied. Modern liberal feminists, like modern liberals generally, have failed to examine the essentially descriptive claims about the human being that underlie their normative model. The liberal claim that human beings consent to transactions in order to maximize their welfare may be false. If it is, then the liberal claim that social value is created through facilitating choice will be false as well. But furthermore, women may be "different" in precisely the way that would render the empirical assumptions regarding human motivation that underlie the liberal's commitment to the ethics of consent more false for women than for men. Thus, it may be that women generally don't consent to changes so as to increase our own pleasure or satisfy our own desires. It may be that women consent to changes so as to increase the pleasure or satisfy the desires of others. The descriptive account of the phenomenology of choice that underlies the liberal's conceptual defense of the moral primacy of consent may be wildly at odds with the way women phenomenologically experience the act of consent. If it is, if women consent to transactions not to increase our own welfare, but to increase the welfare of others, if women are different in this psychological way, then the liberal's ethic of consent, with its presumption of an essentially selfish human (male) actor and an essentially selfish consensual act, when evenhandedly applied to both genders, will have disastrous implications for women. For if women consent to changes so as to increase the happiness of others rather than to increase our own happiness, then the ethic of consent, applied evenhandedly, may indeed increase the amount of happiness in the world, but women will not be the beneficiaries.

And indeed, the liberal ethic of consent does, oftentimes, have less than happy consequences for women. The magnitude of the disservice should be obvious to anyone who can resist the staggeringly seductive liberal urge to imply an increase in subjective happiness from the objective act of consent. The rather inescapable fact is that much of the misery women endure is fully consensual. That is, much of women's suffering is a product of a state of being that was itself brought into being through a transaction to which women unquestionably tendered consent. A woman's experience of marital sexuality, for example, may range from boring to irritating to invasive to intensely painful. Similarly, a female employee may experience the sexual advances of an employer as degrading. But the fact is that the wife was not brought to the altar in shackles nor the employee to the place of employment in chains.[11] Put affirmatively, the conditions that create our misery—unwanted pregnancies, violent and abusive marriages, sexual harassment on the job—are often traceable to acts of consent. Women, somewhat uniquely, consent to their misery. An ethical standard that ties value to the act of consent by presumptively assuming that people consent to their circumstances so as to bring about their own happiness and by so doing thereby create value leaves these miserable consensual relationships beyond criticism.

11. I do not mean to deny—indeed I mean to highlight—the extent to which the choices we make occur within a context of compulsory heterosexuality. But that does not negate the fact that within that context these choices are relatively unfettered. If we are going to address the causes of our misery, then, we must attack the context, not the choices themselves, for signs of bondage.

The liberal feminist is—must be—deaf to the above claim. For the liberal feminist, women and men are the same on the only dimension that should be of concern to law: women and men both create value through their individual and presumptively selfish choices. This is the empirical equality, meaning identity or sameness, behind the liberal legal feminist's normative commitment to equal freedom and equal respect. Reflecting a not necessarily admirable respect for the virtue of consistency, liberal feminists must and do simply deny the extent to which women consent to their sufferance of misery. For the liberal and for the liberal feminist as well, it just can't be.

Phenomenological Critique of Liberal Feminism

I want to suggest in this section that many women, much of the time, consent to transactions, changes, or situations in the world so as to satisfy not their own desires or to maximize their own pleasure, as liberal legalism and liberal legal feminism both presume, but to maximize the pleasure and satiate the desires of others, and that they do so by virtue of conditions that only women experience. I will sometimes call the cluster of other-regarding, other-pleasing motivations that rule these women's actions the *giving self*, so as to distinguish it from the *liberal self:* the cluster of self-regarding rational motivations presumed by liberal legalism. Thus my descriptive claim is that many women much of the time are giving selves rather than liberal selves. If we take the liberal's description of the motivational core of the human being as accurate and central, then this motivational difference between most men and many women implies that women who define themselves as giving selves are not human.

I believe that women become giving rather than liberal selves for a range of reasons, including our (biological) pregnability and our (social) training for our role as primary caretakers,[12] but in this section, I will focus on only one causal hypothesis, which (I think) has great explanatory force. The causal hypothesis is this: women's lives are dangerous, and it is the acquisitive and potentially violent nature of male sexuality that is the cause of the danger. A fully

12. See Chodorow, *Reproduction of Mothering* and Dorothy Dinnerstein, *The Mermaid and the Minotaur: Sexual Arrangements and Human Malaise* (New York: Harper and Row, 1976).

justified fear of acquisitive and violent male sexuality consequently permeates many women's—perhaps all women's—sexual and emotional self-definition. Women respond to this fear by reconstituting themselves in a way that controls the danger and suppresses the fear. Thus: women define themselves as giving selves so as to obviate the threat, the danger, the pain, and the fear of being self-regarding selves from whom their sexuality is taken.

The danger, and hence the fear, that women live with is very hard for others (men) to acknowledge or understand for two reasons. First, both the objective danger and the subjective fear are different. The danger and the endangered fear are pervasive rather than sporadic conditions of our lives. There is a world of difference between the threat of sporadic violence (with which men are familiar, from barroom brawls to wars), and hence sporadic fear, and a threat of pervasive violence, and hence definitional fear. One responds to sporadic fear and the threat of sporadic violence by changing one's behavior. One moves to a safer neighborhood, one fights back, one runs away, one cowers, or whatever, but one knows that the barroom brawl, the mugging, or the war will be over, and that when it is over, the state of normalcy—safety—will return. By contrast, one responds to pervasive fear and pervasive threat not by changing one's behavior, but by redefining oneself. Women cannot eliminate the danger our sexuality poses by moving to a safer neighborhood, any more than blacks can respond to the danger their color poses by moving to a safer race. Nor will the danger cease when the war ends. We respond to the pervasive threat of violent and acquisitive male sexuality instead by changing ourselves, rather than responding to the conditions that cause it.

The danger, the violence, and the fear with which women live and that informs our self-definition are invisible, which is the second reason they are misunderstood. They are not a part of men's world, externally or internally. They are obviously not a part of their internal world: men, unlike women, do not experience the fear of violent sexuality as a part of their self-definition. They will not, because they cannot, understand the kind of defining fear with which women live by reference to shared experience. Furthermore, women's definitional fear is not a part of their external world: the danger and the threat that causes it are largely, to them, invisible. Left and liberal men do not see women shake with fear. They do not see women getting harassed on the street; when men accompany women, as all women know, harassment stops. For the same reason, they do not see women sexually harassed at work. They do not see women battered in the home. They do not see women being raped, by strangers, dates, or husbands. They do not see women violated, abused, and afraid. To these men, violence against women, the pain women feel as a result of it, and the fear of its recurrence, are invisible. It is not surprising that the claim that women's lives are ruled by fear is heard by these men as wildly implausible. They see no evidence in their own lives to support it. This simple fact, more than anything else, I believe, commits women and men to live in two separate realities.

This invisibility and the ignorance it produces is almost as damaging as the fear itself. It has several manifestations, every one of which now constitutes a serious stumbling block for feminist progress. One manifestation, for example, is the male reaction to the increasing visibility of the problem. As anyone who reads *Newsweek* knows, the amount of violence in women's lives is not just higher, but much higher, than has until very recently generally been thought. Surely it's fair to say that the percentage of women who have been violently (and privately) abused at some point in their lives is higher than most of "us" used to believe. The probable incidence of sexual abuse of young girls is not .02 percent, as it was comfortably thought until very recently, it is far higher. The probable incidence of wife abuse is not .1 percent, (did anyone ever really think that?), it is far higher.[13]

---

13. The amount of "private violence" in any society is by definition not known. *Time* put the point this way:

> [W]hen statisticians turn to private violence, the numbers become iffy, approximate in the extreme. Are there 650,000 cases of child abuse annually, or a million? Or 6 million? Bona fide experts, extrapolating and just guessing, variously cite all those figures and others. It is said that every year two million women are beaten by their husbands, and it is also said that nearly six million are. Pick your figure. A Justice Department survey counted 178,000 rapes during 1981, but for every woman who reported a raped to the police, perhaps nine or maybe 25 did not. It is beyond dispute, however, that extraordinary numbers of women and children are being brutalized by those closest to them. (Kurt Anderson, "Covery Story: Private Violence," *Time*, 5 September 1983, 19)

The editor of *Sisterhood Is Global* elaborate:

> Approximately 2 million to 6 million women each year are beaten by the men they live with or are married to; 50–70% of wives experience battery during their marriages; 2000–4000 women are beaten to death by husbands each year; in 1979 40% of all women who were killed were murdered by their partner . . . 25% of women's suicide attempts follow a history of battery; wife

Here's a sex difference I've noticed: when women see these newly reported high percentages, they are outraged at the violence, and when men see the same numbers, they are outraged at what they perceive as unethical and wild inflation of statistics. I find this sex difference profoundly disturbing.

How does a pervasive and largely invisible danger, and an equally pervasive and invisible fear, affect women's lives? Women cannot and do not live in a state of constant fear of male sexual violence any more than workers can live in a state of constant fear of material deprivation. One way (there are others) that women control the danger—and thus suppress the fear—is by redefining themselves as giving selves. Most simply, a woman will define herself as a giving self so that she will not be violated. She defines herself as a being who gives sex, so that she will not become a being from whom sex is taken. In a deep sense (too deep: she tends to forget it), this transformation is consensual: she consents to being a giving self—the dependent party in a comparatively protective relationship—for self-regarding liberal reasons; she consents in order to control the danger both inside and outside of the relationship, and in order to suppress the fear that danger engenders. Once redefined, however, and once within those institutions that support the definition, she becomes a person who gives her consent so as to ensure the other's happiness (not her own), so as to satiate the other's desires (not her own), and ultimately so as to obey the other's commands. In other words, she embraces a self-definition and a motive for acting that is the direct antithesis of the internal motivational life presupposed by liberalism. The motivation of her consensual acts is the satisfaction of another's desires. She consents to serve the needs and satiate the desires of others.

I have no interest in arguing that all women are giving selves all of the time. I want to suggest in the next few subsections that enough women have lived with enough fear and danger in their lives as to justify the inference that significant numbers of women have

battery injures more U.S. women than auto accidents, rape or muggings; every 18 seconds a woman is beaten by her husband severely enough to require hospitalization. Police spend 1/3 to 1/2 of their time responding to domestic violence calls; 97% of spouse abuse is directed against wives. Battery is a cross-class, cross-race problem. (Robin Morgan, ed., *Sisterhood Is Global: The International Women's Anthology* [Garden City, N.Y.: Anchor Press/Doubleday, 1984], 704)

defined themselves in a way that undercuts the commitment to the ethical primacy of consent that underlies liberal feminist legal theory. In the following sections I will describe some of the life environments that render such a self-definition plausible. I will discuss only those environments in which I have lived. Thus, the descriptions that follow are exemplary of the types of fear that have at some point in my life determined my self-definition. Toward that end, I will discuss the effect of domestic violence, promiscuous and threatening heterosexuality, and the fear of rape and street hassling on a woman's self-definition. The list is obviously not exhaustive; it excludes, because I have not myself lived through it and do not fully understand it, how stranger rape itself (instead of the fear of it) and incest affects a woman's self-perception.[14]

Abusive Domestic Relationships: Fear and Consent

Del Martin begins her book *Battered Wives* with the following letter from a battered wife:

> I am in my thirties and so is my husband. I have a high school diploma and am presently attending a local college, trying to obtain the additional education I need. My husband is a college graduate and a professional in his field. We are both attractive and . . . respected and well-liked. We have four children and live in a middle-class home with all the comforts we could possibly want.
>
> I have everything except life without fear.
>
> For most of my married life I have been periodically beaten by my husband. What do I mean by "beaten"? I mean that parts of my body have been hit violently and repeatedly, and that painful bruises, swelling, bleeding wounds, unconsciousness, and combinations of these things have resulted.
>
> I have had glasses thrown at me. I have been kicked in the

14. The best description of stranger rape to my knowledge is in Lynne N. Henderson, "The Wrongs of Victims' Rights," *Stanford Law Review* 37 (1985): 953–66. For powerful descriptions of incest, see Bass and Thornton, *I Never Told Anyone*.

> abdomen when I was visibly pregnant. I have been kicked off the bed and hit while lying on the floor—again, while I was pregnant. I have been whipped, kicked and thrown, picked up again and thrown down again. I have been punched and kicked in the head, chest, face and abdomen more times than I can count.
>
> Few people have ever seen my black and blue face or swollen lips because I have always stayed indoors afterwards, feeling ashamed. I was never able to drive following one of these beatings, so I could not get myself to a hospital for care. I could never have left my young children alone, even if I could have driven a car.
>
> Being beaten is a terrible thing; it is most terrible of all if you are not equipped to fight back. I recall an occasion when I tried to defend myself and actually tore my husband's shirt. Later, he showed it to a relative as proof that I had done something wrong. The fact that at that moment I had several raised spots on my head hidden by my hair, a swollen lip that was bleeding, and a severely damaged cheek with a blood clot that caused a permanent dimple didn't matter to him. What mattered was that I tore his shirt! That I tore it in self-defense didn't mean anything to him.
>
> My situation is so untenable I would guess that anyone who has not experienced one like it would find it incomprehensible. I find it difficult to believe myself.[15]

How do women respond to the total fear that accompanies the daily violence that characterizes an abusive domestic relationship? What does such fear teach you? A woman cannot live in a state of terror every day, and what a battered woman learns in an abusive marriage is how to define herself in such a way that she can on occasion suppress the fear. Thus, the near-universal response to the pervasive fear with which a battered woman lives is to redefine herself as a giving rather than a liberal self. The battered woman is a giving self for another within an abusive marriage, to precisely the extent to which it is too frightening and dangerous to even contemplate being for oneself. As a giving self, she consents to everything, absolutely, and at all levels of being, and she does so for the subjectivity

15. Del Martin, *Battered Wives* (San Francisco: Glide Publications, 1976), 2–3.

of the other, and the survival of herself. The other must live, and that is why you are. If you are going to be at all, you are going to be for him. And you are going to be, so you are going to be for him.

One woman explains:

> Fear (a) My husband was physically violent three times. . . . [H]e and I [sat] in a crowded restaurant where we were both well-known, me listening to him demolishing my character, that of my parents and friends, and when I resisted and insisted on leaving, he threatened to kill me. And I believed him, I sat there, I smiled, . . . and I was terrified.
>
> (b) Fear of my sanity—I felt myself fragmenting—much like in descriptions of schizophrenia. Bits of me seemed to be breaking off and floating away, and it was always more of a problem to catch them and get them back, like catching soap bubbles.
>
> Confusion. Why had he married me? What did he want? . . . Who had he married? It wasn't me. Who had I married? Was it him?
>
> Isolation—Identity Loss—Loss of Confidence—Misery. All these go together. They merge and feed one upon the other. . . . I cried, I stormed, I took on his description of me, I wilted under the pressure of how to correct these so obviously irritating characteristics. But, was he, himself at fault. No, for I tried to be understanding.
>
> It's a long time after now—ten years. . . . With an understanding of feminism came a way of absolving myself of failure, of eccentricity, of non-conformity. Yet, I remain bruised—I keep my guard up, because . . . I'm afraid at times that the next punch will splinter me forever.[16]

The redefinition of self as giving in an abusive marriage is the literal death of a woman's liberal subjectivity. She learns to consent for the satiation of the other's desires. That becomes the meaning of consent. This does not make her an altruistic person; this makes her a negative. She will even remember herself as such:

16. Dusty Rhodes and Sandra McNeill, eds., *Women against Violence against Women* (London: Onlywomen Press, 1985), 232–34. Subsequent references, abbreviated *WA*, are given in the text.

> I don't find it difficult to come to certain theoretical conclusions based on my experiences—but I still feel as if I'm standing apart and outside the experience—no amount of theorizing or analyzing can describe the complexities of emotional feelings I experienced during my marriage. When I analyze or theorize it's almost as if I am talking and thinking about another person—not myself. . . . I can't remember anything except six months of negative feelings. . . . I was afraid I would go mad. (*WA*, 232)

She teaches herself that this negative mode of being is inevitable:

> When I was eight, my father remarried. My new mother . . . shielded me from some of my father's most brutal outbursts. [One day I asked her why she put up with my father's violence.] "Claudia, that's the way men are. You just have to take it."[17]

And finally, she teaches herself that the apparently human face she shows the world is a fraud; you are not truly human, you are other. A giving self, being for another, has no entitlement to truth. You have relinquished the self-validating, self-creating, and self-verifying connection between word and experience. You learn, in other words, to lie to yourself and to others. You become the lie:

> Well-educated, well-to-do people don't discuss such things. I became a super cover-up artist. Shielding five children from the fact that their father took swipes at their mother was easy compared to the elaborate excuses designed for friends. [When a friend told her of her abuse by her husband, she was appalled and felt pity and disgust.] I couldn't allow myself the solace of confiding to her that I was a fellow sufferer. Perhaps pride stood in my way. My reaction to her disclosure merely reinforced my vow never to discuss my own situation with anyone.[18]

"Very few people understand this kind of fear," says Erin Pizzey, in *Scream Quietly or the Neighbors Will Hear*.[19] This is not right—

17. Quoted from Martin, *Battered Wives*, 79.
18. Ibid., 79–80.
19. Ibid., 78.

a lot of women understand this kind of fear. But with the exception of Vietnam veterans, no white, heterosexual man I have ever known knows how it feels to be afraid all of the time. Most women as well lack this knowledge. But many women—and there are many battered women—know what it means to define oneself in such a way as to make it possible to live with the truth that tomorrow you may die. If the day-to-day decision to stay in such a marriage is "consensual," the price is unconscionable: for the gain of controlling fear, you give up your subjective life.

Promiscuous Heterosexuality: Fear and Consent

Many more women, however, know the fear and the threat of violence implicit in promiscuous heterosexuality. A "date" with a man who is utterly—aggressively—uninterested in your subjective well-being, and at the same time, utterly consumed by his expectation and his felt compulsion to have you is a frightening encounter. But the fear of violence in promiscuous heterosexuality, when it is there, is always disguised and always confused. One woman explains:

> [I]t is considered quite O.K. and normal for a man to try to persuade a woman to have sexual intercourse. He asks her to dance, she accepts. (She wants to, she doesn't want to but she's afraid of hurting his feelings, she's afraid of making him angry, she wants a man to dance with.) He asks her out, she accepts. (She wants to, or she doesn't want to, but all her friends have got blokes, she's afraid of making him angry, he might feel hurt, she cannot go out if she's on her own.) He kisses her. He puts his hand on her leg, her breast, her cunt. He wants to see how far he can go. She lets him. (She wants to, or she doesn't want to but he's taken her out after all, and spent money on her, she needs a lift home, she doesn't want to seem a prude, he might be angry.) He asks her to sleep with him. She accepts. (She wants to, or she doesn't want to but she thinks she might as well, she can't back off now, it might be O.K., she's flattered that he wants her, he might be angry.)
>
> Or she refuses. He tries to persuade her. He tells her he loves her. He says she doesn't love him. He calls her a prude, immature, frigid. He says he needs sex. . . . Each time she finally tells him

> to stop, breaks away, he gets angry, he rages, he sulks, he tells her how bad it is for men to be left "excited." (Prick-teaser!) He teaches her to suck him off. He works toward his goal, which is her vagina. He means to have, to possess this woman.
>
> This isn't rape this is normal everyday stuff. The magazines call it young love. (*WA*, 27–28)

And another describes her own memories:

> I want to talk particularly about the violence I have experienced from men. . . . When I was in my early teens I naively believed myself to be the inheritor of enlightened and liberating attitudes to sex. We had the pill and as far as I could see the double standard was diminishing, making it easier for women to be sexually active and assertive. Unlike my mother who was told never to say yes it was unpopular amongst girls I knew then to ever say no. We were controlled by men's demands. . . . Throughout my teens I variously had sex with men in the backs of cars, at the fairground, under the pier and the lavatories a few times. Violence was implicit in many of these sexual encounters. I remember my arms being locked above my head so I could not move; I remember being bruised and bitten and scratched. I remember moments of rising panic when I thought the man was actually going to hurt me badly. (*WA*, 229)

One way (there are others) that a young girl can respond to the "rising panic" she feels on a date is by defining herself as giving. A straightforward, sensible, protective reaction to someone who is indifferent to your subjectivity, and at the same time must have you as an object, is to hide your subjective self and objectify and then give your sexual self for his pleasure and your safety. The subjective experience of a date rape for a giving self is the experience of giving what must inevitably—definitionally—be given. The empty stares and the overdeveloped biceps are not as threatening—the sex that is the culmination of the date will not feel like a rape—if the girl had defined herself in such a way that sex just is "that which is given to the other." To withhold consent (and thus invite a rape) once she redefines herself as giving is not just unliberated or prudish; it is definitionally excluded. It will be followed by guilt and confusion. It will feel intolerably unnatural, like doing something perverted and in violation of one's reason for being. To be is to be sexually giving.

The woman quoted above accounts for her consensual participation in these multiple and violent sexual encounters:

> Frequently I was either uncomfortable or in actual pain but I did not know how to protest or refuse. I had non-voluntary sex quite a few times particularly when I was drunk and the men were reckless as to whether or not I had willed it in the first place. Quite often I suffered from thrush and cystitis, but I would never tell men to stop because I was in pain. During that time I often felt sick with guilt and with confusion but I still confused my constant sexual availability with liberation and freedom of choice. A couple of times I allowed men to bugger me and one of these times I bled so much I thought I had hemorrhaged. (*WA*, 228)

There is a fine line between the feeling of being threatened by an implied threat of force and the feeling of the sheer inevitability of sex. Nevertheless, they are, for the self-regarding women, distinctively different experiences: the first is frightening and the second is deadening. By contrast, for a woman or girl who had defined herself as giving and her sexuality as that which is to be given, there is no line. She will never experience the anxious, ambiguous fear of rape by a "date." But nor will she experience consensual sex as pleasurable, or if she does, it will be only incidentally so. She consents to sex for his, not for her, pleasure. The sex that culminates these dates will be consensual, but it will also be uncomfortable, unpleasant, painful, or dangerous. It will invite venereal disease (genital sex); bleeding and hemorrhaging (anal sex); gagging and nausea (deep oral sex); bruises, lacerations, and welts (sadomasochistic sex); and unwanted pregnancy. The giving self will not experience this pain as a reason to withhold consent, for she is not, by self-definition, a being who consents to sexual encounters for her own pleasure or withholds consent if she foresees pain. She unquestionably consents, but not to satiate her own desires. She consents to satiate the desires and feed the pleasure of the other.

The Rape Threat: Fear and Consent

Almost all women, including those who have never experienced unwanted sex or battery, have experienced the fear of rape. The working paper on rape from the Women Against Violence Against Women (WAVAW) conference elaborates:

> The fear of rape is always with us. It affects our lives in countless ways—not only in that we are afraid to walk the streets late at night, but in all our dealings with men, however superficial these might be. . . .
>
> This makes us self-conscious about our bodies, the way we sit and stand and walk—when was the last time you saw a woman sit sprawled across a bus seat the way men do all the time? We keep our knees together, our legs crossed, our faces neutral. Somewhere in our minds we are always aware that any man—every man—can, if he wants to, use the weapon of rape against us.
>
> And men know it too. The man who mutter obscenities at us in the street knows it, the local greengrocer who insists on calling us love . . . knows it, the wolf-whistling building workers know it, the man reading page three on the tube and grinning at us knows it. At one point on Reclaim the Night in Soho, we were confronted by a large group of men shouting "We're on the rapist's side—we're with the rapist." They didn't really need to tell us. We already knew. (*WA*, 25)

One way that (some) women respond to the pervasive, silent, unspoken, and invisible fear of rape in their lives is by giving their (sexual) selves to a consensual, protective, and monogamous relationship. This is widely denied, but it may be widely denied because it is so widely presumed. It is, after all, precisely what we are supposed to do. One woman describes her embrace of this option thusly:

> The brutality and coldness of (promiscuous heterosexual) experiences were instrumental in persuading me to have steady and secure relationships with men. I did not feel safe with lots of different ones. The threat of men's violence drove me into couple

> relationships. I feel ambivalent about these men. They were not unmitigated bastards and they did afford me protection. My mother would often mutter ominously about the world not being a safe place for women and my experiences could only confirm this. Being alone I felt, at times, besieged and up for grabs. Being with one man sheltered unwelcome attention from men in the streets, at parties, etc. (*WA*, 227–28)

Women who give themselves to a monogamous relationship in order to avoid the danger of rape from others, often end up giving themselves within the monogamous relationship so as to avoid the danger of rape by their partner. These women, and it is anyone's guess how many there are, acutely feel the loss of identity that such a giving entails. "L" begins her story:

> I got married in 1970, I was 19 and so was he. I found marriage a great strain at first adjusting myself to fit in with his personality, character, needs and wishes. Somehow I seemed to know this is what I had to do. . . . [M]ainly I was losing my name and "gaining" his. I didn't at that time realize I had a choice. (*WA*, 234)

Such women are in a constant state of duress, but they will only occasionally, and only dimly, experience it as such. A woman who learns to give herself in monogamy so as to obviate the fear and danger of marital rape will not experience the sex itself as frightening: the sex is what she gives to avoid the danger of rape. Such a woman controls danger and fear, but in exchange she gives—she alienates—her power to seek her own subjective pleasure through her own volition: the gift of one's sexual self under duress severs the connection between pleasure and volition. By giving yourself and your sexuality in order to ensure your safety from danger, you lose the power to bring about your own pleasure. L continues:

> In the main I was enthusiastic about sex, the physical pain seemed to stop, or perhaps I got used to it. Even then, though, I remember not always wanting to do it when he did, maybe I was tired, or just not in the mood but I wouldn't say no because he might be hurt or upset. I didn't at the time feel particularly resentful about this. . . .

> It was only after my first child was born . . . that sex began to be a problem. . . . I began to resent the sexual demands my husband made. . . . As well as this I was working full-time so I felt generally harassed. But I had been advised . . . not to neglect my husband. So I didn't. I sexually serviced him, and it began to feel just like that. If I said no, as I sometimes did, there would be either a row, well into the night, or silence which might last for days. Either way my tension and strain increased so I learned to be available, even if I didn't want to. It was quicker in the long run, so I could get some sleep.
>
> I remember feeling all kinds of hostile feelings against him when he invaded my body. . . . But I couldn't really articulate it, I felt trapped. . . . I was like some kind of automaton. . . . On and on it went with me totally drained of energy, but still I was expected to "have sex." In fact I did, without enthusiasm, just as another chore, like doing the ironing or bathing the kids. . . .
>
> I didn't like most of the things he did to me, but I felt a little that I was supposed to. I faked liking what he did, including buggery which I found painful, but still he kept doing it. (*WA*, 235–36)

Finally, and paradoxically, she gives away her own safety when she gives herself for safety. Protection from someone who is himself a source of danger is whimsical. The point at which the monogamous woman begins to feel that the sex in such a relationship is coercive, is precisely the point at which she has begun to redefine herself as self-regarding rather than giving. The sex begins to look and feel more like rape—to feel scary—instead of feeling boring and unpleasant and deadening. L describes this transformation—from "bad sex" to rape—thus:

> I could catalogue all the separate incidences of rape—that is, doing it against my will—but its [*sic*] too painful for me to recall it. In fact my experience is fairly commonplace. No major brutal acts, just a generalized abuse of my integrity. . . .
>
> It's well over a year since I left, and I think I'm beginning to recover. It's hard whilst it's happening to you to realize that you are being exploited, fucked-over and constantly raped. Because the effect of it all is to reduce your ability to fight back, or even

> to see what its [*sic*] about. My confidence was constantly undermined and eroded. . . . It's all those years of rape—perhaps subtle rather than brutal, but rape nevertheless. I was lucky I got out after ten years of marriage. Its [*sic*] only now that I can see what effect it had on me. It was rape and I couldn't name it. Had I known I'm sure I would have got out sooner. Rape in marriage is an issue, naming it is the first step in a campaign which could stop the misery of millions of women's lives.

Street Hassling: Fear and Consent

Finally, for exceptionally privileged and protected young women and girls who do not learn elsewhere the threat under which they live, street hassling gets the message across. It is a potent daily reminder of the quality of the state-of-nature outside the protective institutions in which they will be expected to encase their lives. Street hassling is not trivial. Sexual assaults and batteries on the street are threatening ("Come sit on my face, bitch. *Hey bitch, I said come sit on my face!* HEY BITCH, I MEAN YOU"), constant (most white men have experienced only a few street assaults by strangers. Many women—perhaps most women who live in urban areas—have experienced hundreds), criminal (they are assaults, and when accompanied by touchings, they are batteries), frightening (look down, cut across the street, shrink into your coat, let your mind go blank, don't look up), unacknowledged (look down, hope it stops, hope no one else hears, hope no one else sees), disorienting and self-alienating (smile so he might stop . . . learn to smile—*to show pleasure*—when you are frightened), uncompensated (of course), and unpunished (ditto). Street hassling is also the earliest—and therefore the *defining*—lesson in the source of a girl's disempowerment. If they haven't learned it anywhere else, street hassling teaches girls that their sexuality implies their vulnerability. It is damaging to be pointed at, jeered at, and laughed at for one's sexuality, and it is infantilizing to know you have to take it. The woman on the street is under the thumb of the abusive man in exactly the way that children are under the thumb of abusive parents. She is an object of his pleasure, his contempt, and his disposal. The subjective experience reflects the treatment. It feels frightening and infantilizing. It always made me feel—still makes me feel—like a helpless and guilty child. I know that I am in the hands of a superior power that will not be even *seen*, much less checked, by those from whom I might expect protection—the state, sympathetic men. When I refuse to let danger inhibit my movement (which is often), I pay a high price. On "public" streets, and on "public" transportation, I can expect to be touched, jeered at, yelled at, sexually ridiculed and exposed. This does not make me feel (primarily) "angry," "wronged," or even "assaulted." It makes me feel sexually ridiculous, exposed, dirty, vulgar, vulnerable, and afraid.

One way that (some) women and girls respond to the jolt of fear, the rising panic, that street hassling engenders is by defining themselves as "giving"; by hiding, suppressing, their subjective selves and then giving away for visual consumption their sexual appearance. She gives up her sexual appearance for visual consumption, in exchange for the safety of her subjectivity. *Thought* stops. *Feeling* stops. She must and does stop thinking and feeling when she is on the street, because it is the thinking, feeling, *subjective* person who is most denied and hence most threatened by harassment. The subjective, thinking, feeling being must hide. What she becomes on the street is visually consumed, given-away sex. To become less fearful (and thereby relatively freer in movement) she separates her sexual appearance from her subjective self, hides the latter, and gives the former away. She gives it away for his pleasure and for her safety.

This quasi-consensual bargain feels horrible. Your body, objectified and separated from your subjective being, becomes dead weight. You hide the subjective identity you value, and you devalue what you can't hide and must give—your objective sexuality. As you do so, you learn self-deception and self-belittlement—you learn to smile when you are in pain. And finally, you learn to hate that which forces this violent rupture of subjective self and objective sexuality, and it is your sexuality that forces it.

We all—men and women—live under a terrifying threat of material deprivation. We spend a great deal of energy warding off that danger and suppressing that fear. We pay our employer to protect us from that threat with our surplus labor value, and we spend considerable time and energy legitimating the employer's authority and right to do so. Similarly, we all live with the threat of criminal violence, pay the state to protect us from the threat, and expend energy legitimating its authoritative right to do so. Both employer and state become authorities whose legitimacy we regularly affirm.

With every such act of affirmation, of legitimization, we become less like the self-regarding character presupposed by liberalism. And, by virtue in part of our continuing affirmation of these authorities, the authorities become increasingly dangerous themselves.

Women, though, and only women, live with a third danger: women and only women must somehow ward off the threat of acquisitive and violent male sexuality. It should not be so hard to understand (*why* is it so hard to understand?) that women develop protective strategies for coping with this additional threat. The means with which we do so—primarily by learning to give ourselves to consensual, protective relationships, within which we then define ourselves as giving—are not the product of false consciousness or brainwashing. But nor are they value-creating, voluntary, and mutual relationships worthy of celebration. They are no less and no more than the product of our victimization: they are coherent, understandable responses to very real danger. Until we create a better world, they are also all we have.

The Giving Self and Liberal Feminism

A liberal feminist theory of law that presumptively values consensual transactions on the assumption that the giving of consent is motivationally self-regarding, without addressing the fear that molds women's self-definition, runs the risk of missing altogether the real causes of women's misery. I will explore only one example.

Sexual harassment of women students by male professors is now recognized as a discriminatory injury and an actionable harm. And, although it constitutes a triumph of radical, not liberal, feminism, the prohibition of coercive, academic sexual harassment is nevertheless fully consistent with liberal and liberal feminist premises.[20] The

20. For a general sense of the difference between liberal and radical conceptions of the harm in sexual harassment, contrast the radical treatment of the topic in MacKinnon, *Sexual Harassment of Working Women,* with the liberal treatment in Dziech and Weiner, *Lecherous Professor*. Both books reflect their authors' passionate conviction that harassment, either in school or at work, is terribly wrong. But there is a vivid difference in the characterization of that wrong. Dziech and Weiner conceive of their mission, I think, as an attempt to uncover a festering but exceptional wound: a few bad apples—the "lecherous professors"—sexually molest a larger number of female students. MacKinnon, by contrast, reveals sexual harassment in the workplace to be continuous with sexuality outside of the workplace. Sex in the workplace, because it is at work, poses a different injury than that outside of work.

sex for a grade that follows sexual harassment by a teacher of a student is characterized by liberals and liberal feminists as coercive because it is for a grade. Thus, whatever other reason might exist for prohibiting sex-for-grade transactions (and there are others), prohibition of these sexual transfers is fully consistent with liberal premises: the sex is a compensable assault because it is nonconsensual.

This liberal feminist reconstruction of what was originally a more radical insight, I believe, rather significantly misses the mark. The greater damage done on college campuses to women, by men, and through sex is precisely what the liberal conception of academic sexual harassment definitionally excludes. Women who are faced with the choice of sleeping with the teacher to get the A they academically earned, or settling instead for a C, have undoubtedly been injured. But with all due respect for the harm done to those students, there is a deeper tragedy, a more profound loss, and a greater harm done daily in campus bedrooms, and these relatively astute women who "know what they should have gotten" are decidedly not the victims. The greater misery, I believe, is the product of the fully consensual and highly regarded romantic attachments of female graduate students and assistant professors, or undergraduates and research assistants. It is a mistake to infer, as the liberal feminist is inclined to do, from the wrongness of coercive, for-grade campus sex that consensual sex between male teachers and female students is therefore *good*. We cannot and should not so infer.

Smart male students view themselves as all sorts of things, including young intellectuals. A good male student will often attach himself to a brilliant professor and will aspire to *be like* him. A smart female student who defines herself as giving *might* attach herself in this way to a brilliant professor and aspire to be like him. But it's not very likely. Unlike the male student, she is far more likely to be attracted to the brilliant professor and aspire not to be *like* him, but to give herself *to* him. In her own way the giving female student will seek the recognition and praise that all students crave, by offering her sexuality. She may be intellectually gifted, and she may perceive herself as such. But to the extent that the female student who is a giving self tries to define herself as an intellectual, she does so at the cost of internal war. For the definition of self as a sexually giving self rather than an academically demanding self is always there, always in competition, always available. For the female student, the intellectual self must fight the giving self, both in external and internal reality. The women who lose this battle have lost far more than the women who lost the A to which they were entitled, and so has the world.

All good students, male and female, love their professor's displays of intellectual brilliance; this is part of the joy of being a student. For the giving woman, however, that love is dangerous and ambiguous. Like male students, she craves recognition by her teachers. Her intellectual self craves recognition for intellectual work done. Her giving self, though, craves the recognition that can only come through the teacher's acceptance of her gift of self. Consequentially, male professors have a power that I suspect they often do not know they have, and when they do, they don't understand it. The male professor, as authority, is in a position to validate one or the other of the woman's conflicting self-definitions. If he reinforces the intellectual self, the woman's self-definition as intellectual is encouraged. If he reinforces the giving self, by accepting the woman's offered sexuality, the woman's internal war is over. The woman receives an authoritative pronouncement to the effect that her contribution to art, history, music, or whatever will be in a form that she has always suspected and even hoped for—that it will be, at root, sexual. Her contribution will not be in the delivery of ideas, which after all will most likely not be the work of genius, but will be instead through her giving of herself to one whose intellectual contribution, unlike her own, may be. She is a jewel whose intellectual talents will be used to make all the more perfect her rare gift. The female student who loves intellect, and who is aware of herself as a sexual being, will not only consent to these romantic entanglements. She will crave them—fiercely, continuously, and with heart, mind, and soul.

The pleasure to be had in such a relationship bears a disconcerting similarity to that of a cocaine high. Furthermore, both are damaging and addictive, although only cocaine is recognized as such. The woman feels pleasure in making a contribution to the culture she respects, even deeply respects, through a fusion of intellectuality and sexuality. It can feel like a mystical blend: a transcendental, transformative experience. Self-objectification can feel beautiful. It feels palpably *meaningful* to enrich the life of someone who is admirable and immersed in a discipline you value by merely *being*, and by giving what you are. The gift of self can feel more significant, universal, transcendental, and religious than the paltry competition for status in the seminar rooms in which one's (ex)-peers are engaged.

The pain of these relationships—as well as the damage they do—far exceeds their high. The woman's self-respect will hit a new low with which she is probably unfamiliar and for which she is totally unprepared, for at least three reasons. First, for a life of such servitude to feel of value, the man being served must be perceived as truly superior. The more skeptical the woman becomes of the man's genius, the more she must downgrade her own potential in order to maintain what is really central to these relationships—the distance between them. Whatever intellectual insecurities she brought with her are multiplied. This is a very bad way to feel about oneself. Second, the life of servitude to genius is likely to be a lazy, privileged, and pampered life. The woman will lose whatever employable skills she once had. She becomes unable to support herself. A given, empty self will not have the self-possession it takes to *work*. This sort of self-imposed, consensual unemployability is debilitating and infantilizing. This is also a bad way to feel about oneself. And finally, the woman who is using the relationship as a means of entrance into a discipline is being manipulative and knows it. This too is not a good way to feel about oneself. The cumulative effect is a smothering blanket of self-contempt. You lose your respect for your intelligence, your competency in the world, and your moral character, and all for good reason: you have lost yourself.

This is not a subtle point, nor an invisible loss. "Falling in love" with high school teachers, college professors, or research assistants really does destroy the productivity, the careers, the earning potential, and eventually the self-respect of many gifted women. Smart women drop out of high school, college, and graduate school (and pretty women are at higher risk) to date, to marry, to help, and to serve those they perceive as intellectual giants. Eventually they learn boredom, the weariness of inactivity, and the self-contempt of nonproductivity. But in spite of its incredible familiarity, most academic men and many academic women do not see this as a harm at all, and if they do see it as a harm, they do not see it as worth discussing. This ignorance must be ideological. My guess is that we cannot see the harm of these consensual relationships to precisely the degree to which we have adopted the blinders of liberalism. It is a harm caused not by coercive, occasional acts, but by the way we have defined the self that consents to the noncoercive relationships in which we engage. It is a harm that a liberal legal regime that resolutely regards the giving of consent as the infallible proxy of an increase in self-regarded and self-assessed value cannot possibly address.

There is no reason that liberalism or liberal legalism need be thus constrained. Liberalism need not commit itself to the narrow normative category of consent, and when liberalism has been at its strongest—when it has been a generous and spirited force for progress—it has not been. There is even greater reason why a liberal feminist theory of law should not be so constrained. A liberal feminism would be truer to not only the guiding historical strengths of liberalism but also to the goals of feminism if it aimed to eradicate the fear that presently dominates women's choices, rather than merely celebrating in the name of formal equality whatever choices we presently make. The stunted self-definitions that women embrace today are at least in part a reaction to fear: the fear we have learned firsthand from the violence in our lives, and the fear we have been taught to harbor. Both feminism and liberalism have been at their best when they have attacked the multiple dangers that rule people's lives. If we could get rid of the danger, we could get rid of the fear; without the fear, our choices would, I have no doubt, take on great meaning. When we are free of fear, we will indeed be strengthened rather than weakened by the "voluntary transactions" we enter. When we are free of fear, we will be truly autonomous. Then our giving selves—if we choose to be such—will be something to admire rather than disparage. For only then will our generosity, our charity, and our communitarian instincts be true to ourselves as well as nurturant of the needs of others.

Radical Feminism and the Ethical Primacy of Power and Equality

Radical feminism begins with a description of women that is diametrically opposed to that embraced by liberal feminism. Liberal feminists assume a definitional *equality,* a sameness between the female and male experience of consensual choice and then argue that the legal system should respect that fundamental empirical equality. In sharp contrast, radical feminists assume a definitional *inequality* of women—women are *definitionally* the disempowered group—and urge the legal system to eradicate that disempowerment and thereby make women what they presently are not, and this is equal. Radical feminism thus begins with a denial of the liberal feminist's starting assumption. Women and men are *not* equally autonomous individuals. Women, unlike men, live in a world with two sovereigns, the state and men, and this is true not just some of the time but all of the time.[21] A legal regime that ignores this central reality will simply perpetuate the fundamental, underlying inequality.

The cause of women's disempowerment, as well as its effect, is the expropriation of our sexuality. Women are the group, in Catharine MacKinnon's phrase, "from whom sexuality is expropriated,"[22] in the same sense that workers are, definitionally, the group from whom labor is expropriated. Women are the gender from whom sex is *taken*. Women *as women* suffer the threat of acquisitive and potentially violent male sexuality. The threat of male violence and violent sexuality both defines the class *woman* and causes her disempowerment and the expropriation of her sexuality, just as the threat of starvation and material deprivation both defines the worker, and causes his disempowerment and the expropriation of his labor.

This much radical feminism shares with feminism generally. Where radical feminism has departed from feminism, I believe, is in the normative argument it draws from the insight that women are, definitionally, the group from whom sexuality is expropriated. The argument, I believe, owes more to radicalism than to feminism. The argument has three steps.

First, radical feminism, like radical legalism, begins with a highly particularized although largely implicit description of the human being. People are, in short, assumed to be such that there exists a correlation between objectively equal distributions of power, including sexual power, and subjectively happy and good lives.[23] Domi-

21. See MacKinnon, "Agenda," 1; and MacKinnon, "Feminism, Marxism, Method, and the State: Toward Feminist Jurisprudence."

22. The exact quote:

> As the organized expropriation of the work of some for the benefit of others defines a class—workers—the organized expropriation of the sexuality of some for the use of others defines the sex, woman. Heterosexuality is its structure, gender and family its congealed forms, sex roles its qualities generalized to social persona, reproduction a consequence, and control its issue. (MacKinnon, "Agenda," 2; see also 14–15)

23. The assumption that powerlessness and subordination are against our true

nation makes us evil and submission makes us miserable; substantive equality will make us both moral and happy; and both claims are true because of, and by reference to, this conception of our essential human nature.[24] Radicals, including radical feminists, are as committed to the equation of objective, substantive equality and subjective well-being, and the view of our nature on which it rests, as liberals are committed to the equation of objective consent and subjective happiness.

Second, both radicalism and radical feminism draw from this depiction of the human being the normative inference that it is the imbalance of power that facilitates expropriation (of work for the radical legalist, of sex for the radical feminist legalist), rather than the expropriation itself, which is *definitionally* bad, and then the further inference that it is definitionally bad *whether or not the expropriation it facilitates is experientially felt as painful.*[25] The strategic consequence follows: radical legal reform should aim to eradicate hierarchy and thereby attain a substantively equal social world. Thus we should oppose not what makes us miserable—the violent expropriation of our work or our sexuality—but the hierarchy of power that facilitates it, for by doing so we will better target the true cause of our misery.[26] We should support not what makes us happy, but what makes us substantively equal, because by doing so we will invariably further our true interest, even if not our felt pleasure. Thus, radical feminism shares with general radical thought a refusal to ground its opposition to expropriation (whether of sex or work) in the subjective suffering of the disempowered that such expropriation entails. Instead, for both groups expropriation must be opposed because it is symptomatic of the true cause of our misery—our material or sexual disempowerment, respectively—reflecting in turn our relative material or sexual inequality. The radical regards expropri-

---

interest is so pervasive in radical discourse that it is rarely explicated. It does not, of course, imply that the powerless can never feel happy. It does, though, imply that our nature is such that in an ideally equal world, we would be happier, more fulfilled, or more fully human.

24. See MacKinnon, "Agenda." This comes through strongly, although still implicitly rather than explicitly, in MacKinnon's exchange with Carol Gilligan, published in "Feminist Discourse, Moral Values, and the Law—A Conversation," *Buffalo Law Review* 34 (1985): 72–77.

25. MacKinnon, "Agenda," 19–20.

26. Ibid., 19. Also see ibid., 25–26 n. 59.

ation suffered by the disempowered as *bad, not* because the expropriation has been shown to be painful, but instead because it is symptomatic of a larger violation of our essential nature, *and hence of our inherent ideal.*

Finally, radical feminists share with all radicals a methodological insistence that the correlation between objective equality and subjective well-being is foundational and definitional; it is therefore *not* something that can be discredited by counterexample. Both groups of theorists accordingly refuse to credit the phenomenological evidence that the essentially descriptive claims that underlie the normative commitment to substantive equality may be false.[27] Thus, to radicals generally, and to radical feminists in particular, the extent to which the disempowered desire anything other than their own empowerment, and anything at odds with an equalitarian idea, is the extent to which the disempowered are victims of false consciousness. Phenomenological reports by the disempowered of pleasure and desire that counter the radical correlation of equality and subjective well-being thus reinforce, rather than cast in doubt, the radical's definitional assumptions. They reflect the permeating influence of our objective condition, not the limit, imposed by subjective pleasure and desire, of normative ideal.

The striking political contribution of radical *feminist* theory has been to extend the umbrella of the normative argument of radicalism

---

27. The problem is succinctly stated in the following passage:

> In order to account for women's consciousness . . . feminism must grasp that male power produces the world before it distorts it. Women's acceptance of their condition does not contradict its fundamental unacceptability if women have little choice but to become persons who freely choose women's roles. For this reason, the reality of women's oppression is, finally, neither demonstrable nor refutable empirically. Until this is confronted on the level of method, criticism of what exists can be undercut by pointing to the reality to be criticized. Women's bondage, degradation, damage, complicity, and inferiority—together with the possibility of resistance, movement, or exceptions—will operate as barriers to consciousness rather than as means of access to what women need to become conscious of in order to change. (MacKinnon, "Agenda," 28)

Consciousness-raising is itself defined restrictively, so as to minimize conflict between commitment to method and the substantive goal of equality:

> In consciousness raising, often in groups, the impact of male dominance is concretely uncovered and analyzed through the collective speaking of women's experience, from the perspective of that experience. (Ibid., 5–6)

Further attempts to deal with the same problem appear at 20 n. 42, 19–20, and 6 n. 7.

to include women as well as men, and thus to address hierarchies of gender as well as hierarchies dictated by class and race. If hierarchy is bad, then hierarchies and sexual hierarchies according to sex and gender are bad; if disempowerment is a prescription for misery, then women's disempowerment is a prescription for misery; and if expropriation is bad, then expropriation of our sexuality is bad.[28] The radical feminist's commitment to gender equality stems from her empirical insistence that in the only respect that should be of concern to radicals, women and men are *the same:* women, like men, *suffer* from relative disempowerment and inequality and will therefore benefit from empowerment and equality. Women, like men, just are such that objective inequality will cause us subjective misery, and objective empowerment—and thus, equality—will be our script for salvation. The legal strategy is directly entailed. Women are made miserable by inequality and enlivened by equality. What we should do with law, then, if we mean to address the problem of women's suffering, is disable the objective hierarchies of gender that cause it. The scope and depth of women's power must be increased, and the sphere of disempowerment must be shrunk. Legal reform should therefore be directed toward a dismantling of gendered hierarchies.

The inclusion of women under the radical's normative umbrella is a great triumph, but it is costly: the adoption of radical legalist methodology by feminist legal theorists has also occasioned a damaging methodological divide between radical feminism and feminism more broadly construed. Radical feminists, true to their radicalism, refuse to consider whether or not the definitional implication it assumes between objective equality and subjective well-being resonates with women's desires and pleasures, and hence whether the conception of human on which that implication is based is true of *women*. The radical feminist, to the extent that she is a radical, will—must—deny that substantive equality in any sphere could ever be less than ideal or that empowerment of women could ever work to our disadvantage. Thus, to radical feminists, that women on occasion take pleasure in their own submissiveness is simply a manifestation of their disempowered state, not a meaningful counterexample to the posited egalitarian ideal. As with radicalism generally, the stated definitional ideal must trump the experiential counterreport.

28. Thus, the persistent parallelism between work and sex, class and gender, Marxism and feminism. See MacKinnon, "Agenda."

For feminists, this radical methodology should raise serious warning signals. First, we should remember that the ideal and the description of essential human nature on which it rests is itself drawn from a male, if Left, intellectual tradition, and is therefore *not an ideal we should readily assume will be true of women*. The ideal, in other words, against which we are judging our own and each other's consciousness to be false may be an ideal that is true of men, but not women. But second, and perhaps more fundamentally, it is feminism's most crucial insight that *our experience* must be primary—and not to be trumped by posited ideals or definitions. As feminists, we should be wary of our attraction to a masculinist ideal, and we should be evermore concerned when that ideal is then employed to run roughshod over experimental insights, painstakingly unearthed from our consciousness.

A Hedonistic Phenomenological Critique of Radical Feminism

Radical feminists' failure to credit phenomenological reports of conflict between egalitarian ideals and women's subjective, hedonic, felt pleasures is generally benign, for one simple reason. The area of conflict is not great. Women want the fruits of substantive equality and increasingly want them regardless of whether the means for getting them implicate equal treatment of the respects in which we are *like* men, or different treatment of the respects in which we are different. Thus, women both want and would be better off with equal pay for work of comparable worth, equal protection of laws, equal voice in governance, equal access to political, educational, and employment opportunities. Women both want and would be better off with special treatment of the different ways in which pregnancy disables us from employment, affirmative action to correct the decades of exclusion from all-male employment opportunities, and nonparallel, have-it-both-ways legislation that at one and the same time mandates the integration of all-male enclaves and the protection of all-female clubs and schools, if that's what it takes. Women want the goods that substantive equality will deliver. Over vast areas of our lives, there is no conflict between our desires, our felt pleasures, and radical feminist ideals.

In one area of our lives, however, namely our erotic lives, there has emerged a conflict between the radical feminists' conception of an equalitarian ideal and women's subjective desire. The radical feminist's commitment to equality, and identification of the expropriation of our sexuality as the consequence of our relative disempowerment, entails the normative conclusion that sexual inequality *itself* is what is politically undesirable. Thus, male dominance and female submission in sexuality *is* the evil: they express as well as *are* women's substantive inequality. But women report, with increasing frequency and as often as not in consciousness-raising sessions, that equality *in sexuality* is not what we find pleasurable or desirable.[29] Rather, the experience of dominance and submission that goes with the controlled, but fantastic, expropriation of our sexuality is precisely what *is* sexually desirable, exciting, and pleasurable—in fantasy for many, in reality for some. This creates a conflict between theory and method as well as between stated ideal and felt pleasure: What should we *do* when the consciousness that is raised in consciousness-raising finds pleasure in what is definitionally regarded as substantively undesirable—sexual submission, domination, and erotic inequality? In the words of one prominent feminist: "how can you maintain that you desire freedom and equality, when fundamentally [what you desire is to be] a slave?"[30] The conflict between felt pleasure and stated ideal has become a dilemma for feminism, but it has created an unprecedented debacle for our very young feminist legal theory, and one that threatens to be fatal.

The dilemma for feminism, I believe, is a real one; but the crisis atmosphere to which this dilemma has led in feminist legal thought, I will argue, is unnecessary. Radical feminist theorists—distinctively, in feminist literature—respond to the conflict between political ideal and subjective, erotic pleasure by adamantly refusing to address it, and it is that refusal more than the dilemma itself that is threatening the survival of radical feminist legal theory. In the feminist legal literature two strategies of avoidance have emerged. The first, advocated by Andrea Dworkin and Catharine MacKinnon, regards the

29. For some descriptions from heterosexual women, see Snitow, Stansell, and Thompson, *Powers of Desire*; and for some descriptions from lesbian women, see Pat Califia, *Sapphistry: The Book of Lesbian Sexuality* (Tallahasee, Fla: Naiad Press, 1980); and Rubin, "Sexual Politics," 28.

30. Maria Marcus, *A Taste for Pain: On Masochism and Female Sexuality* (New York: St. Martin's, 1981), 210. Subsequent references, abbreviated *TP*, are given in the text.

undeniable reality of the pleasure many women find in the eroticization of controlled submission as simply an example, perhaps an example par excellence, of the false consciousness of the oppressed.[31] The desires reflected in fantasies of erotic domination are false definitionally—they are false because the object of desire is submission, and submission is precisely what is definitionally *un*desirable. The second strategy—advocated by Sylvia Law and Nan Hunter—constitutes in essence a retreat to liberal principles. Fantasies are private and beyond political analysis; the role of law should be to expand, not shrink, the options available to women, including the option, if freely chosen, of masochistic desire, fantasy, practice, and pleasure.[32]

I will examine in another section the pornography debate that these two feminist responses have generated. Here, I want to focus on what the two factions share: *both positions, at critical theoretical junctures, abandon feminist practice*. As a result both positions definitionally exclude the very issue that should be of greatest concern to feminists, and that is the meaning and the value, to women, of the pleasure we take in our fantasies of eroticized submission. The MacKinnon position that the pleasure in erotic submission is false because sexual submission *is* that which is undesirable resolves by definitional fiat what should be resolved by experiential, particularized, contextualized investigation—and that is what these fantasies of eroticized submission mean, what their value is in our lives, and what they can tell us about the desirability as well as the nature of sexual equality and power. The Law/Hunter position that fantasies are free choices that—again definitionally—must like all other choices be respected hides the same issues, but this time in the name of liberal tolerance rather than radical equalitarianism.

This abandonment by feminist theorists of the phenomenological realm of pleasure and desire is a function of liberal and radical legalism, not true feminism. It reflects the extent to which we have embraced the ideals of legalism, whether we regard those ideals as substantive equality, liberal tolerance, privacy, or individual auton-

31. See MacKinnon, "Agenda." Also see E. Morgan, The Eroticization of Male Dominance/Female Submission (1975); and Adrienne Rich, "Compulsory Heterosexuality and Lesbian Existence," *Signs* 5 (1980): 631–60.

32. See the amicus brief filed by Nan Hunter and Sylvia Law on behalf of the Feminist Anti-Censorship Taskforce, in the United States Court of Appeals for the Seventh Circuit, in American Booksellers Association v. William Hudnut, No. 84-3147 (1985).

omy, rather than the methodology of feminism—careful attention to phenomenological narrative. It reflects too the extent to which we have allowed liberal and radical norms drawn from nonfeminist traditions to become the criteria by which we judge the narratives of our lives that emerge from consciousness-raising, *instead of the other way around*. More than any other issue, the pleasure that we obtain from the eroticization of submission poses an indissoluble conflict—or exposes an indissoluble conflict—between feminist method and feminist-legalist ideals, whether that legalism is radical or liberal. Hiding this conflict under the rug, whether in the name of liberal tolerance or radical equality, does far more harm than the conflict itself could ever inflict.

Equalitarian Ideals and Erotic Submission

Consider these two quotes, juxtaposed by the Danish radical feminist Maria Marcus in the introduction to her book on female masochism, *A Taste for Pain*:

> "We regard our personal experience, and our feelings about that experience, as the basis for an analysis of our common situation. . . . The first requirement for raising class consciousness is honesty, in private and in public, with ourselves and other women." Sisterhood Is Powerful (Redstockings Manifesto)
>
> "And Sister, if you can't turn on to a man who won't club you and drag you off by the hair, that's your [hang-up]. Keep your hang-ups the hell out of this revolution." Sisterhood Is Powerful (Lilith's Manifesto) (*TP*, dedication page)

The contours of the conflict between stated ideal and felt pleasure, and between method and theory, with which radical feminism is now grappling, I believe, are starkly brought out in Marcus's detailed, moving, and candid account of her own profoundly ambivalent reaction to *The Story of O*.[33] *The Story of O* is, in Marcus's phrase, a "masochistic pipedream" (*TP*, 197). Written pseudonymously in the midfifties, it is without question the unsurpassed modern masochistic

33. Pauline Reage, *The Story of O* (New York: Grove Press, 1965).

text. It is a stunning piece of pornography. Marcus summarizes the plot thusly:

> Chateau Roissy is owned by a secret brotherhood, and there Rene abandons his lover to the inhabitants and their regime. Briefly, this aims to turn the women who come there into utter slaves, with the aid of force, whips and rape. These means are used according to carefully arranged and familiar rituals—performed sometimes by the gentlemen, sometimes by the servants—and in the course of a few weeks O has become what they wish her to be. She has learned to obey the rules of the mansion, which are all concerned with her three orifices—never to close her mouth; always to be dressed so that she is freely accessible, including from behind. The three orifices are the only things of hers that are of importance, so they no longer belong to her, but only to the men. She may not use her mouth to speak with (except when asked to do so) and neither is she allowed to look on a man's face—she may not raise her eyes above the level of his genitals, her lord and master. . . .
>
> Sir Stephen (her Master) treats her with a mixture of chivalry, contempt and cruelty. He mainly makes use of the orifice most subject to shame . . . he whips her or has her whipped, he lends her to others and talks about her in most brutal terms to the others. . . .
>
> *The Story of O* is the best pornographic book I know for a sadomasochistic public. Just listen to how O is shown the whip:
>
> Her hands were still pinned behind her back. She was shown the riding-crop, black, long and slender, made of fine bamboo sheathed in leather, an article such as one finds in the display-windows of expensive saddle-makers' shops; the leather whip—the one she's seen tucked in the first man's belt—was long, with six lashes each ending in a knot; there was a third whip whose numerous light cords were several times knotted and stiff, quite as if soaked in water, and they actually had been soaked in water, as O was able to verify when they stroked her belly with those cords. . . .

Marcus quickly alludes to the very general conflict between pleasure and democratic political ideal that she perceives to be at least in part the novel's subject matter:

> O's compulsive submissiveness goes against all the ideas we live by in Western democracies, in which every human being is born free and equal and this freedom and equality must not be suppressed. *The Story of O* says the opposite, that some people, possibly all people, are born into inequality and bondage, and can only be happy by losing their false freedom and equality and giving themselves over to submissiveness and slavery. (*TP*, 204)

But Marcus is clear, *The Story of O* is not a story about democracy; it is a "fable about women" (*TP*, 209). She is equally clear that O's masochistic pleasures and desires, like the rest of ours, are socially constructed:

> The Story of O is simply the story of a woman as male society sees her. . . .
>
> O has everything. She is the unaggressive, passive, penis-less little creature adapting to the role offered to her. She accepts all pain as part of her condition. She has an unconscious need for punishment, connected with the fact that her original sadism has turned inwards to become masochism. . . . She is faithful to her feelings, and she has no especially strong superego, which is demonstrated by her accepting no morality except what at any given moment she feels most fits the occasion. She is basically a narcissistic creature reflecting her body and feelings, but she has learnt that she is forbidden to touch her clitoris. She can play with women, but only give herself, and thus know fulfillment as a woman, with men. . . .
>
> O becomes the image of the *natural woman* and many readers will feel (whether they dare admit it openly or not) that it is good and right . . . and that all genuine women belong there. . . . Readers will feel all that, and trust their feelings, for feelings are natural, and anyone who doubts feelings, and starts talking about feelings being influenced by external forces, is at best a cold and bloodless creature in the clutches of the intellect. (*TP*, 206–7)

The analysis would be fine and comfortable if it stopped there; but it does not. Marcus does not simply condemn O and the society that created her. She has an intensely empathic and sexual response to *The Story of O*:

> When I first read *The Story of O*, it filled me with a mixture of sexual excitement, horror, anxiety—and envy. I read it many times, each time with the same feelings. But gradually, as I had the good fortune to plunge to some extent into acting out an "Imitation of O," my envy, anyhow, lessened, because . . . one imitates O with overstepping a boundary into a state which is not particularly enviable.
>
> But I must still say that Pauline Reage is right—the description is correct and I understand O. I understand her pride in the weals from the whip. . . . He owns me. I'm worth owning. Look what he makes me put up with. Look how strong the man who loves me is. Look I'm valuable. I *exist*. I understand that O comes to feel an inner peace, strength, dignity, security and psychic energy in this particular way, an energy that is nothing like anything else I (O) know. (*TP*, 207)

The Story of O, Marcus concludes, is *the* text with which radical feminists must concern themselves, and the magnitude of female readers' responsive, empathic, and erotic response to the text is the issue with which radical feminism must come to grips (*TP*, 209).

Radical feminists have responded, I believe, to the conflict between pleasure and ideal posed by the undeniable female eroticization of sexual submission in three characteristic ways. First, some feminists claim that there is no conflict between stated ideal and felt pleasure because feminist consciousness-raising, properly understood, has revealed the falsity of these pleasures. Thus there is no contradiction between feminist methodology, consciousness-raising, and feminist goal, sexual equality. What the methodology reveals is that the pleasure had in sexual submission is false.

The second response (which was, until very recently, the near-standard feminist response) is simply to abandon feminist methodology. One way of maintaining the ideals of freedom and equality is by abandoning whatever methodology brought you to the conclusion that you enjoy being a sexual slave. If that methodology is feminist consciousness-raising, then so much the worse for consciousness-raising.

The third possible response to the conflict between the pleasure we take in erotic domination and our equalitarian ideals is to put our ideals in abeyance—maybe they are what is false—and hold true to consciousness-raising. This is the position for which I will argue. First I want to comment on the two feminist responses that I think fail.

What I have identified as the first response—the dismissal of the desire for erotic submission and the pleasure obtained from it, as instances of false consciousness *as revealed by consciousness-raising itself*—is, I believe, wildly out of line with the methodology of consciousness-raising, as that method is more widely understood in feminist practice. There is a striking and revealing discontinuity between the criteria by which fantasies of erotic submission are judged as "false," and the criteria by which other felt desires are discovered through consciousness-raising to be false. Feminist consciousness-raising (and the correlative menacing of "false" in the phrase "false consciousness") is governed, I believe, by three methodological principles. First, a woman discovers the falsity of her felt pleasures and desires in consciousness-raising *when she discovers that they are not her own*, when she discovers, quite literally, that she has been seeking the pleasure of others, not herself. The desire and the pleasure had from the desire's satisfaction are subjected to a test of *source*, not substance: Whose desire is it? Whose pleasure is it? Second, she discovers the falsity of her desires when she discovers, again quite literally, that she has been lying, either to herself or others. Thus, the desire and its attendant pleasure are tested by reference to its *genuineness*, not its substance—is it truth or falsehood? The desire (or the pleasure) is discovered to be false when she discovers that what she has been calling desirable is *not* in fact, *to her*, desirable. And third, and perhaps most centrally, she discovers the falsity of her desires when *she herself*, not outside observers, feels their falsity. It is when the subject herself discovers the dysfunction between her purported desire and her discovered identity that the desire is felt to be false and is rightly abandoned.

The feminist position that the desire for and pleasure obtained in erotic submission are false, I believe, flagrantly violates all three of these methodological principles. First, the judgment that women's desires for erotic submission are false is typically made by reference to the *content* of those desires, not their source. The desire for eroticized submission is false because of the content of the desire itself, not because it has been discovered to constitute, in masked form, the desires of others. Second, the desire is judged false not because it is determined to be *a lie*, not truly felt to be pleasurable but only reported as such, but solely because of its content, solely because it is a desire for sexual submission. And, finally and most revealingly, with the noteworthy exception of Justine's and Danu's statements quoted above, the discovery of the falsity of these desires has not typically come from the women who have them, but almost always from the women who do not. The desire is judged to be false, not because the subject herself has come to feel it as false, but because someone else has come to judge it as such. The judgment of falsehood is almost always against the will as well as the opinion of the woman who has the desire. This truly is a profound departure from feminist methodology that is truly offensive; consciousness-raising is not about the imposition of judgments of truth or falsity on the desires of others.

I do not believe that on the basis of a truly feminist consciousness-raising methodology these desires would inevitably be discovered to be false. First, they do not ring of the giving self. The women who have desires for, construct fantasies of, and take pleasure in erotic submission are rather clearly expressing desires, fantasies, and pleasures that are their own. In Maria Marcus's description of her own experience, and her ambivalent response to it, for example, there is nothing to suggest anything other than full ownership of either the desire or the ultimate pleasure:

> Then one day he was there, my Black Prince—my dream lover, the sadist, just like in fairy tales when someone waves a wand. Everything went of its own accord. I didn't even have to provoke him. He did everything I had hoped for in my fantasies. He spoke quietly and menacingly and he beat me, and while in bed, forced me to do humiliating things. I was taken up as high as never before.
>
> But not quite to the top.
>
> I was completely disoriented when this was repeated several times.
>
> . . . I was even more disoriented when shortly after that, I had

> my first orgasm. An orgasm within marriage, after nearly twenty years of active sexual life, after experiencing childbirth and achieving professional success. . . .
>
> I kept wondering what it all meant. . . .
>
> First of all, a colossal tension had been released. The miracle had happened and the prince had been there. . . . He had opened a door into that forbidden room for me. . . .
>
> Secondly, I am sure that prince of mine took me to places where I had never been before, probably right to the beginning of the path and perhaps even quite a way up it—so high that for the first time I didn't immediately register it consciously, I think that glimpse etched itself in so that I did not forget it again. (*TP*, 118–19)

It could, of course, be argued that fantasies of erotic domination are false for the straightforward reason that their verbal articulation reveals them to be such. Pleasure is not pain—they are opposites—and anyone who confuses the two is for that reason alone sustaining false desires. However, the crux of the feminist claim that the pleasure had in fantasies and enactment of erotic submission is false is not that the pleasure is logically incoherent. It is that the pleasure is quite literally *false*, not contradictory: submission is felt to be pleasurable, *but it is not*. Submission is thought to be desirable, *but it is not*. The pleasure is *therefore* on some level a lie, either to others or oneself. And yet, if we examine the accounts of the pleasure had in erotic submission and domination for indicia of lying by any criterion other than content, the charge is singularly hard to substantiate. In this passage, Maria Marcus elaborates on O's enjoyment of her submission, and Marcus's own identification with that enjoyment:

> What [O] finds is that she is becoming happier and happier, happy over the way she is being used, happy over being whipped, happy over not being allowed to speak and happy not to move. . . .
>
> How can she describe the joy, the inner peace and dignity and cleanliness she feels after being whipped and soiled by the sweat and semen of the men and her tears? . . .
>
> At one moment, O is standing naked in a room, two men

> looking at her, and she is waiting obediently for them to give her orders. But something is wrong. She looks appealingly up to Sir Stephen: He understood what the trouble was, smiled, came up to her and, taking her two hands, drew them behind her back and held them pinioned there in one of his. She slid back against him, her eyes shut, and it was in a dream. . . .
>
> Not until the moment O (I) becomes freed of her body, of the use of her arms, of the right to decide for herself, of the right of her own desires—not until the moment I (O) lose my identity, do I find my own identity. Not until that moment is there no longer anything to doubt. Not until that moment have I found my place in a system. . . . At last I can be secure, strong, bold, proud, clean, filled with a great inner peace. At last I find myself—because I have lost myself. At last I have become—O. (*TP*, 202–4)

There is much to be disturbed about in this passage, both in O's reaction and in Marcus's, but it is difficult to find any lies.

Most radical feminists, however, who have encouraged the dismissal of fantasies of erotic domination have justified that dismissal not by reference to criteria stemming from feminist methodology at all, but by reference to feminist and suprafeminist substantive normative standards. To these feminists, the bringing to consciousness of the pleasure women feel in erotic submission simply represents the *limits* of consciousness-raising as feminist methodology. That the dismissal of pleasure cannot be justified by reference to the methodological criteria of consciousness-raising represents not an argument against the dismissal of pleasure, but an argument for abandoning, at precisely that point, the methodology. Thus, it is simply not the case that we should validate whatever emerges in consciousness-raising; there are and should be external criteria or external norms, such as equality or autonomy, by which the content of our pleasures and desires should be judged. Those norms, in turn, are derived not from our felt pleasures, even when those pleasures are fully and correctly identified as our own—but from our political ideals. Where felt pleasure conflicts with derived ideal, ideal must trump; where feminist method reveals antifeminist pleasure, feminist method must cease. In short, if we desire sexual submission, then so much the worse for the primacy of desire, even if—especially if—those desires are revealed to us through feminist consciousness-raising as being very much our own.

Marcus eventually endorses something like this position. Her ultimate suggestion for the fate of female sexual masochism reflects a strongly felt *moral* and even medical judgment that the pleasure, if incorrect, must go:

> Even if we are cured of our authoritarian masochism, we may still suffer some sexual masochism. As long as we do, it will also be used to keep us down, and it will be interpreted as evidence that inwardly we long to submit ourselves to a ruling power. And many women may retain their faith in the link with authoritarian masochism. So if for no other reason, we should do something about it together.
>
> We should try to analyze the origins of sexual masochism, and *even if we cannot, still try to find out how to cure it*—in ourselves and in others. We could set up self-help groups with the aim of mapping muscular tensions that arise when we become sexually stimulated, with or without masochistic elements. We could try to divert sexual arousal so that it does not have to take the route through the head, enabling it to spread unhindered to our soft relaxed receptive sexual organs, *without being soiled by fantasies that we feel are destructive and degrading*.
>
> I think we should plump for the physical way, because the psychic way is so intangible and complicated that it would demand too much of us. But together, in groups, we might be able to cope with the physical track, in the way we have learned to cope with so much else.
>
> If we do it together, we may learn to cope with the violent physical dramas that would presumably take place when resistance is swept away and orgasm threatens to break right through. For we know each other and we know ourselves. . . .
>
> *The aim must be to allocate our problems—our female masochism—their right place and no more. . . . [W]e have to deal with sexual masochism and if possible dispose of it*—not because it is shameful, but because in itself *it is much we can well do without. . . . I will try to be cured of my sexual masochism*, or

else to live with it without feeling compromised when faced with the women's movement or the rest of the world. (*TP*, 252–60)

This abandonment of consciousness-raising as method and its concomitant dismissal of women's internal lives as a criterion of value in favor of an objective political agenda has at least three costs. First, it has already done and will continue to do enormous damage to our integrity. As Adrienne Rich has eloquently argued, one of women's most disabling problems is that women *lie*.[34] For a multitude of reasons, we lie to ourselves and to others. And one thing women lie about more than any other, perhaps, is the quality and content of our own hedonic lives. We tell others we are happy when we are not; we tell others that our marriages are good when they are in fact brutal; we tell others we are orgasmic when we are not; we tell others we are sexually fulfilled when we are deprived. We smile on the street, we express pleasure, when we are being threatened and feeling pain. One reason we lie, perhaps more than any other, is to fulfill the politically dictated expectations of others. We say we are flattered, happy, fulfilled, orgasmic, because the social and political visions of others demand that we should be so. This lying has hurt us. We lie so often we don't know when we are doing it. We lie so often we lack the sense of internal identity necessary to the identification of a proposition's truth or falsity. We lie so often that we lack a self who lies. We just *are* lies; we inhabit falsehood. Our lives are themselves lies.

Consciousness-raising, more than any other feminist methodology, has given women a means by which to break the chain of deception in which we live. By learning to identify the falsehoods we utter, we have learned to create a self who can assert a truth. Consciousness-raising is the discovery of the power of *truth*, not just *a* truth. When we abandon consciousness-raising we run the risk of losing truth. We run a high risk of losing ourselves again in yet another morass of deception. We run the risk of once again living a lie. We run the risk of once again having to *feel* subjectively what it is forbidden to *be* objectively, and we will once again end up paying the piper. I am not willing to take that risk.

34. Adrienne Rich, *On Lies, Secrets, and Silence: Selected Prose, 1966–1978* (New York: Norton, 1979).

Second, if feminists abandon consciousness-raising as a method in favor of an authoritatively pronounced objective ideal, many women will pay by forgoing a source of sexual pleasure. This is not a trivial sacrifice. When we deny what gives us sexual pleasure, and when we thereby deny ourselves that sexual pleasure itself—when we deny both truth and pleasure—we deny not just one but two important aspects of our selves. We become, yet again *not entitled;* this time—and, let's not forget, not for the first time—not entitled to sexual pleasure. We become, once again, sexually *errant*. (God damn: Wrong *again!*) We become, if we forgo the sexual pleasure we have earned to own, once again, the conveyors of sexual pleasure for others, and once again, our role will be dictated by someone else's conception of sexual right and wrong.

Third, if we give up on feminist consciousness-raising, we will be giving up a method of self-creation that has, for many women, *worked*. We have learned through consciousness-raising to trust our experiences. We have learned to give meaning to those experiences, and to validate the meanings they teach. We have learned to assert hidden experiences as meaningful—full of meaning. By giving meaning to the past, we have acquired some sense of control of the future. If we now shift ground, if we now begin to test the validity of our lived experiences by reference to political ideals, we run the risk of forgetting. We run the risk of forgetting the exhilaration of self-affirmation and self-creation. We run the risk of forgetting the pleasure of shared trust. We run the risk of forgetting the importance of learning to identify, acknowledge, and act on the desires we have painstakingly learned to honor as our own. We run the risk of giving ourselves once again, this time for principle rather than protection.

The third response to the problem posed by women's enjoyment of erotic submission, endorsed by a small but growing number of radical feminists, is to understand rather than judge these pleasures in their historical context and in their full experiential truth. The first requires study of history; the latter requires information that can only be gained through consciousness-raising, and with no political prejudgments. Such an understanding, I believe, is essential to any dynamic future for radical feminism. First, only by such a process will we achieve any meaningful understanding of these pleasures, but we will not achieve that so long as we allow stated ideals to trump and silence felt pleasure. But second, I believe, only by understanding our felt pleasures will we achieve any meaningful understanding of our stated ideals. We cannot possibly give content to the substantive equality we seek until we understand the erotic appeal of submission. If we can identify what human needs are met through eroticized submission, perhaps we can better understand and identify the human needs that will be met or frustrated through political, legal, and economic equality.

Jessica Benjamin describes the danger of this explanatory and nonjudgmental approach:

> [An analysis of the controlled, ritualized, rational form of violence characteristic of sadomasochism] is probably not applicable to all forms of violence, or even all male violence against women. . . . There are a great many other forms of violence against women which do not partake of this rational character, in which women are simply assaulted and cannot successfully defend themselves. The danger is that even in such cases women blame themselves and feel guilty for prosecuting the assailant. This makes the topic of rational violence or erotic domination, where participation is voluntary or only a fantasy, seem to some a subtle apology for all male violence.[35]

She then warns of a deadened future if we fail to meet the danger:

> A politics that denies these issues, that tries to sanitize or rationalize the erotic, fantastic components of human life, will not defeat domination, but only play into it. The power of a fantasy, the fantasy of rational violence, must be attributed to the interplay of great social forces and deep human needs. Finding the means to dissolve that fantasy, so as to tolerate the tension between true differentiation and mutual recognition, will be no easy achievement.[36]

On this issue no less than any other, women must face the high

35. Jessica Benjamin, "The Bonds of Love: Rational Violence and Erotic Domination," in Eisenstein and Jardine, *Future of Difference*, 42.

36. Ibid., 66.

risks posed by honesty if we are going to avoid the sure dead end of self-deception.

The Erotic Appeal of Submission

I believe that sexual submission has erotic *appeal* and *value* when it is an expression of *trust* and is damaging, injurious, and painful when it is an expression of *fear*. Here, I want to emphasize—I hope not overemphasize—the value of sexual submission when it is an expression of trust, because that, I believe, is the source of the pleasure women find in voluntary and fantasized erotic submission, in all of its forms. Absolutely pliant obedience, the willingness to transform one's subjectivity into another's object, is sexually arousing (for some) when it enables the submissive subject to transcend her own selfhood, and thereby to abdicate her responsibility for her own action. That this total abdication of responsibility can be erotic, I think, reflects a genuine human truth and a deep human need. It can be pleasurable and exhilarating and sometimes so much so that it is sexually stimulating to forgo authorship of one's actions. When we grant power to another to control, to author, our acts, that grant *may*—and I have argued in the last section often does—express a deep-seated and forgotten (or not so forgotten) fear. But it might not. It *might* be trustworthy. That placing trust in one who is stronger is felt by some to be intensely pleasurable, and that the fantasy of doing just that is felt by many more to be so, should teach us something.

Jessica Benjamin's powerful interpretation of *The Story of O* is complex, but on this central point (I think) she is in agreement. Thus, Benjamin says of O:

> If we accept the idea that O's consent to pain and enslavement is a search for transcendence, we still want to know why she chooses this form, rather than the possibility of mutual, reciprocal giving of self. [The answer may be that the form she chooses] allows one partner to remain rational and in control, while the other loses her boundaries. In fact, it is the master's rational, calculating, even instrumentalizing attitude which excites submission. . . . The pleasure, for both partners, is in his mastery. Were both partners to give up self, . . . this disorganization of self would be total. . . . O could not then experience her

> loss of control as controlled loss. She could not safely give in to her urge to lose control.[37]

Benjamin concludes:

> I believe that we are facing unbearably intensified privatization and discontinuity, unrelieved by expressions of continuity. Given that social structure and instrumental culture enforce individual isolation so rigidly, the transgression which attempts to break it may necessarily be more violent. . . . The more rigid and tenacious the boundary between individuals and the more responsible each individual for maintaining it, the greater the danger it will collapse. If the sense of boundary is established by physical, bodily separation, then sexual and physical violence (if not in reality, in fantasy) are experienced as ways of breaking the boundary. *The fantasy as well as the playing out of rational violence does offer a controlled form of transcendence, the promise of the real thing. Sadomasochistic imagery may be popular because it embodies this promise of transcendence without its fearful reality*. Similarly, if masochists far outnumber sadists, it may be because people are in flight from discontinuity and rationality—especially men who have been charged with upholding it.[38]

Are the desires to "know and be known," to trust another, to blend in identity, at least sometimes expressed in the eroticization of submission and dominance, of any value, and do they express anything of value? Or are they soiled by their extremity, by their expression in forms that implicate "sweat and semen," whips and whiplashes, marks of obedience, and of objectification? *When* (if ever) and *why* (if ever) are these desires and the pleasure felt in their satiation beautiful? When are they *not* "muck we could well do without?" If they cannot, as I have argued they cannot, be entirely dismissed as false, can they be in any sense affirmed as truth? *It's a close question*. Minimally, as Jessica Benjamin has argued, they remind us of the hedonistic limits, the limits of pleasure, pain, and desire, upon the otherwise near-relentless quest by both feminist and nonfeminists for

37. Ibid., 53–58.
38. Ibid., 65.

the fruits of liberal individualism—of subjective autonomy, of severe differentiation, and, in Benjamin's language, of "discontinuity and rationality."[39] That so many women and more than a few men undeniably take pleasure in controlled objectification may be testimony to the limit of the desirability of the pure subjectivism endorsed by virtually all forms of liberalism, including feminist liberal legalism. In a parallel fashion, the fact that many women and more than a few men take pleasure from sexual submission can be read as a critique of the absolutist commitment to substantive equality endorsed by radicalism of all forms, including radical feminism. The trust expressed by the submissive party *in a controlled* and unequal sexual encounter is such a high pleasure that it is erotic. That *fact*, that the trust felt by the submissive party in controlled inequality *is* pleasurable, should serve to remind us that to the extent that absolute equality comes at the cost of the trust of which human beings are capable, often expressed in the consensual abandonment of autonomy and relinquishment of control over oneself to another, that equality will come at a cost.

The lesson of the pleasure in eroticized submission is not that we should forsake either individualism or equality as ultimately undesirable. Nor is it the case that the woman who enjoys fantasies of erotic domination would enjoy literal servitude, or for that matter thinks she would. The lesson—the truth—of the erotic pleasure many feel in controlled submission may be this: while we crave liberal autonomy and radical equality, while we crave the freedom that the liberal feminist pursues and the equality the radical feminist envisions, *at least in this society as it is presently constituted, we also crave, because we also need, the capacity to trust one another, including those who are stronger than we are*. The weak and the strong are in fact interdependent in this society—we *aren't* equally autonomous individuals—and that means the weak need to be able to depend on the strong. The capacity to safely depend on another, to look after one's own well-being, is a desirable state, and it is no great mystery that it is pursued as pleasure. When we test the limits of our capacity to trust, of our willingness to embrace absolute dependency, and when we discover erotic pleasure lurking at that limit, we give expression to our desire to be able to trust someone who is strong and trustworthy, which may be simply a human, and not just female, need.

39. Ibid.

Either trust or fear can prompt us to submit to the will of the other. Trust is enlivening, and fear is deadening. There is a difference. It is a subjective, internal, hedonic difference. It is the difference between the battered woman's consensual endurance—motivated by fear—of beatings, and the lover's consensual enjoyment—motivated by trust—of controlled submission. The first submission is deadening, the second (can be) enlivening. It is a difference we will only be able to *see*, much less understand, if we look at our *internal* lives. From an external perspective, this difference may be muted. From an internal perspective, it is glaring.

There is, *of course*, a danger in this. There is a danger in the pleasure of submission just as there is a limit to the desirability in the nonsexual world of relationships of dependence and trust. *The Story of O*, to its credit, makes this quite clear. Any reading of O, Marcus rightly insists, that celebrates the very good trip at the beginning, but fails to come to grips with the very bad trip at the end, is a betrayal of O:

> [It] is a game with high stakes, and you never get anything for nothing. O does not know this. But Pauline Reage knows very well, which is why *The Story Of O* is such a strong book, because she shows both sides, the gains *and* the losses.
>
> How does O pay?
>
> She sells with her own body, the right to her own body, her own pleasure. She sells her ability to speak. . . . She sells her relations with other people. For those lives isolated from the world about her. She particularly sells her relations with other women, for she can only betray them. . . . She sells her ability to stand on her own. She sells her ability to act, and her will, her responsibility and her individuality. She sells her emotions and finally her own death. She has nothing left. . . .
>
> On the way, O feels a security she cannot do without and cannot acquire in any other way. But at the bitter end, she is alone, disguised as an animal, . . . dumb, without feeling. If it were ever a good trip, it ends as a bad one. She has given herself up and has received nothing in exchange. Only the rest of them have gained. (*TP*, 207–8)

At the end of the story, O is dead, but her subjectivity dies long before that "bitter end," as has, I suspect, most women's erotic enjoyment of her exploits. At some point O becomes a real slave, not a play slave, and I suspect it is at that point that, for most female readers, the book loses its erotic appeal and becomes a nightmare. At some point, O becomes entirely devoid of subjectivity; at some point she can no longer control her relinquishment of self. But this leaves questions, not grounds for condemnation. At *what* point does the pleasure become deadly? Is the ending true to the character development that preceded it? Are we running the risk that O runs if we take pleasure in her exploits? In our own lives, at what point should we unequivocally seek to disown, to shed, our pleasures as coming with too high a risk of danger? When the pleasure is no longer pleasure, when it is no longer backed by trust? When it has given way to a numbing terror, when it is backed by fear? Or at an earlier point, when we suspect that such a transformation might occur? Or even at an earlier point, when in someone else's judgment, such transformation might occur?

I believe these questions should be undertaken and answered. *At some point* in O's progression, she crosses a volitional threshold: at some point she is no longer able to leave. At some point she also crosses a hedonic threshold: at some point she no longer feels pleasure. If we can specify when and why that occurs, we can better understand why her story (up until that point) is so erotic, as well as why her story (past that point) is so frightening. If we do that, I believe, we will better understand the reason we take pleasure in sexual submission, and that understanding, in turn, may lead us to a deeper understanding of the value of trust and submission. More importantly, it will clarify the danger, evidenced by our empathic and frightened response to O's eventual enslavement and death, of sexual submission past the threshold. That understanding, in turn, can only clarify the basis of our pure political commitment to equality.

Radical Feminist Legal Reform: The Pornography Debate

As I said at the outset of this section, the radical feminist's refusal to engage in phenomenological critique of the ideal, substantive equality, she proposes, is usually benign, for the straightforward reason that generally there is no conflict between our felt pleasures, once we have correctly identified them, and radical feminist ideals of political and substantive equality. Occasionally, though, her refusal to check stated objective ideal against felt subjective pleasure will result in a misfire. The feminist antipornography movement is a now-notorious instance of just such a misfire.

Catharine MacKinnon asks, again and again, why feminists are defending the rights of pornographers.[40] The question is a very good one: if the antipornography ordinance devised by MacKinnon and Andrea Dworkin offends the First Amendment rights of pornographers, let the ACLU make the argument. I believe that the First Amendment issue for feminists is a sincerely felt feminist concern. The FACT (Feminists Against Censorship Taskforce) women, I'm sure, do genuinely fear that censorship will hurt women (as opposed to hurting pornographers) more than pornography hurts women, and they may be right. I also believe, though, that the First Amendment is not the only reason feminists are opposing the ordinance. I want to suggest another reason and, thereby, suggest how we might repair the damage caused by the conflict among feminists.

The MacKinnon-Dworkin antipornography ordinance and the theory behind it defines and targets pornography as the subordination of women through sexually explicit graphic or textual means.[41] *Subordination* is (unfortunately) not defined, but nevertheless the ordinance rests on the clear normative premise that it is bad.[42] Furthermore, to "submit" is to consent to one's subordination. Sexual submission, then, is likewise bad. More directly, sexual submission is bad because submission itself is bad, and submission is bad because equality is good, and equality is good because people, definitionally, simply are such that equality is good. Yet many women, including some feminists and some lesbians, don't *feel* sexual submission as

40. At the 1985 National Conference for Women and the Law, as well as in any number of other forums. She has not, to my knowledge, addressed the issue in print.

41. The model ordinance I am using is reprinted as appendix A in "The MacKinnon/Dworkin Model Anti-Pornography Law," *New England Law Review* 20 (1985): 759–62. See sec. 2 of that document.

42. We badly need radical feminist definitions of *subordination, submission, inequality, power, and powerlessness*. If these words are to have the normative meanings generally associated with them in male progressive or radical legalism, we need a feminist defense of that endorsement. If they mean something different, we need to hear the difference. Gilligan makes the same point in MacKinnon and Gilligan, "Feminist Discourse," 74.

bad. In fact, many women feel sexual submission as pleasurable, as so pleasurable as to be erotic, and as so erotic as to be orgasmic. And many women have come to this understanding of themselves and of their pleasure through consciousness-raising sessions. The antipornography ordinance has defined the depiction or expression of sexual submission as objectively bad, when for many women both the thing expressed and its expression is subjectively pleasurable. The ordinance raises the conflict between objective ideal and subjective pleasure, and the result has been chaos.

First, a historical reminder—it was not always thus. When the antipornography campaign commenced in the late seventies and early eighties, there was *widespread* feminist consensus on the evil of pornography. That consensus, it now goes without saying, has dissolved. Why? One reason might be this: in the early days of the campaign feminists understood the evil of pornography to be that it causes *violence* (and more specifically sexual violence) against women.[43] Now, antipornography advocates urge that the evil of pornography is not that it causes *violence* against women, but that it *subordinates* women, on the theory, no doubt, that the former is symptom, the latter is root cause. The shift from violence to subordination has splintered the movement, for, I think, primarily the reason noted above: subordination is taken to be both reflected in and caused by sexual submission, and consensual, controlled, sexual submission, is hedonically, for many, pleasurable.

This is the lesson I draw: we might be able to rebuild a consensus

43. Pornography is characterized in both the model ordinance and in the Minneapolis and Indianapolis versions as sex discrimination and as central in creating and maintaining sex as a basis of discrimination. The first charge presents a highly controversial theory of the relation between the depiction of discrimination and discrimination itself—between Little Black Sambo and racial oppression—while the latter presents a counterintuitive and counterhistorical thesis about the multiple causes of women's oppression.

Contrast this claim: "Pornography leads to violence against women and is central in maintaining sex as a basis for permissible violence." This latter claim may be equally controversial among feminists but it is also, I believe, more intelligible. Whether true or false, it does not rest on undefined terms. And, for that reason, it gives us a better idea of how to draw lines. I believe, for example, that sexism, discrimination, and sexuality are so pervasive in this culture that practically every depiction of sexuality in the popular media fits the Minneapolis definition. But only a discrete subcategory of that literature even arguably causes violence. It shouldn't be impossible—the Meese Commission has at least made the attempt—to define the boundaries of that subcategory.

on pornography by focusing our attention on the harm we want to eradicate, rather than on the classification or description of the thing we want to prohibit. I suggest we go back for a moment to what we know of our own pleasure and pain and *trust* it. What we all know—and by "all" I mean, on some level, all women—to be undeniably painful is the expropriation of our sexuality that is motivated by *fear,* sexual submission under threat or memory of sexual compulsion, the ever-present threat of that expropriation, the fear that the threat engenders, the danger with which we consequently live, and the torture we endure when the fear proves to have been horrifically well grounded. When we give ourselves because we have been taught to *and the teacher is fear,* the giving is *not pleasurable*. It is painful. The transaction is neither erotic, pleasurable, nor valuable; it is damaging and deadening. Both the coercive *and the consensual* relinquishment of control expressed in sexual relationships that are grounded in fear are damaging, painful, unpleasant, deadening, and not at all erotic. Relinquishment of control over one's body that is motivated by fear is damaging *whether or not the external indicia of consent to the relationship or transfer are present*. Pornographic literature that facilitates by legitimating *either* the violent expropriation of our sexuality or fear-induced *giving* (so as not to be one from whom sexuality is taken) hurts us. It damages us. It injures us. If pornography proximately causes that injury and the proximity is provable, it should be civilly actionable.

By contrast, the relinquishment of authority and responsibility expressed in masochistic sexual fantasy and controlled masochistic practice at least sometimes constitutes a willed sexual submission motivated by *trust*, not fear. When motivated by trust, that submission can be pleasurable, erotic, and therefore valuable. Erotic literature that facilitates sexual fantasies or consensual practices (or understanding of those fantasies) that express and give rise to the experience of trust, can, I think, be pleasurable, erotic, and of value regardless of the content of the fantasy or the practice.

There is no contradiction in holding both of these positions simultaneously. They pose a difficult question of causation, but that's a far cry from a disabling *contradiction* between theory and method or ideal and pleasure. We need to know what pornography hurts and endangers us and what pornography frees or enlivens us. This may be a very difficult factual question; it may be too difficult, but it does not give rise to a contradiction. Fire too sometimes warms and sometimes burns, but it is not, after all, *always* hard to know the difference between warmth and burns. We need to know whether we can differentiate and describe the subcategory of what is now overdefined as pornography that hurts women by encouraging, validating, or legitimating the violent expropriation through fear of our sexuality. Mounting evidence suggests that violent, pictorial pornography does precisely that, and if so, we should pursue a world that is rid of it. But we should be clear: it is the *injuries* that pornography causes, the violent expropriation of our sexuality, that is the "muck we can live without." The injury pornography causes is the expropriation, through violence, force, coercion, terror, and fear, of our sexuality. If pornography injures us in this way, then we should rid ourselves of it, but not because it embodies or expresses a pleasure we have defined as undesirable. We should be rid of it because, and to the extent that, we discover that it hurts.

I have no doubt that a lot of pornography injures us in just this way. I have no doubt that pornography can precipitate sexual violence, because it has happened to me. I know that pornography legitimates sexual coercion and cruelty. I also know that women are coerced to participate in pornography, and I know that the violence depicted in pornography is, more often than we would like to think, a recording and not a simulation of real violence. I also, though, have no doubt that some pornography, as defined under the MacKinnon-Dworkin ordinance, is pleasurable to women and occasionally profoundly so. The depiction of sexual domination and submission is for many women sexually arousing, and for some women it constitutes an important avenue of sexual release. Women do find pleasure in sexual submission, occasionally in its graphic representation, and often in its textual description. The understanding and eradication of the sources of women's suffering is obviously an important feminist goal. But it is also, or ought to be, an important item on any feminist agenda to facilitate the exploration of women's sources of pleasure. Women take pleasure, and often intense pleasure, in erotized submission. Whatever causes women pleasure without causing attendant pain is something we should celebrate, not censure.

Empirically, we need to know what subcategory of pornography as it is now defined significantly contributes to the violent expropriation of our sexuality. That is the injury, and *that* pornography should be actionable. As the WAVAW insists: NO WOMAN WANTS THAT. Sexual violence, and the harm it does, is the evil facilitated and sometimes proximately caused by pornography. When we respond to violence, we give ourselves in fear: that is never pleasurable and never felt to be such. But pornography that depicts sexual relationships of domination and submission that does not legitimate or encourage the violent, forced, coercive expropriation of sexuality—even if it depicts unquestionably hierarchical sex—regardless of content and regardless of whether we call it S-M porn, butch-fem porn, soft-core porn, romance, or erotica—may well be relatively harmless, is probably a pleasure for many, and might be liberating for a few. If it is harmless, we ought to enjoy it if we want to, learn from it if we can, and otherwise leave it alone. The sexual violence that pornography may cause, not the erotic domination it may depict, should be the key to what is actionable (and whether it is actionable) for the simple reason that it is the sexual violence in our lives, and not erotic domination, that hurts us.

I think the crisis in radical feminism that the pornography debate has engendered is false, for this reason. First, it is at least possible that on this issue we can have it both ways. Many of us are debating the pornography issue without having looked at much of it. We have a category in mind that might not be a sensible category. If we *look* at what is presently and too broadly defined as pornography, we might discover that the pornography that hurts us, the pornography that contributes to the violent expropriation of our sexuality, is not so hard to distinguish from the pornography that doesn't hurt us and that might be pleasurable, the description of controlled erotic submission. For example, it may just be *true*—the Meese report suggests it is—that pictures are more prone to cause violence than words, and that violent pictures are more prone to cause violence than nonviolent pictures. It may also be true—sales of pornography to women suggest it is—that *words* are erotic in the way described above while pictures of dominance and submission are not. *The Story of O*, unquestionably violent, is, as Marcus suggests, a "lyrical poem" (*TP*, 200). Whatever else it is, it is *words*.

It also, of course, may not be true. *The Story of O*, no matter how erotic as text, might be proximately causing literally untold misery—silenced, actual, fearful, terrifying enslavements—and *no woman wants that*. If it is, then we cannot have it both ways, and as Wendy Williams has said in a different context, where we can't have it both ways we have to think carefully about which way we want to have it.[44] In my own mind, I have no doubt: if *The Story of O* is being reenacted in real life on some farm somewhere in the hills of Kentucky right through to the bitter end, then we can all live without *The Story of O*. For me, this is not a close question, although it may be for others. But again, this poses a choice, and even if it is a hard choice, that is a far cry from a disabling contradiction. Erotic energy, no less than clean, cheap nuclear energy, comes with a price, and the price of both energies may be too high.

Finally, we should draft an ordinance that properly targets the real injury without offending First Amendment principles; first because we have to and second because those First Amendment principles further more than they hinder feminist goals. We *need* at least some of this literature, and we need it for genuinely liberal as well as genuinely feminist reasons. First, we need to understand our ideals better than we presently do. The sexual high many women reach from controlled objectification, domination, and submission might stem from the pleasure of trust that can accompany inequality. Then again, it might not. But either way it would be nice to *know*. There may be contained in that pleasure the kernel of a critique of our dominant ideals of individual autonomy and equality. If we really believe that the personal is political, that should not sound ludicrous. It might, of course, be both nonludicrous and wrong: all that might be contained in our pleasure is a reflection of the extent of our debasement. But we won't know one way or the other unless we think about it, and we won't think about it so long as we regard the subject as taboo. One way to start thinking about it is to come to grips with the erotica, the textual representation of controlled sexual domination and submission, that pleases us.

Conclusion: Women's Difference, and an Alternative Standard for a Feminist Critique of Law

Although liberal and radical legalism are typically contrasted, as I contrasted them in the bulk of this chapter, I want to suggest in this conclusion that the proxies for well-being of liberalism and radicalism,

44. Williams, "Equality Crisis," 175, 195.

choice and power respectively, are so at odds with women's subjective, hedonic lives because liberal and radical legalism share an assumption. They share a vision of the human being, and therefore of our subjective well-being, as autonomous. The liberal insists that choice is necessary for the true exercise of that autonomy, and thus is an adequate proxy for subjective well-being, while the radical insists the same for power.[45] But this strategic difference should not blind us to their commonality. Both the liberal and the radical legalist have accepted the Kantian assumption that *to be human* is to be in some sense autonomous, meaning, minimally, to be differentiated, or individuated, from the rest of social life.

Underlying and underscoring the poor fit between the proxies for subjective well-being endorsed by liberals and radicals—choice and power, and women's subjective, hedonic lives is the simple fact that women's lives, *because of our biological, reproductive role*, are drastically at odds with this fundamental vision of human life. Women's lives are *not* autonomous; they are profoundly relational. This is at least the biological reflection, if not the biological cause, of virtually all aspects, hedonic and otherwise, of our difference. Women, and *only* women, and *most* women, transcend *physically* the differentiation or individuation of biological self from the rest of human life trumpeted as the norm by the entire Kantian tradition. When a woman is pregnant her biological life embraces the embryonic life of another. When she later nurtures children, her needs will embrace their needs. The experience of being human, for women, differentially from men, includes the counterautonomous experience of a shared physical identity between woman and fetus, as well as the counterautonomous experience of the emotional and psychological bond between mother and infant.[46]

45. Liberal feminism's embrace of "pro-choice" rhetoric as the language in which to couch their advocacy of reproductive freedom is the most obvious reflection of this commitment. The claim that "a woman has the right to control her own body" similarly reflects the liberal's belief that choice is central to our physical, as well as legal claim to autonomy.

MacKinnon's belief that women's relationality reflects our victimization, not our essence, is vividly conveyed in her exchange with Gilligan in the Buffalo symposium. See MacKinnon and Gilligan, "Feminist Discourse," 74–76.

46. I am describing the way women's lives are, not the way they should be or have to be. If men became more nurturant of children, they too would become less autonomous. My general point is that whatever subclass of adult human beings nurture the young will be relatively less autonomous than the subclass that does not.

Our reproductive role renders us nonautonomous in a second, less obvious, but ultimately more far-reaching sense. Emotionally and morally women may benefit from the dependency of the fetus and the infant upon us. But *materially* we are burdened rather than enriched by that dependency. And because we are burdened, we differentially depend more heavily upon others, both for our own survival and for the survival of the children who are part of us. Women, more than men, depend upon relationships with others because the weakest of human beings, infants, depend upon us.

Thus, motherhood leaves us vulnerable: a woman giving birth is unable to defend herself against aggression; a woman nursing an infant is physically exposed; a woman nurturing and feeding the young is less able to feed herself. Motherhood leaves us unequal: because of her distinctive nurturing role, a mother is either stronger or weaker than those to whom she is closest. She is stronger than the infant, and because of her nurturing response to the weak infant she is herself weaker than her autonomous brother. Most assuredly, then, a mother is not *autonomous;* she is both depended upon and thereby dependent on others. She depends upon others, as others who are weaker depend upon her. To whatever degree the reality of or potentiality for motherhood defines ourselves, women's lives are relational, not autonomous. As mothers we nurture and are nurtured by an interdependent and hierarchical natural web of others.

The goals the liberal and radical seek, increased freedom and increased equality, respectively, are surely intended to benefit the subjective well-being of human beings. That is, they are intended to benefit the subjective well-being of autonomous creatures. If it is true that women's lives are differentially more relational than autonomous, and if autonomy is a necessary attribute of a human being, then women's difference rather abruptly implies that women are not human beings. Politics that are designed to benefit human beings, including liberal and radical legalism, will leave women out in the cold.

This is not a novel insight: that women are not human as human is now conceived has in a sense always been the dominant problem for feminism. But the two characteristic ways in which modern feminists have responded to this dilemma are both, I think, flawed. The liberal feminist's solution is to deny it. The fact that women become pregnant, give birth, and nurse infants is a difference that *does not count*. It does not make us any less autonomous than men.[47] For

47. As Sylvia Law says, "An assimilationist vision that ignores differences

reasons that by now should be familiar, this response does not work: if the last half-century has taught us anything at all, it is that this liberal strategy of denial is a disservice.[48] If we embrace a false conception of our nature, we can be sure of only one thing, and that is that legal reform based on such a conception will only occasionally, and then only incidentally, benefit real instead of hypothetical women.

The radical feminist's proposal is that we seek to *become* autonomous creatures. We are indeed not autonomous, but what that reflects is our lack of power—our social, political, and legal victimization—not our essential nature. To the extent that we become autonomous by gaining power, we will *become* the beneficiaries of the legal system designed to promote the well-being of just such people.[49] This radical vision is at root deeply assimilationist. By gaining power, we become equal; as we become equal, we become less "relational"—meaning less victimized. As we become less relational, we become more autonomous, and as we become more autonomous, we become more like human beings—more like men. Radical assimilation, though, has costs no less weighty (and no less familiar) than liberal denial. There is no guarantee that women can become autonomous human beings, no guarantee that women want to, and at heart, no persuasive argument that women should.

A very new and promising response, which does not fit easily within the liberal and radical models, is that feminists should insist on women's humanity, and thus on our entitlement, and on the wrongness of the dominant conception of what it means to be a human being. We should insist, as Christine Littleton has argued, for an equal "acceptance of our difference."[50] This third course is surely more promising—it has truth and candor on its side—but without hedonistic criticism it is insufficient: *Which* differences are to be accepted? If the root of our differences is that our lives are relational

between men and women does not help us to reconcile the ideal of equality with the reality of difference." Sylvia Law, "Rethinking Sex and the Constitution" *University of Pennsylvania Law Review* 132 (1984): 955–1040. See also Ann C. Scales, "Towards a Feminist Jurisprudence," *Indiana Law Journal* 56 (1981): 375–444.

48. See Law, "Rethinking Sex."

49. Compare MacKinnon, who wants to "get the boot off of women's necks," with Dinnerstein, who wants to share the burden of child rearing. Both view women's lack of autonomy as the obstacle to full participation in society, and accordingly as the cause of women's misery. Compare MacKinnon and Gilligan, "Feminist Discourse," with Dinnerstein, *Mermaid and the Minotaur*.

50. See Christine Littleton, "Toward a Redefinition of Sexual Equality," *Harvard Law Review* 95 (1981): 487.

rather than autonomous, which is reflected in our differential endurance of pain, or is our differentially negative self-esteem, then acceptance of those differences will backfire. We need more than just acceptance of our differences; we need a vocabulary in which to articulate and then evaluate them, as well as the power to reject or affirm them.

My proposal is that we address the multiple problems posed by our differences from men by adopting a critical method that aims directly for women's subjective well-being, rather than indirectly through a gauze of definitional presuppositions about the nature of human life that almost invariably exclude women's lives. We should aim, simply, to increase women's happiness, joy, and pleasure, and to lessen women's suffering, misery, and pain. As feminist legal critics we could employ this standard: a law is a good law if it makes our lives happier and less painful and a bad law if it makes us miserable or stabilizes the conditions that cause our suffering. A shift toward this direct hedonism, I believe, would do four things for feminist legal theory.

First, a move toward hedonistic criticism would free us from false conceptions of our nature. Our present quality discourse (whether cast in terms of equal freedom or equal power) has forced us to accept dominant visions of the human being whose equality we seek. By forgoing proxies for subjective well-being that are in turn derived from those visions, and insisting instead on pleasure and pain, happiness and misery, joy and sorrow as our central normative categories, we can remain agnostic toward varying definitional conceptions of who we are.

Second, a move toward hedonistic criticism would facilitate an unclouded articulation of the quality of women's hedonic lives. When we try to squeeze descriptions of our lives into the parameters laid out for us, the results are often not just distorted, but profoundly anomalous. We are trying too hard to assimilate, in our theory as well as in our professional and personal lives.

Third, I believe, a shift toward a discourse that would focus attention on the pain in women's lives, and away from the oppression and subordination we suffer, would make us more effective. If we are ever going to make progress in alleviating women's misery, surely an important goal for feminists, we must insist loudly upon the normative significance of our hedonic lives. To draw an analogy, Martin

Luther King argued again and again that the essence, the dominant fact, of the Negro's life is *pain*, that that fact would not change until the white liberal would come to *share* it, that he would not share it until he *felt* it, that he would not be able to feel it until he understood it, and that he would not understand it until the *Negro* succeeded in bringing the pain to the surface—until he could make its content palpable.[51] Only then would the pain be mitigated. I believe that the same is true of women: the fundamental fact of women's lives is pain, that fact will not change until men share it, which will not in turn occur until its meaning and content are communicated. If we are ever to do anything about the pain of women's lives—the violence, the danger, the boredom, the ennui, the nonproductivity, the poverty, the fear, the numbness, the frigidity, the isolation, the low self-esteem, and the pathetic attempts to assimilate—we must first make the feel of that pain palpable, and hence shared. But we will not even attempt to do so as long as we embrace models of legal criticism that deny the relevance of subjective pain and pleasure, happiness and suffering, joy and sorrow to the critical evaluation of law. The liberal and radical legalisms to which feminist legal theory is now wed do precisely that. They both assume the sufficiency of an objective proxy, either choice or equality, for subjective well-being. By doing so, they virtually ensure the irrelevance of rich descriptions of felt pain and pleasure to a feminist criticism of law.

Lastly, by forcing into the public discourse descriptions of women's subjective, hedonic lives, the conception of the human being assumed by that discourse, the substantive description of experienced human life that the phrase *human being* denotes, might change so as to actually include women. For this reason alone, women need to develop descriptions of the quality of our hedonic lives.

There are two problems. Women's subjective, internal pain, because it is so silent and invisible, and because it is so different, is quite literally incomprehensible. To state the obvious: men do not understand, have not shared, have not heard, and have not felt the pain, the numbing terror, of an unwanted pregnancy. They have not heard, shared, or felt the tortuous violence of a stranger rape or the debilitating, disintegrating, and destructive self-alienation of marital rape. Men do not know that women's frigidity—our endurance of

51. See, e.g., *The Words of Martin Luther King, Jr.*, ed. Coretta Scott King (New York: New Market Press, 1983), 22.

unpleasant, unwanted, nonmutual, and nonetheless fully "consensual" sex—is not only neither funny nor a sexual disorder, but is painful, and thus injurious. Relatedly, men have no conception of what "nonviolent" forms of rape are even *about*, for the simple reason that they have no sense of what could possibly be painful about sex when it is not accompanied by a threat of violence. This communication breakdown is not slight or incidental; it is total. Men's conception of pain, of what it is, is derived from a set of experiences that *excludes* women's experience. When women and men talk about pain (and, to a lesser extent, about pleasure), we are employing vastly different experiential referents.

The second problem is this: women have a seemingly endless capacity to lie, both to ourselves and others, about what gives us pain and what gives us pleasure. This is not all that surprising. If what we need to do to survive, materially and psychically, is have heterosexual penetration three to five times a week, then we'll do it, and if the current ethic is that we must not only do it but enjoy it, well then, we'll enjoy it. We'll report as pleasure what we feel as pain. It is terribly difficult to get to the bottom of these lies, partly because we convey them not just with our words, but with our bodies. It is now a commonplace that women don't "feel at home" with male language—but this is no wonder, when what we've mainly learned to do with it is lie.

Both problems strike me as surmountable. Women must start speaking the truth about the quality of our internal lives. The pain women feel may be unique, but women and men (I believe) are alike in this way: both women and men resist pain when it is our own, and (most) women and (most) men will sympathetically resist pain suffered by others, when that pain is meaningfully communicated. And even if that is unduly optimistic, it is at least clear that *without* a clear articulation of the content and meaning of our pain, it will not be sympathetically resisted by men who do not share it. But more fundamentally, women will come to recognize the truth about our inner lives only when we start to speak it. Women's inner reality simply does not fit the Kantian conception of human nature that underlies so much of our liberal and radical legalist commitments. It is only by starting with our own experiences that we will be able to develop a description of human nature that is faithful to our lived reality, rather than one that ignores it. From that set of descriptions, and only from that set of descriptions, can we construct or reconstruct our own political ideals, whether they be autonomy, equality, freedom, fraternity, sisterhood, or something completely other and as yet unnamed.

Chapter 5

Economic Man and Literary Woman: One Contrast

The law-and-literature movement has been with us long enough that it is now possible to speak seriously of a "literary analysis of law,"[1] just as it has become possible, and even standard, to speak of an "economic analysis of law." It is also standard, of course, to speak of that abstract character who has emerged from the economic analysis of law: "economic man." In these brief comments, I want to offer one contrast of the economic man that emerges from economic legal analysis with the "literary person" that is beginning to emerge from literary legal analysis. I will sometimes call the latter person, in the interest of rough justice and somewhat in the interest of accuracy, "literary woman."[2] The literary woman posited by literary legal theorists is coming into her own, and she is at least beginning to operate as a check on the excesses of economic man run wild.

I should add by way of caveat that these comments are intended to be programmatic and tentative. I am not suggesting and do not believe that the comparative vision of literary woman that I will describe in this chapter is the only, or even the most, representative vision of humanity and human nature that has emerged from the

1. James Boyd White has used the phrase "literary view towards law," although in a slightly different context and toward a somewhat different end. See James Boyd White, "Economics and Law: Two Cultures in Tension," *Tennessee Law Review* 54 (1987): 161–201.

2. In the interest of rough justice, I use the word *woman* to include men as well as women, *she* to include the male pronoun, and *womankind* to include mankind. In the interest of accuracy, women's moral voice seems to be distinctively tied to the moral value of empathy I discuss in this chapter, and the literary method of narrative. See generally Carol Gilligan, *In a Different Voice: Psychological Theory and Women's Development* (Cambridge: Harvard University Press, 1982); Suzanna Sherry, "Civic Virtue and the Feminine Voice in Constitutional Adjudication," *Virginia Law Review* 72 (1986): 543–616.

law-and-literature movement. I do think, though, that it is a vision we ought to pursue. The idealized literary person, sometimes explicit, but most often implicit in much of our literary legal analysis, stands in sharp contrast to her closest interdisciplinary cousin, economic man. For that reason alone, the vision of human nature she represents has tremendous moral promise. We ought to begin to make good on it.

Literary Woman and Economic Man

The economic man posited by modern legal economists (and to a lesser degree by liberal legalists) is a relatively complex figure. I want to focus here on only two of his major attributes, both of which sharply distinguish him from literary woman. First, economic man is an infallible "rational maximizer of his own utility."[3] This attribute subdivides into two subparts, one cognitive and the other motivational: economic man invariably knows what is best for himself,[4] and he inevitably is motivated to seek it.[5] He knows his own subjective welfare perfectly and pursues it relentlessly. He is the infallible judge, for example, of whether he would prefer pushpin to poetry, alcohol to nutrition, or heroin to shelter. He knows best not only whether a Coke or a Pepsi would yield him greater pleasure, but also whether a liberal education or an apprenticeship would better prepare him for life. His preferences perfectly mirror his subjective welfare, and his choices perfectly mirror his preferences. Thus, he relentlessly chooses what he prefers, prefers what he wants, wants what he

---

3. Thus, Posner claims in the introduction to *The Economics of Justice*:

> [The tool of law and economics] is the assumption that people are rational maximizers of their satisfactions. . . . Is it plausible to suppose that people are rational only or mainly when they are transacting in markets, and not when they are engaged in other activities of life, such as marriage and litigation and crime and discrimination and concealment of personal information? . . . I happen to find implausible and counterintuitive the view that the individual . . . will act rationally in making some trivial purchase but irrationally when deciding whether to go to law school or get married or evade income taxes or have three children rather than two or prosecute a lawsuit. (*EJ*, 1–2)

4. This assertion sometimes takes the tautological form that the individual's preferences are definitionally what is best for her or him, and sometimes take the more substantive form that the individual has superior access to the sorts of knowledge required to make the judgment of what is best. The view is concisely criticized in Mark Kelman, "Choice and Utility," *Wisconsin Law Review* (1979): 769.

5. This assumption is the target of chap. 1 in this volume.

desires, and desires what will maximize his subjective well-being. He is perfectly rational.

The second distinguishing attribute of economic man is what I call his "empathic impotence." Although economic man is perfectly rational with respect to knowledge of his own subjective well-being, he is at the same time utterly incapable of empathic knowledge regarding the subjective well-being of others.[6] He is unable, in economic terms, to compare the "relative intensity" of the subjective pain of another with either his own pain or with that of others.[7] Although the technical, jargonistic language of the law-and-economics movement hides the point, the insistence that economic man is unable to make "intersubjective comparisons of utility," when translated into common parlance, amounts to no more than an admission (rather than an assertion) that he lacks even minimal empathic skills. Economic man is peculiarly incapable of the empathic knowledge, quite common to the rest of us, that his neighbor's broken leg hurts more than his own hangnail;[8] or that a child's discomfort while eating a healthy diet is less than the pain she will feel if she eats nothing but sugar; or that the pain an impoverished buyer might sustain when the law deprives him of the freedom to contract to purchase a television set on burdensome credit terms is less than the pain that buyer would sustain in the future when he loses essentials such as food and clothing he would otherwise be able to purchase.[9] He cannot empathize with the other sufficiently to make these comparisons.

---

6. See generally Lionel Charles Robbins, *An Essay on the Nature and Significance of Economic Science*, 2d ed. (London: Macmillan, 1935). The modern claim that we cannot compare interpersonal utilities constitutes a significant departure from the classical utilitarian position that such knowledge is both possible and the basis of utility summations across persons. The modern economist's insistence that we are incapable of knowing anything whatsoever about the internal states of others seems to be driven primarily by the quest for objectivity and quantification. The view has been heavily criticized in both the philosophical and legal literature. See, e.g., John Rawls, *A Theory of Justice* (Cambridge: Belknap Press, Harvard University Press, 1971), 90–92; Bruce A. Ackerman, *Social Justice in the Liberal State* (New Haven: Yale University Press, 1980); Kelman, "Choice and Utility," 778–79.

7. See generally Kelman, "Choice and Utility," 778–79, and the authorities cited therein.

8. Ibid.

9. Economic attacks on judicial interference with consumer preferences in the private market on the basis of unconscionability and voter preferences in the public sphere on the basis of unconstitutionality are typically premised either in whole or in part on this assumption. See, e.g., Richard A. Epstein, "Unconscionability: A

Thus, one way—surely not the only way—to describe economic man is that he is both peculiarly *capable* and peculiarly *disabled:* he knows everything there is to know about his own subjective life, and nothing whatsoever about the subjective lives of others. He is as incapable of error regarding his own subjective self-interest as he is incapable of knowledge regarding the subjectivity of others. Empathy is as foreign to him as rationality is familiar. Economic man is, in short, a rational, self-regarding Hercules, and an empathic, other-regarding weakling.

Now, as I and countless other critics of the law-and-economics movement have argued elsewhere, the first of the economist's assumptions regarding our nature, the Herculean rationalism of economic man, is almost surely false.[10] We are not invariably rational maximizers of our utility in either the cognitive or motivational sense: we do not always know what is best for ourselves, and we are not invariably motivated to seek it. I will not repeat these debates here. I do want to note, however, that, although we should not need literature, law, or a movement to tell us this simple truth, it is nevertheless one of the abiding strengths of the law-and-literature movement, as well as of literature more generally, that the literary person assumed by literary critical theory has helped us see this.[11] While reading narrative literature, a reader recognizes dimensions of a character's subjectivity to which the character himself is blind and constantly discovers dimensions of her own character as well, of which she was previously unaware. As Gadamer rightly insists, we "discover ourselves" as we engage in dialogue with texts, and part of what we discover in the text as well as in ourselves are wants, needs, prejudices, desires, and even preferences that we did not know

Critical Reappraisal," *Journal of Law and Economics* 18 (1975): 293–315; and Robert Bork, "Neutral Principles and Some First Amendment Problems," *Indiana Law Journal* 47 (1971): 1–35.

10. See, e.g., Kelman, "Choice and Utility"; and chap. 1 in this volume.

11. Even those critics of the law-and-economics movement who do not identify themselves as literary-legal theorists rely heavily on the notion that a narrative view of personal identity is radically opposed to the economist's discrete, moment-by-moment vision of what it means to be a human "chooser." Mark Kelman, more clearly than any other, has made this assumption explicit. It certainly is not merely a coincidence that he is also a novelist. See Kelman, "Choice and Utility"; Mark Kelman, "The Past and Future of Legal Scholarship," *Journal of Legal Education* 33 (1983): 432–36; Mark Kelman, "Spitzer and Hoffman on Coase: A Brief Rejoinder," *Southern California Law Review* 53 (1980): 1215–23 (citing 1221).

we had, and for which we had no plausible explanation, so long as we focus narrowly on our individualist histories.[12] This process of self-discovery would be literally meaningless if we were as knowledgeable of our subjectivity as is economic man. But we simply are not; we remain a mystery to ourselves throughout adulthood, not just in our early years of minority. Indeed, for most of us, culture has the great value it has, in large part, because it is the means by which we learn who we are.[13] Put simply, we just do not know ourselves as well as economic lawyers insist. Literature is one means by which we can glimpse this truth.

Nor are our motivations relentlessly rational, as countless critics of the law-and-economics movement have also argued. Again, although we should not need literature to tell us this obvious fact, the sharply contrasting vision of human nature offered by the law-and-literature movement surely has helped us see it.[14] In fact, literary woman has the potential to correct a misimpression created by the nonliterary critical attacks on economic man as well. Critical legal studies critiques of economic man often proceed on the unnecessarily limiting assumption that while we are not motivationally unidimensional as the economists insist, we are dual-motivational; that is, we possess altruistic, other-focused communitarian needs and desires as well as egoistic, self-serving, individualistic desires. The complexity of literary woman reminds us, however, that this too is a false duality. We have many kinds of needs, desires, and motivations, not just one as the legal economists insist, and not just two as their communitarian critics sometimes imply. Unlike economic man, literary woman is indeed at times altruistic, as the communitarian critics of economic man insist, but she is also at times masochistic, automatic, submissive, selfish, oppressive, and perhaps sadistic.[15] Indeed, we *have* literature in large part because our characters are multidimensional and worth exploring. Their complexity is a constant surprise, both to ourselves and to others.

12. See generally Hans-Georg Gadamer, "On the Problem of Self Understanding," in *Essays in Philosophical Hermeneutics,* trans. J. C. B. Mohrverlag (Berkeley: University of California Press, 1976).

13. For the clearest statement from James White, a seminal literary theorist, of the shortcomings of the economic model of motivation and self-knowledge, see White, "Economics and Law," 173, 180–81, 191–94.

14. White, "Economics and Law."

15. See chap. 1.

In short, the literary woman emerging from our literary analysis of law is no Herculean rationalist. Her character is multimotivational, which is why it is worth exploring, and she does not know herself, her own subjectivity, as well as she might. She is sufficiently complex so that as a character, she is worth portraying, and as a reader, she is worthy of dialogue; she is educable.

We can sharpen the contrast between economic man and literary woman even further, however, by focusing on economic man's second distinguishing attribute. Although not as frequently controverted, the second of the economist's assumptions, that we are incapable of making interpersonal comparisons of utility, is also almost surely false.[16] The ability to make such comparisons is, in simpler language, the ability to empathize with the pains and pleasures, the joys and sorrows, and the happiness and suffering of others. The claim that we are incapable of making such comparisons is simply the claim that we are utterly nonempathic.[17] If we cannot intersubjectively compare utility, we cannot know the joys and sorrows of our neighbor, our friends, our spouses, our cocontractors, our colitigants, our families, our coworkers, our employees, our lovers, or our community. But the economists's claim here is surely incorrect. We can and routinely *do* make intersubjective comparisons of utility. We can know the subjective lives of our neighbors, both those who are close to us and those who are not. We are not incapable of this knowledge. Indeed, the capacity fcr this knowledge is a large part of what makes us human.[18] The sharply contrasting vision of human nature embodied in literary woman provides a means (one means) by which we can understand this truth. Through reading, hearing, and telling stories, we *do* precisely what economic legal analysis insists we are incapable of doing. We reach an empathic understanding, a grasping, of the subjectivity, the pain, the pleasure, the happiness, or the sadness of the other. When we read with understanding, we not only understand that happiness or pain, but to some degree we take it on as our own.

16. See Kelman, "Choice and Utility," for the related argument that knowledge we undoubtedly possess regarding the categorization of goods belies the claim that we cannot know anything about the nature of the consumer, but only about the objective processes of the chooser.

17. I explored the connection between the capacity for empathy and the economist's assertion that we are incapable of interpersonal comparisons in chap. 7.

18. For a persuasive and eloquent argument to this effect, see Lynne N. Henderson, "Legality and Empathy," *Michigan Law Review* 85 (1987): 1574–1653.

Literary woman, then, unlike economic man, is not a Herculean rationalist. Neither is she an empathic weakling: she is fully able to make intersubjective comparisons of utility. Empathic ability is the very competence that is assumed, that *must* be assumed, by both writer and reader if narrative communication is to be meaningful. Indeed, the idealized literary person posited by literary legal theorists is distinctively capable in just this way: the literary person has a virtually infinite empathic potential.[19] She has a virtually infinite ability to understand the subjective being of the other, even where such empathic knowledge is most difficult: with the person of different racial heritage, different family history, different intelligence, or different ambitions, goals, happiness, and sorrow.[20] The primary attribute of the idealized literary person is her intersubjective empathic competence. Thus, while literary woman may be rationally inept, her empathic ability is truly Herculean. It is literary woman's empathic competence, not shared by economic man, that constitutes her moral promise. To that promise, and how we might fulfill it, I now wish to turn.

The Moral Promise of the Literary Person

That the intersubjective comparison of utility or, in short, empathy is possible, does not imply that it is easy. In some cases, empathy *is* easy. We can easily compare the pain of a pinprick with the pain of a dislocated shoulder.[21] But it is a tremendous mistake to conclude,

19. On the centrality of narrative to empathic ability, see Henderson, "Legality and Empathy"; Kelman, "Choice and Utility," "Past and Future," and "Spitzer and Hoffman"; Sherry, "Civic Virtue"; Gilligan, *In a Different Voice*. For a related argument to the effect that narrative and the capacity for storytelling are central to moral virtue, see Alisdair C. MacIntyre, *After Virtue: A Study in Moral Theory*, 2d ed. (Notre Dame, Ind.: University of Notre Dame Press, 1984).

20. Examples, of course, are endless, but two must be mentioned. In *Beloved* (New York: Plume, New American Library, 1987), Toni Morrison provides a striking—as well as a strikingly accessible—description of the internal subjectivity of escaped slaves in pre-Civil War days. In (I think) equally stunning literary style and language, law professor Patricia Williams has provided invaluable descriptions of the internal subjectivity of modern people of color. Patricia J. Williams, "Alchemical Notes: Reconstructing Ideals from Deconstructed Rights," *Harvard Civil Rights-Civil Liberties Law Review* 22 (1987): 401–33.

21. I owe this example to Mark Kelman. See Kelman, "Choice and Utility," 780.

as do many critics of economic man, that because interpersonal comparisons are obviously possible in many cases, they are therefore always straightforward and simple. Oftentimes and probably in those cases in which it matters most, intersubjective comparisons of utility are profoundly difficult. Often when empathic understanding is most urgently needed, it is hardest to achieve. Empathy is hard when we try to empathize with that which we never have experienced ourselves, or never could experience.[22] Empathy is hard when the personality with which we try to empathize, the subjectivity we are trying to grasp, is radically different from our own.[23] It is very difficult, for example, for a member of the racial majority in a racist society to empathize with the subjective pain of a racial minority. I suspect that most of us who think we do understand this pain in fact do not.[24] It is very difficult for a heterosexual to understand the magnitude of the pain experienced by a homosexual living in a homophobic society.[25] To take a more local issue, it is very difficult for a white man to empathically grasp the magnitude or nature of the pain of being the only woman or black on a law faculty.[26] It is not impossible, but it is difficult. It is difficult to empathize with the pain of those who are most different from us.

Now, the way that the literary woman achieves the empathic bridge in the hard case, the means by which she gains access to the other's subjective life, is metaphor and narrative. This is the one vital

22. The adamant refusal of the "white male heavies" in the critical legal studies movement (as elsewhere) to come to grips with this deceptively simple point is the reason, plain and simple, that so many women, people of color, gays, lesbians, and other "different" and differently oppressed groups are enraged by the internal dynamics of the movement.

23. See generally Henderson, "Legality and Empathy"; Martha Minow, "Justice Engendered," *Harvard Law Review* 101 (1987): 10–95.

24. Legal theorists, litigators, and judges of color have always, of course, understood this, but recently legal academics have begun to respond to the problem with greater use of metaphor, narrative, remembrance, anecdote, and even fantasy. See, e.g., Williams, "Alchemical Notes"; Derrick A. Bell, *And We Are Not Saved: The Elusive Quest for Racial Justice* (New York: Basic Books, 1987); Charles Lawrence, "The Id, the Ego, and Equal Protection: Reckoning with Unconscious Racism," *Stanford Law Review* 39 (1987): 317–88.

25. For a powerful description, see Richard Mohr, "AIDS, Gay Life, State Coercion," *Raritan* 6 (1986): 38–62. Henderson argues that the refusal to even attempt empathic identification with gay men accounts for the disastrous outcome in *Bowers v. Hardwick*. Henderson, "Legality and Empathy."

26. See Bell, *And We Are Not Saved*.

lesson that the literary person, and hence the literary analysis of law, can uniquely teach us: she can teach us how to empathize in the hard case. It is for this teaching that the law-and-literature movement is singularly significant. For like the metaphor, good narrative literature *is* the bridge to empathic understanding, and the literary person knows this.[27] Metaphor and narrative are the means by which we come to understand what was initially foreign. Narrative is the communication that facilitates the profoundly difficult intersubjective comparison of utility when more ordinary means fail. In political contexts, we rely on metaphor when our differences leave us desperate, when nothing else works and we have no other choice. "It was as though a curtain had dropped on my self-hood," Martin Luther King stated, describing the pain of segregation.[28] We might translate King's utterance in this way: "It is unlike anything you have ever experienced, so I will try a metaphor." And the metaphor is a good one. The white listener comes slightly closer to understanding a black man's pain, to grasping it, to seeing it, to feeling it, and most important, to assuming it as her own. Like all good metaphors, this one helps us understand the inexplicable. It helps us see what is hidden. By doing so, it helps us grow.

By now, it is no secret that as a culture we are in danger of losing the humanistic perspective that cultural traditionalism in general, and literature in particular, has to offer. As lawyers, we should be particularly wary of the serious risk this danger entails. If we *as lawyers* lose the literary voice, the literary insight, the literary vision of our humanity, if we lose the law-and-literature movement, we will have lost an important and even vital interdisciplinary and critical perspective on law. But there is something greater at stake, I believe, than the loss of a critical perspective. If we let go of our literary self in our relentless quest for technocratic efficiency and bureaucratic competence, we all, lawyers and nonlawyers alike, risk losing our ability to build a community. For although it is surely possible, both in practice and in theory, to make interpersonal comparisons of util-

27. This is, for example, a constant theme, perhaps the only constant theme, in James Boyd White's writing, from *Legal Imagination: Studies in the Nature of Legal Thought and Expression* (Boston: Little, Brown, 1973). I don't know any other legal theorist who has said this as often, or as eloquently. See also Henderson, "Legality and Empathy"; Minow, "Justice Engendered."

28. Quoted in Stephen B. Oates, *Let the Trumpet Sound: The Life of Martin Luther King, Jr.* (New York: Harper and Row, 1982).

ity, it is also surely possible that we can become incapable of making them, particularly in those hard cases when it matters most. Although we are today empathically competent, that can surely change. We can surely *become* the person posited as economic man. We can become unable to make intersubjective comparisons of utility. We can become incapable of empathy. We can become hardened to others. We can surely become unable to listen to, understand, or respond sympathetically to the subjective anguish of others. But we do not have to, and the insistence that we do not have to and that we ought not to is the central, unique, and irreplaceable contribution of the law-and-literature movement. We can fulfill the empathic promise of the literary person rather than the egoistic danger of economic man. We can become more capable, not less capable, of intersubjectively comparing utilities. We can become more, not less, empathic; more, not less, able to understand the subjective lives of others who are radically different from us and respond sympathetically to those lives. We do so, in part, by reading and appreciating the narrative stories of the lives of others.

Let me give an example of the type of question a narrative or literary perspective can help us answer. How does it feel to be an adult survivor of incest, or, more broadly, a survivor of childhood sexual abuse? How much lingering physical, psychic, emotional, and moral pain is involved? How bad is the pain? How does the "intensity" compare with other pains? What are the implications for adult life? How does it affect one's integrity? How does it affect one's sense of self? Does it damage one's capacity to tell the truth? Does it preclude adult trust, in either oneself or others? Obviously, these are questions regarding the subjectivity of the other, and they are questions for which, as lawyers, we need answers. If for no other reason, the legislator needs to know how much of our collective resources to expend on the problem of sexual abuse of children. To answer that question, we need to understand the subjectivity of the abused.

In connection with work I have been doing on the relationship between heterosexuality and violence, in the past two years I have read many narrative accounts of incest and sexual child abuse, and I still do not know the answers to these questions. But my reading has taught me that the answers to these questions are, in principle, *knowable*. I am now convinced that even those of us who have never had this crushing experience can empathize to some extent with those who have. I do not know whether the nonabused majority can ever fully understand the "relative intensity" of that abiding and utterly internal and subjective pain, or of the damage that lingers into adulthood, or of the sorrow that grows from a profound trust having been demolished, or of the sense of loss arising from a security that should be an entitlement of childhood forever being destroyed. I am not sure we can perfectly assess the "intensity of this disutility," or compare its intensity with others. But with metaphor and narrative, when all else fails, we try. With metaphor, narrative, and a willingness to listen, we can succeed to some extent.

Let me try to prove the point. In a remarkably powerful account of her survival of childhood abuse, contained in an equally remarkable book,[29] Lillian Kelly uses both metaphor and narrative to communicate the intensity of her experience of both abuse and survival. She begins with a metaphor to communicate the intensity of the abuse: "Aside from the fear, confusion, and shame, the molestation was as if I'd passed through an enormous threshold, *as big as birth*."[30] She then uses an allegory to convey the intensity of the aftermath.

> Some years after (it's always "before" and "after," isn't it?), during my senior year of high school, my close friend received two antique vases in the mail. One arrived whole, the other hopelessly shattered. My friend labored, sometimes passionately, sometimes indifferently, all through that year piecing together the delicate porcelain. When her cat knocked the half-completed reconstruction from her desk, breaking it in new places, I think my friend saw it as a minor and interesting setback, while I despaired.
>
> She completed the project, but the vase she produced could hardly be called complete. Tiny and large chips, once part of the original, had inevitably been lost, hidden in the packing material, or carried away by a little sister. This vase was more a product of my friend's labor than that of the original artist. Strangely though, the new vase, for all its disfigurement, scars, chips, and ragged lip, for all the horror of the shattering and an imperfect mending, when set beside its unblemished twin, was

29. Ellen Bass and Louise Thorton, eds., *I Never Told Anyone: Writings by Women Survivors of Child Sexual Abuse* (New York: Harper and Row, 1983).

30. Ibid., 197.

> the more splendid of the two. My friend presented her vase to me as a graduation gift, and I have it still.[31]

Although entirely metaphorical, or perhaps because it is entirely metaphorical, this description, better than most I have read, communicates powerfully both the comparative intensity of the pain of abuse and the subjective experience of survival. Both the injured child and the heroic, courageous adult that emerges from this short account become members of my community, a part of my sense of self. Because she shared her story, her injury has become my injury, my burden, and part of my responsibility, and her heroism has become part of my human potentiality. I understand, better than before, the magnitude of her pain and the momentousness of her strength.

The knowledge we learn in this way—knowledge of the subjectivity of others, gained and pursued through metaphor, allegory, narrative, literature, and culture—is a peculiar sort of knowledge, but it is absolutely essential to any meaningful quest for justice, legal or otherwise. It is the knowledge that facilitates community, and the capacity for that knowledge is the capacity that makes us social. Without it, we would not crave, much less attain, justice. But it is not rational knowledge. Knowledge of the other's subjectivity is not rationally acquired, and it cannot be rationally calculated, quantified, aggregated, or compared. It is knowledge that moves us rather than informs us. We make room for this knowledge in our heart, not in our head. Knowledge of others, empathically acquired through metaphor and narrative, becomes a part of our sense of self, our sense of the other, and our sense of union with him. Without knowledge of this sort, we cannot attain true community, and without true community, we cannot attain any meaningful justice.

Martin Luther King unknowingly underscored the centrality of narrative and literature (as well as their close cousins, demonstrations and street theater) to moral progress when he explicitly ties empathy to justice in this passage:

> In this final analysis the white man cannot understand the Negro's problem, because he is a part of the Negro and the Negro is a

31. Ibid.

part of him. The Negro's agony diminishes the white man, and the Negro's salvation enlarges the white man.

What is needed today on the part of white America is a committed altruism which recognizes this truth. True altruism is more than the capacity to pity; it is the capacity to empathize. Pity is feeling sorry for someone; empathy is feeling sorry with someone. Empathy is fellow feeling for the person in need—his pain, agony, and burdens. I doubt if the problems of our teeming ghettoes will have a great chance to be solved until the white majority, through genuine empathy, comes to feel the ache and anguish of the Negroes' daily life.[32]

Conclusion

Why, then, should lawyers read literature? Why teach this stuff? What does it add to the legal curriculum? As Richard Posner asks, why use fiction to make a point that could be proved, or disproved, with the empiric tools of social science?[33] Answers to these and related questions presently proliferate, surely masking (but never very well) endemic and massive insecurity over the utility of humanistic discourse to legal education. This may be because we have overlooked what is most central. Perhaps the most important use of literature, for lawyers, is the most obvious one, but the least mentioned in modern discussion of the law-and-literature movement. Literature helps us understand others. Literature helps us sympathize with their pain, it helps us share their sorrow, and it helps us celebrate their joy. It makes us more moral. It makes us better people. The literary person, like economic man, is surely only one of the many persons we might become. But, unlike economic man, she is also someone we can unabashedly claim that we should become. She represents not just our cultural heritage, but more importantly (and relatedly) she represents our potential for moral growth.[34] She is the possibility within all of us for understanding, for empathy, for sympathy, and most simply, for love.

32. *The Words of Martin Luther King, Jr.*, ed. Coretta Scott King (New York: New Market Press, 1983), 22.

33. Richard A. Posner, *Law and Literature: A Misunderstood Relation* (Cambridge: Harvard University Press, 1988).

34. John Gardner, *On Moral Fiction* (New York: Basic Books, 1978).

Chapter 6

Disciplines, Subjectivity, and Law

Given the postmodern disillusionment with reason, how should we criticize or evaluate a law? How should we go about criticizing law, if not by reference to general principles derived from reason? What does it mean, given the "death of reason," to ask whether a particular law—say, a statute outlawing surrogacy contracts, or a judicial decision requiring the busing of schoolchildren to achieve integrated schools, or a law criminalizing sexual sodomy, or a constitutional provision or constitutional interpretation invalidating state statutes that criminalize abortions on demand—is a good law or a bad law, a just law or an unjust law, a moral law or an immoral law? How are we to evaluate laws, constitutions, judicial decisions, statutes, or legal interpretations, if we have lost faith in the Enlightenment ideal of holding acts of power up to the critical light of reason? If, as the Enlightenment ideal holds, our moral norms are (or should be) the products of reason, and if, as the postmodern critics of reason insist, the product of reason we call moral knowledge is itself a product of power, then how can we criticize the law, which is itself indisputably a product of power?

By exposing the purportedly apolitical or neutral Enlightenment standards of reason, morality, generality, and justice as themselves intensely and inevitably political, the modern critics of reason may indeed have liberated legal criticism from a false straitjacket of disingenuous neutrality. But have they also rendered all forms of criticism of both law and extant positive morality incoherent? And if they have, is not the almost certain ultimate political consequence of this gigantic unmasking of reason not popular liberation, or anything even remotely like it, but rather a political stagnation, moral complacency, and muting of the critical voice such as we may never have previously encountered? Does not moral progress depend entirely on the possibility of moral criticism, and does not the possibility of moral criticism depend entirely on the difference, and on their being a difference, between the power that is the object and the reason that is the method of criticism? Have we won freedom from one false savior, the method of reason, at the cost of all criticism, and hence at the cost of moral, societal, and political progress? If we give up on reason, have we given up on criticism?

Before going on to consider answers to this question—how do we criticize, or morally evaluate, law, if not by reference to reason—let me specify more precisely what I take to be excluded by the postmoderns' exclusion of reason as a possible answer. The postmodern critique of reason, as it relates to legal discourse, has sought to explode two particular rationalist faiths. First, it has exploded the philosophical notion that we can articulate, in some sort of Kantian fashion, noncontingent, categorical, abstract moral principles that are discernible through reason alone, and that can then be used as a standard against which to evaluate contingent, particular, and utterly concrete legal commands.[1] The postmodern critique of reason renders incoherent what used to be called (in a more rationalist time) deontological arguments about a law or a legal system's moral merit. The deontologist typically argued that if a law cannot be deductively derived from a categorical moral truth or an abstract principle of justice, then the law is unjust, bad, or unwise. Thus, if, for example, a statute or a judicial decision forbidding surrogacy contracts violates a categorical moral imperative that individuals should be allowed to do as they wish with their bodies so long as those actions do not hurt others, then the law or decision that forbids surrogacy contracts is unjust. The postmodern critics of reason have attempted to show that there simply are no categorical, noncontingent, and nonpolitical natural truths of justice or morality. Those truths, according to the modern critics of reason, are themselves inherently political and contingent; they are no more noncontingent, abstract, or categorical than

1. For the most general statement of the postmodern and pragmatic critique of traditional Kantian philosophy, see Richard Rorty, *Philosophy and the Mirror of Nature* (Princeton: Princeton University Press, 1979). For applications to legal criticism, evaluation, and evolution, see Roberto Mangabeira Unger, *The Critical Legal Studies Movement* (Cambridge: Harvard University Press, 1984); and Joseph William Singer, "The Player and the Cards: Nihilism and Legal Theory," *Yale Law Journal* 94 (1984): 1–70; J. M. Balkin, "Deconstructive Practice and Legal Theory," *Yale Law Journal* 96 (1987): 743–86.

the very concrete and particular legal norms they are being used to judge. Deontological moral criticism of law is at best incoherent and at worst self-serving, if it is true as the postmodern critics claim that there are no categorical moral truths that can serve as the major premises of deontological arguments.

The second rationalist faith exploded by the critique of reason is the notion that there are empirical, contingent, but nonetheless universal and knowable truths, or facts about human nature, that can, in turn, ground a knowable conception of the human good, and that can itself then be used as a standard against which to judge particular laws or particular legal systems. This critique renders incoherent what used to be called teleological arguments about a law or a legal system's morality. The teleologist specifies a conception of the moral good by identifying some aspect of human nature with which the good is identified, and then criticizes a law or legal system by asking whether it furthers or frustrates that good.[2] If, for example, a Supreme Court decision requiring busing furthers communal diversity, or a constitutional interpretation invalidating antiabortion laws furthers individual autonomy, and if diversity and autonomy are necessary aspects of the good life because they complement some aspect of our intrinsic human nature, then that decision and that constitutional interpretation are both good, or just. The second prong of the postmodern attack on reason shows that such purportedly universal facts of human nature are in fact not general at all, but, rather, are true only of particular human communities, or subcommunities, or interests or cultures, or races, or classes, or genders. The critics have succeeded through these demonstrations in casting doubt upon the notion of any shared human nature to be discovered as a basis of criticism, much less a human nature that is knowable. If the critics are right that the conception of the good and of human nature used as foundations are conceptions and descriptions of some empowered subcommunity, and not of the human species as a whole, then teleological moral criticism of law is at best incoherent and at worst self-serving. The conception of the good serves a particular political agenda—the ends of power—rather than the ends of reason or the good of the human community.

The question left by the postmodern critique, then, is whether

2. For an excellent example of teleological legal criticism, see William W. Fisher, "Reconstructing the Fair Use Doctrine," *Harvard Law Review* 101 (1988): 1661–1795.

and how we can criticize law, if not by reference to reason, by which is meant either categorical moral truths divined by pure reason or, alternatively, a theory of the good in turn grounded in universal but concrete truths about human nature, derived through rational methods of empirical inquiry. Put in terms of disciplines, the question is this: To what source of wisdom, to what discipline, should the legal critic turn, if not to traditional moral philosophy, the disciplined study of abstract truths of morality, and if not to traditional social science, the disciplined study of empirical truths of human and societal nature? This is the central question, I believe, for the legal academy in our generation. I believe that neither mainstream nor progressive legal scholars have managed to answer it, and that the failure has led to what can be called a moral crisis in modern law schools.

The first and shortest section of this chapter quickly reviews the major response to the question that has emerged from the legal academy, an answer I will call *legal authoritarianism*. The second and major section will critically examine in greater detail a more promising set of responses. Those responses are presently being propounded and explored by the developing interdisciplinary movements in U.S. law schools. The various interdisciplinary movements now overtaking the traditional legal academy, I will argue, constitute and even have their genesis in an attempt to answer the question posed above. That attempt, however, has been largely unsuccessful, and the reason for that failure is the main topic of the second section of this chapter. The third section, drawing heavily on the lessons to be learned from both the promise and failure of interdisciplinary legal studies, suggests my own response.

Legal Authoritarianism

From the perspective of traditional legal scholarship, the question posed by postmodern critique is both peculiar and dangerous. The peculiarity is this: for the vast majority of both doctrinal and theoretical legal scholars, it is not now and has never been *reason*, meaning either abstract morality or a view of human nature, that does or should constitute the standard against which particular laws, decisions, or doctrines should be judged. For most legal scholars, it is law itself, the legal system taken as a whole, rather than either the dictates of reason, or norms of morality derived from knowable human nature, that is the proper moral standard or baseline against which to judge particular legal acts or decisions.[3] Law is, after all, a normative and critical system of some subtlety and considerable complexity, with numerous axioms and critical habits of thought. It is surely possible, whether or not justifiable, to judge the value of a law by reference to the law's own internal critical and normative apparatus. We can ask, for example, whether the decision in a particular contracts case, say a decision that a surrogacy contract is unenforceable because unconscionable, is or is not in line with the development of contracts principles more largely defined. Furthermore, if we feel that our contract law, taken as a whole, is properly and morally grounded in a respect for individual freedom and dignity, then our legal analysis of the implications of contract law from the particular case might constitute a moral analysis as well. To decide or criticize the legality of the opinion will feel like a critique of the morality of the opinion as well, if we feel confident in the morality of the legal standard that forms the baseline of the legal analysis. Similarly, constitutional theorists typically take it as an article of faith that the Constitution, itself a legal document, constitutes a moral as well as legal criterion against which to judge particular laws. An argument against the constitutionality of a law is consequently typically felt by both legal theorist and constitutional lawyer to have moral as well as legal import. This attitudinal stance toward the morality of law dominates mainstream contemporary jurisprudence. For better or worse, most legal scholars hold some form of the view that the total universe of authoritative legal rules and principles constitutes the relevant moral norm against which to judge the morality as well as the legality of particular legal rules or laws.

The effect of the dominance of this sort of legalism in contemporary legal education, pedagogy, and scholarship—despite the occasional intrusions of other disciplines and the growing chorus of dissenting voices—is that, at least in the moral sense, legal theory is decidedly in a pre-Enlightenment stage of development, not Enlightenment, and certainly not post-Enlightenment. The morality of law,

3. The most powerful and sophisticated explanation of this idea comes from Ronald Dworkin. See R. M. Dworkin, *Law's Empire* (Cambridge: Harvard University Press, 1986); *A Matter of Principle* (Cambridge: Harvard University Press, 1985), and *Taking Rights Seriously* (Cambridge: Harvard University Press, 1977).

according to most members of the legal academy, is not judged by reference to norms culled from reason; instead, law is typically judged by reference to the dictates of legalism. More simply, for the legally trained, particular acts of power are typically criticized by reference to other particular acts of power. Indeed, this nonrationalist, pre-Enlightenment, attitude toward the moral authority of law is so thoroughly ingrained in legal education and scholarship that it, rather than the faith in reason so characteristic of the Enlightenment and of other disciplines and professions, may well be the determining characteristic of the "legalistic mind."[4] To put one's faith in the morality of legal authority, rather than in reason, may be what is meant by the phrase "think like a lawyer." To think like a lawyer, in other words, might mean that one has learned to take an essentially legalistic and at root authoritarian stance toward the entire enterprise of legal thought and criticism.

That legal authoritarianism is so entrenched in legal education and scholarship suggests the danger in the postmodern critique of reason: it will further entrench authoritarian and self-referential instincts of the legal academy. Legal authorities of all sorts—the legal system, legal doctrine, precedent, the rule of law—are bound to become all the more appealing as bases for the moral criticism of particular laws, as the possibility of a critical morality derived from some source other than power (such as reason) comes under attack. With the postmodern critique of reason, in other words, the tendency to view legal authority itself as a sufficient standard against which to criticize particular laws or legal decisions need no longer rest solely on a head-in-the-sand refusal to consider the teachings of philosophical or empirical sciences. It can rest, instead, on a sophisticated skepticism that philosophical studies and empirical sciences have nothing normative to offer.

We see this reinforcement of self-referential authoritarianism, I believe, in the increasing number of scholars who have begun to develop a distinctively postmodern form of legal neopragmatism as a self-consciously normative response to the modern attack on reason.[5] The new legal pragmatism can best be understood, I think, as

4. Some mainstream legal theorists are more forthright about this than others. See, e.g., Paul Carrington, "Of Law and the River," *Journal of Legal Education* 34 (1984): 222–28.

5. Examples include Singer, "Player and the Cards"; John Stick, "Can Nihilism

yet another attempt to ground the criticism of law in preexisting legal materials, but this time the legal self-referencing is justified not by a belief in the omnipotence or benevolence of law, but rather by the brute force of necessity. Thus, the argument of the modern legal pragmatists seems to be that the modern critique of reason leaves us with no choice. For these scholars, the critique of reason that now preoccupies the humanistic and social-scientific disciplines has made the preexisting and relatively unthinking legalistic tendency to shy away from a reasoned critique of law, an attitude we ought to be ashamed of, entirely respectable. If the postmodern critique of reason is right, the argument goes, there simply is no alternative. Power is all there is.

As I argued in chapter 3, this pre-Enlightenment, authoritarian attitude of the legal academy is deeply mistaken, whether implicitly endorsed by the centrist mainstream or explicitly embraced by the progressive Left or Right. Authority of any sort, including legal authority, simply cannot be the basis of criticisms of power. We have no more reason to assume the morality of the holder in due course doctrine, or contract law, or the Constitution, or the First Amendment, or any other of our most general legalistic principles than we have to assume the morality of the particular law or decision we are criticizing. Therefore, we have no reason to simply employ general legal principles, laws, or systems as the baseline of moral critique of more particular acts of law. If, as the postmodern critique suggests, we cannot criticize law by reference to norms culled from reason, then we must, indeed, look elsewhere for the basis of legal criticism. But we should not look to authoritative legal materials themselves. Authority, particularly legal authority, is not an alternative to reason.

The Interdisciplinary Movement

The modern attraction to interdisciplinary work in U.S. law schools today stems in large part, I believe, from the hope that in other academic disciplines we will find what we have not found in either law or traditional moral philosophy, namely, normative standards

Be Pragmatic?" *Harvard Law Review* 100 (1986): 332–401; Joan C. Williams, "Critical Legal Studies: The Death of Transcendence and the Rise of the New Landells," *New York University Law Review* 62 (1987): 429–96; *AP*; Richard A. Posner, "The Jurisprudence of Skepticism," *Michigan Law Review* 86 (1988): 827–91.

external to both power and abstract reason with which we might criticize law. Interdisciplinary work is largely motivated, in other words, by the hope that in other disciplines we will find a response to the postmodern challenge. Thus, the interdisciplinary scholars operate on the not unreasonable assumption that other disciplines might supply answers to the questions "how ought we lead, legislate, judge, or advocate"; "how should we use law to do good"; "how do we criticize law"; and "how can we improve upon it."

To be more specific, both of our two major interdisciplinary movements, the thirty-year-old law-and-economics movement and the much newer law-and-humanities movement, have their genesis, at least in part, in attempts to provide a basis for criticism of law that is itself freed of the influence of either traditional moral philosophy or professional legalistic norms. The law-and-economics movement, most notably, is firmly grounded in the recognizably postmodern skeptical conviction that, for various reasons, neither general legal norms themselves nor philosophical verities can be usefully employed as the basis of evaluation of particular laws. Rather, the only knowable baseline of normative criticism, and hence the only source of value, is the desires, preferences, and choices of particular individuals. The value of a law should therefore be judged by reference to its conduciveness to the creation of opportunities for individuals to create value by acting on their preferences. Consequently, economics—the systematic study of preferences—rather than law or philosophy is the discipline that must be at the heart of the moral criticism of law. Although predating the arrival of philosophical postmodernism and politically anathema to its most prominent representatives, the law-and-economics scholars were and are motivated by skeptical convictions that are strikingly similar to those that move the postmodernists. According to the law-and-economics scholar no less than the postmodern critic of reason, neither philosophy nor law can provide the baseline for the normative criticism of law. The legal critic must look elsewhere, and for the legal economist, that means to the preferences of individual consumers.

The law-and-humanities movement similarly has its genesis in a recognizably, and this time self-consciously, postmodern attempt to provide a basis for moral criticism and thinking about law, legal practice, and the profession that is freed of the blinding constraints and biases of the false universals of both traditional moral philosophy and professional law and legalism. Indeed, it is worth stressing that, despite the dramatic and obvious differences between the positivistic methodology of economics and the interpretive and hermeneutic methods of the humanities, both movements take as their point of departure the same set of skeptical convictions, themselves commonly rooted in the skepticism that has given rise to the postmodern critique of reason. For the legal humanist, no less than the legal economist, agrees with the postmodern critic that neither abstract truth nor general legal norms can or should constitute the basis for criticism of positive law. Whereas the economist turns to individual preferences as the source of value, and hence the basis of criticism, the legal humanist instead turns to the wisdom encoded in a culture's texts and explicated by their interpreters—in general, we might say, to a culture's canonical and interpretive community—as the source of value, and hence the basis of criticism of its positive law. The value of a law, then, according to the legal humanist, should be judged not by reference to its conduciveness to the creation of opportunities for individual consent, as for the legal economist, but rather by reference to its conduciveness to the creation of opportunities for meaningfully free participation in the culture's canonical and interpretive community. Neither philosophy nor law, according to both the law-and-humanities movement and the postmodern critique of reason, can provide the baseline for normative criticism of positive law. Only the interpretive community, the subcommunity engaged in dialogic and equal interpretive practices, can provide a standard or source of moral value.

And yet—this is the central paradox I wish to explore—in spite of their genesis in undeniably critical impulses, both the law-and-economics movement, and increasingly, I fear, the (newer) law-and-humanities movement, are rightly known in legal academia not for their critical stance toward law, but for their celebration of it. Whatever might have been their initial critical impulse—or better, in spite of their initial critical impulse—both interdisciplinary movements have come to embrace and reflect conservative if not reactionary or regressive politics, a general acquiescence in the order of things, and a sometimes quite explicit tendency to establish themselves as apologists for the current legal order. Thus, the law-and-economics movement is known not for its individualist, pluralist, or anarchic critical edge, but for its adoring and noncritical attitude toward economic markets and the individual preferences those markets both produce and satisfy. Similarly, the law-and-humanities movement, according to a growing chorus of critics, is constituted not by a communitarian critical perspective but by an adoring and noncritical attitude toward the dominant perspectives and needs of the literate, pontificating interpretive community and a deference toward the canonical texts, both legal and literary, that support that perspective. Law, of course, is a central structural support of both economic markets and canonical culture, so the interdisciplinary scholars' adoration of markets and classics and their dominant interpretations is quickly translated into a complacent, acquiescent, accepting, or simply noncritical stance toward law. Despite their original critical impulse, and despite healthy dissenting wings of both movements, both the law-and-economics movement and the law-and-humanities movement seem to have succumbed to the authoritarian impulse that dominates the mainstream legal academy.[6] If we believe the charge of complacent conservatism made by the critics of the interdisciplinary scholars, then we should conclude that the hope that other disciplines might provide a source of critical insight about the morality of law, legalism, or particular laws has turned out to be illusory.

The criticism of both movements, of course, is somewhat overstated: there are at least a few progressive legal economists,[7] and there are more than a few profoundly critical, even radical, legal humanists. Nevertheless, there is enough easily demonstrated truth in the charge that it deserves explanation. The question I want to pose, then, is not whether both of these movements tend toward conservatism and complacency (which I will take as a given), but rather why: Why has the critical weight of both of these two par-

6. For a critique of the conservative bias in law and economics, see Mark Kelman, *A Guide to Critical Legal Studies* (Cambridge: Harvard University Press, 1987). For criticisms of the emerging conservatism of the law-and-humanities movement, see David Kennedy, "The Turn to Interpretation," *Southern California Law Review* 58 (1985): 251–75; Susan Mann, "The Universe and the Library: A Critique of James Boyd White as Writer and Reader," *Stanford Law Review* 41 (1989): 959–1020; and Robert Weisberg, "The Law-Literature Enterprise," *Yale Journal of Law and Humanities* 1 (1988): 1–68.

7. For the former, see generally Bruce A. Ackerman, *Reconstructing American Law* (Cambridge: Harvard University Press, 1984). For the latter, see, e.g., Robert M. Cover, "Nomos and Narrative," *Harvard Law Review* 97 (1983): 4–68; Richard Weisberg, *The Failure of the Word: The Protagonist as Lawyer in Modern Fiction* (New Haven: Yale University Press, 1984).

ticular interdisciplinary movements gravitated toward celebration rather than criticism of legal culture; acquiescence in, rather than dissent from, professional norms and life? Why have both movements become conservative, rather than critical, in the contemporary legal academy? In both cases, I will submit, the answer lies in the story of each movement's profoundly ambivalent relationship to its moral and philosophical origins, and a similarly ambivalent response to the postmodern critique of reason that has put that philosophical base into doubt. Each movement's story, however, is quite distinctive. Let me start with the law-and-economics movement.

As is now fairly well understood, the law-and-economics movement had its inception in a partial embrace and a partial rejection of the politics, moral values, and methods of classical utilitarianism. The moral standard against which all acts of power should be judged, according to the classical utilitarian, is the individual, and more specifically, the individual's subjective happiness. Lawmaking, of course, is one realm of power, and should therefore be subject to the same evaluative standard as any other act of power. According to the nineteenth-century classical utilitarians, then, if a law promotes individual happiness, it is a good law; if it promotes pain or unhappiness, it is a bad law. Laws should be criticized or praised, quite simply, by reference to their conduciveness to the happiness of the lives of the individuals they affect.

By the early twentieth century, classical utilitarianism had splintered into a bewildering range of utilitarian-inspired theories, one of which turned out to have critical importance for the rise of the law-and-economics movement. From the general utilitarian criterion developed by Bentham, James Mill, and the other classical liberals, a few of the English classical liberals of the late nineteenth century and a much larger number of the legal realists and pragmatists of the early twentieth century went on to develop a powerful method of legal criticism that might best be called *ideal-utilitarian*. That method had two steps. First, by reasoning inductively on the basis of judgments about the relative subjective happiness of different sorts of lives under differing conditions, the legal realists and some of the English liberals believed, one should be able to formulate a conception of the ideally happy—or, to use a modern term, an ideally flourishing—life. After comparing the subjective happiness incident to a sufficient number of sorts of lives, a critic should be able to say, for example, that some degree of personal autonomy, the opportunity to engage in meaningful work, the opportunity to forge and pursue one's own life project, intellectual stimulation, provision for minimal physical needs, involvement in the community's political and cultural life, and the protection of intimate relationships are all essential components of a subjectively happy individual life. One should be able to determine, in other words, that the ideally happy life is constituted by particular, knowable (although debatable), contingent, relatively general, but nevertheless nonuniversal attributes and determine the conditions under which such lives would be most likely to thrive. From such general, tentative, and pragmatically grounded descriptions of the content of the good life, the early twentieth-century legal realists and pragmatists hoped eventually to forge an ideal of individual life and happiness against which not only particular laws, but also legal systems, constitutions, and forms of government could then be criticized.[8] The second, critical step would then readily follow: a law or legal system that contributes to the conditions necessary to the facilitation of the ideal life—some measure of autonomy, social involvement, privacy, meaningful work, security against want and need—is a good law. A law or legal system that frustrates such lives is bad.

The modern legal economist's response to the legal realists' utilitarian method of legal criticism was and is strikingly ambivalent. The legal economist (unlike the modern liberal legalist) continues to embrace the classical utilitarian ideal of individual subjective happiness as the goal of law. Law should indeed maximize individual well-being, as classical utilitarians and the legal realists after them held. The legal economist, however, sees an insurmountable problem of knowledge with the ideal utilitarian's use of any particular, idealized conception of the good life as a guiding critical norm. The problem with the ideal-utilitarian standard of the good life as a measure of the value of law is not so much political, its valorization of one form of life over another, as it is epistemological. The ideal-utilitarian mandate to maximize individual happiness by ascertaining

8. The literature here is vast. For a representative sampling, see Morris Raphael Cohen and Felix S. Cohen, *Readings in Jurisprudence and Legal Philosophy* (New York: Prentice-Hall, 1951). See John Dewey, *Individualism, Old and New* (New York: Minton, Bach, 1930); and John Stuart Mill, *On Utilitarianism* (New York: Dutton, 1951), for examples of ideal-utilitarian accounts of the good and the good life.

its necessary conditions and then criticizing law by reference to whether it impedes or facilitates those conditions, according to the modern legal economist, requires the moral critic to perform the impossible: namely, to specify an ideal conception of happiness that is in turn based on information gleaned from a comparison of the pure subjectivity of other individuals. Thus, the ideal-utilitarian wants to posit, on the basis of comparisons of different lives, that an autonomous life is subjectively happier, as well as morally better, than an enslaved one, or that a politically engaged life is similarly happier as well as better than an atomistic one, or that an educated life is more stimulating then one lived in ignorance—that Socrates unhappy, to paraphrase Mill, is happier than a pig satisfied. But these sorts of comparisons, from the demanding, skeptical, and (in retrospect) postmodern perspective of the legal economist, simply cannot be done. We cannot know anything about the subjective state of other individuals and, hence, the relative feel of autonomy to slavery, or education to ignorance; we cannot crawl inside A or B's skin and see how either of them is feeling under divergent life conditions. Knowing that something pains me will not help me determine whether something pains you, since I am me and you are you. Knowing that I am made happy by meaningful work, intellectual stimulation, or political involvement tells me nothing at all about what makes you happy, and hence nothing at all about the nature of happiness itself. It is therefore impossible—whether or not politically wise—to generate the sorts of general, inductive judgments about the conditions of a subjectively happy life necessary to meaningful ideal-utilitarian criticism.

To generalize the point, individual happiness, the realists' ideal-utilitarian goal of law, according to the modern economist, is an utterly subjective, idiosyncratic, and individualist quality and is therefore utterly unknowable. We do not have and cannot rationally acquire the kind of data we need to apply the standard of criticism for which the ideal-utilitarian argued. There is no way, then, according to the legal economist, that we can criticize the merits of particular laws by reference to their conduciveness to the components of a happy or flourishing life because there is no way we can meaningfully specify the content of such a life. The classical utilitarian was right to put forward the individual's subjective happiness as the goal of law, but the utilitarian-inspired legal critics of the early twentieth century were wrong to assert the possibility that one could specify the necessary conditions of happiness, and then use those specifications as the standard for the rational moral criticism of law. The legal critic cannot rationally do what the ideal-utilitarian urges.

I want eventually to question whether the legal economists are right to be so skeptical of our ability to know the subjectivity of others and, hence, skeptical of the ability of the legal critic to specify a fairly general account of the content of happiness and then ascertain whether and how much a law impedes or furthers the conditions that foster happy lives. But first I want to stress that it is precisely this claim, that there is an insurmountable epistemological problem with critical ideal-utilitarianism, that defines, unifies, and distinguishes the modern law-and-economics movement from its utilitarian and legal realist predecessors. The legal economist typically endorses the classical utilitarian's conviction that our legal system ought, indeed, maximize the subjective happiness of affected individuals. That is a proper legal goal. But because we cannot perceive, understand, measure, gauge, or in any other way rationally compare the subjective lives of other individuals, according to the legal economist, we cannot rationally evaluate laws by whether or not they foster the necessary conditions for subjective, individual happiness. The goal of law, individual happiness, cannot become an objective standard of legal criticism, because its constituent components, autonomy, political engagement, stimulating work, and so on, can never be known. Happiness, in short, cannot be an object of rational knowledge. Individual subjective welfare is the goal of law, but because it is essentially unknowable, it cannot serve as the standard for rational criticism of law.[9]

What, then, should we do? It is here that the science of economics enters the picture and solves the legal economist's epistemological dilemma. We need to forgo the search for the nature or content of human happiness, the legal economist argues, but it does not follow that we should relinquish either the goal of happiness itself or, more importantly, the method of rational inquiry. Rather, what we need to do is replace the utilitarian's nonquantifiable, noncomparable, and essentially unknowable standard of subjective happiness with a stan-

9. See, for an example of a legal-economic attack on the subjectivity, irrationality, and idiosyncrasy of classical utilitarian legal criticism, Posner's discussion of Bentham in *EJ*, 31–48.

dard that is knowable, quantifiable, and comparable and, hence, subject to rational inquiry—namely, the preferences, choices, and consensual transactions of particular, individual consumers. We cannot know what makes someone happy, but we can know what each particular individual wants. More concretely, given the vast differences between people, we cannot know that autonomy, work, or social engagement will, as a rule, contribute to individual happiness, but we can know what any particular individual chooses, prefers, and will pay for. The solution, then, to the epistemological problems posed by utilitarianism and legal realism is straightforward: we need to displace unknowable happiness with knowable objective wealth. Rather than maximize happiness, we should aim to maximize wealth, and we should criticize a law by whether or not it does so. Thus, Richard Posner, the most committed proponent of the value of wealth maximization, is led to sharply distinguish the modern legal economist's interest in value and wealth from the utilitarian's use of happiness as a guiding critical norm.

> The most important thing to bear in mind about the concept of value is that it is based on what people are willing to pay for something rather than on the happiness they would derive from having it. Value and happiness are of course related. . . . But while value necessarily implies utility, utility does not necessarily imply value. The individual who would like very much to have some good but is unwilling or unable to pay anything for it—perhaps because he is destitute—does not value the good in the sense in which I am using the term value.
>
> Equivalently, the wealth of society is the aggregate satisfaction of those preferences (the only ones that have weight in a system of wealth maximization) that are backed up by money, that is, that are registered in a market.

Economics, we might say, with its minimalist claims about human nature, is the quintessential postmodern science, and law and economics, with its minimalist claims about what is or is not desirable, is the quintessential postmodern system of value.

It is, then, a continuing commitment to the Enlightenment ideal of the possibilities and values of rational inquiry, combined with distinctively postmodern doubts that there is any such knowledge about happiness that can be rationally acquired through philosophy or social science, that defines the methodology of the law-and-economics movement. A lingering Enlightenment commitment to rational method combined with postmodern doubt requires, for the legal economist, that legal criticism be grounded in the objective discipline of economics rather than in the politics, irrationality, and ethical indeterminacy of idealism, philosophy, or the social sciences. For although we cannot know, through either philosophical investigation or scientific inference, the nature of happiness itself, through the methods of economics we can rationally know and can objectively quantify, compare, and maximize the preferences, choices, and wealth of other individuals. Such knowledge requires neither abstract truth and deduction, nor universal claims of human nature. Preferences, wealth, and choices, unlike happiness, are objective, measurable, observable, quantifiable phenomena. Since we cannot objectively and rationally know the nature of another's happiness but can know his or her objective behavioral preferences and choices, we should then seek to maximize not subjective well-being but rather his or her preferences, choices, and wealth. Preferences and choices are preferred standards of criticism not only because they are good evidence of the individual's subjective happiness but more importantly because they are knowable. Only by maximizing wealth can we hope to fulfill the mandate of utilitarianism.

It is also, however, precisely this commitment to preferences, choices, and wealth—grounded not in utilitarian ethics but in an independent and postmodern skepticism regarding the possibility of attaining knowledge about the subjectivity of others—that ultimately unhinges legal economists from their classically liberal and individualistic base and steers them instead toward modern conservatism. By substituting particular instances of objectively manifested consent, preferences, and wealth for the general conditions of subjective flourishing, happiness, pleasure, or well-being, to say nothing of autonomy, meaningful work, social engagement, and intellectuality, the law-and-economics movement has converted ideal-utilitarianism, at its inception, a potentially profoundly critical ethic—into first libertarianism and then conservatism. For, as countless critics—modern, postmodern, and otherwise—of the law-and-economics movement have now pointed out, our preferences and our consensual transactions no less than our markets are themselves the products of hierarchies of power that are in large part constructed by law.[10] Our preferences, our choices, and the transactions to which we give our consent reflect both our individual and our social histories, including present distributions of wealth and power, the prejudices of our upbringing, the pettiness or cramped meanspiritedness of our social peers, the xenophobia of our society, and the current state of our law. They hardly constitute an Archimedean point freed of the influences of power from which we can rationally criticize law. To the extent that preferences, choices, and consensual transactions reflect preexisting distributions of power and wealth, the criticism of law by reference to our choices is not less political than the criticism of law by reference to constructed ideals. It is also, to that extent, an inherently and inevitably conservative enterprise.

It is, then, not all that surprising that the law-and-economics movement has emerged not as the voice of radical individualism, or liberalism, or ideal-utilitarianism, but instead as the voice of conservatism in the legal academy. Both our private preferences reflected in the market and our public preferences reflected in participatory politics are a product of the orderings of our present world, including our legal world. The preferences, choices, consensual transactions, and existing desires of the individual in which the legal economist puts such faith do not provide a basis for moral criticism of law that is independent of the authority of law itself. Those preferences and choices are themselves the products of power, including legal power. To criticize power by reference to preference is ultimately to hold up power to power. Holding power up to power—the familiar authoritarian response—is no alternative to the Enlightenment scholar's illusive quest to hold power to the critical light of reason.

A parallel story can be told of the emergence of the much newer, 1980s law-and-humanities movement, and its unfolding transformation into yet another voice of conservatism in the legal academy. Although the law-and-humanities movement is far more diffuse than the law-and-economics movement, the story of the legal humanist's attempt to answer the postmodernist's challenge is nevertheless in many ways analogous to that of the legal economist's. Like the legal

10. See Kelman, *Critical Legal Studies*, 151–85; Cass R. Sunstein, "Legal Interference with Private Preference," *University of Chicago Law Review* 53 (1986): 1129–74; Margaret Radin, "Market Inalienability," *Harvard Law Review* 100 (1987): 1849–1937, and chaps. 1 and 7 in this volume.

economist's ambivalent ties to classical and ideal-utilitarianism, the law-and-humanities scholars are also ambivalently both attracted to and repelled by an underlying ethical and political philosophy. The participants in the modern law-and-humanities movement, for the most part, partially embrace and partially reject the modern civic republican's ideal of communitarian happiness, health, well-being, or virtue, just as the law-and-economics movement partially embraces and partially rejects the utilitarian's ideal of individual happiness, health, well-being, or flourishing. The conservatism that is now characteristic of so much law-and-humanities scholarship has its genesis in that ambivalence.

Modern civic republicanism, as a normative ideal, is a far more contemporary ethic than utilitarianism, but the two movements nevertheless have noteworthy structural similarities. The modern civic republican holds that the standard against which all acts of power should be judged is not individual health or happiness, as the utilitarian holds, but rather communitarian well-being, health, or happiness.[11] Like the utilitarian's individualism, the modern republican's communitarian normative goal is subjective: it is the subjectively felt happiness, or well-being, of the community (rather that the individual) that the lawmaker should seek to maximize. At the same time, and again like the utilitarian, the civic republican's method aims at some objectivity: just as the ideal-utilitarians developed various objective conceptions of the ideally happy individual life, civic republicans have developed objective or ideal conceptions of what constitutes a happy community. Communitarian happiness, for most modern republicans, is constituted by particular, knowable, contingent, culturally variable, but nevertheless specifiable attributes just as, for the ideal-utilitarian, individual happiness is constituted by particular, knowable, contingent, nonuniversal, but nevertheless fairly general characteristics. A good community, according to various modern republican conceptions, is a diverse, vibrant, self-governing, nonoppressive, deliberative, respectful, egalitarian, and caring community, and if a law promotes it, then it is a good law. A bad community, correlatively, is a homogenous, intolerant, deadened, oppressive, dis-

11. See, e.g., Cass R. Sunstein, "Beyond the Republican Revival," *Yale Law Journal* 97 (1988): 1539–59; Frank Michelman, "Law's Republic," *Yale Law Journal* 97 (1988): 1493–1537; Mark Tushnet, *Red, White, and Blue: A Critical Analysis of Constitutional Law* (Cambridge: Harvard University Press, 1988).

respectful, hierarchical, violent, and uncaring community, and again if a law promotes it, then it is a bad law.

From such general descriptions, republicans have begun to forge an account of ideal community life from which not only laws and legal systems, but also political systems and constitutions, can be criticized. Legal systems and community judgments that foster diverse, equal, tolerant, deliberative, self-governing, and vibrant communities can be presumed to promote communitarian well-being, while laws that foster hegemony and intolerance—such as antisodomy or miscegenation laws—are properly criticized on that account.[12]

Now, although it is considerably more murky than the relationship of the law-and-economics movement to classical utilitarianism, the law-and-humanities movement has a similar relation to the communitarian standard of value embraced by civic republicanism. Thus, many of our most prominent modern legal humanists, including thinkers as diverse as Stanley Levinson, Owen Fiss, and James Boyd White, agree with the civic republicans that the subjective health and well-being of the community, rather than the subjective happiness of the atomistic individual, ought be the goal of law. The humanistic thinkers tend to locate the common thread that connects them with their rejection, on this basis, of economic patterns and methods of thought.[13] But the sharp differences between the legal economists and the legal humanists may have blinded us to their similarities. One such similarity is simply that the relation of legal humanism to civic republicanism is more similar than dissimilar to the relation between economic legalism and utilitarian individualism. For, just as the legal economist sees a problem of knowledge with the ideal-utilitarian's insistence that one can meaningfully compare different subjective experiences and construct an objective standard of the good life, the legal humanist sees a problem of knowledge with the civic republican's claim that one can compare the worth of different conceptions of communitarian good and construct an objectively knowable standard of community value. How are we to know, asks the skeptical legal humanist, particularly the legal humanist most influenced by post-

12. Thus, Michelman criticizes antisodomy laws on the basis of civic republican ideals in "Law's Republic."

13. See Owen M. Fiss, "The Death of Law?" *Cornell Law Review* 72 (1986): 1–16; James Boyd White, "Economics and Law: Two Cultures in Tension," *Tennessee Law Review* 54 (1987): 161–202.

modern developments, whether participation, equality, tolerance, diversity, oppression, respect, care, hierarchy, or violation are criteria of a good or bad, healthy or unhealthy, happy or unhappy community? What is good for one community, after all, may be bad for another. How are we to know, then, whether a particular community or a particular description of an ideal community is an intersubjectively good or bad community? How are we to make these intercommunitarian judgments of utility?

Thus, just as the economists objected to ideal-utilitarian standards of criticism on the ground that the individualistic ideals it constructed required an inaccessible knowledge of the subjective lives of individuals, so the legal humanists fear that the communitarian ideals of civic republicanism require an inaccessible intercommunitarian knowledge of the well-being of other communities.[14] Drastically obscured by profound differences between these two movements is the fact that the objection in both cases to the creation of objective standards from comparisons of subjective experience of others stems from precisely the same source. Like interpersonal knowledge, the kind of intercommunitarian knowledge required by republicanism can neither be derived from abstract principles of moral truth, nor from empirically sound general truths of human or social nature. Neither form of knowledge—the interpersonal kind demanded by utilitarianism nor the intercommunitarian kind demanded by republicanism—can be derived from reason. Therefore, the knowledge critical republicanism requires, like the knowledge ideal-utilitarianism requires, is not possible. The law-and-humanities movement, like the law-and-economics movement, has its genesis in its response to precisely this problem of knowledge. Participation in the law-and-humanities movement, for many if not most, is primarily motivated by a search for a more public, and hence more knowable, criterion of communitarian value than that propounded by traditional political theorists, just as the law-and-economics movement begins with a search for a more public, and hence more knowable, criterion of individualistic welfare than that put forward by classical and ideal-utilitarian philosophers.

How is the problem solved? Like the legal economist (and unlike

14. See generally James Boyd White, "Is Cultural Criticism Possible?" *Michigan Law Review* 84 (1986): 1373–87, and "Thinking about Our Language," *Yale Law Journal* 96 (1987): 1974.

the postmodern theorist), the legal humanist remains committed to the general ideal of knowledge freed of the influence of power as the Archimedean point of reference from which meaningful criticism can proceed, and rational inquiry as the method by which such knowledge can be obtained. The legal humanist therefore needs a disciplined proxy for the unwieldy and politicized notion of community value, just as the legal economist sought out a proxy for individual well-being. At this point, modern critical literary theory enters the picture and solves the problem of knowledge. Heavily influenced by critical literary theory, the legal humanists find the proxy for communitarian well-being in the community's interpretive health and prowess. Just as the process of choosing and the preference that is its product serve as an objectively knowable proxy for subjective individual happiness for the modern legal economist, so the legal humanists find their criterion of subjective, communitarian value in the process of interpretation. The mere presence of an interpreted text evidences, for the legal humanist, the presence of minimal communitarian values, in a sense that strikingly parallels the legal economist's insistence that a fulfilled preference, or a choice, evidences an increase in individual personal well-being. For the existence of an interpreted text—a produced, heard, understood, and interpreted communication—at least evidences whatever equality and tolerance between speaker and listener is required for communication and interpretation to have successfully occurred. That may well be a considerable degree of equality and openness, both of which are certainly components of subjective community health. A community that vigorously produces, reads, discusses, interprets, and criticizes central and unifying shared texts is, therefore, a good community.

The legal humanist is thus moved to displace the civic republican's subjective, unknowable good, healthy community, and the participation, egalitarianism, diversity, and tolerance that are its constituent parts, as the standard of legal criticism, substituting the notion of the interpretive community: a community that is actively engaged in criticism, interpretation, and debate of its central, unifying texts is a good community, while one that is not so engaged is not. The notion of the interpretive community, after all, does not produce the problem of knowledge that plagues the subjective values behind the republican's criterion of communitarian well-being: interpretation is almost by definition a public, knowable, accessible process, and can be studied in a disciplined way, namely through the various disciplines of the humanities, just as objective, public, accessible preferences can be studied by economics. A law that facilitates the interpretive community, a law that furthers dialogic and interpretive values, is, therefore, a good law, and a law that frustrates such values is bad.

Thus, the legal humanist typically endorses the procedural values of unimpeded dialogue, communication, and fair hearing. In a representative passage, James Boyd White explains:

> Law-and-humanities studies teach us that we should continue to do what we have always done, which is to engage in the kind of conversation in which disagreements and misunderstandings are addressed, always imperfectly and always incompletely but not always without accession of understanding. Of course not all conversations go equally well. Implied in what I have said is that our attention must continuously be given to the quality of the conversational process: to our openness to the views of another, to our willingness to revise our own terms, to our readiness to learn more fully the degree to which, whenever we speak, we say more than we mean or know. Who am I to you, and you to me? With what attitude toward each other and toward our languages do we speak? What are our voices? If we can get these things right, the rest of what we care about, or ought to care about, will follow.[15]

Law, then, should be judged by whether it facilitates this interpretive and textual conversation. Judged by that standard, White concludes, Anglo-American legalism scores quite highly:

> As for law, it too partakes of the radical uncertainty of the rest of life, the want of firm external standards. But it is also a special way of living on these conditions, a way of making standards internally, out of our experience, as we make ourselves in our talk. The law is in fact a method of cultural criticism and cultural transformation, as well as cultural preservation. . . . [T]he law has been by far the best and most powerful method of cultural

15. White, "Cultural Criticism," 1384.

> criticism American society has had. . . . The main reason for this . . . is that the law is the structure multivocal, always inviting new and contrasting accounts and languages.[16]

My claim, then, is that the law-and-humanities movement has its inception in an attempt to transform the civic republican's critical communitarian standard from something unknowable—community happiness, health, or well-being—into something objective and knowable. Like the republican, the legal humanist remains committed to the proposition that a law should promote community values (such as openness, equality, diversity, and tolerance), but goes on to argue that law ought to be criticized not directly by reference to its tendency to creat morally worthy, egalitarian, open, and tolerant communities but rather by reference to whether or not it creates opportunities for textual production, readings, interpretation, conversation, and dialogue. The interpretive community becomes the lodestar of a good community, just as, for the economist, well-functioning markets and individual preferences and consensual transactions become the lodestar of individual well-being. Hence, for the legal humanist, the critical test of law is its capacity to create conditions conducive to the flourishing of the interpretive community: a community actively engaged in the production and interpretation of communicative texts. The legal humanist substitutes a commitment to interpretive practices as the criteria of value against which we should criticize law for the communitarian's intersubjective and unknowable healthy community, just as the economic legalist substitutes a commitment to preference, choice, and markets for the utilitarian's unknowable standard of individual happiness.

Again, I will ultimately question whether the legal humanist is right to be skeptical of the civic republican's ability to compare different communities' intersubjective well-being, and hence to construct ideals of communitarian well-being. But first I want to stress that it is precisely this skepticism, this doubt that we can know the community directly, that defines and unifies modern legal humanism and distinguishes it from contemporary civic republicanism, no less than the parallel skepticism regarding the accessibility of individual well-being distinguishes the law-and-economics movement from utilitar-

16. Ibid., 1386.

ianism. The legal humanist, like the civic republican, ultimately values community and holds to a communitarian standard of legal criticism: a law is a good law if it makes a good community. Unlike the republican, however, and clearly reflecting the influence of postmodern theory, the legal humanist is skeptical of our ability to know or specify the nature of the good community (as well as our ability to know and specify the nature of anything else), just as the legal economist is skeptical of our ability to know or specify the content of individual happiness. Since we cannot know what constitutes the intersubjective well-being of a community, we should seek instead either to mirror the lessons of canonical culture or to maximize the community's textual and interpretive productivity. If a law creates conditions that further the production, interpretation, and criticism of texts, it thereby furthers communitarian values. Laws should be criticized, then, by reference to their tendency to encourage or frustrate the well-being of the interpretive community. The interpretive community solves the problem of knowledge that plagues republicanism, no less than individual preference and markets solve the problem of knowledge that plagues utilitarian individualism.

It is also, however, precisely by substituting the interpretive community for the good community, that the legal humanist not only makes communitarian value susceptible to the reasoned critical attention of the humanities, but also converts it first into cultural traditionalism, and then into conservatism. For, as numerous postmodern and poststructuralist critics of humanism have argued, a high degree of textual interpretive activity is no more indicative of the presence of an egalitarian or tolerant or healthy community than is the existence of a fulfilled preference indicative of an increase in individual well-being. To put the same point slightly differently, writers and readers or speakers and listeners can communicate across, create, reify, and reinforce conditions of oppression, conformity, xenophobia, and hierarchy, just as individuals can contractually or freely consent within conditions of extreme inequality. Abstractly to value textual and interpretive productivity is ultimately to value whatever matrix of power is conducive to that particular form of productivity.[17] To value or criticize a law by reference to its capacity to generate inter-

17. This is a central insight of modern critical social theory. See generally Michel Foucault, *Discipline and Punish*, trans. Alan Sheridan (New York: Pantheon, 1977), and *The History of Sexuality*, trans. Robert Hurley (New York: Pantheon, 1978).

pretive and textual productivity within the interpretive community it creates and from which it derives is ultimately to criticize one act of power by references to others.

My hypothesis, then, very generally, is that in spite of the vast differences between these two movements—one is committed to libertarian and individualist goals while the other is committed to republican and communitarian goals; one is generally identified with the political Left and the other with the political Right; and one is allied with the humanistic disciplines of critical theory and the other with the social scientific discipline of economics—both the law-and-humanities movement and the law-and-economics movement have gone through similar patterns of development, crisis, reformulation, critique, and capitulation, and the end result in both cases has been a reversion to the legal complacency that both movements were initially well poised to avoid. Let me review that cycle. First, both movements are initially defined by their endorsement of overtly subjective or intersubjective goals, coupled with a rejection of the use of idealistic descriptions of the objective content and conditions of those goals as standards of legal criticism. Thus, the law-and-economics movement endorses the classical utilitarian's insistence that subjective individual well-being is the goal of law, but rejects the related legal realist's ideal-utilitarian claim that one can specify the nature of individual well-being in a way that can then serve as an evaluative standard for legal criticism. Rather, preference and choice, according to the legal economist, must serve as critical stand-ins. We should aim to maximize preference and choice (and criticize law by reference to whether or not it does so) rather than well-being, because preference and choice, unlike well-being, are measurable, quantifiable, knowable, and, hence, susceptible to the rationalist tools of the economic discipline. Similarly, the law-and-humanities movement endorses the civic republican's identification of subjective communitarian well-being as the goal of law, but rejects the republican's insistence that one can identify the nature of communitarian well-being in a way that can serve as the standard of legal criticism. Rather, communitarian interpretivism must serve as the critical standard instead. We should aim to nurture the community's interpretive productivity (and criticize law by reference to whether or not it does so) because a culture's interpretive practices, rather than comunitarian well-being, are susceptible to the critical and knowable standards of humanistic discourse. In both cases, it is the combination of partial endorsement and partial rejection of overtly subjective critical standards that defines the movements.

Second, both movements reject the use of individual and community happiness (or well-being) as the standard of legal criticism for much the same reason. In both cases, the interdisciplinary legalist is skeptical that the critic can attain or articulate any meaningfully general knowledge of the nature, content, or conditions of individual or community well-being. The result is that in both cases, the criterion of criticism—individual well-being on the one hand, communitarian well-being on the other—raises, in the eyes of the interdisciplinary scholar, a crisis of rationality. If we understand rationality to mean a commitment to the knowledge obtained through deductively sound and empirically verifiable propositions, then both the utilitarian and the republican standards require a sort of knowledge that cannot be rationally acquired. The ideal-utilitarian standard of the good life requires an unattainable knowledge of the comparative subjective well-being of individuals, and the civic republican ideal of the good community requires intersubjective knowledge of the comparative well-being of communities. Neither sort of knowledge, however, can be obtained through deductive inferences or empirically verifiable propositions. The sort of knowledge required for the moral standard against which the law is to be judged for both the ideal-utilitarian and the modern communitarian is not attainable.

Both modern interdisciplinary movements, law and economics and law and humanities, have their interdisciplinary inception in a response to this perceived epistemological crisis. Both endorse a particular goal, individual and communitarian well-being, as the goal of legalism. But both have come to view that goal as incapable of rational assessment or description. Neither individual nor communitarian well-being can be an object of rational knowledge, and consequently neither can serve as an Archimedean standard against which law should strive. Both movements, then, displace the original ideal as the basis against which law should be criticized with a more public standard that can be rationally knowable. For happiness the legal economist substitutes objectively knowable individual preferences, choices, and opportunities for consent. Under the legal economist's standard, whatever law maximizes one's preferences and one's consensual transactions (rather than one's well-being) is a good law, and whatever minimizes fulfillment of one's preferences or opportunities for consent is a bad law. Similarly, the legal humanist displaces the republican commitment to communitarian well-being with a commitment to the promulgation of texts and interpretations. Under the legal humanist's standard, whatever law maximizes the opportunity for dialogic participation in communitarian textual conversation is a good law, and whatever law frustrates such textual communication is a bad law. The community's interpretive productivity, unlike the worth of the community's values, can be objects of rational knowledge; it is possible, at least humanistically if not scientifically, to study a community's interpretive practices, even if we can never know that community's inner life.

In both cases, it is this displacement of the unknowable ideal of individual or community happiness with an object of rational knowledge—generated in turn by both a profound skepticism about the possibility of rational understandings of the nature of happiness, and continuing commitment to the Enlightenment ideal of rationality and discipline as the means by which knowledge is acquired—that defines the interdisciplinary legal movement. By substituting the purportedly unknowable ideals of individualistic and communitarian well-being with objective, quantifiable preferences and consensual transactions on the one hand, and communicative texts on the other, the scientific discipline of economics became central to the critical task of liberalism, and the humanistic disciplines of literature and literary theory became central to the critical work of communitarianism. Subjective, irrational ethics became tamed by disciplined knowledge. It is also, however, precisely this displacement of subjective ethics with the object of rational knowledge that proved to be fatal to both interdisciplinary movements' critical potential. In an effort to avoid irrationalism, both movements, at their inception, moved toward a standard amenable to disciplined rational inquiry as the benchmark of legal criticism. The legal economist moved away from individual subjective well-being to wealth maximization; the legal humanist moved away from intersubjective communitarianism toward interpretivism. But neither preferences, the lodestar of value to the legal economist, nor interpretive productivity, the lodestar of value for the legal humanist, can survive the postmodern critical assault on reason. Preferences and interpretations, no less than the worldly and transcendental knowledge that is the product of empirical and philosophical inquiry, are products of power, including legal power. Neither a community's interpretive practices nor our individual preferences are any more moral than the politics that produce them. When the economic and humanistic interdisciplinary scholars criticize law by reference to individualistic preferences on the one hand, and communitarian textual productivity on the other, they have both embraced a version of legalistic authoritarianism that their political forebears set out explicitly to avoid.

Sympathy, Intersubjectivity, and Intercommunitarianism

Is there any way that this circle can be broken? Put in terms of politics, the circle is this. In an attempt to escape the apparent irrationality of utilitarian and republican critique, the interdisciplinary scholars moved toward normative standards that they hoped would be more susceptible to disciplined analysis—preferences and markets for the legal economist; cultural texts and interpretations for the legal humanist. Those standards themselves, however, are no less hopelessly politicized by virtue of their rationality as the overtly political base from which each movement fled. Put epistemologically the circle is this. Both movements are conceived as attempts to provide alternatives to the impossibility of certain types of knowledge: the impossibility of knowing what utilitarianism requires, the conditions and contents of individual happiness, and the impossibility of knowing what republicanism requires, the conditions and content of community well-being. Both were then led by the force of that conviction to the development of more knowable standards and, hence, to interdisciplinary methods and commitments. The apparent objectivity of those standards, however, no less than the reasonableness and rationality of those interdisciplinary commitments, have quickly come to be understood as entirely dependent upon the extent to which the standards and disciplines in question recreate, reify, and legitimate existing hierarchy. Whether viewed epistemologically or politically, the outcome of the circle of subjectivity, irrationality, knowledge, discipline, and regression has been the same. Both movements have come to represent, in the modern legal world, a legal conservatism that may be culturally or economically sophisticated but is indistinguishable from the legal authoritarianism of the traditional, unidisciplinary legal scholar. Both movements moved from openly political, liberatory, and critical analysis to an apparently neutral, reasonable, disciplined, nonpolitical methodology, and both have wound up with a purportedly apolitical but, in fact, intensely conservative commitment to the values and mainstays of the status quo.

I want to suggest one possible way out of the circle of irrationality to discipline to regression, which is that we reexamine the crisis of knowledge that in each case started the circle rolling. We need to put back into consideration the possibility of knowledge of the subjectivity of both the individual and the community, which constituted, in turn, the basis of the ideals against which law was to be criticized. It is skepticism toward the possibility of knowing the nature of another individual's or community's subjective life that prompted first the legal economist and then the legal humanist to abandon individual and community well-being in favor of markets and interpretive practices as the standard against which law should be critically measured. But it is worth noting that the turn to alternative disciplines in each case was driven not only by postmodern doubt about philosophy and empirical science, but also by an Enlightenment-based faith in the methods of rationality: the interdisciplinary scholars insisted not only that individual and community happiness were, by their nature, not subject to rational inquiry, but that we should therefore substitute in their stead standards that would be susceptible to rational inquiry—wealth, for the economists; interpretations, for the humanists. Thus it was faith in rationality no less than skepticism toward claims of philosophical and scientific knowledge that drove the legal humanist and legal economist toward the interdisciplinary positions that now seem themselves to be so riddled with the politics of regression. That faith, however, may have been misplaced—the basis of it has now surely been put into doubt by postmodern scholars—and, if so, then that arguably misplaced faith might suggest a way out of the circle. If we have truly come to doubt the purifying moral power of rational inquiry, then surely we ought also to reexamine the rationalism-inspired doubts that led us to the conviction that it is not possible to know another's subjective welfare, or what it is to inhabit another's community. Rather than reject the criteria of individual and community well-being as standards of evaluation because they cannot be objects of rational inquiry, we might more profitably question the insistence on rationality as our standard of what is knowable.

Thus, it may indeed be true that we cannot rationally know the subjective feel of another individual's welfare or a community's health and cannot therefore rationally specify the nature of the good individual and communitarian life. If we are exclusively committed to rational methods of inquiry then we will have to displace those objects of knowledge with something else. But if, as now seems to be the case, we are no longer convinced of the virtues of rationalism, then we ought to consider arational means of understanding the subjectivity of individuals or of communities that are worthy of attention and respect. Our relentless and apparently failed quest for rational knowledge might have blinded us to other ways of knowing.[18] Rather than despair the failures of rational inquiry, we should explore those possibilities. In other words, the insistence on rational knowledge and, hence, on objects of rational knowledge, may have blinded us to the possibilities within the human spirt for arational and arationally acquired forms of undisciplined knowledge and insight.

Furthermore, and finally, it may be that knowledge and those insights, arationally acquired, that lie at the heart of an answer to the postmodern challenge. It may be, in other words, that arational knowledge is at the root of the ideals—individual autonomy, communitarian tolerance, and the like—that should and can constitute the standards against which we should judge legal and political acts of power. If we truly have come to realize, or believe, or suspect, that reason does not and cannot provide us with an independent standard against which to judge acts of power, then we ought at least to consider the possibility that other human attributes, capacities, and abilities might do or provide what reason cannot.

Let me give a couple of specific examples of what I mean by the claim that arational knowledge might constitute the real basis of a moral criticism of law and then make a couple of general concluding observations. First, the legal economist may be right to doubt that we can rationally know the subjectivity of other individuals and thus formulate an ideal conception of the good life on the basis of information rationally acquired through comparisons of those lives. But it does not follow from this doubt that we cannot know and compare the subjectivity of others and construct individualistic ideals on the basis of those comparisons. The source of our knowledge of the other may not be rationality, either understood as general norms of reason

18. Feminist studies are beginning to open up this possibility. See Mary Belenky et al., *Women's Ways of Knowing* (New York: Basic Books, 1986).

or as empirical claims about nature. Rather, the source of our knowledge of this subjectivity may be our utterly arational capacity for sympathy.[19] When we sympathize with the other, we open our hearts to his or her subjective predicament, rather than our minds to his or her behavioral choices and preferences. We sympathetically come to know the feel of his or her subjective pain, or the quality of his or her subjective pleasure. The knowledge we acquire through sympathetic sensitivity to the subjectivity of the other cannot, indeed, be quantified or calculated. It cannot become an object of rational knowledge. But that does not mean that such knowledge does not exist. It does exist. We can and do sympathize with others. We can, do, and should use our knowledge of the subjectivity of others, sympathetically and arationally acquired, in forming our ideals about what life should be like, and hence in forming our normative judgments about law.

Similarly, the legal humanist may be right to insist that we can never rationally know the quality of a community's life, but wrong to believe that it follows that we cannot know and hence compare the quality of communitarian life and form ideals on the basis of such knowledge. Again, it may have been wrongheaded to think that this sort of knowledge is rationally acquired. We know the qualitative feel of oppressive, tyrannical, violent communal living, and we know the qualitative feel of liberating, tolerant, egalitarian, robust, nurturing, caring, and vibrant community life, and we know that the first is a bad way to live in communities and that the second is a good way. We can judge a community's subjective well-being in the same way that we can judge an individual's. We open our hearts to the quality of the community members' lives. We can know more about the quality of a community's values than whether they are conducive to the production of public, communicative texts and interpretations, just as we can know more of the subjectivity of an individual's life than whether he or she has and acts on his or her

19. This is, of course, an old as well as a new claim. Adam Smith, among other thinkers of the Scottish Enlightenment, was impressed by the role of sympathy in the acquistion of moral knowledge. See Adam Smith, *The Theory of Moral Sentiments* (Oxford: Clarendon, 1971). Recently, feminist legal theorists have explored the role of sympathy and empathy in legal judgment. See Lynne N. Henderson, "Legality and Empathy," *Michigan Law Review* 85 (1987): 1574–1653; Martha Minow, "Justice Engendered," *Harvard Law Review* 101 (1987): 10–95. I explore the connection between this strand of feminist legal theory and legal critique in chap. 5.

preferences. Our communitarian life extends well beyond that which we textually express, just as our individual subjective life is far richer than that which is embodied in our preferences, and we can acquire an appreciation of that nontextual life, just as we can understand to some degree the quality of an individual's subjective life that is not reflected in his or her preferences. The knowledge we sympathetically acquire of the quality of nontextual life in particular communities might not be capable of rational, humanistic, literary analysis. But it does not follow that it does not exist.

In legal culture, we use this knowledge of the subjectivity of the individual and collective other when we argue that an unconscionable contract ought not be enforced, even though both parties consented to it, or that a community's or majority's textual moral commitment, enacted in law, ought not be honored, even though it fairly represents its will. We use this knowledge of the subjectivity of the individual or community life when we argue the merits of paternalistic legislation, or of judicial intervention into markets, or of nontextual constitutional protection of fundamental interests in which the majority of the public at any given time seem to have no perceived stake. Indeed, we must have considerable faith in our arational knowledge of the subjectivity of the other. We rely on such knowledge when we conclude that the other's expressed individual preference, or the community's articulated textual belief, is ill-advised, and that the contract or statute to which it gave rise ought not be enforced, by reference to our sense of the true, subjective welfare of the individual or communitarian other—even, at times, a quite distant other.

Thus, we use arational, sysmpathetic knowledge of the other not only when we criticize acts of power of distant lawmakers, but also acts of power that emanate from others themselves, such as a contractual commitment or a majoritarian preference. If this is a worthwhile thing to do—if our arational critical practices can indeed by justified—then the legal economist and the legal humanist are wrong to deny the practicability of the methods of criticism made possible by individualistic utilitarianism and communitarian republicanism. The legal economist and legal humanist turned away from subjective criteria of criticism because of their skeptical conviction that such criteria could ever become objects of rational knowledge. But maybe that skepticism was not, after all, well grounded. Perhaps subjective goals, individual happiness and a healthy community, can also be standards of criticism even if they can never be objects of rational knowledge. Perhaps, as the postmodern critics urge, our insistence on rationality was ill conceived. If it was, then we should reexamine the viability of overtly political and subjectivist criticism of the sort propounded by classical utilitarianism and modern civic republicanism. Moral criticism of law might be properly grounded not in abstract reason, nor in general truths, nor in the dictates of preexisting law, nor in naked power, but rather in the sympathetic judgments of the heart.

Once we recognize this capacity for sympathy, and the role it plays in our capacity for moral knowledge, we will also, perhaps, better appreciate its distinctive failings—most notably the perverse dependence of our capacity to build sympathetic feelings of solidarity, community, and wholeness with some upon principles and practices of exclusion of others. With an understanding of the extent to which our moral commitments, ideals, and, hence, critical judgments about law are grounded in sympathy for the others in our lives, we might consequently better appreciate the failings and limits of that capacity and thereby improve the quality of our moral lives themselves. Ideally we might learn to use the tools of sympathetic identification and learning to counter the limitations of our moral sentiments. The end result could be a far richer, even if no less constructed, moral understanding of the impact of our law on the quality of the subjective lives of the individuals and communities it may, indeed, in part construct, but which it no doubt affects. We should not be deterred from the project by the perceived irrationality of the human capacity at its core.

Those of us in the nonmainstream interdisciplinary legal academy who have tried to answer the question posed by postmodernism—how should we criticize the law, if not by reference to reason, and if not by reference to the law itself—have gone wrong, I believe, in our conviction that we should look to other academic disciplines for normative guidance. We should, indeed, be looking for guidance outside the legal academy, and it is surely true that other disciplines have much to offer. But we have relied too heavily on other disciplines, and on the idea of discipline that underlies them, for an articulation of our ideals. We should instead look to our sympathetic understandings both of the ideal community central to civic republicanism and the ideal individual central to liberal utilitarianism and the commitments to freedom, welfare, tolerance, nurturance, egalitarianism, individualism, and communitarianism that compete within and between them. No doubt if we do so, we will quickly realize that other academic disciplines are indispensable to our ability to achieve, articulate, enrich, and defend our moral convictions. We do indeed, most emphatically, need stories and metaphors to understand the subjectivities of lives not our own, particularly of those silenced lives that, for whatever reason, find themselves outside the perimeters of the dialogic interpretive community but not outside the reach of the law's coercive force. Similarly, we do indeed need economics to appreciate the far-flung and invisible consequences of our policies and desires, and we do indeed need theories of interpretation to come to grips with the inevitable limits of our understanding. But our moral beliefs and ideals themselves must come from the politics and struggles of the heart, not the disciplines of the mind. It is those moral convictions, grounded not in reason but in love, nurtured not in the head but in the heart, borne not in discipline but in the bonds of community, and realized not in the constraint of rationality but in the work of free individuals, that should inform our critical, and particularly our radically critical, sensitivities.

Chapter 7

Taking Preferences Seriously

Growing numbers of modern conservative legal theorists argue, for different and sometimes conflicting reasons, that judges should take the revealed preferences of either private contractors, or public legislators, or both, very seriously indeed.[1] Over the last decade, the most prominent of these theorists have become appellate judges,[2] and as a consequence, respect for revealed preferences increasingly is becoming a norm of judicial decision making, and not just a theoretical construct. Thus, Judges Richard Posner and Frank Easterbrook of the Seventh Circuit, as well as former judge Robert Bork of the D.C. Circuit (all potential or past Supreme Court nominees), have argued that when the desires to which preferences give expression are satisfied, value is created, and therefore, a judge who uses her power to identify and then satiate objectively revealed preferences has exercised her power morally.[3] For the conservative legal theorist, satisfaction of the preferences of individuals is the source of value, and hence the key to moral decision making, both judicial and otherwise. Respect for the preferences of others, according to these conservative theorists turned judges, is therefore a judge's primary moral duty.

1. See, e.g., Richard A. Epstein, *Takings: Private Property and the Power of Eminent Domain* (Cambridge: Harvard University Press, 1985), 149, 252–53; Robert Bork, "Neutral Principles and Some First Amendment Problems," *Indiana Law Journal*, 47 (1971): 1–20; Frank H. Easterbrook, "Method, Result, and Authority: A Reply," *Harvard Law Review*, 98 (1985): 627–29; Frank H. Easterbrook, "Legal Interpretation and the Power of the Judiciary," *Harvard Journal of Law and Public Policy* 7 (1984): 94–99; Frank H. Easterbrook, "Statutes' Domains," *University of Chicago Law Review* 50 (1983): 544–52; Richard A. Epstein, "Unconscionability: A Critical Reappraisal," *Journal of Law and Economics*, 18 (1975): 294. See generally Anthony T. Kronman and Richard A. Posner, *The Economics of Contract Law* (Boston: Little, Brown, 1979).

2. Judges Posner and Easterbrook are on the 7th Circuit, and Judge Bork formerly was on the D.C. Circuit.

3. See generally Richard A. Posner, *The Economics of Justice* (Cambridge: Harvard University Press, 1981), 88-115; Bork, "Neutral Principles," 1–20.

Preferences should be regarded seriously, according to the conservative legalists, because of two distinct (and somewhat conflicting) conservative commitments with two distinctive normative implications for the ethics of adjudication, one in the realm of private law and the other in the realm of constitutional law. First, some conservative theorists base their respect for preferences in libertarian principles. According to these libertarian conservative legalists, judges should not interfere with our private or primary preferences that are revealed through our consensual, contractual choices in the marketplace of goods and services.[4] Judges should therefore refrain from paternalistic intervention into private contract, even when they clearly have the legal authority to intervene.[5] Assuming the judge has a legal choice in the matter, for moral reasons she should neither refuse to enforce a contract on the grounds that it is contrary to public policy or unconscionable nor imply into those contracts mandatory, nonwaivable terms that would paternalistically protect the contracting party against his own freely chosen, albeit unwise, preferences. The improvident, but voluntary preferences reflected in our bad contractual choices—such as consumer contracts for nonessential luxury goods with onerous, cross-collateral credit terms, or sales contracts for cheap but unwarranted household products, or sales contracts for babies or sex, or service contracts for our reproductive capacities—should be given the same respect as any other contractually bargained-for promise or obligation. All our contracts reflect our private preferences, which in turn reflect our private desires, which, if satisfied, will produce value. Judges should enforce contracts as written.

Second, other conservative theorists ground their respect for preferences in the more modern conservative commitment to judicial restraint. For these theorists, as for their libertarian colleagues, respect for preferences is the key to moral decision making. But for this second group this basic principle has implications in the public realm and not just in the private. These "judicial constraint" legal conser-

4. See Kronman and Posner, *Economics of Contract Law*, 253–61; Epstein, "Unconscionability," 293–95. See generally Epstein, *Takings*.

5. See Kronman and Posner, *Economics of Contract Law*, 253–61; Epstein, "Unconscionability," 293-311; Charles T. Goetz and Robert E. Scott, "Liquidated Damages, Penalties, and the Just Compensation Principal," *Columbia Law Review* 77 (1977): 593–94.

vatives believe respect for preferences implies that judges should not interfere with the second-order or external or simply the social preferences of communities regarding the type of conduct that we ought, as a society, indulge or disallow.[6] Just as the libertarian conservative legalist argues that in the private sphere, unwise individual preferences should be honored and if need be enforced against later regret, so the judicial restraint conservative legalist argues that in the public sphere as well, our unwise social preferences—for prohibitions against homosexual sodomy, for laws criminalizing abortion, for tolerance of private racial discrimination, or for the criminalization (or decriminalization) of pornographic expression—must also be regarded as sacrosanct. They too reflect preferences that in turn reflect desires that, if fulfilled, create value. Therefore, the same principled respect for preferences of others entails that judges should refrain from nonmandatory constitutional interpretation that paternalistically upsets a community's social preferences.[7]

Thus, we might generate this principle of conservative legalism: judges should take preferences as inviolable in the two spheres in which they are most clearly revealed: private contracting and public lawmaking. Sometimes, of course, these conservative commitments to individual liberty and judicial restraint might conflict: a community may prefer that an individual's preference—say, to ride a motorcycle without a helmet—ought not be respected and enact legislation reflecting that communitarian and antilibertarian preference. In such a case, the conservative legalists will divide, depending upon whether they view individual liberty or judicial restraint as the more fundamental conservative commitment. But, however they decide such cases, we have come legitimately to expect that conservative judges and theorists generally will be guided by a respect for preferences, both public and private. For the conservative legalists, constitutional principles that narrow the realm of permissible legislative decision making and contract principles that narrow the scope of permissible contract should all be narrowly construed and for essentially the same reason. The judge should neither rewrite a contract nor overturn the legislature's will, because both the private contract and the public law are means by which our preferences are revealed,

6. See Bork, "Neutral Principles," 9–11; Easterbrook, "Method," 627–29.
7. Ibid.

and satisfaction of those preferences is in turn the means by which value is created.

Two recent cases exemplify the growing influence of the legal conservatives' respect for preferences upon our habits of adjudication and, therefore, upon our substantive law. In both cases the reviewing court expressed precisely the respect for revealed preference and hence the hostility to judicial paternalism advocated by the legal conservatives. First, in *Bowers v. Hardwick* the justices of the United States Supreme Court upheld Georgia's antisodomy statute, clearly aimed at criminalizing consensual homosexual conduct, against constitutional attack.[8] The Supreme Court unquestionably had the legal authority to strike the legislation, but it chose not to do so. The Court could have ruled on either privacy or equal-protection grounds that a statute criminalizing consensual homosexuality violates the constitutional rights of homosexuals. More specifically, the Court could have held that Georgia's antisodomy statute violated the equal protection clause of the Fourteenth Amendment had it found that because homosexuals are a hated and irrationally maligned minority, antihomosexuality legislation is analogous to legislation based on a "suspect classification" and therefore should be struck unless it serves a compelling state need.[9] Alternatively, the Court could have ruled that antihomosexuality legislation violates a fundamental right to privacy, by analogizing consensual homosexuality to the consensual, nonreproductive heterosexuality implicitly protected in the Court's reproductive freedom cases, from *Griswold v. Connecticut* to *Roe v. Wade.*[10] Instead, the Court upheld the statute, and it did so at least in part because of a newfound moral duty to eschew intervention and defer to the community's social preferences.

Second, *In re Baby M*[11] upheld a private contract for surrogacy motherhood against a range of attacks by the later-regretful gestational mother. Again, the New Jersey trial court judge unquestionably

8. 478 U.S. 186 (1986).

9. For a general discussion of the meaning of "suspect classification," see Regents of Univ. of Cal. v. Bakke, 438 U.S. 265, 290–91 (1978). On striking the legislation in the absence of compelling need, see Bowers, 478 U.S. 196 and n. 8. The Court did not address this argument, but noted that the plaintiff might have brought an action under the equal protection clause.

10. 381 U.S. 479 (1965); 410 U.S. 113 (1973).

11. 217 N.J. Super. 313, 525 A.2d 1128 (1987), aff'd in part and rev'd in part, 109 N.J. 396, 337 A.2d 1227 (1988).

had the legal authority to strike the contract.[12] The choice to the trial court was a clear one. The trial judge could have ruled that this contract was either unconscionable, illusory, or a violation of public policy. More specifically, the judge could have found that the surrogacy contract was violative of public policy by analogizing a contract for the sale of a woman's reproductive capacity to a contract for the sale of body parts or to the sale of a baby, both of which are outside the realm of permissible contractual freedom.[13] Alternatively, the trial judge could have found that the surrogacy contract as written was unconscionable and could then either strike the contract, or imply into it a mandatory one-month grace period after the birth of the baby within which the gestational mother could change her mind.[14] Again the judge had ample precedential authority to paternalistically strike or modify the contract and chose not to in part because of a felt moral duty to eschew intervention and to defer to the preferences of private contracting parties.

Thus, both the trial court judge in *Baby M* and the Supreme Court justices in *Bowers v. Hardwick* refused to intervene paternalistically, and in both cases, the judge or justices hearing the cases justified that refusal, in part, by invoking the sovereignty of preferences and the consequent impropriety of judicial paternalism. In both cases, the courts' perceived moral obligation to refrain from impermissible judicial paternalism ultimately determined the litigants' legal entitlement. Neither court explicitly employed conservative arguments to justify their refusal to act paternalistically. But the outcomes of both cases, and the courts' cavalier dismissal of paternalistic grounds for intervention, nevertheless demonstrate the growing

12. In fact, the reviewing appellate court reversed the trial court and did indeed strike the contract. See In re Baby M, 109 N.J. 396, 337 A.2d 1227 (1988).

13. See, e.g., James B. Boskey, "The Damage Done by the Baby M Ruling," *New Jersey Law Journal* 119 (1987): 585, 604; "Surrogacy-Baby Selling," *American Bar Association Journal* 73 (1 June 1987): 38–39; "A Judicial Mistake," *L.A. Daily Journal*, 2 April 1987. See generally W. Marshall Prettyman, "Provisions Violate Public Policy," *New Jersey Law Journal* 119 (1987): 333–34.

14. See Barbara Cohen, "Surrogate Mothers: Whose Baby Is It?" *American Journal of Law and Medicine* 10 (1984): 262; Mark Rust, "Whose Baby Is It? Surrogate Motherhood after Baby M," *American Bar Association Journal* 73 (1987): 55–56; see also Martha A. Field, *Surrogate Motherhood* (Cambridge: Harvard University Press, 1988), 84–109; "The Rights of the Biological Father: From Adoption and Custody to Surrogate Motherhood," *Vermont Law Review* 12 (1987): 115–16 (discusses recent New York legislation on surrogate parenting).

influence of conservative legalism on judicial attitudes. Conservative legalist arguments against judicial paternalism are reshaping the fundamental principles of the ethics of adjudication and through them, of contract and constitutional law as well.

This chapter argues generally for judicial paternalism, in both the contractual and constitutional spheres. I will conclude that the judiciary's newfound obligation to defer to contractual and legislative preference, exemplified in cases like *Hardwick* and *Baby M*, does not constitute a defensible moral impulse, conservative, liberal, or otherwise. Rather, an absolutist judicial deference to preference in cases such as these constitutes a moral failure. Thus, like many other critics of a preference-based morality, I will conclude that judges should not take either individual or communitarian preferences quite so seriously. However, I will also contend that although the arguments against the wisdom of many of our private and public preferences put forward by contemporary critics of conservative legalism are convincing, their affirmative case for judicial paternalistic intervention is seriously incomplete. I will accordingly offer what I believe is a more complete defense of judicial paternalistic intervention.

Part 2 below outlines what I take to be the conservative legalists' major arguments against judicial paternalism. Part 3 outlines the major criticisms that have been made of the conservative legalists' case and then explains why those criticisms are incomplete. Parts 4 and 5 put forward my affirmative defense of judicial paternalism. My thesis will be that the moral as well as motivational basis for paternalistic judicial intervention into both private contracts and public legislation is the judge's sympathetic understanding of the subjective well-being, aspirations, goals, values, and plights of the litigants before her. Thus, in the sparse language of the legal economists, judicial paternalism rests on an "interpersonal comparison of utilities" and on the knowledge gleaned from those comparisons. I will then argue that this sympathetic response to the subjectivity of the other is not only what justifies judicial paternalism, but also what distinguishes it from legislative paternalism. Because of the much-maligned structure of the adversarial system of trial, judges are peculiarly well positioned institutionally to make precisely these sorts of sympathetic judgments. The case-by-case nature of adjudication, the immediacy of the litigants' narratives, and the reliance on flexible precedent all suggest that judges may be better situated than legislators to make morally justified paternalistic decisions in this way. I determine that far from being impossible, as the conservative legalists insist, an interpersonal comparison of subjective utility is the act of love, care, and sympathy that constitutes the essence of judicial paternalism.

In the conclusion I briefly explore the role of sympathetic judgment in the context of the two particular decisions mentioned above: first, the *Baby M* case involving a contractual preference for surrogate motherhood; and second, the *Hardwick* case involving a legislative preference for the criminalization of homosexual sodomy. I will argue that in both cases, the judge's or justices' refusal to intervene paternalistically in the manifested preferences of the litigants-individual preferences manifested in the private contract in the first case, and communitarian preferences manifested in the public legislation in the second was unjustified. In each situation, the court could have intervened as a legal matter and should have intervened as a moral matter. In each, the court's failing to do so constituted a failure of sympathy, a refusal to care, a turning away from the other, and accordingly, a breach of the court's moral role.

Taking Preferences Seriously

The conservative legal theorists' two major arguments against judicial paternalism, in both the public and private spheres, rest squarely on a utilitarian moral base. Thus, both arguments assume that when judges have a choice—when the law is unclear, or when the law delegates to the judge some degree of discretion—judges should decide cases in whatever way maximizes the subjective well-being of all affected parties.[15] That utilitarian maxim alone, however, does not counsel against judicial paternalism. Both of the legal conservatives' arguments against judicial paternalism couple the utilitarian premise that judges should decide cases so as to maximize utility with particular empirical claims about our human nature.

The first argument stems loosely from the law-and-economics tradition and plays the greater role in libertarian reasoning against judicial intervention into private sphere contractual decision making.

15. Epstein is the only law-and-economics theorist who labels himself a utilitarian. See Epstein, *Takings*, 334–38. The rest adopt some modified version. See *EJ*, 48–88.

The argument is simply that our revealed preferences are generally rational, by which is meant that for the most part every individual and every community will desire—and hence prefer—that which is in his, her, or its true interest (*EJ*, 1–2). We desire that which will increase our subjective well-being, and we manifest those desires in our preferences. If the judge ought to maximize well-being, and if our preferences are rational, then the judge, like any other moral actor, ought to respect our revealed preferences. They are the most reliable guide to what she is morally obligated to maximize: our subjective well-being. (*EJ*, 1–2; *ES*)

The second argument rests not on the assumed rationality of the litigants' preferences, but rather on a narrow vision of the competencies of the judge as a moral actor. This contention, which, unlike the first, has been unexamined and undercriticized by critics of legal conservatism, stems from the separate discipline of welfare economics. Although not accepted uniformly by all legal conservatives, it has nevertheless played a significant role in legal conservative arguments against judicial intervention in both the public and private spheres. The argument is as follows. We are each different. My subjective life is unlike your subjective life. What I feel as pleasure, you may feel as pain. As a result of our differences, I can never simply assume that what I feel as pleasurable you will also feel as pleasurable because I cannot experience your sensations. Like every other moral actor, I cannot make these interpersonal comparisons of utility.[16] I cannot, for example, assume that the pain I feel from your insult, your pornography, or your loan-sharking contract, is greater than the pleasure you experience in making the insult, consuming the pornography, or charging usurious interest because I cannot assume that you and I feel pleasure from the same things, to the same degree, and in the same ways. I cannot know, to take more mundane examples, that the pain you feel upon breaking your leg is greater than

16. The classic formulation of this claim is in Lionel Charles Robbins, *An Essay on the Nature and Significance of Economic Science*, 2d ed. (London: Macmillan, 1935), 138–54. See also Bork, "Neutral Principles," 10 n. 20. See generally Amartya Kumar Sen, "Interpersonal Comparisons of Welfare," in *Choice, Welfare, and Measurement* (Cambridge: MIT Press, 1982); Harsayni, "Cardinal Welfare, Individualistic Ethics and Interpersonal Comparisons," *Journal of Political Economy* 63 (1955): 309; Tibor Scitovsky, "The State of Welfare Economics," *American Economic Review* 41 (1951): 303.

the pain I feel (or a third party feels) from a pinprick.[17] I cannot know that a hot and tired tennis player will be more refreshed by a cola than the spectator sitting in the shade. The subjectivity of the other is cognitively impenetrable. Therefore, although the judge is charged with the duty of maximizing subjective well-being, she cannot know what the subjective well-being of the other is like. The judge, then, faces a dilemma. Although the comparative quantity, quality, and intensity of felt pain and pleasure ultimately determine what the judge ought to do—she ought to maximize pleasure and minimize pain, and the intensities of each do count—there is no way she can know the nature, quality, quantity, or intensity of each individual's subjective experience under each alternative outcome.

The judge must therefore employ some sort of knowable, objective, behavioral proxy for the unknowable, subjective quality she is obligated to promote. In the private sphere, contract fills this role. Although a judge cannot know anything about our subjective states, she can know our objective behavior. And, assuming that our preferences are rational, she can draw powerful inferences from our behavior. For example, if Johnny has bubble gum and Susan has candy, and they agree to a trade, then a judge can infer from that agreement (given that Johnny is rational) that at least at the point of trade, Johnny thought he would enjoy the candy more than he would be hurt by giving up the bubble gum, and Susan the reverse. Furthermore, if the two contractually agree to trade at some point in the future, the judge can infer that at least at the time of contracting Johnny expected that he would enjoy the promised performance more than his own performance would cost him.[18] Thus, Johnny's objective, knowable contractual choices behaviorally manifest his unknowable subjective utility. The judge, then, who is concerned with maximizing the well-being between Johnny and Susan, will not forcibly redistribute the goods, but will take whatever action is necessary to permit their free, contractual exchange. Similarly, a judge concerned with maximizing subjective well-being cannot directly know the nature of a consumer's subjective enjoyment of purchased goods, or of a seller's or producer's subjectively felt costs. But, assuming the rationality of

17. I owe this example to Mark Kelman. Mark Kelman, "Choice and Utility," *Wisconsin Law Review* 1979 (1979): 779.

18. See Kronman and Posner, *Economics of Contract Law*, 1–2, 5–7.

preferences, the judge can know that at least the buyer thinks that she (the buyer) will enjoy an item purchased more than she would have enjoyed the money paid. The judge can know that a seller expects to enjoy the price more than the resources consumed by the cost of his performance (Cf. *EA*, 66–98, an analogous tort law example). The judge concerned with maximizing subjective utility, then, will enforce contracts as written.

In the public sphere, votes serve (roughly) the same proxy function as do contracts in the private. The reviewing judge in the public sphere is disabled from comparing subjective utilities across groups just as, in the private sphere, the judge is disabled from comparing the subjective utility of alternative distributions for the same individual.[19] The reviewing judge cannot know, for example, whether the majority who are disgusted by homosexual conduct will be in greater pain over such conduct should it be permitted, than would be the homosexual minority should their activity be criminalized. The judge cannot penetrate the subjectivity of either group. She can, though, know how they vote. Barring a structural defect in the representational system, she can infer from those votes the subjective utility to each group of the challenged legislation.

Thus, both of the conservatives' arguments against judicial paternalism follow not from utilitarianism alone, but from utilitarianism coupled with one or the other or both of these two claims regarding our human nature: that we are each rational maximizers of our own utility and unable to gauge the subjective utility of others. When the judge has a choice, she should exercise power in whatever way will maximize the subjective well-being of both the litigants before her and the larger class of persons who will be affected by her holding. But, because she cannot compare their interpersonal utilities, she cannot do so by maximizing the subjectivity that is unknowable to her. The judge is thus empathically impotent; she cannot penetrate their subjective awareness. Because their preferences are rational, however, she doesn't have to. The contractor and the voting citizen manifest their unknowable subjectivity in their quite knowable contractual and legislative choices. The moral judge should then defer to those choices. There is no room for paternalistic intervention in

19. For an example of the interplay between judicial decision making and public and private decision making, see Bork, "Neutral Principles," 9–11; Easterbrook, "Method," 627.

either the contractual or the constitutional context. The moral but nonempathic judge relies on neutral, amoral mechanisms, contracts and voting, to aggregate subjective and unknowable utility and thus to dictate the morally required result.

Pro-Paternalism

The joint dependence of the legal conservatives' case against judicial paternalism upon a particular utilitarian theory of what morality requires on the one hand, and a particular view of human nature on the other, obviously invites two lines of attack. Liberal legal theorists who abhor utilitarianism, such as Laurence Tribe, Paul Brest, and Ronald Dworkin, all attack the economists' case against paternalism for its dependence on what those critics assume to be the inadequacy of its underlying moral theory: utilitarianism.[20] Value, the liberal theorists argue, is not a function of subjective well-being, as conservative utilitarians incorrectly assume. Therefore, whether or not preferences accurately reflect well-being, the economic arguments against judicial paternalism fail. A good judicial decision is not necessarily the decision that maximizes well-being; rather, a good judicial decision is the decision that protects rights. It follows that a judge might intervene into a contractual or legislative preference to promote some competing value, such as autonomy, equality, justice, or fairness. The judge can intervene into preferences, but not on the basis of the preference holders' true interest. Rather, the judge intervenes on the basis of some nonutilitarian value, which may or may not converge with the parties' true interest.

The merit of this antiutilitarian (and nonpaternalistic) argument for judicial intervention is beyond the scope of this chapter, other than to note that the liberal argument (at times) rests on the false assumption that utilitarian morality alone entails an unswerving respect for preferences, and hence judicial passivity in the face of contracts or legislation.[21] The second critical attack on the economists'

20. See, e.g., Paul Brest, "The Fundamental Rights Controversy: The Essential Contradictions of Normative Constitutional Scholarship," *Yale Law Journal* 90 (1981): 1102–5; R. M. Dworkin, "Is Wealth a Value?" *Journal of Legal Studies* 9 (1980): 216; Laurence H. Tribe, "Constitutional Calculus: Equal Justice or Economic Efficiency?" *Harvard Law Review* 98 (1985): 598.

21. I have criticized this argument elsewhere. See Robin West, "In the Interest of the Governed: A Utilitarian Justification for Substantive Judicial Review," *Georgia Law Review* 18 (1984): 469–528.

argument against judicial paternalism, and the attack with which I will be primarily concerned in this chapter, comes from a range of theorists who generally accept (or do not challenge) the legal conservative welfare-maximizing assumption about the scope of the judge's role. According to these critics, a good judicial decision may well be the decision that maximized well-being. However, it is not necessarily the case, as the legal conservatives assume, that the way to maximize well-being is by satiating as many preference-driven desires as the judicial machinery permits. An individual's preferences may or may not accurately reflect that person's actual well-being. When they do, preferences should be respected; but when they do not, preferences can justifiably be set aside, and on purely utilitarian grounds. I will call this second group *antipreference critics*.

The Argument against the Sovereignty of Preference

According to the antipreference critics, our preferences may fail to reflect our true interest for any number of reasons. First, and most importantly for the antipreference critics, our preferences are themselves heavily influenced by, if not the product of, extant social structures, including public law and private contracts, and it is therefore circular to justify enforcement of the latter by reference to the former.[22] Those social structures may themselves be antithetical to our interest, as may be the preferences to which they give rise. For example, my inclination to consent to a surrogacy contract may indeed accurately reflect my preferences, but my preference for money over the exclusive use of my reproductive capacities may itself be a product of a culture that excessively (and to my detriment) commodifies aspects of my being—including my labor as well as my sexuality and reproductive life.[23] If so, then it will not necessarily follow from my preference for a surrogacy contract that surrogacy is indeed in my best interest. Similarly, a community's political preference to live in a society free of homosexuality may reflect not the community's true interest, but the influence of a homophobic, xenophobic, or simply bigoted social

---

22. See, e.g., Kelman, "Choice and Utility," 772–78; Cass Sunstein, "Naked Preferences and the Constitution," *Columbia Law Review* 84 (1984): 1694–95. See generally Margaret Jane Radin, "Market-Inalienability," *Harvard Law Review* 100 (1987): 1849–37.

23. See Radin, "Market-Inalienability," 1921–37.

milieu.[24] If respected, such a preference may play to the society's worst instincts, and far from serving or increasing its well-being, may narrow its members' sense of humanity and stunt the community's growth. In both cases, preferences may indeed be a function of the individual or majority's assessment of its own subjective well-being, but that assessment itself is the product of a powerful ideology, which itself originates in the interests of a particular class, race, and gender that has anything but individual or societal true interest at heart. If I am downtrodden, my contractual preferences may reflect that state: I may prefer commodities, services, or wages that justify that subordination, thereby reducing my uncomfortable cognitive dissonance with the status.[25] If I am oppressed, my political preferences may reflect, promote, and further my state of oppression. In such a case, my preferences have been shaped by that state of oppression, rather than by a vision of myself that I could conceivably and profitably become.[26] Similarly, if many of the members of a community are oppressed, limited, uneducated, or ill-informed, then the community's or majority's collective political preferences will be distorted as well.

In all these scenarios, the antipreference critics argue, the individual's or the community's preferences—for surrogate parenthood, for antihomosexual legislation, for higher wages instead of a share of ownership—may be "irrational," meaning simply that they are for distributions of power, wealth, or resources that will not promote the individual's true interest or the true interest of society. In each case the preference is for a commodity, a contract, a labor agreement, or a piece of legislation that the individual or the community believes will further true self or social interest, but which will not in fact do so. In each case, then, the judge who is committed to maximizing well-being should not be barred from intervention by an absolute commitment to the rationality of preference. Some preferences do not reflect true interest. The judge thus committed should set ideologically soiled preferences aside in favor of individual or societal true interest.[27]

24. See Sunstein, "Naked Preferences," 1693–1705.

25. Ibid.

26. Ibid.

27. See Cass Sunstein, "Legal Interference with Private Preferences," *University of Chicago Law Review* 53 (1986): 1130–31; Sunstein, "Naked Preferences," 1691–93.

The image of human nature that emerges from the critics' attack on preferences contrasts sharply with that assumed by the legal conservatives. According to the conservatives, the individual is almost entirely his own creation. Although the individual is assuredly a part of his society, the influence its social structures have over his subjective, intentional life is virtually nil. The individual's subjectivity comes with a protective force shield, so to speak, that keeps out extraneous influences. Other than for a few narrowly drawn exceptions (primarily the preferences of minors and mental incompetents), the individual's preferences, intentions, dreams, ambitions, desires, and plans of life are presumed to be entirely his own.[28] My preferences are my own, my scheme of the good life is my own, my values are my own,[29] my intentions are my own, and my ambitions are my own. I own them in much the way and with the same rights of exclusively as I own my furniture. According to the critics, in sharp contrast, the individual and her preferences are the creation of the society and more specifically of the society's web of hierarchical relations that constructs her. There is no "force field" protecting my subjectivity; my boundaries are fluid. My preferences are in no meaningful sense my own, no matter how strongly I may feel them to be. Although preferences are the obvious target of the critics' attack, the same is true of my wants, desires, ambitions, or dreams: what I feel most to be my own—my private world of intentionality—turns out to be least my own. I am inevitably locked in a web of influence, and my intentions, ambitions, dreams, ideals, and desires—no less than my preferences—reflect the web.

These two conceptions of human nature imply sharply contrasting visions of the rationality of the individual's preferences (and inferentially, of communitarian preferences). According to the legal conservatives, the individual is rational in a motivational as well as a cognitive sense (*EJ*, 1–9). The world, particularly the legal one, presents him with a series of choices, possible payoffs, and possible sanctions: if he commits a crime, he may reap a benefit, but he must also serve the time. It is his choice. If he enters into an unenforceable

---

28. This presumption gives rise to the basically pejorative phrases "possessive individualism" or "atomism."

29. The commitment to the subjectivity of value is cogently criticized in Mark Kelman, *A Guide to Critical Legal Studies* (Cambridge: Harvard University Press, 1987), 64–85.

contract, it may go as planned, but there is some chance that it will not, in which case the unenforceability of the contract will lower the contract's value. Perhaps then he should pay more and purchase a contract that is enforceable. Again, it is his choice. If he steps out into the street, he may reach his destination safely, but he may be hit by an uninsured motorist—perhaps he should take out first-party insurance (*EJ*, 95). On the other hand, if he favors risk, perhaps he should not. It is his choice. The individual amasses all of this information about the outside world and plans his future accordingly. He knows his true interest, he knows his degree of attraction or repulsion to risk, and he can calculate probabilities as well as the next person. He wants to increase his subjective well-being, and he constantly assesses the outside world and the options it presents him with this goal in mind. He is always choosing, even when he does not know it. He is competently self-regarding (*EJ*, 1–9). He is not a saint, but neither is he a burden (the central these in *ES*, 1432–38). He chooses what he prefers, he prefers what he wants, he wants what he desires, and he desires what is in his interest. Therefore, his interest is best promoted by leaving him with whatever his choices have yielded.

According to the critics, by contrast, the individual who holds preferences is deeply irrational. What he wants and desires is not to further his interest, but to comply with the social structures—physical, psychic, economic, and affective—in which he finds himself. Therefore, the social world presents the individual not with a series of possible payoffs and sanctions from which he chooses what will best promote his interest, as the conservatives insist, but rather with a series of hierarchically ordered mandates.[30] The individual generally is inclined to obey these mandates, and more importantly, generally is inclined to accept whatever ideological claim renders obedience to those mandates that are morally and rationally sound.[31] This acceptance may be a good thing, depending on the norm, or it may not be, but either way, it is not a process of rational calculation. It is a mode of obedience and compliance, the aim of which is to minimize cognitive dissonance. It represents not an assessment of self-interest, but an

30. See, e.g., Kelman, *Critical Legal Studies*, 130; Sunstein, "Legal Interference," 1138–39, 1145–51; and chap. 1 in this volume.

31. See, e.g., Robert W. Gordon, "New Developments in Legal Theory" in *The Politics of Law: A Progressive Critique*, rev. ed., ed. David Kairys (New York: Pantheon Books, 1990).

inculcation of those beliefs that are necessary to render obedience psychologically as well as morally defensible. Often this process is morally unproblematic: if the authority is itself benign and rational, then the irrational compliance of the socialized individual is morally unproblematic. Sometimes, though, these authorities are not so benign, and the beliefs—and hence the preferences—with which they leave the individual are not so unproblematic. These problematic preferences—for wages over a share of ownership in a collective bargaining agreement, for sexual harassment on the job, for contractual freedom to sell one's reproductive capacity, for a society free of homosexuals and homosexual influences—are also a product of authoritatively inculcated beliefs. Their origin lies with authorities that are anything but benign or rational. Their origin lies in ideological structures produced by powerful hierarchies, submission to which is not necessarily in the individual's self-interest.

To return, then, to the language of the legal conservatives, the individual's preferences, view of herself, and her subjective life in general are neither cognitively nor motivationally rational. She constructs her preferences on the basis of cognitive beliefs systemically inculcated and generated by the hierarchies (some defensible, some not) in which she lives and works: she is motivationally inclined not to egoistically promote her own self-interest, but rather to comply with the demands of her social world. Depending upon the value of the social norm under which she acts, that compliance is either altruistic, communitarian, masochistic, or all three. However, it is not rational, and the aim is not self-interest.

The critics' view of the individual, of the relationship between the individual and her society, and the motivational and cognitive rationality of her preferences has sharply contrasting implications for the judge interested in promoting the individual's true well-being and faced with contractually or legislatively manifested preferences that run counter to the true interest of the people that hold them. For the antipreference critic, the individual's (or the community's) perceived self-interest bears little or no relation to her true interest. It possesses a stronger relation, in fact, to the social structures that oppress than to any truly rational conception of well-being. The judge interested in promoting well-being should not, then, simply set out to give the individual or the majority what she or it thinks they want. The judge ought not to take either contractually or legislatively revealed preferences so seriously if she is interested in promoting societal or individual well-being, in both the private (contractual) context[32] and in the public (constitutional) one.

The Critical Case for Paternalism

How, though, should the critically minded judge proceed? On what basis should the judge decide that a contractually revealed preference is not truly in the parties' best interest, or that a legislatively revealed public preference would not truly promote societal well-being? How does the judge acquire knowledge of societal or individual true well-being? More concretely, if she cannot rely on preferences as a stable guide to well-being, on what should she rely? There are, I think, roughly two possible ways to attain the sort of knowledge of true interest that conceivably could ground any act of paternalistic intervention, including judicial paternalism. The first way—indeed the most obvious possibility and the position for which I will argue in the next two sections of this chapter—is that the judge acquires this knowledge by doing precisely what the legal conservatives argue cannot be done: in the private law context, the judge discerns the individual's true interest by sympathetically placing herself in the individual's shoes and seeing how it would feel to live with the choices that person has made, as opposed to some unchosen alternative. The judge imaginatively assumes the party's life situation as her own and then renders a judgment that reflects that sympathetic knowledge. In the public sphere, the judge sympathizes with the affected sections of the community in roughly the same, albeit more attenuated, fashion. In economic language, the judge makes a direct and intensely interpersonal comparison of subjective utility and decides, on the basis of that comparison, whether the community's true interest will be promoted by respecting its initially stated preference, or whether some unchosen alternative would be more conducive to the community's true interest.

For whatever reasons, the most prominent modern critics of preference sovereignty have not vigorously pursued this possibility.

32. For the private context, see generally Duncan Kennedy, "Distributive and Paternalist Motives in Contract and Tort Law, with Special Reference to Compulsory Terms and Unequal Bargaining Power," *Maryland Law Review* 41 (1982): 563–658. For the public context, see, e.g., Sunstein, "Legal Interference," 1133–35.

Rather, they have argued (sometimes explicitly, sometimes implicitly) that a judge should make paternalistic determinations by reasoning deductively from a detailed and ideological conception of "human flourishing"[33] in the private sphere and from a rich notion of civic virtue in the public sphere. The judge ought to decide whether to enforce a contract, or to uphold a piece of constitutionally contested legislation, by determining whether it is consistent with a developed vision of what it means for human beings to flourish, or for a community to exhibit the characteristic traits of civic virtue. Thus, according to the critical conception, a judge inclined to rule that surrogate-motherhood contracts are unenforceable might justify her decision to overrule the potential contractors' preference to the contrary by reasoning that contracts to rent out one's reproductive capacity, like contracts to sell body parts, are inconsistent with the self-respect and self-possession essential to a truly flourishing human life.[34] Similarly, a judge inclined to rule that antisodomy statutes violate a fundamental right to privacy and are therefore unconstitutional might justify that decision on the grounds that, the legislative preference notwithstanding, homophobic legislation interferes with a rich conception of civic virtue.[35] The judge reasons deductively from a rich but general description of virtue or human flourishing to an assessment of the merits of the particular contract or proposed legislation before her. If the contract or legislation is compatible with civic virtue or the project of human flourishing, it should stand; if not, it should be struck.

I am entirely sympathetic to this argument as far as it goes, but as it stands, it is seriously incomplete. Beyond the obvious problems of vagueness and indeterminacy, there are at least three difficulties with the critics' suggestion that judges should decide whether to intervene paternalistically into contracts and legislation by reference to descriptions of civic virtue and human flourishing. The first is descriptive, the second normative, and the third logical. The first problem is simply that this is not in fact the way that paternalistic,

33. See, e.g., Michael J. Perry, *Morality, Politics, and the Law: A Bicentennial Essay* (New York: Oxford University Press, 1988), 19–23; Radin, "Market-Inalienability," 1903–20. For a thorough discussion of Michael Perry's book, see "Symposium: Michael J. Perry's *Morality, Politics, and the Law*," *Tulane Law Review* 63 (1989): 1283–1679.

34. Radin, "Market-Inalienability," 1928–36.

35. Sunstein, "Naked Preferences," 1690–91.

interventionist judges reason. As a description of judicial paternalistic practice, the critical conception simply fails. The growing influence of legal conservatism and of the law-and-economics school notwithstanding, we do have a fairly well-developed body of interventionist case law, both in contract doctrine and in constitutional law, and in virtually none of it do judges reach their paternalistic decisions by holding preferences up to a test of human flourishing.

Relatedly, and tellingly, the flourishing and virtue standards for judicial paternalism do not do justice to the distinctive institutional particularity of judicial decision making. Unlike a legislator, a judge both reacts to, and is normally primarily responsible for, a litigant's particular dilemma, and not to contested, abstract, and general visions of human flourishing and civic virtue. Putting the point prescriptively, the human flourishing–civic virtue standard is simply too ambitious a role to accord with the brute institutional facts of judicial decision making. Judges do not approach cases with developed visions of how lives ought to be led or of what civic virtue requires of communities. There is nothing in prior case law, the judicial process, or in the judicial temperament that indicates that they should or could begin to do so.

The second problem is political. The suggestion that preferences should be discounted on moral grounds when they conflict with the demands of a flourishing human life or a vision of civic virtue does nothing to undercut the legal conservatives' claim that judges, distinctively, should exercise restraint in the face of settled preferences. There is no reason, in short, to suppose that judges are better equipped to define human flourishing and civic virtue than are contractors or legislators. Even if the descriptive claim that certain preferences may undercut the development of a society that encourages the flourishing of human life (and particularly social life) is true, it does not follow that judges are equipped institutionally to determine what the contours of the ideal might be. Without such an argument, one should leave the task of delineating the content of flourishing and the meaning of civic virtue either to individual determination or to the more overtly political legislative body. The claim that preferences are sometimes a poor proxy for well-being, combined with the contention that a vision of human flourishing and an understanding of the demands of civic virtue—rather than deference to preferences—should guide the exercise of power do indeed constitute the major premises of a strong case for paternalism. But they do nothing to further the cause of judicial paternalism as opposed to legislative paternalism; if anything, it cuts against it.

Third, and most important, the claim that judges should paternalistically upset private or public preferences by reference to a rich description of civic virtue and human flourishing rests on an inconsistent attitude toward the morality of power. The reason the critics distrust individual and group preferences is that they are the all-too-predictable product of hierarchies of power. The relatively powerless prefer outcomes that are often detrimental to their true interest because they have been unduly influenced by a worldview (and a correlative conception of their place within it) that is the product of illegitimate, capitalist, racist, professionalist, or patriarchal power. Why, given the profound distrust of power that underlies the critics' critique of the normative role of preferences, should we trust a vision of human flourishing articulated, delineated, and then imposed by powerful judges?[36] Judges are admittedly free of the influence of majoritarian power (at least federal judges are), so presumably their vision of flourishing and their conception of civic virtue will not reflect the power of the majoritarian mob. However, there is no reason to suppose that the judicial vision of virtue and the judicial conception of flourishing will not reflect the power of the purse, the white race, and the patriarch; indeed, critical legal studies and feminist histories themselves overwhelmingly indicate that they almost surely will, as they most assuredly have in the past.[37]

In fact, the critics' reliance on a rich conception of flourishing and virtue to guide judicial paternalistic decision making perversely underscores rather than undercuts at least one aspect of the conservatives' case against judicial paternalism. The critics are rightly suspicious of the conservatives' faith in the revealed preferences of individuals and majorities. Also for good reason, the critics eschew liberal, rights-based arguments for intervention into those preferences. In the critics' view, this leaves politics as the only alternative, and in this, I believe, they are mistaken. For as the critics and the

36. Of the critics, Paul Brest is most sensitive to this problem. See Paul Brest, "Who Decides?" *Southern California Law Review* 58 (1985): 664–69; Paul Brest, "Interpretation and Interest," *Stanford Law Review* 34 (1982): 768–69.

37. See Robert W. Gordon, "Critical Legal Histories," *Stanford Law Review* 36 (1984): 93–95.

legal economist insist, visions of what it means to flourish and conceptions of what civic virtue entails are political ones, and a dispute between conflicting visions of what it means to flourish or to exhibit virtue is an overtly political debate.[38] But, unless they say much more, the critics have not shown that a judge's vision of flourishing or virtue should trump a legislative or contractual choice based on a conflicting vision. Thus in the contractual sphere, the claim that preferences can justifiably be set aside when they reflect a desire to live a sort of life that is at odds with the demands of human flourishing might indeed suggest a basis for interference with contract, but it does not provide support for judicial intervention. In the legislative sphere, the claim that political preferences reflected in legislation may be distorted by ideology or other impermissible determinants similarly does not imply that the judiciary might better make these judgments than the legislature. The critics insist that political hierarchy soils preference; yet, they continue to insist that the judge should overturn individual and legislative preferences on the basis of overtly political visions. Without more, it is difficult to see why.

Taking Welfare Seriously

Another way to justify paternalistic intervention into contracts or legislation that reflect settled preferences, one much closer to actual judicial practice, is by reference to the judge's understanding of the parties' true subjective well-being and true interest obtained directly from the parties before her. The judge obtains this understanding by sympathetically listening to the litigants' narratives and being open enough to their stories to allow herself to be moved. Duncan Kennedy alludes to something of this sort when he argues that the motivational basis of judicial paternalistic intervention in contract law is love or empathy.[39] I think this point is essentially correct, but I want to extend it. The empathic interaction and identification with the parties that a trial or appeal facilitates, I believe, also provide the knowledge necessary to justify judicial intervention, as well as account for the

38. See Brest, "Interpretation," 773; Kelman, "Choice and Utility," 796–97; see also Radin, "Market-Inalienability," 1880–87 (alienation and commodification debates derived from conflicting free market, liberal, Marxist, and evolutionary-pluralist political visions).

39. Kennedy, "Distributive and Paternalistic Motives," 563.

judge's paternalistic motivation. Thus, my claim is that paternalistic judicial intervention into revealed preferences is informed and justified not by a detailed description of human flourishing or civic virtue, but by a sympathetic understanding of the parties' true interest.

By sympathetic understanding, I mean a direct apprehension of the subjective suffering or well-being of the other. A sympathetic understanding is more than a simple appreciation, and less than an assumption, of the suffering of another.[40] It is a direct understanding of another's pain, sorrow, or suffering. Adam Smith captures what I mean by the phenomenon of sympathy and its role in our moral life in this passage:

> By [an act of sympathy] we place ourselves in his situation, we conceive ourselves enduring all the same torments, we enter as it were into his body, and become in some measure [the same person with] him, and thence form some idea of his sensations, and even feel something which, though weaker in degree, is not altogether unlike them. His agonies, when they are thus brought home to ourselves, when we have thus adopted and made them our own, begin at last to affect us, and we then tremble and shudder at the thought of what he feels. For as to be in pain or distress of any kind excites the most excessive sorrow, so to conceive or to imagine that we are in it, excites some degree of the same emotion, in proportion to the vivacity or dulness of the conception. That this is the source of our fellow-feeling for the misery of others, that it is by changing places in fancy with the sufferer, that we come either to conceive or to be affected by what he feels, may be demonstrated by many obvious observations. . . . When we see a stroke aimed and just ready to fall upon the leg or arm of another person, we naturally shrink and draw back our own leg or our own arm; and when it does fall, we feel it in some measure, and are hurt by it as well as the sufferer. The mob, when they are gazing at a dancer on the slack rope, naturally writhe and twist and balance there own bodies, as they see him do, and as they feel that they themselves must do if in his situation. Persons of delicate fibers and a weak constitution of body, complain that in

40. For a rich description, see Lynne N. Henderson, "Legality and Empathy," *Michigan Law Review* 85 (1987): 1574–87.

> looking on the sores and ulcers that are exposed by beggars in the streets, they are apt to feel an itching or uneasy sensation in the [corresponding] part of their own bodies. . . . [T]hat horror arises from conceiving what they themselves would suffer, if they really were the wretches whom they are looking upon, and if that particular part of themselves was actually affected in the same miserable manner. . . .
>
> Neither is it those circumstances only, which create pain or sorrow, that call forth our fellow-feeling. Whatever is the passion which arises from any object in the person principally concerned, an analogous emotion springs up, at the thought of his situation, in the breast of every attentive spectator. . . . In every passion of which the mind of man is susceptible, the emotions of the bystander always correspond to what, by bringing the case home to himself, he imagines, should be the sentiments of the sufferer.[41]

The ability to sympathetically understand (and respond to) another's pain—described by Smith as the essence of a moral act—implies, in modern jargon, the ability to interpersonally compare subjective utilities, as well as the ability to act on them. If Smith is right in his claim that we can sympathize with the subjective misery, pain, suffering, joys, and pleasures of others, then the modern legal conservatives are simply wrong in their claim that we cannot make interpersonal comparisons of utility. When we sympathize with the pain of another, as Smith describes the process, we acquire a sense of the subjective feel, intensity, quantity, quality, and perhaps most crucially, the importance of that pain as felt by the other. This knowledge of the other's subjectivity can then become the basis of our comparison of the intensity of the pain felt by that human being with that of another, or of ourselves, or of the same individual under an alternative distribution of resources. Further, it is that comparison, in turn, that determines my final moral commitment (if not my action): I commit myself to resist the suffering inflicted upon this woman, or upon these men, by this distribution of power or wealth because their pain is greater or weightier than the suffering of others, or because it is greater or weightier than the pain the same individuals would feel were resources

41. Adam Smith, *The Theory of Moral Sentiments* (Oxford: Clarendon, 1971), 2–5.

to be distributed otherwise. According to Smith, and contrary to the legal conservatives, not only can we make these interpersonal comparisons, but it is by virtue of our capacity to do so that we can make moral decisions.

Smith's description of sympathy entails a conception of the moral actor and the moral decision that radically diverges from that assumed by the modern legal conservatives who purport to write in the spirit of Smith's work. Both Smith and the legal conservatives envision an actor whose primary duty is to maximize the good, and both conceive of the good to be maximized as involving, centrally, the subjective welfare or well-being of others. Although Smith views the human ability to sympathize with the subjectivity of others as the very capacity that facilitates moral action, legal conservatives adamantly insist that there simply is no such capacity. That difference, in turn, entails divergent conceptions of the moral act. From the modern legal conservatives' point of view, the actor who wants to use her power morally—in such a way as to promote the good—does so by deferring to whatever vision of the good is embraced by the parties affected by her decision. The act in which she is engaged is therefore the essentially passive act of deference. From Smith's point of view, by contrast, the moral act is an active one of sympathy with the subjective experience of the other. It rests on an understanding of the nature, intensity, and importance of the pain or pleasure implicated for the other by her decision. The act is active, not deferential: the moral actor sympathizes and decides; she does not defer.

There is an equally profound difference, however, between the conception of the moral actor who is moved by her sympathetically acquired knowledge of the subjectivity of another entailed by Smith's account of sympathy, and the moral actor as conceived by the position assumed by the antipreference critics. Unlike the modern conservatives, neither Smith nor the critics view the preferences of the affected parties as the definitive test of subjective well-being, and therefore, neither views the moral decision as essentially an act of deference to the preferences of the other. But the similarity ends there. According to the critics, the knowledge of the other's welfare required by the moral decision is a deductive inference from a detailed, holistic conception of human flourishing. The actor begins with a worked-out vision of the good and applies that vision to the particular situation facing her. According to Smith's conception, by contrast, the knowledge of the other's welfare required by the moral decision is an inference drawn directly from her knowledge of the subjectivity of the other. That knowledge is gained (in part) by her sympathetic understanding of the subjective intensity, nature, and importance of the pain or pleasure others will feel as a consequence of her decision. She does not have, nor need she have, a rich conception of human flourishing or of the good. She need have only a sensitivity to the interests of the other, the empathic ability to comprehend the nature of that subjectivity, and the moral, other-regarding inclination to act on the knowledge sympathetically gained.

Later in this section and in the next one, I will argue that a sympathetic assessment of the subjective experience of contractual and legislative choices is the best moral justification of judicial (as opposed to legislative) paternalistic decision making. First, though, I want to specify more precisely what I mean by a sympathetic judgment, as well as by the interpersonal comparison of utilities that the sympathetic judgment grounds. As many modern moral philosophers have argued, and as (nonlegal) economists generally concede: we can make these comparisons, and we do make these comparisons, every day. We can sympathize with one person's subjective grief and another's subjective annoyance, compare the two subjective experiences, and decide the former is of greater weight, magnitude, intensity, and importance than the latter, even when neither subjective experience is reflected in a contract, a vote, or a price. We can even make comparisons of the intensity of that most arbitrary of subjective experiences, namely culinary taste: we might compare Johnny's revulsion to the taste of candy with Susan's indifference and decide that Johnny hates the candy more than Susan likes the bubble gum. We can do this even if neither party has committed to the trade. We make these comparisons in much the way Smith describes in the above passage. We look at Johnny's scrunched-up face, and we share with him a pale version of his nauseated reaction to what is causing his physical response.

In a similar way, the assumptions of the libertarian legal conservatives notwithstanding, we can sympathize with the subjective consumption of additive goods, of dangerous but cheap consumer goods, or of onerous cross-collateral credit terms. Similarly, we can sympathize with the subjective experience of alienation—through commodification—of highly personal services and attributes. We can say with some confidence, for example, that the subjective experience of consuming addictive drugs is ultimately misery and that this is true regardless of the preference (or the opinion) of the addicted purchaser. Our knowledge of this truth might come from beliefs we have acquired about the effects of drugs on the addict's life and on the lives of those around him. But it need not. It might also come from a direct and sympathetic response to a particular drug addict's plight. If we have known drug addicts, have worked with addicts, have lived with addicts, or have seen drug addicts on television, we can sympathize, somewhat, with their subjective plight: we know their subjectivity is misery because we see it in their faces. Similarly, we can say, although with perhaps less confidence, that the subjective alienation and commodification of sexuality—the subjectivity of prostitution—is dehumanizing, regardless of the manifested preference of the streetwalker to the contrary. Again, we could conceivably reach the conclusion that prostitution is not in the prostitute's best interest by examining the effect of prostitution on her life. Alternatively, though, we could reach the same conclusion by sympathizing with the subjective life of a concrete, particular individual. A face-to-face encounter with a particular individual can leave a mark. We can make the other's agonies, as Smith says, to some degree our own. By seeing the individuality, the particularity, of the other, we can assume the feel of her burdens, and by doing so we come to sympathetically understand them. When we understand them, we can better assess the impact of drugs, prostitution, surrogacy contracts, and helmetless motorcycle rides upon the quality of life for those who make these choices.

If we can make these sympathetic leaps of imagination, then we can surely make the interpersonal comparisons of utility on which, according to the legal conservatives, morally responsible paternalistic intervention would depend, if only it were possible. If we can sympathize with the subjectivity of the addict, then we can also decide that the pain, for her, of enduring withdrawal is less than the misery she will sustain over the course of a life of addiction. If we can sympathize with the financial devastation following an accident involving a cheap but unwarranted product, then we can decide also that the pain, for the consumer, of the economic devastation is greater than the pain he would endure by being forced to pay a higher price in exchange for a mandatory warranty. If we can sympathize with the subjectivity of the prostitute, then we can also decide that the pain, for her, of a life of prostitution is greater than the pleasure reaped from the compensation for the sexual transaction. If we can sympathize, in the way Smith describes, with the subjective suffering and joys of others, then we can do what the legal conservatives claim we cannot: we can evaluate held preferences (both individual and social) directly against a standard of the preference holder's true subjective well-being.

Why, then, are the modern legal conservatives so drawn to the radically counterexperiential claim that these comparisons, and the sympathetic judgments on which they rest, are in principle impossible? The answer may have to do with the incredibly exalted role we accord to rationality in modern legal discourse. The sympathetic judgments that facilitate interpersonal comparisons of utilities have a least four attributes, all of which render them incompatible with widely accepted modern conditions for rational choice. First, and perhaps most important, the sympathetic judgments that ground interpersonal comparisons of utility are not acts of reason. The knowledge we attain of the subjectivity of others by sympathizing with their particular circumstances is not rationally acquired. It is acquired sympathetically: it is gained through the heart, not the head. It is an act of care, not of reason. The sympathetic act is simply not rational. Therefore, it is not surprising that the legal conservatives—who worship rationality—regard such judgments as impossible.

Relatedly, sympathetic judgments do not yield knowledge that readily lends itself to quantification. When we make a sympathetic judgment, we do so on the basis of a feel we have acquired for the subjective life of the other. When we decide that one person's pain or suffering outweighs that of another, or outweighs the pain the same person will feel under an alternative distribution of resources, we do so on the basis of conflicting feelings we have internalized, not on the basis of utilities that we have compiled, quantified, and aggregated. When we sympathetically feel the intensity of someone else's pain, we neither quantify that pain, nor calculate the cost of remedying it. The moral response to a sympathetic comparison of the subjective feel of others' experience is indeed a weighing of the importance and quality of conflicting experiences. But it is not a quantification. The moral decision rests on a felt balance, not on a calculated comparison.[42]

42. See Lynne N. Henderson, "The Dialogue of Heart and Head," *Cardoza Law*

Second, we sympathize with particular, concrete persons and are moved to combat the harm that confronts them far more readily than we sympathize with groups, situations, or "hypotheticals."[43] (Relatedly, because we tend to sympathize with concrete, particular individuals, narrative, far more than argument, triggers sympathetic responses.) We may be morally committed to fighting world hunger for any number of reasons, and we may have reached that resolution by any number of routes. But if we see, work with, or know hungry people, we are more likely to sympathize with their plight than if our knowledge is limited to what we know of unseen and unknown groups of starving peoples in third-world countries.[44] Similarly we may understand the logic (or even grant the wisdom) of acknowledging a woman's right to a first-trimester abortion, but we sympathize with particular, struggling women whom we have known as they work their way through decisions regarding pregnancies. We sympathize with those with whom we come in contact. The closer to our "circle of care," the more readily we understand and share their subjective struggles.[45]

Third, the sympathetic judgment is not information; it is not simply a judgment about the suffering of others. It presupposes, as well as facilitates, a commitment to oppose the cause of the other's subjective suffering, as well as an understanding of it. When we sympathize with the suffering of another, we understand what she's going through, but we do not just understand it, we are also moved to lessen it. When we sympathize, we share in the pain and commit ourselves to resist its source. The act of sympathy is completed not by the act of understanding, but by this further commitment.

Fourth, and quite contrary to the impression Smith creates in the passage above, neither sympathetic judgments nor the interpersonal comparisons they ground are automatic. In fact, they are often extremely difficult. Sometimes, of course, it is relatively easy to sym-

---

Review 10 (1988): 130–39; Henderson, "Legality and Empathy," 1592; see also Nel Noddings, *Caring: A Feminine Approach to Ethics and Moral Education* (Berkeley and Los Angeles: University of California Press, 1984), 46–48. See generally Carol Gilligan, *In a Different Voice: Psychological Theory and Women's Development* (Cambridge: Harvard University Press, 1982).

43. See Henderson, "Legality and Empathy," 1575–84; see also Martha Minow, "Justice Ungendered," *Harvard Law Review* (1987): 10–95.

44. Noddings, *Caring*, 46–48; Henderson, "Legality and Empathy," 1584.

45. Noddings, *Caring*, 46-48.

pathize with the other, just as sometimes it is easy to interpersonally compare utility; the examples Smith uses are such cases. But sometimes it is not easy at all. As is commonly acknowledged, it is easier to sympathize with those most like us, and those closest to us, and it is difficult to sympathize with—to understand the subjectivity of—those least like us or farthest from us. It is also easier to sympathize with someone who is experiencing an event with which we are familiar, than it is to sympathize with someone who is experiencing something of which we have no firsthand knowledge. At the extreme, it is simpler to sympathize with a more or less universal experience than with a unique or idiosyncratic experience. It is easy to understand that a broken leg hurts more than a pinprick, for the sympathizing party might herself experience both (or even better may have already experienced both). She can readily make the imaginative leap required to compare the intensity, duration, and importance of these two subjective experiences of pain. It is much more difficult, though, for a heterosexual to understand the intensity, duration, quality, or ultimately the importance of the suffering entailed by an antisodomy statue. Heterosexuals as a group have little sense of what if feels like to be stigmatized or prosecuted because of an erotic orientation. Similarly, it is difficult for whites to understand, sympathetically and directly, the nature of the pain that racial segregation entails; this is why Reverend King felt it necessary to employ the literary devices of metaphor and demonstration (street theater) to bridge the cognitive as well as the motivational gap between black pain and white apathy (see chap. 5). It is not impossible to sympathize with those least like ourselves, but it is harder. It requires more effort. It requires a more flexible imagination. It requires a bigger heart.

For all these reasons—their arationality, their particularity, their affectivity, and their difficulty—sympathetic judgments regarding the subjectivity of others do not play much of a role in public decision making. To some extent, this is justifiable: to whatever extent morally responsible policy analysis demands quantifiable and ascertainable costs and benefits, sympathetic judgments of subjective suffering and pleasure are not likely to play a dominant role in the analyses and perhaps should not. However, it simply does not follow from their justifiable absence in policy analysis that intersubjective comparisons of utility and the moral acts of sympathy that Smith describes upon which they rest are not at the root of other types of moral action, including judicial paternalistic intervention into both contractual and majoritarian preferences. Popular wisdom notwithstanding, judges may not be engaging in policy analysis when deciding cases, and if they are not, then judicial decision making should not be constrained by principles of rationality appropriate to that sphere.

On the contrary, the knowledge of the subjectivity of others, knowledge attained by sympathetically acquired assessments of intersubjective well-being, is not only possible, but may well be the prerequisite of morally justifiable judicial paternalism. The familiar and clearly paternalistic decision in *Williams v. Walker-Thomas Furniture Co.*[46] might serve as an illustration. In *Williams*, Judge Skelly Wright found, in effect, that the subjective misery of economic disaster for welfare consumers implicated by a cross-collateral credit term was so great that the disutility of the risk of its occurrence could not possibly be offset by the presumably lower price facilitated by such a term. Wright essentially compared the subjective utility (to the buyer) of the contract as written with the subjective utility of the hypothetical contract that would be drawn were the questionable term to be struck and a compensatory increase in price to occur. Using Adam Smith's language, Wright sympathized with the buyer's subjective experience of the contract as written and then sympathized with the buyer's hypothetical subjective experience of the hypothetical contract in its alternative form with the offending term struck. By deciding to strike the credit term, he in essence held that the former experience, the subjective experience of the contract as written, was one of unwarranted and unjustified suffering, buyer's preferences notwithstanding.

Of course, Wright's paternalistic decision that this sort of term in this sort of contract was unenforceable affected a large class of people, not just the litigant contesting the term. By ruling that the cross-collateral term was unenforceable (or, more precisely, potentially unenforceable), Wright in effect overruled the preference of an unspecified class of potential buyers who would prefer to buy the good at the lower price and bear the burden of the onerous credit term. As legal economists have repeatedly pointed out, the ruling in *Walker* deprived this class of buyers of the freedom to manifest this preference in a contract. As such, the decision constitutes a loss in

46. 350 F.2d 445, 449–50 (D.C. Cir. 1965).

efficiency. However, it does not follow that it was therefore unjustified. The justification for the paternalistic decision was Wright's belief that the suffering caused by the credit provision was just too great in relation to the decrease in price that the term facilitated. The suffering the term caused was not compensated by the price reduction facilitated by the credit provision.

A judge might ground a decision to paternalistically strike surrogacy contracts, or imply a one-month grace period into them, in the same way. As in *Williams*, a judicial ruling invalidating or modifying these contracts would constitute a loss in efficiency. The price of the promised performance would presumably go down: the surrogate's performance with the mandatory one-month term would be worth less (to the adoptive parent) than the surrogate's performance without the mandatory term. A class of potential surrogates would therefore be deprived of the freedom to contract for the service at the higher price. But the loss in efficiency might nevertheless by justified. Being forced to relinquish one's child is universally understood as a terrible experience. Even if we have never lived through it, it does not take too great an imaginative leap of sympathetic identification with the later-regretful gestational mother to understand the intensity of the anguish and torment of such an experience. A judge could come to understand that the painful experience of the later-regretful surrogate, like the experience of the defaulting welfare buyer in *Walker*, would be so profound, so thorough, and so anguish ridden, that the higher price the contract would yield without the mandatory grace-period term could not possibly compensate for that suffering. Using the economists' jargon, the subjective disutility of the contract as written to the subsequently regretful surrogate dwarfs the subjective disutility of the contract-as-modified. The comparison of these interpersonal utilities is not only possible, but stark. In Smith's terms, a judge could sympathize with each of these hypothetical contractors, form a commitment to resist the source of the greatest pain, and for that reason paternalistically require the mandatory grace-period term.

Of course, a sympathetic understanding of subjective welfare does not constitute the only basis on which a judge might justify a decision to modify surrogacy contracts. Another possible argument that a judge might make for intervention into the surrogacy industry is of the sort put forward by the critics discussed above. Surrogacy contracts contemplate a distribution of services and resources that drastically conflicts with the demands of a flourishing life. Surrogacy contracts, like the purchase of addictive drugs, under this argument, should be unenforceable for any number of idealistic reasons: they degrade the human personality; they commodify that which ought not be commodified; they blur the distinction that should be maintained between family and market. If these claims are true, then these contracts should be unenforceable regardless of whether anyone ever comes to regret the contract, once made. (This might be called "paternalism-plus.") Under the various arguments from human flourishing it is the contractual arrangement itself that is objectionable, not the suffering caused by the later-regretted decision.[47] I will call these arguments, collectively, idealistic.

In the next section, I will argue that sympathy rather than idealism should ground judicial paternalism. First, though, I want to note three institutional reasons why judicial paternalism in both private and public law is more likely to be motivated by sympathy than by idealism, and similarly is more likely to be grounded in knowledge of the other's subjective well-being than in a utopian vision of ideal association. First, simply by virtue of the litigation process, a judge deals with particular experiences of particular people (not a class of transactions) told to her in a more or less narrative way, and for that reason alone, judicial paternalism is more likely to be grounded

47. In fact, many (not all) of the arguments presently being put forward by feminists and others against surrogacy contracts rely upon these sorts of idealistic arguments. Both in amicus briefs in the Baby M case, and in the legislative arena, feminists have argued that surrogacy contracts, even assuming they are efficient, exploit the surrogate mother by manipulating a preference that she has come to have solely by virtue of her economic disenfranchisement. Through the guise of consent, these arguments claim, surrogacy contracts create a breeder class of women to create a source of alternative gestation for wealthy women seeking to avoid the dangers and inconveniences of childbearing. They reshape the institution of the family, and they will lead to a society that devalues life by commodifying it. They constitute a threat to the seriousness of the regard with which we take fellow citizens. They further the splintering of the reproductive function into various sellers who are paid for providing various goods and services, including the fertilized egg, gestation, and delivery services, and, after birth, nursing and child-raising services. This splintering is a serious threat to women's already vulnerable status as equal citizens. For all these reasons, the surrogacy industry poses an obstacle to our attainment of a society in which we all truly flourish. Unlike cost-benefit analyses, these idealistic arguments are truly paternalistic and therefore heavily disfavored by the legal economists. See generally Radin, "Market-Inalienability," 1928–36.

in a sympathetic response to those stories than in an assessment of the demands of an ideally flourishing or virtuous life.[48] Unless the nature of the litigation process changes drastically, a judge is not likely to prioritize idealist visions of association over the litigants' own narratives. A judge has a face-to-face, human interaction with the litigants that extends over a period of time. She is in a relationship with litigants, not constituents. Even an appellate judge comes to know the litigants as the origins of particular, individual stories. A judge, unlike a legislator, is faced with an individual rather than a group, a narrative rather than an abstraction, and a particular dilemma rather than a cluster of competing political visions. Unlike the legislator, she is involved in a direct, human relationship with particular people. Rightly or wrongly, by virtue of institutional design alone, the paternalistic judicial decision is more likely to reflect a sympathetic response to individuals and their stories, while the paternalistic legislative decision is more likely to rest on a utopian vision of the demands of some ideal form of our social life.

If sympathy has any role to play in moral decision making, then this bias toward particularity might represent what is worthy and unique about judicial paternalistic policy-making, and not (as is often argued) what is dangerous about it. Due to the particularity of the judicial process, the judge has the opportunity at least to grasp for the subjectivity of the parties before her, to understand the feel of their lives, respond to their story, further their welfare, and listen to their arguments. The legislator, by contrast, has the opportunity, and perhaps the duty, to do much the opposite: when making policy, the legislator must resist, not indulge, the urge to overparticularize. She must be sensitive to distant ramifications of her decisions. In terms of cost-benefit analysis, the legislator ought to treat each affected party much as Jeremy Bentham insisted: each person counts for one and no more than one.[49] She should assess the costs and benefits of the proposed contract to each affected party equally. In terms of utopian politics, she should proceed much as our critics insist: she can and should weigh our legislative and contractual demands against the strictures of our ideals. It is simply bizarre, though, to impose

48. See Judith Resnik, "On the Bias: Feminist Reconsiderations of the Aspirations for Our Judges," *Southern California Law Review* 61 (1988): 1877–1944.

49. See Jeremy Bentham, *Jeremy Bentham: Ten Critical Essays*, ed. Bhikhu C. Parekh (London: Cass, 1974).

either the economists' Benthamic stricture or the idealists' utopian commitments on a judge. Certainly, the judge must be attentive to both the class of persons affected and the idealist visions either furthered of frustrated by her holding. But in important respects, a judge is more like an ideal parent than like an ideal legislator: unlike the legislator, but like the parent, her primary attention is directed to the particular, subjective narrative of the individuals before her. Unlike the legislator, but like the parent, she feels enormous pressure to act responsively in that relationship. She could not, should not, and typically does not treat the litigants as one and no more than one—as on par with all other persons who might find themselves in similar circumstances. The basis for any paternalistic ruling she may be inclined to make for this reason alone is more likely to be a sympathetic response to the litigants' subjective plight than a deductive inference from either implicit or explicit visions of the social good.

A judge is more likely to ground a paternalistic decision on a sympathetic response to the subjective experience of the litigants before her than on an inference drawn from a rich description of civic virtue or human flourishing for a second institutional reason as well. Unlike the legislator, a judge deciding whether to intervene paternalistically into, say, the surrogacy industry will hear at length from one contractor who has come to regret the decision. The primary data, then, for the judge's decision that an individual's preference in a contract is or is not ill-advised is a party who at that very moment regrets the contractual preference and is suffering the consequences of that regret. In the public-law realm, a judge deciding whether to intervene into a communitarian preference for, say, an antisodomy statute will hear at length from a representative of the burdened minority who will feel the brunt of the majority's will. The judge not only can but must respond to the subjective experience of these particular litigants. The primary data for legislative decision making (whether paternalistic or not) by contrast, is not, need not be, and probably ought not be a particular contractor who has come to regret the decision, or the particular minority burdened by the proposed legislation. A legislator would be within bounds of democratic process to decide that a contract so drastically conflicts with her vision of a flourishing life that it should be unenforceable, even if no one ever came to regret the contract, or that legislation ought be passed despite its effect on subgroups.

In an eloquent article in the *Harvard Law Review*, Professor Margaret Radin lays out the idealistic basis for what I would call "legislative paternalistic intervention" in the private sphere: there are certain things we simply should not sell, Radin argues, such as body parts, sex, and our freedom, and this proscription holds whether we momentarily want to do so and whether we would ever regret it if we did.[50] It would be perfectly sensible (although perhaps not politic) for a legislator to ground a paternalistic judgment against sales of body parts, sex, or freedom on Radin-like grounds: the felt desire of some persons to enter into these contracts reflects a false consciousness, poisoned by the influence of a patriarchal culture, that wrongly insists on the commodification of too many aspects of our lives, and that that cultural vision, as well as the particular contractual preference it inculcates, frustrates the development of a flourishing life. The legislator, one would hope, would have strong reasons for saying as much, but whatever the argument, it would be well within the bounds of democratic politics for her to so decide—subject, of course, to constitutional check: legislative determinations of these sorts run the danger of violating constitutional rights of privacy.[51]

The judge, though, operates in a different arena and reaches her decision in response to different pressures. The judge need not decide that a contested contract is contrary to the demands of a flourishing life or that a majoritarian preference is contrary to the demands of civic virtue to find a basis for invalidating either. Rather, a judge can base her paternalistic decision to strike a contract or majoritarian preference on the finding that the contested contract provision is ill-advised because of the suffering it has caused *this* person who has later come to regret the decision, or that the majoritarian preference is ill-advised because of the disproportionate suffering it causes *this* minority. The judge's decision to place a contract term outside of the bounds of permissible contract will most likely rest on her sympathy with the particular, perhaps unique, subjective experience of the one now-regretful contractor in the courtroom. In a parallel sense, the judge's paternalistic decision to find a majoritarian preference uncon-

50. Radin, "Market-Inalienability," 1936–37.

51. See Field, *Surrogate Motherhood*, 46–47.

stitutional typically rests on her sympathetic assessment of the subjective experience of the burdened minority. It need not rest on a purported conflict between the preferences of the nonregretful contractor and the equally hypothetical vision of what it means to live a flourishing life or on a conflict between the majoritarian will and civic virtue.

Finally, there are political as well as institutional reasons that judicial paternalism is likely to be grounded in sympathy while legislative paternalism (over both contractual and majoritarian preference) is more likely to be grounded in idealism. The conservatives' discomfort with idealistic intervention notwithstanding, legislators generally do debate the value of our preferences by reference to articulable political ideals (as well as vice versa). For all the reasons put forward by the critics of preference sovereignty, this debate is entirely proper: we need to debate the value of not only surrogate contracts, but of our other preferences as well, including our "preference" for pornography over censorship, for prostitution, for motorcycle helmets and seat belts, for abortion, and for homosexuality. We need to debate the value of these preferences by reference not just to the authority of our traditions (both constitutional and otherwise) but also by reference to our conflicting utopian visions of the good life. We need these debates to answer the questions, but more importantly, we need these debates to reassert the primacy, or at least the importance, of ideals to our private and public choices. It does not follow, though, that idealistic debate of this sort has a meaningful role in adjudication. In fact, it is precisely this form of judicial speculation that most sharply raises the specter of undue judicial control over our choices in the private sphere and of our political will in the public.

For political as well as institutional reasons, then, judicial private-law paternalistic decisions not to enforce a contract are rarely justified on the grounds that such a contract interferes with a contestable vision of human flourishing. This is not surprising: a politically more palatable alternative and, I will argue, morally more palatable alternative is readily available. To take an easy case for sympathetic judicial paternalism—we all have arms, legs, livers, and kidneys, and we all can imagine how it might feel to part with them. It is not so difficult to conclude that it would feel so awful to be separated from one of these aspects of oneself that no amount of money would compensate, and that therefore, no contract, for any amount of money, for the sale of such a commodity would truly promote the seller's well-being. The stated legal grounds for a decision to disallow such contracts may be that they are per se unconscionable, presumptively coerced, a violation of human dignity, or contrary to public policy. But whatever the legal grounds, the moral grounds for judicial intervention should not be so hard to discern (or to distinguish from idealistic grounds): anyone with an ordinary amount of sensitivity, including a judge, can make the imaginative leap and assess the subjective feel of being separated from one's children, body parts, or sexuality against one's will. The judge can (more or less) sympathize with the situation of the postperformance contractor and say, with some confidence, that any preference for a trade that commodifies these parts of ourselves is misguided and that it is so seriously misguided that the judge is morally required to disallow the trade, preferences notwithstanding.

Idealism is possible in the public sphere as well, but it is typically a politically unwise justification for judicial intervention into societal preferences. Thus, the Supreme Court surely had the power to overturn a majoritarian preference such as that expressed in the antisodomy statute at stake in *Hardwick* on overtly idealistic grounds. A community may decide that for idealistic reasons it should criminalize homosexuality while the Court might decide, on idealistic grounds, that preference notwithstanding, a decent community should strive for a society free of the homophobia such a legislative preference for criminalization reflects. Because the Court gets last say, the judicial vision would trump the legislature's. However, although the Court might have the power to justify review in this way, it would be unwise to do so, and in fact it rarely does so. It is just this sort of head-on-head conflict between judicial and legislative idealistic vision that most clearly raises the fear of judicial tyranny, just as does, in the private sphere, the head-on-head conflict between judicial wisdom and the individual self-regarding preferences expressed in contracts. It is this sort of judicial paternalism that is typically the target of the conservative complaint that judicial activism offends democratic ideals.

Paternalistic review of the majority's homophobic preference on straight welfare grounds, by contrast, is more firmly rooted in the justified and traditional province of the judiciary. A majority's preference for forbidding homosexuality such as that reflected in a sodomy statute, for example, might indeed be at odds with any defensible description of civic virtue. But such an overtly political argument is not the only possible justification for judicial intervention. A court might be prompted to intervene in a case like *Hardwick* not by a particular vision of ideal society, but instead by an immediate concern for human suffering. The community might be wrong in thinking that the sodomy statute will maximize well-being. Criminalizing this form of sexual intimacy will cause many people much hardship. If that hardship is sufficiently great, it may outweigh whatever benefit criminalizing the offending conduct affords the heterosexual majority. If it does, then judicial intervention might be morally justified on traditional welfare-maximizing grounds.

Justified Judicial Paternalism

In the private sphere, surrogacy contracts, contracts with onerous cross-collateralization, contracts for the purchase of dangerous consumer goods with damage disclaimers shielding the manufacturer from liability for personal injury loss, contracts for the sale of our sexuality, and contracts for the sale of body parts should all be held unenforceable, and for sympathetic, rather than (or in addition to) idealistic reasons. In each of these exchanges, the postcontractual subjective suffering the contractor voluntarily agreed to bear is of such magnitude, intensity, and importance that it outweighs the benefits that the contract otherwise bestows. In each of these cases, the preferences revealed in these contracts are a poor proxy for the individual's true subjective welfare. Further, a paternalistic judicial decision to override the revealed preference can be justified by the profundity or intensity of the suffering entailed by the contractual risk the vulnerable party voluntarily agreed to bear.

Our two classic instances of paternalism in contract law—*Henningsen v. Bloomfield Motors, Inc.*[52] and *Williams v. Walker-Thomas Furniture*[53]—rest implicitly, although not explicitly, on a straight welfare rather than idealist justification. As many commentators have noted, in neither case did the judge even attempt to justify his pater-

52. 32 N.J. 358, 161 A.2d 69 (1960).
53. 350 F.2d 445 (D.C. Cir. 1965).

nalistic decision on efficiency-based grounds. Nor did either judge justify his paternalistic intervention by reference to overarching conceptions of human flourishing. Rather, what seems to have mediated the move in both cases from the premise that the party's preference (at the time of the contract) for the contested term was irrational to the conclusion that the term should be struck was a direct and immediate sympathetic identification with the subjective anguish and difficulty of the vulnerable party's postcontractual plight. Thus, from Judge Skelly Wright's statement of the facts in *Walker-Thomas*, Wright apparently was struck hard by Mrs. Williams's plight of having to feed, clothe, and support herself and seven children on $218 a month.[54] A purchase of a $514 stereo set on credit terms that burdened the security of prior purchases made this always difficult task next to impossible.

Similarly in *Henningsen*, Judge Francis was swayed by the postcontract subjective dilemma of the vulnerable party: the plaintiff had contractually relinquished a right to recover for extensive personal injury damage caused by the defective automobile in exchange for a price deduction that could not conceivably compensate for the anguish subjectively sustained upon occurrence of the risk. In both cases, the judge apparently reached the paternalistic decision to strike the contract by sympathizing with the plight of the party before him. Further, the particularity and contextualization afforded by the structure of litigation facilitated, rather than frustrated, the decisions to intervene paternalistically. Judge Wright was moved to intervene upon hearing one woman's story of impoverishment, and similarly Judge Francis was moved to intervene upon hearing one couple's story of injury.

Likewise in the public sphere, societal legislation that in recent years has been constitutionally most vulnerable—legislation criminalizing abortion and mandating racial segregation—has caused considerably more suffering than it has prevented, and for that reason alone the Court's decision finding both preferences unconstitutional are morally justifiable. Majoritarian preferences for segregated schools and transportation systems, for the criminalization of homosexuality, for the economic disenfranchisement of the homeless and impoverished, and for the criminality of abortion are all suspect preferences: the community that holds them has very likely misassessed the intensity

54. Ibid., 447.

and the import of the subjective experience of the burdened class. The African American's experience of a segregated world; the homosexual's experience of an antisodomy statute; and the woman's experience of the physical difficulty, financial expense, and emotional heartache of raising children in the midst of poverty are all hard to grasp if we have not had the experience ourselves. The subjective feel of the suffering sustained by those oppressed and to varying degrees silenced groups is, to say the least, not well understood by those with power in this society. When the suffering that a societal preference entails is neither universal nor well understood, the possibility of even well-intentioned error is high. Correlatively, the case for paternalistic intervention into that preference is strong.

Just as judges are peculiarly well suited to hear and to sympathize with descriptions of extraordinary and intense subjective suffering brought on by unwise contractual choices, so judges are also well suited to hear and to sympathize with unique and uniquely ill-heard accounts of intense suffering sustained by minorities and oppressed groups by virtue of a majority's preference. Both the trial and the appeal present an opportunity for an oppressed group or a victimized party to describe the subjective feel of a previously unheard minority experience and to do so in a rich, narrative, and detailed manner. Putting the point more generally, a public trial is one mechanism by which a private, unnamed, misunderstood, trivialized, uncounted, or ignored pain can become public, named, understood, and counted. A trial, for its many drawbacks, facilitates rich descriptions of our uniquely private and subjective lives. It provides an opportunity for an otherwise silenced litigant to win the sympathy of someone in a position of power. Thus, to return once again to *Hardwick*, a reviewing judge might decide on sympathetic grounds both that the legislative, idealistic, paternalistic judgment that a flourishing society cannot tolerate consensual sodomy is itself based on a suspect preference (such as racial bigotry, homophobia, sexism, national chauvinism, or sexual prurience) and is therefore not a good proxy of societal well-being, and that the suffering endured by homosexuals as a consequence of the idealistic legislative sanction outweighs, in importance, whatever benefit accrues by virtue of the legislative decision. A judge who decides to intervene paternalistically and strike the legislation on these grounds is justified in doing so.

Brown v. Board of Education and *Roe v. Wade*[55]—the two major

55. 347 U.S. 483 (1954); 410 U.S. 113 (1973).

paternalistic constitutional decisions of the past quarter century invalidating societal preferences—are at least consistent with, if not overtly exemplary of, this model of paternalistic judicial intervention. On this account, *Brown* is best understood as a sympathetic response to the pain caused the burdened group by the majoritarian preference for associational freedom and a belated recognition that that pain outweighs in importance, profundity, and intensity whatever pain the white majority feared from a regime of forced association.[56] *Roe* is best understood, on this account, not so much as a case protecting privacy, but as acknowledging, again belatedly, the distinctive suffering of a disempowered minority group—pregnant women who wish to end their pregnancies. In both cases the availability of judicial review provided a burdened group an opportunity to communicate to the empowered majority the subjective feel of a largely unrecognized, and to some extent unknown, subjective experience of a particular majoritarian preference: a preference for racial purity in the first case and for an intolerance of reproductive freedom in the second. Both *Brown v. Board of Education* and *Roe v. Wade* provided opportunities to correct for these societal failures of the heart.

It goes without saying, I believe, that a judge who seizes the opportunity of a trial or an appeal to listen to a previously unheard narrative is well within the legitimate legal bounds of her professional role. What is not so clear is that she is also thereby fulfilling a moral ideal. By expanding her own judicial, sympathetic understanding of the individual subjective lives of the litigants before her, she serves a role for the community of which she is a part. For these trials, no less than the paternalistic judgments to which they sometimes lead, expand not just the judge's but also our societal sense of sympathy with the outsider. They instruct us to include that person's suffering, in its uniqueness, as a cost when we assess whether we wish to approve or sanction some part of the community's conduct. The paternalistic judicial decision grounded in a sympathetic listening can thereby improve the moral quality of our social lives.

Conclusion

The legal conservative's argument that judges should not intervene into private and public preferences is based partly on the false claim

56. See Henderson, "Legality and Empathy," 1593–1609.

that our lives, our selves, and our subjective experiences are so utterly unique that a judge cannot possibly come to understand, and hence sympathize with, the subjective suffering and joy of others. This claim is belied not only by our everyday experience, but by judicial practice as well. Of course, we often choose not to sympathize with the suffering of others, and it is easy to rationalize this failure with the false claim that because of some inherent limitation of the human psyche, we cannot sympathize with others. But we should recognize this rationalization for what it is. The refusal to sympathize with the suffering of others, whether engaged in by judges or others, constitutes an act of will. It does not reflect an inherent limitation on our moral capacities.

In both the Supreme Court's decision in *Hardwick* and the New Jersey trial court's decision in *Baby M*, the reviewing bench could have, but did not, evaluate the impact of these voluntary preferences on the parties whose lives were most profoundly affected by these individual and societal choices. In both cases, the judge and justices deferred to preference and shunned paternalistic intervention. Neither bench even sought an understanding of the subjective state of the party suffering the burden of the preference to which the court deferred. Both written decisions carry the mark of this peculiar and even grotesque form of insensitivity. Justice White's opinion in *Hardwick* exhibits either a perverse refusal to acknowledge pain or a striking ignorance of the subjective plight of homosexuals in a society that criminalizes the activity most conducive to the intimacy we all agree is essential to a meaningful, pleasurable, and good life. The trial court's opinion in *Baby M* similarly reveals a stark insensitivity to the desperation of a woman who is forced to sell a child to whom she has given birth. Both opinions reek of an intentional and aggressive refusal to come face-to-face with human pain, and both seek to justify this refusal with a cavalier reference to the dignity and the sovereignty of individual and societal preferences. In the name of rationality and reason, both judge and justice refused to become sympathetically engaged with the persons before them. Both benches dispensed deferential, efficient, and rational opinions, and both did so by refusing to employ their arational, sympathetic imagination and their nonrational capacity for compassion. The decisions evidence not so much a libertarian moral respect for preferences as an adamant closing of eyes and ears to the well-being of others. In both cases, they are failures of the heart, and because of that, uncoincidentally, they are legal failures as well.

As the legal conservatives fear, sympathetic, compassionate decision making without the check of reason and respect for liberty might well degenerate into a tribal and totalitarian nightmare. But a regime of reasoned, rational, and efficient decisions unchecked by the demands of love raises an equally horrific vision. In fact, unsympathetic decision making devoid of compassion is offensive to the ideal we vaguely intend by the illusive phrase "rule of law." The judgment at the center of the utterly legalistic determination that case A is sufficiently analogous to case B so as to fall within the scope of case B's precedent is surely a sympathetic one. We must understand the subjectivity, the equities, and the "feel" of the parties involved in case B before we can declare it like A. When we say A is like B, we do this interpersonal act; we make these comparisons. We declare A like B, and we profess ourselves enough like the human actors in A and B to make this declaration. If we ever truly come to believe, as well as assert, that we are unable to make interpersonal comparisons of utility, we will have declared ourselves unable to engage in evolutionary, precedential legal analysis as well.

The *Hardwick* and *Baby M* decisions thus represent not just a failure of compassion, sympathy, and human identification, but, I believe, a failure of judicial decision making—traditionally and constitutionally conceived—as well. In *Hardwick*, the Supreme Court could have decided, but did not, that if recreational, nonreproductive heterosexuality is protected against state intrusion, as the Court had implied in both *Griswold v. Connecticut* and *Roe v. Wade*, then homosexuality should be protected as well. *Griswold* and *Roe*, sympathetically read, protect not family rights, but indeed, their very opposite: they represent an endorsement of the intimacy, pleasure, and growth to which decidedly nonfamilial and nonreproductive sexuality is conducive. To decide that homosexuality is within the sphere of that precedent would have required a court to see that homosexuality, no less than already protected nonreproductive heterosexuality between either married or nonmarried partners, is also conducive to intimacy, pleasure, and growth, and hence something to be valued, not criminalized. Such a finding would have in turn required the sympathetic, not the intellectual, judgment that homosexuals and heterosexuals are similarly situated vis-à-vis their capacity for expressions of sexual intimacy: that they are like us; that we are like them; that we are not so different; that we can understand their need for privacy and their need for nonintervention vis-à-vis the state; that we can understand that their desires are not terribly different from the desires of the couple in *Griswold* for sexuality freed of the burden of reproduction; that we can understand, therefore, that *Hardwick*, in the way that counts, is similarly situated with *Griswold* and within the scope of that precedent. An expansion of *Griswold*, in other words, would have required the judge to look behind the differences between himself and the homosexual defendant Hardwick, between his own marriage and Hardwick's relationship, between his desires and Hardwick's, between homosexuality and heterosexuality, to their shared humanity. A decent reading of the precedent would have required a sympathetic understanding of the subjectivity of homosexuality.

To return to the sparse language of the legal conservatives, to decide the case for Hardwick would have required an interpersonal comparison of utility, thus mandating what Judge Bork has insisted we cannot do: the Court would have had to weigh the suffering of Hardwick against the homophobic desires of the majority. To decide *Baby M* for Mary Beth Whitehead, the court would have had to weigh the suffering of Whitehead against the desires of other surrogates for a contract price free of the influence of mandatory terms. To assess the significance of Whitehead's suffering or Hardwick's plight, the judge or justice in each case would have had to imagine himself in the place of those litigants: How would it feel to lose one's child because of an earlier promise? How would it feel to be drawn to a criminal form of sexual intimacy, criminalized because of a societal preference? The judge who has had neither experience would have to ask, imagine, analogize, listen, and feel her way to an answer. She would have to do precisely what Smith insisted we can and must do if we are to be moral creatures: look past our differences and understand the suffering of others by reference to our shared human aspirations, fears, pains, and pleasures. The ability to look past difference to the humanity that we share is necessary to any sensibly evolving notion of constitutional entitlement and private obligation. If we lose that ability, we will have lost more than the ability to care. We will have lost the constitutional and common-law traditions of true respect and community that depend on it.

Part 3
The Narrative Voice in Law and Jurisprudence

Chapter 8

Jurisprudence as Narrative: An Aesthetic Analysis of Modern Legal Theory

It is now a commonplace that lawyers and legal theorists have much to learn from literature.[1] We surely can learn something about the law from great works of literature that deal with legal themes, such as Kafka's *The Trial* and Melville's *Billy Budd*.[2] But apart from the law depicted in literature, legal theory itself contains a substantial narrative component that can be analyzed as literature. Modern legal theorists persistently employ narrative plots at strategic points in their arguments, relating romantic sagas about mythical commanders and communities and saturating their writings with realistic anecdotes from lawyers' and judges' subjective experiences of law.[3] Fictive

1. See generally "Interpretation Symposium," *Southern California Law Review* 58 (1985): 1–752; "Law and Literature Symposium," *Texas Law Review* 60 (1982): 373–586; Harold Suretsky, "Search for a Theory: An Annotated Bibliography of Writings on the Relation of Law to Literature and the Humanities," *Rutgers Law Review* 32 (1979): 727–39.

2. See, e.g., Richard Weisberg, "How Judges Speak: Some Lessons on Adjudication in *Billy Budd, Sailor* with an Application to Justice Rehnquist," *New York University Law Review* 57 (1982): 1–69; Judith Schenck Koffler, "Capital in Hell: Dante's Lesson on Usury," *Rutgers Law Review* 32 (1985): 608–60. Shakespeare appears to evoke the most interest among legal scholars. See, e.g., Jack Benoit Gohn, "*Richard II*: Shakespeare's Legal Brief on the Royal Prerogative and the Succession to the Throne," *Georgetown Law Journal* 70 (1982): 943–73; J. D. E., "Shakespeare and the Legal Process: Four Essays," *Virginia Law Review* 61 (1975): 390–433.

3. See, e.g., Bruce A. Ackerman, *Social Justice in the Liberal State* (New Haven: Yale University Press, 1980) (twenty-first century spaceship community); Jeremy Bentham, *Introduction to the Principles of Morals and Legislation*, in *The Works of Jeremy Bentham*, ed. Sir John Bowring (1843; rpt., New York: Russell and Russell, 1962), 1:146 (using anecdote to illustrate wisdom of ordinary citizens); R. M. Dworkin, *Taking Rights Seriously* (Cambridge: Harvard University Press, 1977), 105–50 (Herculean judge); Jerome Frank, *Law and the Modern Mind* (New York: Coward-McCara, 1935), 100–117 (tales of the judging process); Lon Fuller, *The Morality of*

protagonists also play an important role in legal theory: Dworkin's heroic Herculean judge and Holmes's one-dimensional "bad man," for example, are central devices by which these jurists convey their conceptions of the meaning of law.

It is not surprising that legal theory should rely so heavily upon narrative form. The subject matter of legal theory is the nature of law. This nature is partly revealed by the content of law—its history and political and economic underpinnings. Examining law as a fact can help us understand what law is and what it is has been in the past. But law is also an ever-present possibility, potentially bringing good or evil into our future. The nature of law is also revealed, then, by our aspirations for and our fear of law: fantasies and nightmares revolving around power, reason, and authority. When we discuss what is, we rely quite naturally upon description and analysis. But when we discuss what is possible, what we desire, and what we dread, we turn to stories about hypothetical communities and the legal actors and forms within those communities.

If legal theories are, in part, aesthetic objects, then we should be trying to understand them in that sense. This chapter argues that the narrative plots, protagonists, and images of major legal theories do, in fact, fall into recognizable literary categories, at least as depicted in a classic work of structuralist literary criticism, Northrop Frye's *Anatomy of Criticism*.[4] In this work, Frye, premiere "formalist"

Law (New Haven: Yale University Press, 1964), 33–38 (King Rex); Oliver Wendell Holmes, *The Common Law* (Boston: Little, Brown, 1881) (narrating the story of Anglo-American law's development); R. M. Dworkin, "What Is Equality? Part 2: Equality of Resources," *Philosophy and Public Affairs* 10 (1981): 285–87 (shipwreck survivors on desert island); Jerome Frank, "What Courts Do in Fact," *Illinois Law Review* 26 (1932): 645–66 (witty, often anecdotal discussion of judicial process and hypothetical cases); Lon Fuller, "The Case of the Speluncean Explorers," *Harvard Law Review* 62 (1949): 616–45; H. L. A. Hart, "American Jurisprudence through English Eyes: The Nightmare and the Noble Dream," *Georgia Law Review* 11 (1977): 969–89 (portraying American adjudication as beset by two extreme illusions); Oliver Wendell Holmes, "The Path of the Law," *Harvard Law Review* 10 (1897): 459–62 (the bad man); Joseph C. Hutcheson, Jr., "The Judgement Initiative: The Function of the 'Hunch' in Judicial Decision," *Cornell Law Quarterly* 14 (1929): 274–88 (relating judge's experiences).

4. Northrop Frye, *Anatomy of Criticism: Four Essays* (Princeton, N.J.: Princeton University Press, 1957). Subsequent references, abbreviated *AC*, are given in the text. For an application of Frye's narrative categories to the writings of nineteenth-century historians, see Hayden White, *Metahistory: The Historical Imagination in Nineteenth-Century Europe* (Baltimore: Johns Hopkins University Press, 1973).

literary critic,[5] demonstrates that four discrete "aesthetic myths" recur in the common plots of poems, movies, novels, plays, comic strips, and other narrative forms. Two of the myths reflect contrasting *methods* of storytelling: romantic and ironic narrative modes (*AC*, 151–58). The other two reflect contrasting *visions* of the world: comic and tragic worldviews (*AC*, 141–50).

Two similar polarities dominate modern jurisprudence. The first polarity concerns conflicting theories of law as either an exercise of reason or an exercise of the will. The second involves conflicting images of law as either a liberating force serving the community or an oppressive tool serving the interests of the powerful. The two theories and two images have generated four major jurisprudential traditions: natural law, positivism, liberalism, and statism. This chapter establishes a correlation between these four major jurisprudential traditions and the four aesthetic myths that Frye identified as permeating great and popular literature. The natural lawyer's and the legal positivist's *methods* of analyzing law fit readily within Frye's descriptions of romantic and ironic narrative method. The liberal and the statist's contrasting *visions* of law can be read as instances of comic and tragic narrative visions.

Part 1 of this chapter summarizes Northrop Frye's analysis of the role of myth in narrative literature and reviews his four core myths and their corresponding literary plots: romance, irony, comedy, and tragedy. Part 2 describes four corresponding jurisprudential traditions: natural law, legal positivism, liberalism, and statism. Parts 3 and 4 argue that each of these jurisprudential traditions is unified

5. Frye has been called "the leading theoretician of literary criticism among all those writing in English today." Harold Bloom, "A Study of the Structure of Romance," *New York Times*, 18 April 1976, sec. 7; see also Robert D. Denham, *Northrop Frye and Critical Method* (University Park: Pennsylvania State University Press, 1978), vii. Frye's books and essays on literature are discussed in *Northrop Frye in Modern Criticism: Selected Papers from the English Institute*, ed. Murray Krieger (New York: Columbia University Press 1966); For a discussion of Frye's formalism, see fifth part of this chapter.

Some critics have attacked Frye's analysis of literature in *Anatomy of Criticism* because they perceive inconsistency in Frye's carrying out his general refusal to pass judgment on the quality of the works he discusses. Frye's work has also been criticized for its canon and for paying too little attention to the texts' historical and social contexts. See W. K. Wimsatt, "Northrop Frye: Criticism as Myth," in Krieger, *Northrop Frye*; Morris Dickstein, "U. and Non-U," *Partisan Review* 36 (1969): 153–56, reviewing Northrop Frye, *The Modern Century* (London: Oxford University Press, 1969).

by either a vision of the world or a narrative method that corresponds to one of Frye's four literary myths. The final section assesses the significance of this correspondence, demonstrating that it is fruitful to address conflicts in legal theory as reflecting aesthetic as well as political and moral differences in the way we view the world. By so doing, we may achieve a better understanding of who we are and why we disagree.

Frye's Four Myths of Narrative Literature

Frye distinguishes four "organizations" of archetypal symbolism in literature (*AC*, 139). First, he describes two "undisplaced" narrative myths reflecting *visions* of the world that are expressed in the *comic* and *tragic* poles of literature.[6] These myths take the form of "two contrasting worlds of total metaphorical identification, one desirable and the other undesirable." Frye calls these the "apocalyptic" and the "demonic," and they can be illustrated by popular conceptions of heaven and hell. The second two organizations are literary methods by which the undisplaced myths are "analogized" to the actual human world; these methods find expression in *romantic* and *ironic* narrative forms. The first analogical method is that of "innocence." By the "analogy of innocence," the pure, undisplaced apocalyptic myth is changed into story by the medium of *metaphor*. The second analogical method is that of "experience." By the "analogy of experience" the pure, undisplaced demonic myth is translated into story by the medium of *realism* (*AC*, 139).

In the apocalyptic undisplaced myth (the comic pole), human as well as divine civilizations flourish. The apocalyptic world is an idealized, indivisible unity, in which God is "One Christ," the members of a political community are of one body, and lovers unite as one flesh (*AC*, 141–43). Community, in its various forms, is infinitely desirable, a natural good, as is the human transformation of nature through work (*AC*, 141).[7]

6. "Undisplaced myths" are narratives that have retained their mythic subject matter and have not been made into "plausible, symmetrical, and morally acceptable" stories for a modern audience (*AC*, 136–38).

7. "The apocalyptic world, the heaven of religion, presents . . . the categories of reality in the forms of human desire, as indicated by the forms they assume under the work of human civilization. The form imposed by human work and desire on the *vegetable* world, for instance, is that of the garden, the farm, the grove, or the

In contrast, the demonic myth (the tragic pole) presents "the world that desire totally rejects" (*AC*, 147).[8] Although the demonic world also has divine, social, and sexual aspects, each aspect is divisive, menacing, and horrific. The world that desire totally rejects is a world in which we are divided and isolated (*AC*, 147).[9]

Frye's third and fourth organizing forms of myth are his two analogies, the narrative methods by which the undisplaced apocalyptic and demonic myths are translated into worldly, recognizable phenomena. The undisplaced apocalyptic myth is translated by the analogy of innocence into an idealized, romantic world. In this narrative method of romance (*AC*, 151–54), apocalypse is made real by the romantic idealization of reality.[10] The undisplaced demonic myth

---

park. The human form of the *animal* world is a world of domesticated animals, of which the sheep has a traditional priority in both Classical and Christian metaphor. The human form of the *mineral* world, the form into which human work transforms stone, is the city. The city, the garden, and the sheepfold are the organizing metaphors of the Bible and of most Christian symbolism, and they are brought into complete metaphorical identification in the book explicitly called the Apocalypse or Revelation, which has been carefully designed to form an undisplaced mythical conclusion for the Bible as a whole" (*AC*, 141).

8. Frye describes the demonic world as follows:

> [T]he world of the nightmare and the scapegoat, of bondage and pain and confusion; the world as it is before the human imagination begins to work on it and before any image of human desire, such as the city or the garden, has been solidly established; the world also of perverted or wasted work, ruins and catacombs, instruments of torture and monuments of folly. And just as apocalyptic imagery in poetry is closely associated with a religious heaven, so its dialectic opposite is closely linked with an existential hell, like Dante's *Inferno*, or with the hell that man creates on earth, as in *1984*, *No Exit*, and *Darkness at Noon*, where the titles of the last two speak for themselves. (*AC*, 147)

9. "The demonic human world is a society held together by a kind of molecular tension of egos, a loyalty to the group or the leader which diminishes the individual, or, at best, contrasts his pleasure with his duty or honor. Such a society is an endless source of tragic dilemmas like those of Hamlet and Antigone. . . . In the sinister human world one individual pole is the tyrant-leader, inscrutable, ruthless, melancholy, and with an insatiable will, who commands loyalty only if he is egocentric enough to represent the collective ego of his followers. The other pole is represented by the *pharmakos* or sacrificed victim, who has to be killed to strengthen the others" (*AC*, 147–48).

10. "The mode of romance presents an idealized world: in romance heroes are brave, heroines beautiful, villains villainous, and the frustrations, ambiguities, and embarrassments of ordinary life are made little of. . . .

In the analogy of innocence the divine or spiritual figures are usually parental, wise old men with magical powers like Prospero, or friendly guardian spirits like Raphael before Adam's fall. Among the human figures children are prominent, and so is the virtue most closely associated with childhood and the state of innocence—chastity, a virtue which in this structure of imagery usually includes virginity" (*AC*,

is translated to the world via the analogy of experience, or the "method of realism" (*AC*, 154–55). Use of the analogy of experience defines what may be called the "ironic mode."[11] Frye generates from these four organizing myths—the apocalyptic, the demonic, the romantic, and the ironic—four thematic categories:

> We have thus answered the question: are there narrative categories of literature broader than, or logically prior to, the ordinary literary genres? There are four such categories: the romantic, the tragic, the comic, and the ironic or satiric. . . . We thus have four narrative pregeneric elements of literature which I shall call *mythoi* or generic plots.
>
> If we think of our experience of these *mythoi*, we shall realize that they form two opposed pairs. Tragedy and comedy contrast rather than blend, and so do romance and irony, the champions respectively of the ideal and the actual. On the other hand comedy blends insensibly into satire at one extreme and into romance at the other; romance may be comic or tragic; tragedy extends from high romance to bitter and ironic realism. (*AC*, 162)

Frye's four pregeneric myths can be schematized as in figure 1.

Frye then distinguishes phases within each of his four categories. Because romance blends into comedy and tragedy, there are phases of romance that are also phases of tragedy or of comedy. Similarly, some of the borderline phases of irony are also phases of comedy at one extreme, and of tragedy at the other. Frye's conception of the mythoi also can be schematized as in figure 2.

---

151). Cities are more alien to the pastoral and rural spirit of this world and the tower and the castle, with an occasional cottage or hermitage, are the chief images of habitation" (*AC*, 152).

11. "[This] treatment of human society reflects . . . Wordsworth's doctrine that the essential human situations, for the poet, are the common and typical ones. Along with this goes a good deal of parody of the idealization of life in romance, a parody that extends to religious and aesthetic experience. . . . Gardens . . . give place to farms and the painful labor of the man with the hoe, the peasant or furze cutter who stands in Hardy as an image of man himself, 'slighted and enduring.' Cities take of course the shape of the labyrinthine modern metropolis, where the main emotional stress is on loneliness and lack of communication" (*AC*, 154–55).

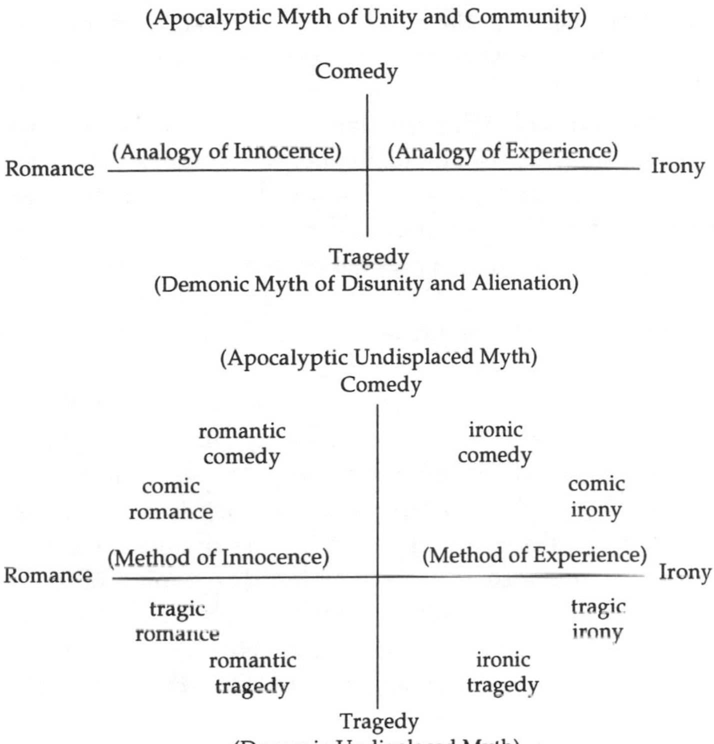

Four Jurisprudential Traditions

Frye's categorization of literary traditions according to contrasting views of the world and methods of narration can be easily fitted to Anglo-American jurisprudence. That jurisprudence can be divided into four traditions, rooted in polar responses to two recurrent questions in legal theory. The first question is philosophical, competing answers to which have generated two *methods* of inquiry. The second question is empirical; the answers have formed two *visions* of our legal world.

The philosophical question has both an analytical and methodological dimension: What is the *analytical* relationship between law and morality, and how *methodologically* do we distinguish legal from moral norms? Natural law and legal positivist responses to this question bear a relation to each other comparable to the contrast

Frye describes between the romantic and ironic modes of narrative literature, which are concerned respectively with the ideal and the actual.

For the natural lawyer, true law, by definition, must meet some set of moral criteria:[12] to St. Augustine, for example, laws that ignore the "eternal" law cannot be just and are therefore not true law.[13] Law incorporates morality, and the "discovery" of law therefore requires the discovery of true morality as well.[14] In aesthetic terms, the natural lawyer employs a "romantic" jurisprudential method. Only in an imaginary apocalyptic world is his ultimate hope realized: only in heaven, or apocalypses, do the legal "is" and the moral "ought" coincide perfectly. Like Frye's romantic, the natural lawyer analogizes this apocalyptic vision of a perfect convergence of law and morality to the imperfect world we inhabit through the ahistorical, "innocent" techniques of metaphor: idealization, reason, and faith. Thus, Plato teaches that the discovery of law, like the discovery of truth and beauty, is the reasoned and nonexperiential grasping of a transcendent, ideal reality.[15] The natural lawyer's philosophical method, like the romantic's narrative method, is theoretically pure and willfully counterfactual. Only moral law is true law. Experience does not ground the theory and method of the natural law traditions; innocence, faith, and reason do.

12. The natural law tradition begins with Plato, who defines law as the "discovery of true reality." Plato, *Meno*, ed. Malcom Brown, trans. W. K. C. Guthne (Indianapolis: Bobbs-Merrill, 1971). Other natural lawyers have claimed that law must, in order to qualify as true "law," accord with moral norms derived from God's law (Augustine), human nature (Aquinas), rights (Dworkin), procedural fairness (Fuller), generality (Wechsler), neutrality (Ackerman), the human good (Finnis), or the community good (Aquinas and Aristotle). See Ackerman, *Social Justice*; St. Thomas of Aquinas, *Summa Theological*, Questions 94–96, ed. T. Gilbey (1964), 75–151; Dworkin, *Taking Rights Seriously*; John Finnis, *Natural Law and Natural Rights* (Oxford: Clarendon 1980); Herbert Wechsler, "Toward Neutral Principles of Constitutional Law," *Harvard University Law Review* 73 (1959): 1–35. But see Finnis, *Natural Law*, 23–365 (the natural law tradition does not require denial of the separation of law from morality).

13. See Herbert Deane, *The Political and Social Ideas of St. Augustine* (New York: Columbia University Press, 1963), 89. During the last forty years of his life, however, Augustine never addressed the proper response to "unjust" temporal laws. He did not suggest that such laws were invalid or that they could be disobeyed. Ibid., 90–91.

14. Augustine's radical assertion is repeated in milder form in Aquinas, *Summa Theological*, 130–33 (Question 96, Reply to Point 4).

15. Plato, *Meno*, 73d.

Legal positivists, conversely, propound an experiential method and a realistic theory.[16] Law is a historical *fact*. As such, it can be discovered only by the study of worldly phenomena. Thus, Austin teaches that law is the "command of the sovereign,"[17] Holmes that law is "what the course will do in fact." The positivists' jurisprudential method is comparable to Frye's ironic narrative method; like Frye's literary ironists, legal positivists analogize their demonic vision to our world by reference to contingent truths born of experience.[18] Only that which is *observable*, is. Experience and skepticism, not faith and reason, ground positivist theory and method.

The second group of basic questions of concern to modern legal theory is empirical. What is the historical relationship between law and morality? Do legal systems tend to satisfy moral criteria or do they tend to be evil? Do they serve forces of liberation or forces of oppression? These are questions about history, human nature, and human societies. The extreme visions underlying the contrasting responses to these questions correlate with the apocalyptic and demonic myths that Frye argues underlie comic and tragic narrative plots.

One of these empirical views echoes Frye's undisplaced demonic myth. In light of the brutality of modern history, it is certainly possible to conclude that positive legal systems more often than not fail to meet even minimal moral criteria, whether the criteria are Kantian, Augustinian, or utilitarian.[19] Like Frye's tragedian, the statist views this history of brutality and oppression as the experiential analogue of our demonic human predicament.[20] The misery heaped upon human beings by human beings, through law and lawlessness

16. See generally H. L. A. Hart, "Positivism and the Separation of Law and Morals," *Harvard Law Review* 71 (1958): 593–629; H. L. A. Hart, "Problems of Philosophy of Law," in *The Encyclopedia of Philosophy*, ed. Paul Edwards (New York: Macmillon and The Free Press 1967), 6:264–76.

17. John Austin, *The Province of Jurisprudence Determined and the Uses of the Study of Jurisprudence* (London: Weidenfeld and Nicolson, 1954), 10–14; Holmes, "Path of the Law," 461.

18. See Hart, "Problems of Philosophy," 272–73.

19. See, e.g., Immanuel Kant, *The Philosophy of Law: An Exposition of the Fundamental Principles of Jurisprudence as the Science of Rights*, ed. William Hastie (Edinburgh: T. and T. Clark, 1887); Deane, *Ideas of St. Augustine*; and Jeremy Bentham, *Of Laws in General*, ed. H. L. A. Hart (London: University of London, Athlone Press, 1970), 31–33.

20. See, e.g., Gustav Radbruch, "Legal Philosophy," in *The Legal Philosophies of Lask, Radbruch, and Dabin*, trans. Kurt Wilk (Cambridge: Harvard University Press, 1950), 43, 112–20.

both, makes perfect sense to the tragic legal theorist; it is hell on earth. Racial, religious, political, and sexual oppression and violence are not perversion of our nature; they are the foreseeable ends of our natural propensity for brutality.

At the other aesthetic extreme, the liberal theorist concludes from history that legal systems and the societies they control tend to improve morally, not degenerate, over time.[21] Auschwitz, El Salvador, and oppression are aberrational; community, progress, and altruism reveal our truer nature. Although imperfect, modern democratic governments do what they ought to do: promote the community's happiness, treat people as ends rather than means, maximize individual freedoms, respect personal autonomy, and encourage community. Aesthetically, these optimistic assessments of recent history, human nature, and law share an apocalyptic vision of human potential and current reality. It follows naturally from the communitarian and progressive assumptions of liberalism that laws do, can, and will promote human welfare; if community is natural and good, then laws and legality are simply a natural and good feature of that human enterprise. The same kind of assumptions, Frye argues, underlies comedy. Liberal, democratic, and humane societies and legal systems appear natural from the aesthetic vantage point of the apocalyptic myth.

These four jurisprudential positions correlate, then, with Frye's fundamental narrative plots. Romantic and ironic narrative modes mirror the natural law and positivist methods in jurisprudence. Comic

21. The liberal state in our culture is distinguished from the conservative not by a neutral stance toward particular definitions of the good life, as Dworkin and Ackerman have suggested, but by the manner in which the "good life" is defined, ascertained, and pursued. Unlike conservatives, liberals are committed to a naturalistic, evolving conception of the good life, rather than a moralistic and static one. As a result, they are committed to an experimental, inductive method of understanding. Liberalism's aim, then, is a naturalistic conception of the good life that is empirically understood and ultimately accessible to all members of the community. These "constitutive goals" sometimes imply a strategy of state neutrality toward the nature of that life and sometimes require the contrary. Whether or not state neutrality is required by liberal commitments depends upon contingent and temporal conditions. But liberalism itself does not require neutrality; at most, given liberal premises, conditions may at various times suggest the wisdom of state neutrality. See Robin West, "Liberalism Rediscovered: A Pragmatic Definition of the Liberal Vision," *University of Pittsburgh Law Review* 46 (1985): 673–738. On moral improvement, see e.g., H. L. A. Hart, "Law in the Perspective of Philosophy: 1776–1976," *New York University Law Review* 51 (1976): 538–51.

and tragic narrative visions correspond to liberal and demonic or statist worldviews, respectively.

But just as narrators combine vision with method (*AC*, 131–40), legal theorists typically combine either a romantic or ironic theoretical method with either a comic or tragic vision of the world. Both the natural lawyer and the positivist may harbor either a demonic or an apocalyptic vision of history and of human society. Similarly, a liberal may employ either a romantic or an ironic jurisprudential method, as may a statist. The combinations of theoretical method and historical vision yield jurisprudential positions, which in turn correlate with the phases Frye finds within his narrative plots.

The natural lawyer who discovers that much of what currently operates as law does not morally qualify as such will be prompted to deny the law's ultimate validity. As Ely notes, for example, our revolutionary Declaration of Independence, unlike the Constitution, is permeated with natural law concepts that deny the validity of the British law of its time.[22] A romantic method coupled with an awareness of the tragic failings of particular states, rulers, or laws is the shared aesthetic stance of the eighteenth-century revolutionary, the twentieth-century civil disobedient, and the transcendental visionary.

Alternatively, the natural lawyer who sees in the present world a legal system that generally comports with moral criteria will be prompted to assert the essential morality of the law—the rightness of extant power. Romantic method coupled with a comic contentment with the present world is the aesthetic stance of the political reactionary. Law becomes a moral good, which therefore ought to be obeyed, simply because it is law.

Like the natural lawyer, the positivist combines a method—an experiential insistence on the facts—with a view of the world. At the cost of symmetry, one can distinguish three jurisprudential and political positions. First, a positivist may combine an experiential historical method with an apocalyptic vision of the world, believing that our legal system is generally good, adequately reflecting both our tolerance of diversity and our social inclination to community. A positivist methodology coupled with a rational belief in human

22. See John Hart Ely, *Democracy and Distrust: A Theory of Judicial Review* (Cambridge: Harvard University Press, 1980), 49.

goodness and social progress forms the comic-ironic aesthetic position of the reformer. It underlies the optimism of liberal and progressive theorists, from the Benthamites through the New Deal lawyers and the American legal realists. Second, the positivist may perceive a demonic reality but nevertheless harbor an apocalyptic vision of our potential for a communitarian future. Our social isolation and alienation are a consequence of changeable and perverse present institutions, not evidence of an essentially atomistic human personality. Because of the wide gap between present reality and social potential, however, radical action, not liberal progress, is all that can deliver us to the promised land. This aesthetic posture—dark, ironic comedy, tinged with awareness of the demonic—characterizes the critical legal studies movement. Finally, at the most tragic extreme, the positivist method can combine with a thoroughly demonic assessment of the world, present and future: law is the will of the powerful and morality does not exist. The modern law-and-economics movement, despite its liberal window dressing, has its roots in this combination of scientific method with a tragic assessment of our communal potential.

Similarly, liberal and statist theorists may also tend toward either an ironic or romantic methodology. A liberal outlook coupled with a romantic methodology results in a reactionary acceptance of the status quo based upon idealized and static assumptions about human nature. By contrast, liberalism coupled with experiential realism yields an acceptance of our social world based upon changing facts of experience. Statism tending toward irony posits only relentless cruelty and suffering as the essence of human experience. Statism combined with a romantic methodology simultaneously posits a demonic present and an idyllic alternative world: either an afterlife or a postrevolutionary paradise on earth.

These positions can be correlated with Frye's literary categories in figure 3.

Just as Frye's literary themes blend at their boundaries with the themes they border, so these jurisprudential schools blend with each other in their more extreme phases. Natural law tends to embrace either a reactionary or a revolutionary plan of action, depending upon the worldview with which it is coupled. Positivism tends toward either a progressive or regressive stance. An apocalyptic view of human nature can be influenced by either a positivist insistence upon an experiential method, or a romantic insistence on an idealized

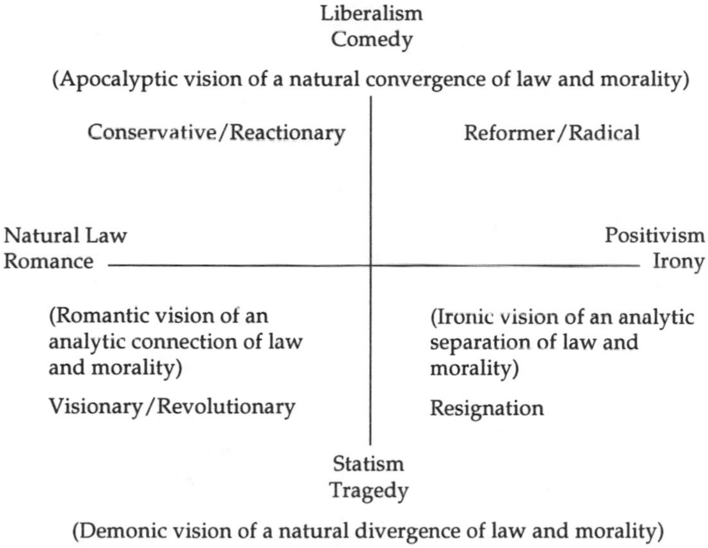

Liberalism
Comedy

(Apocalyptic vision of a natural convergence of law and morality)

Conservative/Reactionary | Reformer/Radical

Natural Law
Romance

Positivism
Irony

(Romantic vision of an analytic connection of law and morality)

Visionary/Revolutionary

(Ironic vision of an analytic separation of law and morality)

Resignation

Statism
Tragedy

(Demonic vision of a natural divergence of law and morality)

methodology. Finally, a demonic vision of human society and legal institutions may be coupled with either a positivist resignation to the status quo or a revolutionary aspiration to a transcendental reality. The major strands of jurisprudential thought thus can be depicted as in figure 4.

Thus, as romance blends with tragedy at one extreme and comedy at the other, natural law blends with revolutionary rhetoric on the one side and a reactionary constitutionalism and individualism on the other. As comedy blends into either romance or irony, liberalism blends, with a romantic equation of the "is" and the "ought" on the one side, and a realistic insistence on their separation on the other. As irony borders upon comedy and tragedy, legal positivism borders upon liberalism and statism. Finally, as tragedy ranges from irony to romance, statism moves from an exhausted realism to inspiration and resolution, closing the circle.

The next two parts of this chapter discuss each of the four major jurisprudential categories, from the contrasting methods of romance and irony to the contrasting visions of comedy and tragedy. First, the family resemblance between the major jurisprudential commitments of each jurisprudential category and the dominant characteristics of its correlative narrative myth are examined. Then the central ambiguity of each jurisprudential category is identified, along with

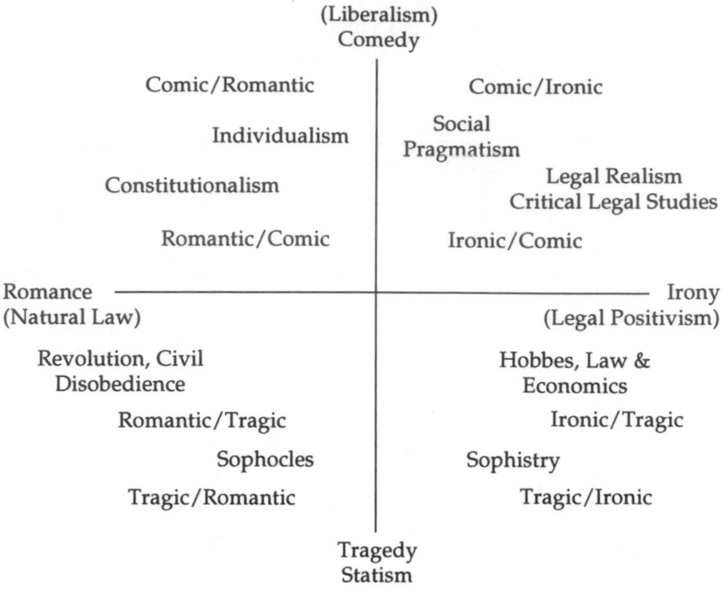

(Liberalism)
Comedy

Comic/Romantic — Comic/Ironic

Individualism — Social Pragmatism

Constitutionalism — Legal Realism, Critical Legal Studies

Romantic/Comic — Ironic/Comic

Romance (Natural Law) — Irony (Legal Positivism)

Revolution, Civil Disobedience — Hobbes, Law & Economics

Romantic/Tragic — Ironic/Tragic

Sophocles — Sophistry

Tragic/Romantic — Tragic/Ironic

Tragedy
Statism

the two major subcategories that the ambiguity entails. Finally, each jurisprudential category is correlated with the phases Frye identifies within each narrative plot. The ambiguity within each philosophical tradition will be discussed in aesthetic terms, for these aesthetic differences have generated much of our modern jurisprudential debate.

Narrative Modes and Jurisprudential Methods

Romance and Natural Law: Good Guys, Bad Guys, and the Rule of Law

Romantic narrative, Frye explains, is characteristically dominated by the description of a mythic quest for an idyllic world (*AC*, 186–87). In romance, heroes are triumphant and rewarded, villains are punished, the comfortable and impeccably moral status quo is restored, and all is right in the end—as it was at the start. The hero embodies moral virtue, and he and it emerge victorious. By the end of the narrative, power and right have inevitably converged (*AC*, 187).[23]

23. "[T]his major adventure, the element that gives literary form to the romance, [is] the quest. . . . A quest involving conflict assumes two main characters, a protag-

Frye explains that romance has both a "proletarian" and a "chivalric" aspect.[24] These elements correlate, in turn, with romance's tragic and comic phases. Tragic (proletarian) romance parallels tragedy's theme of disunification: the hero is inevitably and irretrievably alienated from the community, despite the hero's hope and the narrator's promise of an ultimate communion. In the tragic phases of romantic narrative, heroic strength and moral virtue are pitted against the corrupt values of a dominant social group. Consequently, Frye explains, the tragic phases of romance explore revolutionary themes: tumultuous endings and new beginnings make room for at least the description, if not the fruition, of new utopias.

Comic romance, by contrast, celebrates the moral virtue of the dominant social group: the heroic and virtuous protagonist protects the group against assault from outsiders. Romance in these phases parallels comedy's "unification" theme: the hero and his society are

---

onist or hero, and an antagonist or enemy. . . . The enemy may be an ordinary human being, but the nearer the romance is to myth, the more attributes of divinity will cling to the hero and the more the enemy will take on demonic mythical qualities. The central form of romance is dialectical: everything is focussed on a conflict between the hero and his enemy, and all the reader's values are bound up with the hero. Hence the hero of romance is analogous to the mythical Messiah or deliverer who comes from an upper world, and his enemy is analogous to the demonic powers of a lower world. The conflict however takes place in, or at any rate primarily concerns, *our* world. . . . The enemy is associated with winter, darkness, confusion, sterility, moribund life, and old age, and the hero with spring, dawn, order, fertility, vigor, and youth" (*AC*, 187–88).

"The characterization of romance follows its general dialectic structure, which means that subtlety and complexity are not much favored. Characters tend to be either for or against the quest. If they assist it they are idealized as simply gallant or pure; if they obstruct it they are caricatured as simply villainous or cowardly. Hence every typical character in romance tends to have his moral opposite confronting him, like black and white pieces in a chess game" (*AC*, 195).

24. "The romance is nearest of all literary forms to the wish-fulfilment dream, and for that reason it has socially a curiously paradoxical role. In every age the ruling social or intellectual class tends to project its ideals in some form of romance, where the virtuous heroes and beautiful heroines represent the ideals and the villains the threats to their ascendancy. This is the central character of chivalric romance in the Middle Ages, aristocratic romance in the Renaissance, bourgeois romance since the eighteenth century, and revolutionary romance in contemporary Russia. Yet there is a genuinely proletarian element in romance too which is never satisfied with its various incarnations, and in fact the incarnations themselves indicate that no matter how great a change may take place in society, romance will turn up again, as hungry as ever, looking for new hopes and desires to feed on. The perennially childlike quality of romance is marked by its extraordinarily persistent nostalgia, its search for some kind of imaginative golden age in time or space" (*AC*, 186).

united in purpose and outlook. The identification of heroic strength and moral virtue serves to reinforce, not overthrow, the values and cohesion of the extant social group. In the most comic phases, the group to be defended is either the society as a whole or some slice of it (*AC*, 201–2).

Schematically, romantic narrative "blends" at one extreme with tragedy, and at the other with comedy (fig. 5).

Natural law scholarship, like romantic narrative, is dominated by a moral quest. Law is the natural lawyer's romantic hero: it is morally virtuous and historically triumphant—it is "sovereign." Law embodies both virtue and power. Like the narrator's portrayal of the romantic hero, every natural lawyer defines law or legality so that the defining attributes of a truly legal sovereignty are themselves moral qualities. Such attributes then morally legitimate as well as define the sovereign's political power. Thus, the political monarch is both sovereign and moral, because divine anointment ensures the justice as well as the power of a monarchical regime. Similarly, the Constitution is both sovereign and moral because of its defining attribute; the higher law content of its substantive provisions, its history, and its traditions both morally legitimate as well as define a constitutional regime. The natural lawyer defines law in such a way as to ensure the moral worth of legal supremacy, just as the narrator of romantic fiction describes the hero in such a way as to ensure the moral worth of his inevitable victory.

Romantic narrative, Frye explains, serves a "curiously paradoxical role" in society (*AC*, 186). Natural law scholarship exhibits the same paradoxical range found in romantic narrative, moving between a reactionary endorsement of the legal status quo and a revolutionary rejection of it. The natural lawyer's insistence that law, properly defined, incorporates the demands of morality entails either a chivalric conclusion—the necessary morality of the current regime—or the revolutionary conclusion—the immorality and hence illegality of the regime. Either the Prince is necessarily good because of his divine anointment, the chivalric conclusion, or, if he is bad, he was not divinely anointed and therefore is necessarily not a Prince, the revolutionary conclusion. These conclusions correlate with the comic and tragic phases of the natural law tradition. Whereas the comic natural lawyer sees virtue in existing power relations, the tragedian finds such virtue only in his dream of an idealized or future world.

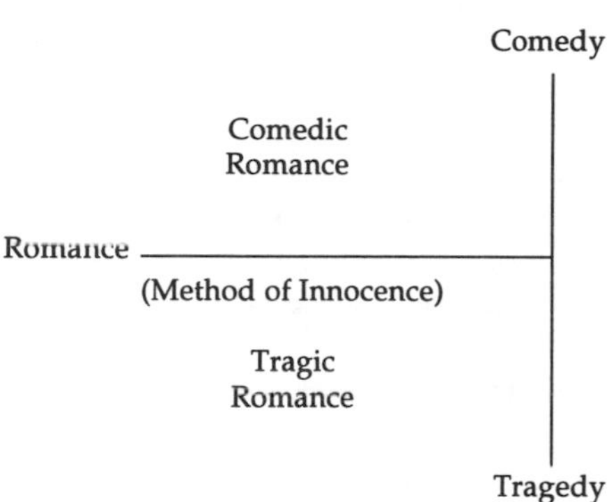

The tragedian thus calls insistently for a revolutionary struggle toward an idyllic future paradise.

Both the chivalric and revolutionary traditions have heavily influenced American legal romanticism. The chivalric inference of morality from the fact of power is reflected in law-review and constitutional literature, as well as popular thinking on law. At the other extreme, the revolutionary inference form the immorality of power to its illegality is a foundation of revolutionary literature.[25] Schematically, American natural law literature covers the same substantive range as romantic narrative (fig. 6).

Tragic Romance: Of Rebirth and Revolution

Law-review scholarship only occasionally explores tragic-romantic themes. This absence is striking although not inexplicable. Legal scholars do not often seek tumultuous changes, new beginnings and endings, or transcendent utopias. Such scholarship lacks the preconditions of tragic romance: an apocalyptic vision of the future, a perception of the present as a living hell, and an innocent, idealistic, ahistorical insistence that we can somehow transcend history to achieve utopia. The perceptions of scholars are less epic and their goals more timid.

American legal literature more broadly defined, however, is replete with tragic-romantic narrative themes. The Declaration of Independence, our document of "tumultuous birth," employs natural

25. See, e.g., *The Writings of Thomas Paine,* ed. Moncure D. Conway (New York: AMS Press, 1967), vol. 1, *Common Sense,* 67; vol. 2, *Rights of Man,* 265.

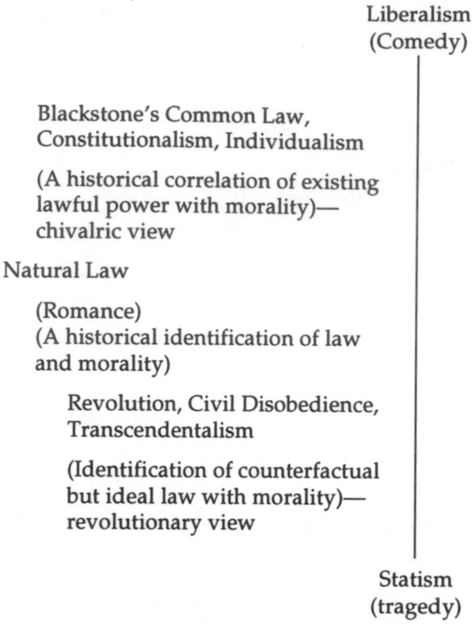

Liberalism
(Comedy)

Blackstone's Common Law,
Constitutionalism, Individualism

(A historical correlation of existing
lawful power with morality)—
chivalric view

Natural Law

(Romance)
(A historical identification of law
and morality)

Revolution, Civil Disobedience,
Transcendentalism

(Identification of counterfactual
but ideal law with morality)—
revolutionary view

Statism
(tragedy)

law logic profoundly tinged with tragic-romantic aesthetic imagery. The Declaration distinguishes true law from the commands of the existing sovereign or of the existing state, defining the former as a transcendent quality that can only be freed by revolutionary action. Law is the justice inherent in our power of reason, not in our will. As narrative, the document tells the romantic story of the birth of a hero, a tumultuous ending and a new apocalyptic beginning. The American Rule of Law is the hero that triumphs over English monarchical authority. The parental authority figures are overthrown and replaced by a lawful, nonparental, and freer political utopia, an orderly society of "desirable law" in which the free and the brave, through heroic and individual action, can exploit the apocalyptic land of milk and honey.[26]

The narrative structure and the aesthetic imagery of apocalyptic writings are drawn upon heavily, if subconsciously, during every period of radical change. The civil-rights movement provides the most recent instance of this reliance. Like the revolutionary Martin Luther King, Jr., distinguishes law from power, defining the former as a

26. See James H. Billington, *Fire in the Minds of Men: Origins of the Revolutionary Faith* (New York: Basic Books, 1980), 9.

transcendent quality released only by revolutionary action.[27] King identifies law not with reason, however, but with love, emphatically echoing the heavenly identification of sovereignty with love that characterizes the undisplaced apocalyptic myth. Aesthetically, King relies almost exclusively on the tragic-romantic imagery of the Declaration of Independence and of the Bible. King's dream, like biblical narrative and the story told in the Declaration, is the story of a hero's moral battle against the demonic world in which we presently live, and toward the "blessed community" of which we are capable. The American dream of freedom and brotherhood is the reality our utopia must contain; alienation and racism are the reality from which we must be delivered.[28]

In King's blessed world, as in every apocalyptic community, the anxieties of our real world have vanished: fertility is victorious over the wasteland; food, drink, bread, and wine are plentiful, the male and female are united, and body and blood are one:

> The dream is one of equality of opportunity, of privilege and property widely distributed; a dream of a land where men will not take necessities from the many to give luxuries to the few; a dream of a land where men do not argue that the color of a man's skin determines the content of his character; a dream of a place where all our gifts and resources are held not for ourselves alone but as instruments of service for the rest of humanity; the dream of a country where every man will respect the dignity and worth of all human personality, and men will dare to live

---

27. King embraced the natural law arguments of both Aquinas and Augustine. See Martin Luther King, Jr., "Letter from Birmingham City Jail," in *Why We Can't Wait* (New York: Harper and Row, 1964), 77–100.

28. "Jesus took over the phrase 'the Kingdom of God,' but He changed its meaning. He refused entirely to be the kind of Messiah that his contemporaries expected. Jesus made love the mark of sovereignty. Here we are left with no doubt as to Jesus' meaning. The Kingdom of God will be a society in which men and women live as children of God should live. It will be a kingdom controlled by the law of love. . . . Many have attempted to say that the ideal of a better world will be worked out in the next world. But Jesus taught men to say, 'Thy will be done in earth, as it is in heaven.' Although the world seems to be in a bad shape today, we must never lose faith in the power of god to achieve his purpose" (Martin Luther King, Jr., "What a Christian Should Think about the Kingdom of God," quoted in Kenneth L. Smith and Ira G. Zepp, *Search for the Beloved Community: The Thinking of Martin Luther King, Jr.* [Valley Forge: Judson Press, 1974], 129).

> together as brothers. . . . Whenever it is fulfilled, we will emerge from the bleak and desolate midnight of man's inhumanity to man into the bright and glowing daybreak of freedom and justice for all of God's children. . . .
>
> It is a dream of a land where men of all races, of all nationalities, and of all creeds can live together as brothers. The substance of the dream is expressed in these sublime words, words lifted to cosmic proportions: "We hold these truths to be self-evident—that all men are created equal; that they are endowed by their Creator with certain inalienable rights; that among these are life, liberty, and the pursuit of happiness." This is the dream.[29]

Comic Romance and Constitutionalism

To the comic-romantic, the identification of power and morality is neither a dream nor the future; it is our present reality. Moral authority is not just an object of desire; it is also the reality that we have and must struggle to preserve. In tragic romance, the hero struggles against the reigning power; in comic romance, the hero's virtue and power mirror the community's dominant values. The hero's undertaking is to defend, not attack, the dominant social group and the values it embraces. As a result, Frye explains, the comic-romantic narrator tends to "hedge"—or identify—existing political power with divine or moral attributes.[30]

Not coincidentally, the hedging of legal authority with divine authority is also a central aesthetic metaphor in comic-romantic jurisprudence.[31] Of course, the comic natural lawyer no longer sees the "fire of the angelic world blaz[ing] in the king's crown" (*AC*, 153). But he does still see or seek the angelic blaze of moral legitimacy in other sources of sovereignty. In American romantic jurisprudence, it is usually the constitutionalist who sees the angelic blaze in existing

29. Address by Martin Luther King, Jr., Washington, D.C., 28 August 1963, quoted in Smith and Zepp, *Search*, 126–27.

30. "We find [in romance] the tendency to idealize the human representatives of the divine and the spiritual world. . . . Divinity hedges the king and the Courtly Love mistress is a goddess; love of both is an educating and informing power which brings one into unity with the spiritual and divine worlds. The fire of the angelic world blazes in the king's crown and the lady's eyes" (*AC*, 153).

31. For example, Dworkin uses a "super-smart" judge as his ultimate legal sovereign. See Dworkin, *Taking Rights Seriously*, 105–30.

power. For the constitutionalist, unlike the revolutionary, legal authority is hedged with right; the romantic identification of law with right is characteristic both of the legal state of which we dream and of the legal state we must defend. As divine ascension both defines and morally legitimates monarchical power, so constitutionalism and the rule of law define and morally legitimate liberal, democratic, and constitutional power.[32]

Romantic stories about how the Constitution came to embody moral right take two familiar forms in jurisprudence: substantive and procedural. The substantive story unambiguously romanticizes the document's content. The constitutional provisions themselves, by virtue of either some miracle or some highly improbable historical accident, embody true principles of morality. Corwin tells the story this way:

> The attribution of supremacy to the constitution on the ground solely of its rootage in popular will represents, however, a comparatively late outgrowth of American constitutional theory. Earlier the supremacy accorded to constitutions was ascribed less to their putative source than to their supposed content, to their embodiment of an essential and unchanging justice. The theory of law thus invoked . . . predicate[s] certain principles of right and justice which are entitled to prevail of their own intrinsic excellence, altogether regardless of the attitude of those who wield the physical resources of the community. Such principles were made by no human hands; indeed, if they did not antedate

32. Constitutionalism's comic vision is in tension with the tragic mythology of the revolutionary. Unlike the revolutionary, the constitutionalist projects an explicit endorsement of the particular institutions that the document defines and thus implicitly endorses the "integrated body" of individuals empowered by the Constitution. The constitutionalist employs not only the romantic form of the monarchist, but also the monarchist's optimistic faith in the good will of the powerful. The revolutionary theorist, or the civil disobedient, does not share the constitutionalist's comic contentment.

King's tragic-romantic justification of civil disobedience, for example, contrasts with the comic-romantic justification offered by Ronald Dworkin. King argues that an unjust law is not a law because it is not in accord with our nature or with God's will, whereas Dworkin argues that an unjust law is not a law because it is unconstitutional. For Dworkin, the Constitution embodies political morality as well as positive legality; our sovereign is in fact the ideal. Dworkin, *Taking Rights Seriously*, 81–130.

> deity itself, they still so express its nature as to bind and control it. They are external to all Will as such and interpenetrate all Reason as such. They are eternal and immutable. In relation to such principles, human laws are, when entitled to obedience save as to matters indifferent, merely as record or transcript and their enactment an act not of will or power but one of discovery and declaration.[33]

Frye tells us that in comic romance, power accompanies moral right (*AC*, 201), and Corwin makes the point explicit: "the *legality* of the constitution, its *supremacy*, and its *claim to be worshipped*, alike find common standing ground on the belief in a law superior to the will of human governors."[34]

Although the stories Dworkin tells in *Taking Rights Seriously* have kept the legend of justice alive, substantive constitutionalism generally has not fared well in the last half of this century.[35] The overtly romantic assertion that the Constitution somehow embodies objective moral truths—that constitutional power is the prerequisite of justice—does not square with a historical, realistic disposition. It is as hard to deny the humanity, and thus the fallibility, of the constitution's authors as to deny the humanity of the king.

But although this particular legend is now less popular, chivalric romance itself thrives in legal theory. The accepted modern constitutionalist story is that the *procedures* the Constitution envisions, rather than its substantive content, ensure the moral legitimacy of constitutional authority. According to the procedural story, law, or constitutional sovereignty, is defined and legitimized not by particular constitutional provisions, but by *processes governed by reason*—just as a monarch is defined and legitimated by the process of divine anointment.

Although Lon Fuller in *The Morality of Law* explored the parameters of procedural, chivalric romance, it was Herbert Wechsler who, as his use of statements by justices Jackson and Frankfurter

33. Edward Corwin, "The 'Higher Law' Background of American Constitutional Law," *Harvard Law Review* 42 (1928): 152 (emphasis omitted).

34. Ibid., 153 (emphasis added).

35. For illustrations of constitutional lawyers' movement away from the substantive model and toward the procedural model, see, e.g., Fuller, *Morality of Law;* Wechsler, "Toward Neutral Principles."

illustrates, elevated the argument and the imagery to the level of nearly pure myth:

> "Liberty is not the mere absence of restraint, it is not a spontaneous product of majority rule, it is not achieved merely by lifting underprivileged classes to power, nor is it the inevitable by-product of technological expansion. It is achieved only by a rule of law." Is it not also what Mr. Justice Frankfurter must mean in calling upon judges for "allegiance to nothing except the effort, amid tangled words and limited insights, to find the path through precedent, through policy, through history, to the best judgement that fallible creatures can reach in that most difficult of all tasks: the achievement of justice between man and man, between man and state, *through reason called law*"?[36]

As in the substantive story, Fuller and Wechsler's procedural constitutionalism, viewed as narrative, exudes a contentment with constitutional institutions as well as a romantic insistence that, through constitutionalism, power, and right converge:

> Having said what I have said, I certainly should add that I offer no comfort to anyone who claims legitimacy in defiance of the courts. This is the ultimate negation of all neutral principles, to take the benefits accorded by the constitutional system, including the national market and common defense, while denying it allegiance when a special burden is imposed. *That certainly is the antithesis of law.*[37]

The analytic difference between the substantive and procedural theories turns on the degree of generality each theorist finds crucial to a moral conception of law. The aesthetic difference between the two theories read as stories also turns on the degree of rationalist detachment from experience that each embraces. Wechsler's story,

36. Wechsler, "Toward Neutral Principles," 16 (quoting Robert Houghwout Jackson), *The Supreme Court in the American System of Government* (Cambridge: Harvard University Press, 1955), 76; and Felix Frankfurter, "Chief Justices I Have Known," in *Of Law and Men: Papers and Addresses of Felix Frankfurter*, ed. Philip Elman (Hamden, Conn: Archon Books, 1956), 158 (emphasis added).

37. Wechsler, "Toward Neutral Principles," 35 (emphasis added).

unlike Corwin's and perhaps unlike Dworkin's, falls in the most comic phases of romance. It is, to borrow Frye's terms, as "reflective, idyllic [a] view" of "contemplative withdrawal" as one can imagine." As in the later works of Shakespeare, Wechsler's narrative voice shows a pronounced tendency "to the moral stratification of characters." His "arrangement of characters"—with judges and legal thinkers on the top of the hierarchy—is "consistent with the detached and contemplative [rationalist] view of society taken in this phase" (*AC*, 202). The judge is detached and contemplative; thus, in Wechsler's narrative, the judge clearly embodies the rule of law.[38]

The Appeal of Romance

Why does chivalric romanticism persist, either in narrative literature or in jurisprudence? Frye attributes its persistence partly to its political function: comic romance reinforces the chivalric morality of the socially powerful.[39] The same is clearly true of jurisprudence: as Bentham noted, the natural lawyer's identification of law with a higher morality almost always serves the ends of the powerful.[40] The claim to virtue legitimates the claim to power. This accommodation no doubt accounts in part for the durability of the natural law tradition.

Shakespeare provides a lovely example of this phenomenon in *Richard II*. As long as heaven guards the right, and as long as King Richard is the deputy elected by the Lord, Richard cannot be deposed, nor is there any reason he should be. Richard himself makes the argument:

> So when this thief, this traitor Bolingbroke,
> Who all this while hath reveled in the nigh
> Whilst we were wandering with the Antipodes,
> Shall see us rising in our throne, the east,
> His treasons will sit blushing in his face,
> Not able to endure the sight of day,
> But self-affrighted tremble at his sin.

38. The criticism of Wechsler's neutral-principles thesis is extensive. For a summary, see Ely, *Democracy and Distrust*, 54–55, 212–13 nn. 58–60.

39. See note 33 and accompanying text.

40. Bentham, "A Commentary on Humphreys' Real Property Code," in *Works*, 5:389.

Not all the water in the rough rude sea
Can wash the balm off from an anointed King.
The breath of worldly men cannot depose
The deputy elected by the Lord.
For every man that Bolingbroke hath press'd
to lift shrewd steel against our golden crown,
God for his Richard hath in heavenly pay
A glorious angel. Then, if angels fight,
Weak men must fall, for heaven still guards
the right.[41]

Similarly, in the romantic conception of sovereignty, moral and legal commitments to a particular rule or ruler are aligned: a law that is constitutional is therefore both valid and just, just as a man divinely anointed will surely be just as well as powerful.[42]

This political explanation, however, is not ultimately satisfying, because the logic of the natural lawyers' claims is easily manipulated. As Bentham also noted, the identification of law and morality can serve the end of anarchy as well as the ends of the powerful.[43] Shakespeare's *Richard II* is finally history, not romance, and in that history, Richard's invocation of romantic imagery eventually works against his sovereignty. If a prince's edict evidences a lack of morality, the prince is not a prince and his edict not a law. Similarly, a properly passed statute that fails to accord due process is a bad law and ought not to be enforced. Natural law, like other forms of narrative romance, serves the revolutionary as well as it serves the reactionary.

And yet, the natural law movement in Western culture has yielded potent, often inspiring, and occasionally profound insights. When natural law is viewed as romantic narrative, this phenomenon is neither paradoxical nor troubling. The natural law traditions in jurisprudence and romantic narrative share deep human roots. The

41. William Shakespeare, "*The Tragedy of King Richard the Second*," act 3, scene 2, lines 47–62, in *The Riverside Shakespeare*, ed. G. Blakemore Evans (Boston: Houghton Mifflin Company, 1974), 821.

42. Dworkin makes the astounding claim in *Taking Rights Seriously* that every sincere moral objection to a law in our culture has a constitutional analogue. This argument seems peculiarly nostalgic and dated. Dworkin, *Taking Rights Seriously*, 206–29.

43. Bentham, "A Fragment on Government," in *Works*, 1:221, 287; see Hart, "Positivism," 597–98.

appeal of both is simply that we *want* power to be loving. The divinely anointed king embodies what not only natural lawyers, but to some extent all of us, still crave: a powerful sovereign who is moral and just; a powerful figure who loves us. Like romantic literature, natural law claims are childlike: they express our deeply felt needs for security, protection, and the perfect love of those who provide it. The quest of the romantic narrator and the constitutionalist is ultimately for a "nostalgic goal": an "imaginative golden age in time and space," when power and morality—law and justice—emanate from the same source (*AC*, 186). The persistence of that quest evidences the depth of our craving for assurance that the story of the community will have a happy ending and that we are being cared for, even if the evidence of our senses—our history—is very much to the contrary.

In reality, we know that we have not even adequately described, much less attained, a society that fulfills both our childlike needs and the demands of our more adult intellects. Perhaps our desire to see power and moral virtue converge will never be satisfied by a particular legal power. But unless and until that political, aesthetic, and primal desire is satisfied, natural law will continue to be a central force in jurisprudence, and romantic literature will continue to thrive.

Irony and Realistic Jurisprudence: The Positivist Separation of Law and Morality

Frye explains that the ironic narrative method, in contrast to the metaphoric and idealistic method of romance, is characterized by a radically empirical commitment: do not expect anything or anyone to be other than he, she, or it appears (*AC*, 154–55). The world is as it is experienced—nothing less, but certainly nothing more. Abstractions are either ephemeral, and therefore unknowable, or false, and therefore misleading. The ironic narrator orders his hero's life pragmatically on the basis of experience, not on the basis of either pretended truths underlying that experience or promises regarding the future.[44] Consequently, ironic narrative is typically dominated by

44. "[Irony and satire are] the mythical patterns of experience, the attempts to give form to the shifting ambiguities and complexities of unidealized existence. We cannot find these patterns merely in the mimetic or representational aspect of such literature, for that aspect is one of content and not form. As structure, the central

skeptical, often satiric attacks on the purportedly complete characterizations of knowledge proffered by various forms of romanticism.[45]

Like the romantic method, the ironic method merges with comedy at one extreme and with tragedy at the other. As a result, Frye explains, the ironic method encompasses a spectrum of realistic narrative visions, ranging from a gentle, generally benign skepticism to a horrific nihilism. In the first comic stages of irony, the ironic narrator couples a comic, communitarian vision of society with his methodological insistence on experiential fact. He consequently employs a gentle, benign, satiric method to expose the shared, communal reality behind religious, moral, intellectual, and literary conventions (*AC*, 229). In the middle stages, social conventions are not just satirized but are stripped away, revealing a shared but often painful human community (*AC*, 232–36). Finally, the most tragic stages reveal the meaninglessness of suffering itself. All moral referents are completely lost; the world suffers, and there is neither relief from nor sense in that ultimate experience (*AC*, 236–39).

The visionary range of the ironic mode can be viewed as in figure 7.

Like the ironic storyteller, the legal positivist employs a radically empirical method that is saturated with experiential fact. The positivist's story of law's sovereignty is rigorously experiential: law is the consequence of legislation and adjudication, both being real events caused by physical forces.[46] Human beings, not disembodied neutral

---

principle of ironic myth is best approached as a parody of romance: the application of romantic mythical forms to a more realistic content which fits them in unexpected ways. No one in a romance, Don Quixote protests, ever asks who pays for the hero's accommodation" (*AC*, 223).

45. "Satire . . . has an interest in anything men do. The philosopher, on the other hand, teaches a certain way or method of living; he stresses some things and despises others; what he recommends is carefully selected from the data of human life; he continually passes moral judgements on social behavior. His attitude is dogmatic; that of the satirist pragmatic. Hence satire may often represent the collision between a selection of standards from experience and the feeling that experience is bigger than any set of beliefs about it. The satirist demonstrates the infinite variety of what men do by showing the futility, not only of saying what they do, but even of attempts to systematize or formulate a coherent scheme of what they do. Philosophies of life abstract from life, and an abstraction implies the leaving out of inconvenient data. The satirist brings up those inconvenient data" (*AC*, 229).

46. See, e.g., John Chipman Gray, *The Nature and Sources of the Law* (New York: Columbia University Press, 1909); Joseph W. Bingham, "What Is the Law?" *Michigan Law Review* 11 (1912): 1–25, 109–21; Holmes, "Path of the Law," 459 ("If

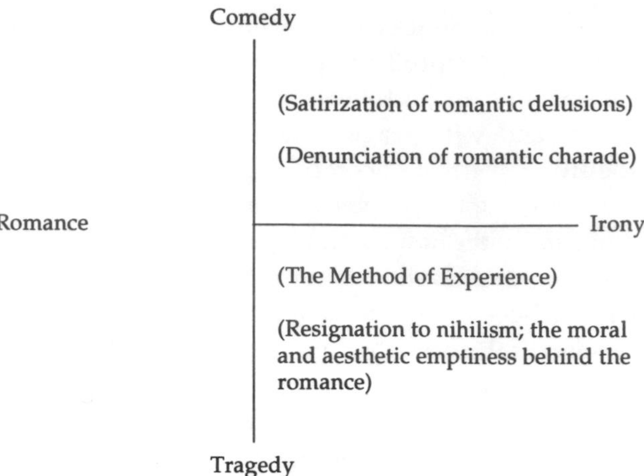

principles, decide cases and enact statutes. Similarly, the practical person experiences jail sentences and damage remedies, not general rules of law, as the essence of law. To the legal pragmatist, whether narrator, theorist, or actor, generalities have no function, no historical impact, no experiential presence, and therefore no meaningful existence. Law is the story of history and experience. In Holmes's famous formulation law is experience, not logic; it is the "story of a nation's development."[47]

What the natural lawyer purports to discover as truth or as "law" are not, then, aspects of the real world, but merely the products of his own introspection. In Justice Holmes's colorful phrase, what we believe as true and eternal is that collection of propositions which

you want to know the law and nothing else, you must look at it as a bad man who cares only for the material consequences which such knowledge enables him to predict"); Joseph C. Hutcheson, Jr., "Lawyer's Law and the Little, Small Dice," *Tulane Law Review* 7 (1932): 1–12.

47. "The life of the law has not been logic: it has been experience. The felt necessities of the time, the prevalent moral and political theories, institutions of public policy, avowed or unconscious, even the prejudices which judges share with their fellow-men, have had a good deal more to do than the syllogism in determining the rules by which men should be governed. The law embodies the story of a nation's development through many centuries, and it cannot be dealt with as if it contained only the axioms and corollaries of a book of mathematics. In order to know what it is, we must know what it has been, and what it tends to become. . . . The substance of the law at any given time pretty nearly corresponds, so far as it goes, with what is then understood to be convenient; but its form and machinery, and the degree to which it is able to work out desired results, depend very much upon its past" (Holmes, *Common Law*, 1–2).

we "cannot help" but believe.[48] Just as the ironic narrator exposes the counterfactual myths underlying romance, the positivist exposes the romantic delusions underlying the natural lawyer's convictions. Holmes's attack on the certitudes of the natural law tradition is a classic instance of the ironist's satirization of the abstractions of romanticism:

> It is not enough for the knight of romance that you agree that his lady is a very nice girl—if you do not admit that this is the best that God ever made or will make, you must fight. There is in all men a demand for the superlative, so much so that the poor devil who has no other way of reaching it attains it by getting drunk. It seems to me that this demand is at the bottom of the philosopher's effort to prove that truth is absolute and of the jurist's search for criteria of universal validity which he collects under the head of natural law. . . .
>
> The jurists who believe in natural law seem to me to be in that naive state of mind that accepts what has been familiar and accepted by them and their neighbors as something that must be adopted by all men everywhere.[49]

More recently, Professor Unger has mocked the modern variant of the romantic's insistent need to identify power as the prerequisite of justice, or in Unger's phrase, "power and perception as right":

> The legal academy . . . dallied in one more variant of the perennial effort to restate power and perception as right. In and outside the law schools, most jurists looked with indifference and even disdain upon the legal theorists who, like the rights and principles or the law and economics schools, had volunteered to salvage and recreate the traditions of objectivism and formalism. These same unanxious skeptics, however, also rejected any alternative to the formalist and objectivist view. Having failed to persuade themselves of all but the most equivocal versions of the inherited creed, they nevertheless clung to its implications and brazenly advertise

48. Oliver Wendell Holmes, "Ideals and Doubts," *Illinois Law Review* 10 (1915): 2.

49. Oliver Wendell Holmes, "Natural Law," *Harvard Law Review* 32 (1918): 41.

> their own failure as the triumph of worldly wisdom over intellectual and political enthusiasm. History they degraded into the retrospective rationalization of events. Philosophy they abased into an inexhaustible compendium of excuse of the truncation of legal analysis. The social sciences they perverted into the source of argumentative ploys with which to give arbitrary though stylized policy discussions the blessing of a specious authority.[50]

Just as natural law embraces the substantive range of romantic narrative, so legal positivism, the jurisprudential method of experience, covers the substantive vision with which it is coupled. The positivist method ranges from gentle satirization of the natural lawyer's theories, through angry denunciation of their deceptions, and finally to resigned acceptance of the finality of perceived reality and rejection of imaginative and spiritual alternatives. Most of the legal realist writings from the first part of this century, as well as the various contemporary forms of legal thinking that are their legacy, combine the ironist's insistence on fact and experience with a comic vision of the communitarian basis of law.[51] That combination is central to comic irony. Most of the critical legal studies movement also combines an experiential or historical method with a communitarian vision of the possible. It differs from legal realism, however, in that it sees horror in the present and comic romanticism as not just delusion but outright deception.[52] Such a combination characterizes Frye's midlevel irony: ultimately comic, but very much aware of its proximity to the demonic (*AC*, 236–37). Finally, the law and economics movement has inherited from Hobbes an experientialism coupled with a denial of the relevance, and perhaps even the existence, of morally superior imaginative worlds.[53] These are the working assumptions of the tragic ironist. The range of visions our jurisprudential method of experience covers thus correlates tightly with the range of vision embraced by ironic narrative (fig. 8).

---

50. Roberto Mangabeira Unger, "The Critical Legal Studies Movement," *Harvard Law Review* 96 (1983): 674–75.

51. See, e.g., Morris Raphael Cohen and Felix S. Cohen, *Readings in Jurisprudence and Legal Philosophy* (New York: Prentice-Hall, 1951), 369–526 (including an excellent collection of realist writings).

52. See, e.g., Unger, "Critical Legal Studies," 575.

53. See, e.g., A. Mitchell Polinsky, *An Introduction to Law and Economics* (Boston: Little, Brown, 1983).

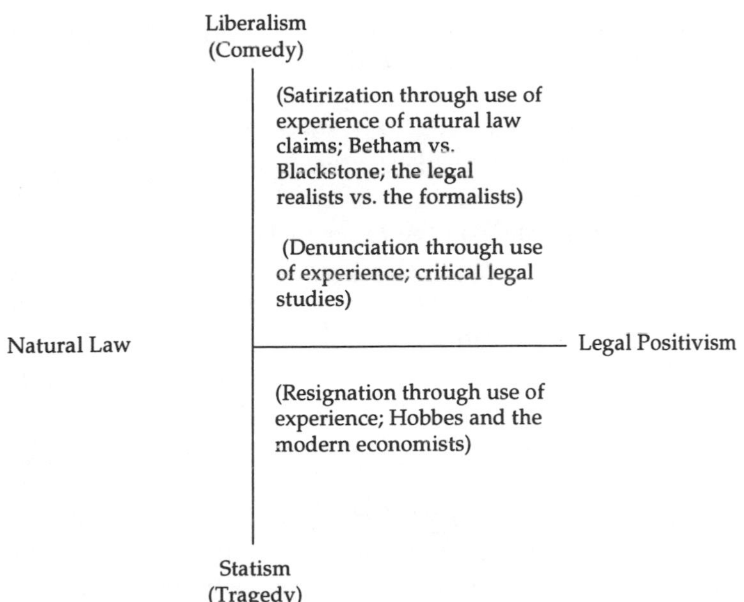

Comic Irony: Reform and Satire

Just as the bulk of our romantic jurisprudence is comic in outlook, so the vast bulk of our ironic jurisprudence, from the reform-minded Benthamites through the American realists to much of the critical legal studies movement, falls within Frye's comic stages of satire.[54] Such positivist jurisprudence, like first-stage narrative irony, uses experience to rebut gently the romantic's claim that law is a function of principled generality, rules themselves, higher moral truths, or the Rule of Law.[55] These romantic mythologies mask the experiential fact that law is a function of the wishes, ends, will, or pathology of whoever is in power. The natural lawyer's romantic belief that through

54. See, e.g., respectively, H. L. A. Hart, *Essays on Bentham: Studies in Jurisprudence and Political Theory* (Oxford: Clarendon, 1982); Robert S. Summers, *Instrumentalism and American Legal Theory* (Ithaca, N.Y.: Cornell University Press, 1982); and Unger, "Critical Legal Studies."

55. For these rebuttals, see respectively Ely, *Democracy and Distrust*, 54–60; Karl N. Llewellyn, "Some Realism about Realism Responding to Dan Pound," *Harvard Law Review* 44 (1931): 1222–24; H. L. A. Hart, *The Concept of Law* (Oxford: Clarendon, 1961); and generally the works of Mark Tushnet, particularly "Truth, Justice, and the American Way: An Interpretation of Public Law Scholarship in the Seventies," *Texas Law Review* 57 (1979): 1307–59.

law we somehow negate the power basis upon which legal systems are built is an illusion. To expose the myths of formalism, the legal positivist, like the ironic narrator, is interested in "anything men do" (*AC*, 229), including that which the romantic natural lawyer would ignore. Bentham's attack on Blackstone's common law, the attacks of Llewellyn, Frank, and Pound on "mechanical jurisprudence," as well as Professor Hart's attack on the romantic constitutionalism of Fuller and Dworkin,[56] all fit easily and obviously within this comic stage of irony. All employ facts—most often anecdotal descriptions of the judicial experience—to satirize and debunk the claimed generality and abstraction of law. Every first-year law school curriculum reflects the continuing dominance of comic irony in our legal culture; benign satire of entrenched authority is what the legal profession knows and teaches best.

In its comic phases, the experiential method and the debunking of idealism are coupled with a liberal, optimistic vision of society and of progress. As a consequence, jurisprudential comic irony is typically the province of the social democrat, at least in this country. The comic ironist wants the source of authority unveiled so that its communitarian basis may be clarified. In the first half of this century, the heyday of comic irony, this ground was occupied by the legal realists. As ironists, the realists criticized entrenched authority, advocating instead an active, highly visible judiciary that would freely discover and then pursue the true social interest. Thus, Holmes saw "public policy" behind the obfuscating rules of the common law; Cardozo looked to the "method of sociology" to account for judicial behavior; and Lasswell and McDougal looked to the new social sciences to provide the tools by which law and the lawyering professions could strengthen the communitarian bond.[57] Holmes described the

56. Jeremy Bentham, *A Comment on the Commentaries and A Fragment on Government*, ed. James Henderson Burns and H. L. A. Hart (London: University of London, Athlone Press, 1977). See generally Hart, "The Demystification of the Law," in *Essays on Bentham*, 21. See also Karl N. Llewellyn, *The Bramble Bush: Some Lectures on Law and Its Study* (New York: Printed for the use of students at Columbia University School of Law, 1930); Jerome Frank, "Mr. Justice Holmes and Non-Euclidian Legal Thinking," *Cornell Law Quarterly* 17 (1932): 568–608; Roscoe Pound, "Mechanical Jurisprudence," *Columbia Law Review* 8 (1908): 605–23; and generally Summers, *Instrumentalism*, 136–56. On Fuller and Dworkin, see Hart, "Law in the Perspective of Philosophy," 49–87, 123–44, 198–222.

57. Holmes, *Common Law*, 35–36, 94–96; Benjamin Nathan Cardozo, *The*

judicial role and the social context that an ironic method and comic vision imply:

> [I]n substance the growth of the law is legislative. And this in a deeper sense than that what the courts declare to have always been the law is in fact new. It is legislative in its grounds. The very considerations which judges most rarely mention, and always with an apology, are the secret root from which the law draws all the juices of life. I mean, of course, considerations of what is expedient for the community concerned. Every important principle which is developed by litigation is in fact and at bottom the result of more or less definitely understood views of public policy; most generally, to be sure, under our practice and traditions, the unconscious result of instinctive preferences and inarticulate convictions, but none the less traceable to views of public policy in the last analysis. *And as the law is administered by able and experienced men, who know too much to sacrifice good sense to a syllogism,* it will be found that, when ancient rules maintain themselves in the way that has been and will be shown in this book, new reasons more fitted to the time have been found for them, and that they gradually receive a new content, and at last a new form, from the grounds to which they have been transplanted.[58]

Thus, the legal realists were consistently both comic and ironic. Their realism led them to uncover the historical, actual grounding of law in the fact of judicial power, a potentially startling and disturbing insight. But their comic optimism reassured them that such power was not to be feared. In Holmes's words again, judges are "able and experienced men" who can be trusted to shape the direction of American social policy.

Today it is a critic of an active judiciary, Professor John Ely, who is our ultimate first-stage satirist and thus our most eloquent democrat.[59] This new development is in a sense a direct consequence

Nature of the Judicial Process (New Haven: Yale University Press, 1921), 98–141; Harold Lasswell and Myre S. McDougal, "Legal Education and Public Policy: Professional Training in the Public Interest," *Yale Law Journal* 52 (1943): 203–95.

58. Holmes, *Common Law*, 35–36.

59. See, e.g., Ely, *Democracy and Distrust*, 54–60 (satirizing constitutional theories based on neutral principles or reason).

of the success of the realist movement: the public-policy basis of judicial opinions has indeed been laid bare. With the apparatus of formalism stripped away, judicial opinions now overtly rest on the moral authority of the authors. Just as the realists distrusted and debunked the moral authority of the academic and often invisible authors of formalism, preferring the conscious and immediate moral guidance of the courts, so Ely distrusts and debunks the judiciary's claim to moral authority, preferring the even more immediate moral guidance gleaned from participatory democracy.[60] Thus, in practice, Ely and the realists are *doing* precisely the same thing, although their conclusions differ. It therefore is hardly surprising that Ely, like the realists he attacks, uses ironic, anecdotal narrative to make his point.

Ely's use of narrative is as skillful as Holmes's. Ely quotes the ironic narrator Philip Roth to refute the romantic natural lawyer's case for judicial supremacy:

> "Well, what may seem like the truth to you," said the seventeen-year-old bus driver and part-time philosopher, "may not, of course, seem like the truth to the other fella, you know."
> "THEN THE OTHER FELLOW IS WRONG, IDIOT!"

and the ironic historian Garry Wills to refute the romantic historian's:

> Running men out of town on a rail is at least as much an American tradition as declaring unalienable rights.[61]

But Ely does not stop with his realistic attack on the natural lawyer. He invokes the same arguments and the same narrative method against the oddly romantic myths that the realists themselves had created. Thus, against the realists' inference of "ought" from "is," Ely employs his most ironic narrative tone and tells this story:

> The explanation [for why one might think a judge ought to enforce her own values in adjudication] seems to involve what might be called the fallacy of transformed realism. About forty

60. Ibid., 87–104.

61. Ibid., 48 (quoting Philip Roth), *Great American Novel* (New York: Holt, Rinehart and Winston 1973), 19; and 60 (quoting Garry Wills), *Inventing America: Jefferson's Declaration of Independence* (Garden City, N.Y.: Doubleday, 1978).

> years ago people "discovered" that judges were human and therefore were likely in a variety of legal contexts consciously or unconsciously to slip their personal values into their legal reasoning. From that earth-shattering insight it has seemed to some an easy inference that that is what judges *ought* to be doing. Two observation are in order, both obvious. The first is that such a "realist" theory of adjudication is not a theory of adjudication at all, in that it does not tell us *which* values should be imposed. The second is that the theory's "inference" does not even remotely follow: that people have always been tempted to steal does not mean that stealing is what they should be doing. This is all plain as a pikestaff, which means something else has to be going on. People who tend to this extreme realist view must consciously or unconsciously be envisioning a Court staffed by justices who think as they do. That assumption takes care of both the problems I've mentioned. It tells you what values are to be imposed (the commentator's own) and also explains (at least to the satisfaction of the commentator) why such a Court would be desirable. But it's a heroic assumption, and the argument that seems to score most heavily against such a "realist" outlook is one that is genuinely realistic—that there is absolutely no assurance that the Supreme court's life-tenured members (or the other federal judges) will be persons who share your values.[62]

Viewed as a narrator, however, Ely is clearly aligned with the realists he attacks. Like them, he uses his stories to "[break] up the lumber of stereotypes, fossilized beliefs, superstitious terrors, crank theories, pedantic dogmatisms, oppressive fashions, and all other things that impede the free movement of . . . society" (*AC*, 233). Ely does to the moral authority of the active judiciary and the myths that surround it precisely what Bentham and the legal realists did to the moral authority of the common law and what historian Garry Wills later did to the moral authority of the Kennedy-era Camelot.[63]

Black Comic Irony: Denunciation and Radicalism

With a slight shift of perspective from reliance on faith and reason to reliance on tangible sensual reality, Frye explains, "the solid earth

62. Ibid., 44.

63. Garry Wills, *The Kennedy Imprisonment: A Meditation on Power* (Boston: Little, Brown 1982).

[of realism] becomes an intolerable horror" (*AC*, 235). This shift of perspective characterizes midlevel ironic narrative. With such a shift, the penetrating insights of legal realism become, to use Dean Pound's phrase, the "cult of the ugly."[64] The persistent gaze of the realist eventually perceives not the fruits of the labor of wise and able men, but the fist of power behind a virtually unchecked judiciary. Dean Pound dramatizes the point through narrative and imagery in the following anecdote:

> I suggest to you that so-called realism in jurisprudence is related to realism in art rather than to philosophical realism. Like realism in art it is a cult of the ugly. . . . [A]n artist commissioned to paint the portrait of one of the outstanding judges of the recent past noted that he had a huge fist and a habit of holding it out before him. Accordingly, as a realist, he painted the fist elaborately in the foreground as the chief feature of the portrait, behind which, if one's gaze can get by the fist, one may discover in the background a thoughtful countenance. The judge did have such a fist and did hold it out in front of him on occasion. But having known him well for years, I doubt if anyone thought about it until the artist seized upon it and made it the main feature of his portrait. The fist existed. But was it the significant feature of the judge? Was reality in the sense of significance in the fist or in the countenance?[65]

Holmes's ideal judge, then, may be perceived and portrayed not as a tool of reason with a thoughtful countenance, but as a fist wielding the power of the legal sanction he controls. The realist judges are, in Professor Cover's telling phrase, "people of violence."[66] With the same shift of perspective, however, Ely's empowered, participatory democracy is similarly transformed, not into a fist, but—perhaps worse—into a "bodily democracy paralleling the democracy of death in the *danse macabre*" (*AC*, 235). Like modern literary irony, modern positivism tends not to be gentle.

Modern positivists share the realists' insistence on experiential-

64. Roscoe Pound, *Justice according to Law* (New Haven: Yale University Press, 1951), 90.

65. Ibid., 90–91.

66. Robert M. Cover, "Nomos and Narrative," *Harvard Law Review* 97 (1983): 53.

ism, but their substantive visions differ markedly. The liberal realist views the discovery of judicial power with a sense of liberation, whereas the critical legal scholar sees no such cause for enthusiasm. Ely views the empowerment of the governed with the democrat's faith in humanity, but the critical legal scholar insists upon the dangers of false consciousness and the potential for majoritarian oppression such empowerment entails.[67] Where the realists saw concentrated power as an opportunity for reasoned reform and ultimately for progress, the critical scholar sees only cause for alarm. The contrast between their criticism of formalism and natural law is equally telling: where the realist saw folly in the romantic delusions of the natural lawyer, the critical scholar sees a demonic deception in the artificiality of formalism. These differences stem not from contrasting methods, but from divergent visions. Like the realist, the critical scholar harbors a passionate vision of an apocalyptic, communitarian potential. But the critical scholar has for the most part abandoned the realists' liberal, optimistic assessment of our history and their faith in our capacity for rational progress toward the future.[68] The central narrative task of the critical legal studies movement, then, is to tell a story that will explain this profound contradiction. On the one hand, we have within our nature and presumably within our grasp the potential for a communitarian utopia, and yet on the other, what we have inherited—what we have in fact created—can only be described as "intolerable horror."

As is characteristic of the ironic mode, the critical legal scholar uses the analogy of experience to tell his story. To the critical scholar, a true understanding of the history of romantic jurisprudence illuminates the dilemma. The history of romanticism and faith in natural law is a history of deceit: the atomistic, alienated, bureaucratic hell in which we live is not, after all, the best social world of which we are capable. Both conservative and liberal romanticism further this massive deception. Romantic descriptions of our social world mask a horrific reality just as legal doctrine masks the oppressive political reality of law. The romantic either misperceives or misrepresents as apocalyptic that which in fact is demonic: he misrepresents as consensus that which is in fact domination, and he misrepresents as

67. Ely, *Democracy and Distrust*, 181–83; Roberto Mangabeira Unger, *Law in Modern Society: Toward a Criticism of Social Theory* (New York: Free Press, 1976), 69.

68. See ibid., 238–39.

inevitable a world that is in fact the product of contingent choices.[69] The hypocrisies of which Holmes, Ely, and others make light are not simply theoretical musings; they are the devil's disguise. In midlevel positivism, as in midlevel irony, awareness of the demonic is never far away. Consequently, denunciation replaces satire and trashing replaces mockery.[70]

The major difference between the critical legal scholar's debunking of formalism and the realist's satirization of generality is not method, which they share, but vision, which leads the critical scholars to a very different agenda for social action. The critical scholar sees a far wider divergence than does the realist between our communitarian potential and our inherited hell.[71] The critical scholar responds to this gulf in one of two ways. Mark Tushnet—like Huck Finn—makes his detachment explicit: if he were a judge, he would, at least in theory, decide cases so as to promote socialism.[72] Roberto Unger takes a more aggressive stance: if the formalist's romantic agenda is not just delusion, but meanspirited deception, then we must aggressively attack and then *transform* the institutions that the perverse choices of the powerful have created. We cannot gradually peel away the pretense of formalism. We cannot slowly evolve from something rotten at the core into something beautiful. Only radical change can alter that which has gone radically sour.[73]

---

69. Unger, "Critical Legal Studies," 674–75, 609–11, 593–97.

70. See, e.g., Alan D. Freeman, "Truth and Mystification in Legal Scholarship," *Yale Law Journal* 90 (1981): 1229–37.

71. See, e.g., Unger, *Law in Modern Society*; Duncan Kennedy, "Form and Substance in Private Law Adjudication," *Harvard Law Review* 89 (1976): 1685–1778; Mark Tushnet, "The Dilemmas of Liberal Constitutionalism," *Ohio State Law Journal* 42 (1981): 411–26.

72. Tushnet, "Dilemmas," 424. Tushnet notes, however, that if he were to become a judge, the role itself would probably change him and cause him to decide cases in a way contrary to that which his theories would compel. Ibid., 425.

73. "[T]he struggle over the form of social life, through deviationist doctrine, creates opportunities for experimental revisions of social life in the direction of the ideals we defend. An implication of our ideas is that the elements of a formative institutional or imaginative structure may be replaced piecemeal rather than only all at once. Between conserving reform and revolution . . . lies the expedient of revolutionary reform, defined as the substitution of one of the constituent elements of a formative context. Only an actual change in the recurrent forms of the routine activities—of production and exchange or of the conflict over the uses and mastery of governmental power—can show whether a replacement of some component of the

The critical legal scholar is in some ways the pure ironist, believing that the hell we have inherited is not the utopia of which we are capable. Though knowledge of history will inform our understanding of the former, only the will to undertake radical action and the courage to transcend and transform historically grounded norms will further our progress toward the latter.

Tragic Realism: Resignation as Method and Vision

In the final and illiberal phases of legal positivism, as in the final tragic phases of ironic narrative, the theorist posits a social world that precludes both the possibility and the intelligibility of either reforms or radical change. In tragic irony, experience instructs our normative alternatives, as in comedic irony, but what this experience teaches is that there is no shared human nature upon which to build a communitarian world. The English reformers, the legal realists, and the critical legal scholars are all simply wrong. We do not have an essentially social, communitarian nature, nor do we have a deeply hidden utopian potential; we truly are nasty and brutish.[74] We have no greater inclination for a liberal, free world in which we enjoy both the differences and the commonalities of others than we have for our own self-destruction. Our present world is vicious, our future will be the same, and both are the result of an unchanging and unchangeable human nature.

Such an aesthetic sensibility is overtly espoused by very few modern theorists, but the covert influence of moral nihilism in the legal academy is pervasive, in both law school classrooms and law reviews.[75] This nihilism is the implicit philosophical justification for

---

formative context has in fact taken place. By affecting the application of state power, a programmatically inspired deviationist doctrine may provide opportunities for collective mobilization that in turn can lead directly or indirectly to revolutionary reform" (Unger, "Critical Legal Studies," 666–67).

74. See Thomas Hobbes, *Leviathan*, pts. 1 and 2 (New York: Liberal Arts Press, 1958), 104–9.

75. Hobbes of course comes closest to espousing this sensibility, and it is interesting how the archmonarchist and archstatist of his day is increasingly invoked as the intellectual forefather of liberalism. See Mark Tushnet, "Legal Realism, Structural Review, and Prophecy," *University of Dayton Law Review* 8 (1983): 809–11; Mark Tushnet, "Legal Scholarship: Its Causes and Cure," *Yale Law Journal* 90 (1981): 1206.

the amorality of the law school classroom on both sides of the podium, and of the courtroom on both sides of the bench. It justifies the amorality of the profession and of the Code of Professional Responsibility. It provides some intellectual credibility for the claim of the legal profession and the legal academy that the lawyer in her professional role can responsibly refuse to take a stand on moral issues.[76]

Perhaps more fundamentally, the modern prevalence of a positivistic moral nihilism provides a distinctively illiberal rationale for our modern fashionable commitment to individualism. This position differs markedly from, although it is often confused with, liberal narrative. As discussed in the next section, both nineteenth-century English liberals and early twentieth-century American radicals embraced individualism because of their optimistic, comic assumption that human nature is constituted such that state authority is *unnecessary*. Today, by contrast, our individualistic distrust of authority is more often premised upon the tragic assumption that human nature is constituted such that moral authority is *impossible*.[77] The former assumption presupposes a communitarian human personality, whereas the latter presupposes an asocial, demonic world. The latter, Hobbesian argument for individualism is grounded not in a love for and a liberal tolerance of the individual but in a demonic assessment of human nature, and a resignation to an alienated asocial coexistence (e.g.,

---

Some works of Bork also approach this sensibility. See, e.g., Robert Bork, Howard Krane, and George D. Webster, *Political Activities of Colleges and Universities: Some Policy and Legal Implications* (Washington, D.C.: American Enterprise Institute for Public Policy Research, 1970); Robert Bork, "Neutral Principles and Some First Amendment Problems," *Indiana Law Journal* 47 (1971): 1–35. Professor David Richards takes up the issue of nihiulism in his article "Terror and the Law," *Human Rights Quarterly* 5 (1983): 183–85.

76. See, e.g., "Model Code of Professional Responsibility," Canon 7, in *1993 Selected Standards on Professional Responsibility*, ed. Thomas D. Morgan and Ronald B. Rotunda (Westbury, N.Y.: Foundation Press, 1973) ("A lawyer should represent a client zealously within the bounds of the law"). See generally Monroe Freedman, *Lawyers' Ethics in an Adversary System* (Indianapolis: Bobbs-Merrill, 1975). But see Richard Wasserstrom, "Lawyers as Professionals: Some Moral Issues," *Human Rights Quarterly* 5 (1975): 1–24.

77. The comic assumption may be traced to Adam Smith's identification of sympathy as the natural human sentiment holding community together (*Adam Smith, The Theory of Moral Sentiments* [Oxford: Clarendon, 1971 1:1–22]). The historical lineage of the tragic assumption dates to Hobbes: hence the increasingly popular appellation of Hobbes as a father of modern liberalism. See note 84.

EJ, 1–115). Through a gross bastardization of the term, this decidedly illiberal stance is today called liberalism by its proponents and its critics alike.

This ambiguity may account for the peculiarly schizoid aesthetic posture of members of the law-and-economics school.[78] To the extent that their normative vision is derived from individualistic liberalism, it is romantic and comic: individual *choice*, like divine anointment, both defines and delegitimates law.[79] Their descriptive vision, however, is at the same time tragic-ironic: the individual whose choice is sovereign is isolated, ruled by arbitrary desire, and essentially selfish; this experiential fact defines one's normative alternatives. Consequently, and confusedly, the tragic, dire convictions of the Hobbesian law-and-economics theorist are espoused with the optimism of the comic and the confidence of the romantic.[80] That may, of course, be precisely because they have reached what Frye calls "the ironic aspect of tragedy" (*AC*, 236). The purportedly impenetrable subjectivity of our values,[81] like the last stages of literary irony, erases all aesthetic distinctions between the beautiful and the ugly, the sublime and the ridiculous, the comic and the tragic. We are what we are, and relief is not even necessary, much less imaginable or in sight. Human alienation is a fact of nature. In its last phase, legal positivism, as in the last phase of tragic irony generally, depicts human suffering as of absolutely no normative consequence.

The Appeal of Irony

The appeal of legal positivism as a method of jurisprudence is not difficult to explain. As Bentham first noted, and as Holmes, the realists, and most recently the critical legal scholars have reiterated, a realistic insistence on the separation of what is from what ought to be is essential to meaningful progress toward fulfilling our

78. See, e.g., *FJ*; Polinsky, *Law and Economics*.

79. See, e.g., *EJ*; Polinsky, *Law and Economics*; Richard A. Posner, "The Ethical and Political Basis of the Efficiency Norm in Common Law Adjudication," *Hofstra Law Review* 8 (1980): 487, 488–502.

80. See, e.g., *FJ*, 362–63 (cheerful account of the benign nature of most race discrimination); Polinsky, *Law and Ecomomics*, viii (joking, comic description of the antihistorical starting premises of economic theory).

81. See Bork, "Neutral Principles," 28–29.

dreams.[82] We must resist the impulse to romanticize the present—to fuse what is with what ought to be—if we intend to transcend or improve our given world. The positivist separation of law and morality, of what is from what ought to be and what could be, is indeed a prerequisite of legal reform whether that reform be radical, liberal, individualist, or communitarian.

Yet positivism must come to grips with its central ambiguities. We might insist upon the separation of law and morality, of what is from what ought to be," because we want to understand our history better, demythologize it, and then work more directly toward normative goals. Alternatively, we might insist that law and morality be separate because of our conviction, or fear, that morality does not meaningfully exist, because moral norms are not as real as sanction-backed legal norms. Aesthetically, this can be described as the difference between tragic and comic irony. Jurisprudentially, it is the difference between a scientific approach to the law coupled with a vision of moral possibility, and a scientific approach to the law coupled with a nihilistic denial of the possibility of such a vision. Politically and humanistically, it is the difference between a historical sophistication that can provide the basis for progress toward our dreams, and a historical insistence that keeps our attention narrowly and exclusively focused on, and limited to, what has been tried, tested, and chosen.

Positivism in its comic phases provides the satire necessary to understand the delusions, the deceptions, and the apologetic core of formalism, as well as the knowledge of the world necessary for responsible striving toward alternative worlds. In its tragic phases, however, irony expresses itself not in healthy satire or unmasking of illusion, but in a dangerous and limiting cynicism; not an enthusiastic embrace of our possibilities, but a resigned insistence on the exclusivity of what has already been determined.

In both narrative and jurisprudence, then, tragic irony represents the death of imagination, and its ascendency in so many fields of

82. Bentham, *Comment on the Commentaries*, 37–58 (see generally Hart, "Demystification of Law," 19, 21–28); Holmes, *Common Law*, 168–76). Among realists, see, e.g., Felix S. Cohen, *Ethical Systems and Legal Ideals: An Essay on the Foundations of Legal Criticism* (New York: Falcon Press, 1933), 14–15; John Chipman Gray, *The Nature and Sources of the Law*, 2d ed., ed. Roland Gray (New York: Macmillan, 1921), 94; Llewellyn, "Some Realism about Realism," 1236–38. See generally Summers, *Instrumentalism*, 176–90. See also Unger, *Law in Modern Society*, 48–58.

thought is a frightening phenomenon.[83] Professor MacIntyre notes that it is not surprising, for example, that the dark ironist Franz Kafka failed to finish so much of his work: tragic irony, although a form of narrative, is in many ways antinarrative; it denies the possibility of a coherent future, so central to storytelling, and thus cannot be finished.[84] The law-and-economics school is similarly antinarrative (as well as antihistorical) and is dangerous in the same way. By insisting upon the exclusivity of the instantaneous present, tragic irony deprives us of the precious opportunity to make moral stories of our own lives.

The allure and the danger of a mindless romanticism, however, are equally strong, and it is as a check against such a danger that positivism has the most to contribute. We need the check of experience against imagination. As storytellers, we combine these two capacities almost instinctively. We imagine a possible ending to our story and check its compliance with what we know. Extant law gives us the beginning paragraphs of narrative. The central moral of the positivist separation of law and morality may be that, to finish the story, we must first envision moral alternatives—employing imagination, knowledge, and moral discourse—before we can possibly pursue them.

Narrative Myths and Jurisprudential Visions

Comedy and Liberalism: From Ritualistic Bondage to Pragmatic Freedom

Frye calls narrative comedy the "mythos of spring" (*AC*, 163). While tragedy envisions an inevitable conflict between the individual and the community, comedy posits the natural compatibility of men and women with each other and with their societies. If human beings are naturally social, then communities, whether they be marriages, families, parties, or states, will promote their members' happiness. Particular societies may fail—some historical communities have undeniably crippled instead of enriched the human spirit—but such failures are

83. Alasdair MacIntyre discusses the reasons for this development in intellectual history in *After Virtue: A Study in Moral Theory* (Notre Dame, Ind.: University of Notre Dame Press, 1980), 46–113.

84. Ibid., 198.

exceptional and temporary. Comedy speaks to our awareness of the potential for happiness inherent in our communitarian associations. The faith of comedy, in direct contrast to that of tragedy, is that the natural inclination of people is toward happiness and sociability, and that the natural movement of social history is toward an expansion and not a diminution of our capacity for joy (*AC*, 163–66).

Literary comedy follows well-established story lines. Comic plots move their characters from old and arid social orders in which form, artifice, and chicanery conspire to suppress the healthy urges of youthful heroes, to young, fresh, and social worlds, in which the freed heroes live relatively happy and naturally harmonious lives. At the outset of comic action, the hero is almost invariably alone, unhappy, and "imprisoned" in some sort of outmoded, foolish, or evil bondage. By the end he or she is engulfed in a happy and freer society (*AC*, 163–64).

Frye describes the arbitrary, formalistic, and stagnant world from which the comic hero breaks free in this way:

> The humor in comedy is usually someone with a great deal of social prestige and power, who is able to force much of the play's society into line with his obsession. Thus the humor is ultimately connected with the theme of the absurd or irrational law that the action of comedy moves toward breaking. . . . Often the absurd law appears as a whim of a bemused tyrant whose will is law . . . who makes some arbitrary decision or rash promise. . . . Or it may take the form of a sham Utopia, a society of ritual bondage constructed by an act of humorous or pedantic will (*AC*, 169).[85]

85. "We notice how often the action of a Shakespearean comedy begins with some absurd, cruel, or irrational law: the law of killing Syracusans in the *Comedy of Errors*, the law of compulsory marriage in *A Midsummer Night's Dream*, the law that confirms Shylock's bond, the attempts of Angelo to legislate people into righteousness, and the like, which the action of the comedy then evades or breaks" (*AC*, 166).

"Thus the movement . . . from a society controlled by habit, ritual bondage, arbitrary law and the older characters to a society controlled by youth and pragmatic freedom is fundamentally . . . a movement from illusion to reality. Illusion is whatever is fixed or definable, and reality is best understood as its negation: whatever reality is, it's not *that*. Hence the importance of the theme of creating and dispelling illusion in comedy: the illusions caused by disguise, obsession, hypocrisy, or unknown parentage" (*AC*, 169–70).

The social world toward which the dramatic action of comedy moves is described in this way:

> Comedy usually moves toward a happy ending, and the normal response of the audience to a happy ending is "this should be," which sounds like a moral judgement. So it is, except that it is not moral in the restricted sense, but social. . . .
>
> The society emerging at the conclusion of comedy represents . . . a kind of moral norm, or pragmatically free society. Its ideals are seldom defined or formulated: definition and formulation belong to the humors, who want predictable activity. We are simply given to understand that the newly-married couple will live happily ever after, or that at any rate they will get along in a relatively unhumorous and clear-sighted manner. (*AC*, 167–69)

Frye explains that comedy "blends into irony and satire at one end and into romance at the other" (*AC*, 177). At one extreme, comedy's optimistic vision is conveyed by a narrative method that is ahistorical, innocent, and metaphorical. At the other, its method depends upon experience and fact. The romantic phases of comedy are characterized by a vision of an ideal, rural, green, and innocent world that occasionally collides with, but generally triumphs over, the real world of experience. As literary comedy moves away from romance and toward irony, its method becomes increasingly experiential and its optimism more tentative. Frye describes the ironic comic's acceptance of society, in contrast to the romantic's, as fragile, quixotic, and contingent (*AC*, 177–80).

A passage from *The Tempest* encapsulates these two methodological extremes of the comedy's optimistic vision. By the end of the play, both Miranda and Prospero embrace the real world of human society and reject their illusory and isolated island existence. The *methods* by which they reach their communitarian commitments, however, contrast sharply. Miranda, raised on an island in relative isolation, innocently and unqualifiedly embraces her newly discovered community of cocitizens:

> Miranda: O wonder!
> How many goodly creatures are there here!
> How beauteous mankind is!

O brave new world,
That has such people in't!
Prospero: T'is new to thee.[86]

Prospero's more sober preference for a concrete and real society over the isolation and illusion of island living follows a lifetime of experience with both worlds. Prospero's longing for real community is not nearly as exuberant or unqualified as Miranda's wide-eyed anticipation, but his appreciation for society is far better informed:

Prospero: Now my charms are all o'erthrown,
And what strength I have's mine own,
Which is most faint: now, t'is true,
I must be here confined by you,
Or sent to Naples. Let me not,
Since I have my dukedom got,
And pardoned the deceiver, dwell
In this bare island, by your spell,
But release me from my bands
With the help of your good hands.[87]

Comedy's methodological range can be schematized as in figure 9.

The political traditions loosely called "liberalism" share comedy's optimistic assessment that democratic societies progress through history from a stage of "ritual bondage" to a state of "pragmatic freedom."[88] At the heart of liberalism is the apocalyptic claim that it is an intrinsic part of our human nature to seek, profit from, and further the welfare of others. Moral government is therefore the norm, the end toward which history naturally moves, whereas antagonistic government is the world of bondage from which we break free. Community is our natural state; it is not a compact into which we enter to avoid the horrific conditions of the state of nature. Communities nurture and enhance the natural inclination and therefore

86. William Shakespeare, *The Tempest*, in *Riverside Shakespeare*, act 5, lines 182–86, p. 1634.

87. Ibid., epilogue, lines 1–10, p. 1635.

88. See text accompanying note 94.

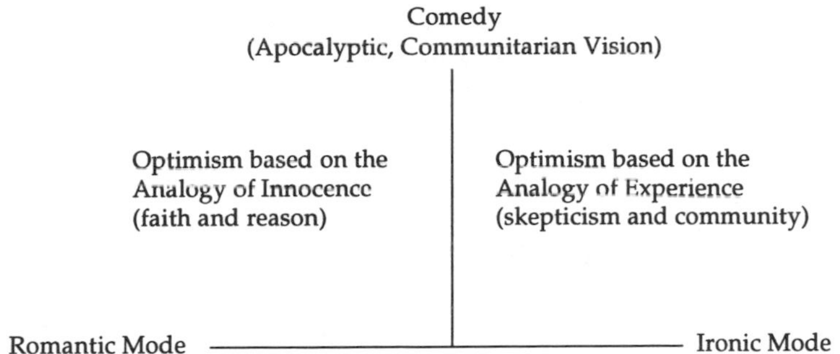

the happiness of their individual members.[89] Political liberalism, like literary comedy, assumes a world in which human nature is naturally good, so that morality need be neither prescribed nor posited. We simply *are* such that moral conduct is natural. In both the world of literary comedy and that of political liberalism, pragmatic freedom is made possible by the natural coincidence of the moral good, the community's good, and the individual's interest.

The apocalyptic comic myth also finds expression in liberal jurisprudence. Like political liberalism, liberal legal theory rests on a comic view of history and human nature: progress is an inherent good, unnecessarily retarded by outmoded dictates of positive morality and law.[90] As literary comic narrative moves from ritual bondage and toward the idealistic, communal utopia of pragmatic freedom, so political and legal liberalism insists that history and our legal

89. See John Stuart Mill, "Utilitarianism," in *Utilitarianism, Liberty, and Representative Government* (New York: Dutton, 1951). Adam Smith also firmly believed that our natural capacity for sympathy was at least as crucial to social living as our inclination to trade. See Smith, *Theory of Moral Sentiments*. Evidence is mounting that the communitarian "moral sense" position of the Scottish Enlightenment heavily influenced Jefferson and the other thinkers of his era. See generally Wills, *Inventing America*, 167–259.

90. This position can perhaps be more easily recognized when viewed in the following way. The legal realists' insight of the 1930s and 1940s was generally accompanied by the empirical claim that the envisioned judicial activism was not a bad thing. Holmes, Llewellyn, Frank, Lasswell, and McDougal all believed that judges wield considerable power, and with clearer thinking could do so more wisely; none suggested that their power be curtailed.

However, this faith in the essential integrity of nonelected poliical figures and the positive portrayal of human nature that faith entailed would be out of place in today's more skeptical intellectual climate. The modern critical legal studies movement is considerably more explicit in its communitarian commitments. See, e.g., Tushnet, "Dilemmas," 411–16.

institutions progress inevitably toward a happy ending. The world of ritual bondage is the artificially rule-bound world of legal science and formalistic jurisprudence. This stale old world of legal formalism suffers from an abundance of rules drawn with fetishistic precision, rules often substantively unrelated to the social world in which they operate.[91] They stunt rather than further the immediate happiness of the community, resting on an illusion of static certainty. Law in liberalism's new world, by contrast, embodies the pragmatic freedom that Frye describes as the resolution of dramatic comedy (*AC*, 170). Law in the new world abandons academic, formalistic thinking; it stems directly from the group or individual affected by the rule in question.[92] The situs of such lawmaking is either the democratic legislative assembly, where rules respond directly to the interests and demands of the governed, the courts, where rules are formed and reformed around immediate facts, fitted to shifting equities and free to change with changing policies, or private contract, where rules of conduct can respond to the changing values embraced by individuals themselves. Thus, the new community's laws reflect only the sense of the community and the spirit of the individual—nothing else.[93]

Liberal jurisprudence has the same methodological range as narrative comedy. At one extreme, the romantic liberal theorist embraces society through the method of innocence: he analogizes the apocalyptic, communitarian myth to the present world through an ahistorical, neutral version of the nature of the world.[94] At the other extreme, the

91. For a classic discussion of this claim, see John Dewey, "Logical Method and the Law," *Cornell Law Quarterly* 10 (1924): 20.

92. See Holmes, *Common Law*, 1–2.

93. In addition to the work of the law-and-economics movement, which has made this principle its guiding light, see Ackerman, *Social Justice*. Ackerman proceeds from a similar assumption but then reaches dramatically divergent conclusions. Dworkin has also embraced a form of the thesis that we cannot evaluate the worth or goodness of plans of life chosen by others. R. M. Dworkin, "Liberalism," in *Public and Private Morality*, ed. Stuart Hampshire (Cambridge; New York: Cambridge University Press, 1978), 127–43.

94. The ahistoricism of romantic liberalism has left it vulnerable to critics from all ends of the political spectrum. See generally the essays from the critical legal studies movement collected in *The Politics of Law: A Progressive Critique*, rev. ed., David Kairys, ed. (New York: Pantheon Books, 1990); and the more careful analysis of liberalism's neutrality principle in Steven Shiffrin, "Liberalism, Radicalism, and Legal Scholarship," *UCLA Law Review* 30 (1983): 1103–1217. From the conservative tradition, see the attack on liberalism's shunning of a community's contingent, shared morality in favor of individualistic relativism, in Patrick Baron Devlin, *The Enforcement of Morals* (London: Oxford University Press, 1965).

ironic liberal theorist embraces society through the method of realism: experience teaches that concrete community is more conducive to happiness than the isolated world to the imagination.[95] Thus, the liberal's optimism is acquired either by an ahistoric, willful ignorance of history, or through an experienced understanding of the nature of community and natural limitations (fig. 10).

Romantic Comedy: Liberalism and the Method of Innocence

Ronald Dworkin's Herculean jurisprudential construct rests quite overtly on the romantic side of liberalism. In this respect, it is representative of the narrative form of the vast bulk of our constitutional jurisprudence. In *Taking Rights Seriously*, Dworkin gives us not only a romantic-liberal narrative, but a romantic *hero* as well, the judge he calls Hercules. Dworkin's substantive view of society is clearly comic: Hercules' world is liberal, apocalyptic, and intensely communitarian. At the highest level, Hercules' law is simply the shared moral consensus of the community.[96] In Frye's terms, Dworkin's narrative method is just as clearly romantic: Hercules rules over a dream world that occasionally "collides with the stumbling and blinded follies of the world of experience . . . with its idiotic marriage law [, its] plots and intrigues" (*AC*, 183–84). By Herculean effort, Dworkin's hero manages to impose the form of desire (*AC*, 184) on the inaccuracies and idiocies of law. This imposition elevates the reader "from a lower world of confusion to an upper world of order," enabling her to "see the action" from "the point of view of a higher and better ordered world" (*AC*, 184). Dworkin's story is a highly formalized kind of American romantic and comic jurisprudence, less rule-bound and yet more orderly than other, less romantic comic visions.[97]

95. Illustrations of this position include Mark Tushnet's adoption of socialist principles and Duncan Kennedy's "existential" embrace of altruism. See Tushnet, "Dilemmas," 424; Kennedy, "Form and Substance," 1717–22.

96. See, e.g., Dworkin, *Taking Rights Seriously*, 90–94.

97. Dworkin's heroic judge decides cases on the basis of enduring principles. By contrast, the far more human judges of Hart and Sacks decide cases on the basis of the "greener," freely formed, and temporary policies. Henry Melvin Hart and Albert M. Sacks, *The Legal Process: Basic Problems in the Making and Application of Law*, tentative ed. (Cambridge: Harvard University Press, 1958), 457–515.

Liberalism
(Comedy)

(Apocalyptic, Communitarian Assessment of Legal Institutions)

Method of Innocence: Ahistorical optimistic romanticization of legal institutions, e.g., the Constitution, the individual, or the courts	Method of Experience: Empirically based optimistic assessment of the grounding of our institutions, e.g., the perceived altruistic or communitarian nature of humanity

Natural Law (Romance) ——————— Positivism (Irony)

Although Dworkin's Hercules and his orderly legal world are representative of most romantic liberalism, it is the liberal's heavily ritualized, romanticized story of the individual—the freely contracting, self-determining economic and political man—that lies on liberalism's last phase romantic fringes. Again, Dworkin relies upon narrative to make the argument. To understand liberalism truly, Dworkin has recently argued, we must imagine, with help from the narrative hypothetical, how a group of shipwrecked, artificially equalized individuals would divide the resources that they have discovered on their luckily plentiful, deserted island:

> Suppose a number of shipwreck survivors are washed up on a desert island which has abundant resources and no native population, and any likely rescue is many years away. These immigrants accept the principle that no one is antecedently entitled to any of these resources but they shall instead be divided equally among them. . . .
>
> Now suppose some one immigrant is elected to achieve the division according to that principle. . . .
>
> . . . Suppose the divider hands each of the immigrants an equal and large number of clamshells, which are sufficiently numerous and in themselves valued by no one, to use as counters in a market of the following sort. Each distinct item on the island . . . is listed as a lot to be sold, unless someone notifies the auctioneer . . . of his or her desire to bid for some part of an item, including part, for example, of some piece of land, in which

> case that part becomes itself a distinct lot. The auctioneer then proposes a set of prices for each lot and discovers whether that set of prices clears all markets, that is, whether there is only one purchaser at that price and all lots are sold. If not, then the auctioneer adjusts his prices until he reaches a set that does clear the markets. But the process does not stop then, because each of the immigrants remains free to change his bids even when an initially market-clearing set of prices is reached, or even to propose different lots. But let us suppose that in time even this leisurely process comes to an end, everyone declares himself satisfied, and goods are distributed accordingly.[98]

It is Dworkin's story, rather than his argument, that is of interest here. The story sets the aesthetic parameters of the debate. Drawing upon a modern tradition rooted in the writings of John Rawls, Dworkin defines liberalism in terms of a mythic, radically ahistorical narrative. Shipwrecked islanders are uniquely disassociated from their past as well as uniquely bound together in purpose. Even more striking, Dworkin's islanders have happened upon a plentiful island. Their problem really is one of fairness and not survival. Liberalism explicitly emerges as the most logical ending of a half-told story.

Bruce Ackerman's imaginative construct takes the same narrative technique several steps further. Instead of "forests in moonlight, secluded valleys and happy islands" (*AC*, 185), Ackerman puts his liberal citizens in the twenty-first century equivalent—a spaceship. Ultimately, these fictive characters agree upon liberalism as a just principle of distribution. Like Shakespeare's Miranda and like Dworkin, Ackerman analogizes his apocalyptic, imaginative myth to our own world by making romantic assumptions about the nature of the real world's inhabitants and the physical world. But whereas Dworkin's assumptions are consistently upbeat—Dworkin's island is plentiful and its inhabitants cooperative—the physical world for Ackerman's space travelers is characterized by scarcity. The spaceship's inhabitants—even the relatively altruistic ones—are concerned with protecting their own interests. Thus Ackerman's bleak starting image:

> So long as we live, there can be no escape from the struggle for power. Each of us must control his body and the world around

98. Dworkin, "What Is Equality?" 285–87.

> it. However modest these personal claims, they are forever at risk in a world of scarce resources. Someone, somewhere, will—if given the chance—take the food that sustains or the heart that beats within. Nor need such act be attempted for frivolous reasons—perhaps my heart is the only thing that will save a great woman's life, my food sufficient to feed five starving men. No one can afford to remain passive while competitors stake their claims. Nothing will be left to reward such self-restraint. Only death can purchase immunity from hostile claims to the power I seek to exercise.[99]

Ackerman then introduces the most creative and optimistic component of his undisplaced myth to resolve the dilemma on the side of comic liberalism. In his imaginary, perfectly liberal state, romanticized, rational individuals exchange their ideas, arguments, and claims to goods in a neutral and orderly dialectic fashion, thereby increasing the rationality and fairness of the community, just as the exchange of goods and services increases its material wealth. Despite their thinly stretched resources, the citizens are ultimately as cooperative as Dworkin's shipwrecked islanders. Ackerman's narrative description of justice in his mythical, ahistoric, and morally neutral liberal state is, at root, a story about the appearance such a romantic and radically counterfactual world would have:

> Even when our power is relatively secure, however, it is never beyond challenge in a world where total demand outstrips supply. And it is this challenge that concerns us here. Imagine someone stepping forward to claim control over resources you now take for granted. According to her, it is she, not you, who has the better right to claim them. . . . How can you justify the powers you have so comfortably exercised in the past?
>
> If I succeed in suppressing the questioner, I may hope to live as the power had never been challenged at all.
>
> It is a tempting prospect which becomes more seductive as my effective power increases. Power corrupts: the more power I have, the more I can lose by trying to answer the question of legitimacy; the more power I have, the greater the chance that my effort at

99. Ackerman, *Social Justice*, 3.

> suppression will succeed—at least for the time that remains before I die. Yet this is not the path I mean to follow. . . . *What would our social world look like if no one ever suppressed another's question of legitimacy, where every questioner met with a conscientious attempt at an answer?*[100]

As is typical of the romantic-comic norm, the characters imagined by Ackerman move from a claustrophobically fetishistic and formalistic society into the fresh air of a well-ordered pragmatic freedom. History, for Ackerman and other romantic liberals, moves inevitably toward a less rule-bound society,[101] just as comedy moves inevitably toward a happy and free society.

Ironic Comedy: Liberalism and the Method of Experience

At its other methodological extreme, the liberal vision is coupled with the method of experience. The experiential liberal, like Shakespeare's Prospero, asserts the empirical claim that, despite our failings, we have the potential to progress toward community. Consequently, the ironic liberal's embrace of community is far more tentative than the romantic liberal's: the ironist knows the contingency—and hence the fragility—of the social bond. For the ironic liberal it is our natural communitarianism, not an abstract and neutral individualism, that underlies our social transactions. The tentativeness, the sensitivity to the absurd, the knowledge that the demonic is never far away, the careful embrace of human nature, the insistence upon verifiable fact, the concern for the future, and finally the belief in the acceptability, sociability, and the rationality of desire all underlie both experiential liberalism and ironic-comic narrative.

On its most ironic fringe, comedy borders tragedy. Such ironic comedy rejects but is very much aware of the undisplaced demonic myth provided by the world of experience. As discussed above, most, but by no means all, of the critical legal studies scholarship as well as some legal realist literature corresponds to Frye's most ironic stage of realistic comedy. The critical theorists, such as Tushnet, either

100. Ibid., 3–4 (emphasis added).

101. See R. H. Coase, "The Problem of Social Cost," *Journal of Law and Economics* 3 (1960): 1–44.

describe a humorous and potentially harmful world that ultimately triumphs over the proffered norm, or else describe such a world and then escape from it,[102] just as Jim escapes but does not conquer the slave society in *Huckleberry Finn*. In this phase of liberalism, as in this phase of comedy, the grounds for optimism are at their most tenuous. As Frye puts it, "[T]he sense of the demonic world is never far away" (*AC*, 178).

Most of the legal realist writings and some of the critical legal scholarship, however, evince the realistic, liberal attributes of the ironic-comic narrative form despite both movements' avowed disaffection for liberalism. First, the critical scholar and the realist both focus on the breaking up of fossilized, formalistic rules, a focus Frye describes as common to all of comedy (*AC*, 167–70). Second, both relentlessly insist on experience, an insistence Frye describes as common to all of irony (*AC*, 223). And third, the realist and the critical legal scholar both assert the existence of a true social community underneath the formalized rules. The existence of such a community is crucial to the comic-ironic narrative norm. Duncan Kennedy explains this convergence when he notes the recurrent coupling of antiformalism with the discovery of communalism recurrent in realistic jurisprudential storytelling:

> It may be useful to take, as a beginning text, the following passage from the Kessler and Gilmore *Contracts* casebook:
>
> > The eventual triumph of the third party beneficiary idea may be looked on as still another instance of the progressive liberalization or erosion of the rigid rules of the late nineteenth century theory of contractual obligation. That such a process has been going on throughout this century is so clear as to be beyond argument. . . . To the nineteenth century legal mind the propositions that no man was his brother's keeper, that the race was to the swift and that the devil should take the hindmost seemed not only obvious but morally right. The most striking feature of nineteenth century contract theory is the narrow scope of social duty which it implicitly assumed. In our own century we have witnessed what it does not seem too fanciful to describe as a socialization of our theory of contract.

102. Tushnet, "Dilemmas," 416–26.

> My purpose is to examine the relationship between the first and last sentences of the quoted passage. What is the connection between the *"erosion of the rigid rules* of the late nineteenth century theory of contractual obligation" and the *"socialization of our theory of contract*?"[103]

From the standpoint of narrative, it is not surprising that the legal realist typically opposed not only the romanticists' insistence upon doctrine, but also the rigid isolated individualism of romantic liberalism. This opposition correlates with the ironic-comic's opposition to comic as well as tragic romance. The ironist methodologically opposes abstraction: law is grounded not in deduced, ahistorical, neutral-principled generality, but in particular, contingent facts inductively drawn from experience. The comic ironist is also drawn to the comic vision of social unification: the foundation of law is not the abstract individual but the particular attribute of communitarianism; it is not the Rule of Law but our ability to build linguistic and evaluative bridges of shared meaning that makes community possible and desirable. Our shared moral world reinforces and reflects that interdependence. Therefore, we must understand our dependence upon each other before we can understand the separateness or the otherness upon which formalist and rights theorists mistakenly insist.[104]

Pure liberalism is poised delicately between these jurisprudential methods of innocence and experience, just as pure comedy is poised between romance and irony. Liberalism in its simplest form paradoxically asserts a naive faith in experience—a nonscientific faith in science—coupled with a more specific experiential belief that

---

103. Kennedy, "Form and Substance," 1686-87.

104. "[C]ommunities of understanding are painstakingly created by people who enter into certain kinds of relations and share certain kinds of experiences. . . . [W]e must develop a shared system of meanings to make either interpretivism or neutral principles coherent. But in developing such a system, we will destroy the need for constitutional theory, predicated as that need is on liberal individualism; the problem identified by Hobbes, Locke, and liberal thought in general disappears in a society in which such a shared understanding exists. In the end we may decide to retrieve individualism in order to reaffirm its insistence on the otherness of other people, but we can do so only after we have thought through the implications of our dependence on each other" (Mark Tushnet, "Following the Rules Laid Down: A Critique of Interpretivism and Neutral Principles," *Harvard Law Review* 96 [1983]: 826-27).

communities exist and will progress precisely because we *can* trust our natural instincts. Morris Cohen eloquently explained and defended this liberal optimism about forty years ago. Cohen's explication of the liberal's insistence on a connection between experientialism and faith in human nature—the convergence of irony and romance through comedy—is in many ways an echo of Frye's description of the pure comedic norm.[105]

Tragedy and Statism: The Inevitability of Conflict

Frye describes the tragic vision as dominated by an inevitable conflict between human inclination and the demands of natural law.[106] The

105. Cohen set forth the experiential focus of liberalism as follows:

> [T]he aim of liberalism is to liberate the energies of human nature by the free and fearless use of reason. Liberalism disregards rules and dogmas that hinder the freedom of scientific inquiry and the questioning of all accepted truths. Prophets, priestly hierarchies, sacred books, and sanctified traditions must submit their claims to the court of human reason and experience. In this way mankind wins freedom from superstitious fears, such as that of magic or witchcraft, and from arbitrary and cruel restraints on human happiness. (Morris Raphael Cohen, *The Faith of a Liberal: Selected Essays* [New York: H. Holt, 1946], 439)

At the same time, he acknowledged that liberalism's decision to submit claims to the court of reason and experience rested on a faith in human progress and toleration. Through this faith, liberalism rebutted the view that "human nature is profoundly and radically sinful and corrupt," a view that led to an "excessive regulation of life by governments" (Ibid., 449).

106. "As for the something beyond, its names are variable but the form in which it manifests itself is fairly constant. Whether the context is Greek, Christian, or undefined, tragedy seems to lead up to an epiphany of law, of that which is and must be. It can hardly be an accident that the two great developments of tragic drama, in fifth-century Athens and in seventeenth-century Europe, were contemporary with the rise of Ionian and of Renaissance science. In such a world-view nature is seen as an impersonal process which human law imitates as best it can, and this direct relation of man and natural law is in the foreground" (*AC*, 208). "It is the admixture of heroism that gives tragedy its characteristic splendor and exhilaration. The tragic hero has normally had an extraordinary, often a newly divine, destiny almost within his grasp, and the glory of that original vision never quite fades out of tragedy. The rhetoric of tragedy requires the noblest diction that the greatest poets can produce, and while catastrophe is the normal end of tragedy, this is balanced by an equally significant original greatness, a paradise lost" (*AC*, 210). "And just as comedy often sets up an arbitrary law and then organizes the action to break or evade it, so tragedy presents the reverse theme of narrowing a comparatively free life into a process of causation. . . . The discovery . . . which comes at the end of the tragic plot is . . . the recognition of the determined shape of the life [the hero] has created for himself, with an implicit comparison with the uncreated potential life he has forsaken" (*AC*, 212).

familiar tragic dilemma is a conflict between a protagonist's heroic will to power and the hierarchy mandated by a felt natural order.[107]

Like comedy, tragedy has received both idealistic and realistic treatment from literary narrators. Frye explains that in the romantic stages of tragedy, the hero's innocence, faith, or reason is pitted against and ultimately transforms a decadent, evil, or fetishistic dominant group. By contrast, in the ironic phases of tragedy, the hero's attributes fail to sway the antagonists. The hero occupies the same debased level as the other characters of the social group, all of whom are lower than the audience. These phases parallel irony's themes of loss of freedom, relentless determinism, and hopelessness.

Tragedy's methodological range can be pictured as in figure 11.

One recurrent, although never dominant, body of jurisprudential narrative presupposes the tragic character of our social world. Because of a flawed human nature, the commands of positive law and the dictates of morality are more likely to diverge than to converge. Like the apocalyptic myth of liberalism, this demonic, tragic view of human nature and the state has received both realistic and idealistic treatment from legal thinkers; however, unlike the liberal vision, very little of the tragic vision can be found in traditional legal literature. The statist who employs a positivist method is confined by his experiential premises: law is as it is, and it is power. By contrast, the tragedian who embarks methodologically on the romantic quest is free to deny the pressing reality of suffering and may assert instead the deeper reality of dimly perceived alternative apocalyptic worlds. The pain we feel is temporal. What is permanent is another world—either an afterlife or a postrevolutionary apocalyptic utopia—in which positive and natural law converge. To feel suffering, whether revolutionary or spiritual, and still to insist upon the romantic myth that ultimately all is as it ought to be is to deny the present and to affirm a transcendent reality.

107. "Anyone accustomed to think archetypally of literature will recognize in tragedy a mimesis of sacrifice. Tragedy is a paradoxical combination of a fearful sense of rightness (the hero must fall) and a pitying sense of wrongness (it is too bad that he falls). . . . [J]ust as the literary critic finds Freud most suggestive for the theory of comedy, and Jung for the theory of romance, so for the theory of tragedy one naturally looks to the psychology of the will to power, as expounded in Adler and Nietzsche. Here one finds a 'Dionysiac' aggressive will, intoxicated by dreams of its own omnipotence, impinging upon an 'Apollonian' sense of external and immovable order" (*AC*, 214–15).

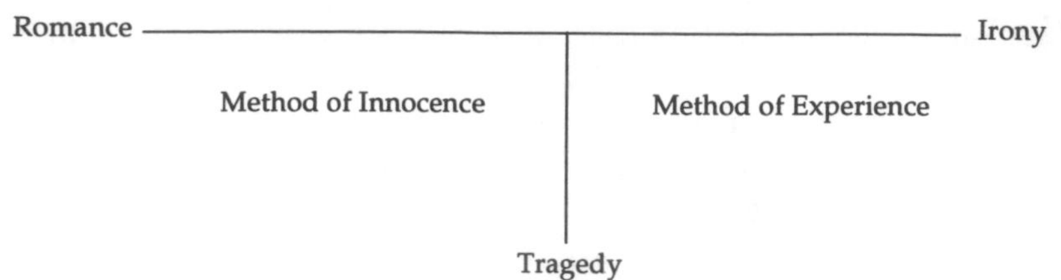

The methodological range of jurisprudential tragedy can be diagrammed as in figure 12.

Visions of Hopelessness: Ironic Tragedy

Viewed as narrative, ironic-tragic jurisprudence, like ironic-tragic literature, harbors an aesthetic mood of hopelessness. Society is and will always be the penal colony, whose inhabitants are both the condemned and the officers. One might think that salvation from the knowledge that our true potential is for cruelty and our true destiny to suffer could be religious: St. Augustine's natural law thesis, for example, is based upon the tragic but intensely romantic biblical myth of the Fall.[108] An ironic, positivist, experiential methodology, however, removes the option of religious salvation. Assuming a relentlessly tragic worldview and a realistic method, there is literally no exit from the tragic insight that the actual purpose of positive law is not to liberate but to oppress.

Franz Kafka best expresses the nature of law from an ironic-tragic point of view. In "The Problem of Our Laws," Kafka describes a legal world in which the "nobles"—the lawmakers and administrators—have "privileged access" to the laws. The "nobles" have no reason to manipulate law to advance their own interest, however, for the simple reason that the laws have always favored this interest:

> Our laws are not generally known; they are kept secret by the small group of nobles who rule us. We are convinced that these ancient laws are scrupulously administered; nevertheless, it is an extremely painful thing to be ruled by laws that one does not know. I am not thinking of possible discrepancies that may arise

108. See St. Augustine, *The City of God*, trans. Marcus Dodds (New York: Modern Library, 1950), 457–64.

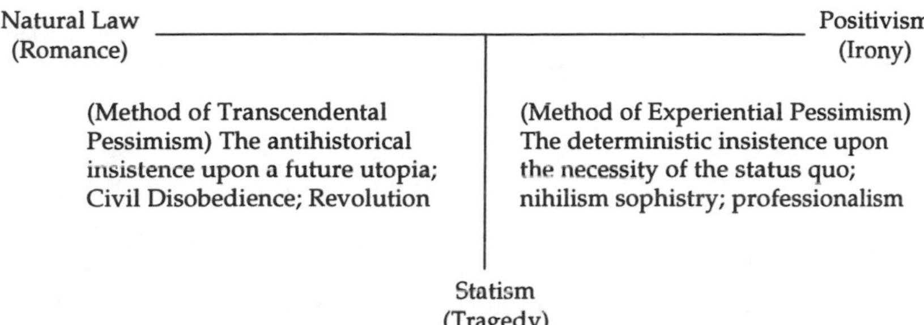

> in the interpretation of the laws, or of the disadvantages involved when only a few and not the whole people are allowed to have a say in their interpretation. These disadvantages are perhaps of no great importance. For the laws are very ancient; their interpretation has been the work of centuries, and has itself doubtless acquired the status of law; and though there is still a possible freedom of interpretation left, it has now become very restricted. Moreover the nobles have obviously no cause to be influenced in their interpretation by personal interests inimical to us, for the laws were entrusted exclusively into their hands.[109]

In such a world, "tradition" has it that the laws exist and "are a mystery confided to the nobility."[110] A small minority of dissenting legal theorists, however, occasionally deny the existence of true law, seeing instead only the arbitrary actions of the nobility. Kafka's "minority of dissent" propounds both the method and the central experiential insight of the American legal realist and critical legal studies movements:

> Some of us . . . have attentively scrutinized the doings of the nobility since the earliest times and possess records made by our forefathers—records which we have conscientiously continued—and claim to recognize amid the countless number of facts certain main tendencies which permit of this or that historical formulation; but when in accordance with these scrupulously tested

109. Franz Kafka, "The Problem of Our Laws," in *Parables and Paradoxes*, bilingual edition, ed. Nahum N. Glatzer, trans. Clement Greenberg et al. (New York: Schocken Books, 1946), 119.

110. Ibid.

> and logically ordered conclusions we seek to orient ourselves somewhat toward the present or the future, everything becomes uncertain, and our work seems only an intellectual game, for perhaps these laws that we are trying to unravel do not exist at all. There is a small party who are actually of this opinion and who try to show that, if any law exist, it can only be this: The Law is whatever the nobles do. This party see everywhere only the arbitrary acts of the nobility, and reject the popular tradition, which according to them possesses only certain trifling and incidental advantages that do not offset its heavy drawbacks, for it gives the people a false, deceptive, and over-confident security in confronting coming events. . . . [B]ut the overwhelming majority of our people account for it by the fact that the tradition is far from complete and must be more fully enquired into, that the material available, prodigious as it looks, is still too meager, and that several centuries will have to pass before it becomes really adequate.[111]

If a party were to denounce the existence of the nobility, Kafka concludes, it would have the support of the people. And yet—and here the tragic implications of Kafka's irony far exceed those of the irony employed by even critical legal scholars—such a movement can never truly come to fruition, for no one can truly denounce the nobility. To do so would be to denounce the one unquestionable law we do have—the law of the nobility—and we cannot deprive ourselves of that one reliable law. Following Kafka's logic, it is a part of our nature to submit, not to a loving authority, as the romantic natural lawyer has it, but to a cruel one:

> This [traditional] view, so comfortless as far as the present is concerned, is lightened only by the belief that a time will eventually come when the tradition and our research into it will jointly reach their conclusion . . . when everything will have become clear, the law will belong to the people, and the nobility will vanish. This is not maintained in any spirit of hatred against the nobility; not at all, and by no one. We are more inclined to hate ourselves, because we have not yet shown ourselves worthy

111. Ibid., 119–21.

> of being entrusted with the laws. And that is the real reason why the party which believes that there is no law have remained so small . . . for it unequivocally recognizes the nobility and its right to go on existing.
>
> Actually one can express the problem only in a sort of paradox: Any party that would repudiate, not only all belief in the laws, but the nobility as well, would have the whole people behind it; yet no such party can come into existence, for nobody would dare to repudiate the nobility. . . . The sole visible and indubitable law that is imposed upon us is the nobility, and must we ourselves deprive ourselves of that one law?[112]

It is one thing, of course, to describe our legal world in tragic-ironic tones, another entirely to endorse the laws such a mythology inspires. Few, if any, modern American theorists would overtly justify oppression with the straightforward assertion that human nature is at root unavoidably sadistic and complementarily masochistic. The unrecognized and unacknowledged presence of an ironic-tragic sensibility may, however, be precisely what has left our legal community so habitually unaccustomed to forming normative judgment of good and evil. In the name of law and legalism we tolerate much evil: Nazis marching in a town of Holocaust survivors; literature, film, and speech depicting the violent and graphic degradation of women; the continuing creation of an ever more firmly entrenched economic subterranean underclass. The danger we must face is that our tolerance of evil will blind us to it.

In the middle of this century, the German legal philosopher Gustav Radbruch warned his colleagues that legal positivism, though the sword of the English legal reformer, often becomes the protective shield of the coward when the positive law it analyzes ought to be not merely reformed, but denounced and defied. The Germanic positivism Radbruch feared embraced state supremacy and exclusivity in much the same way that modern positivist legal practitioners in America embrace political and economic individualism. For the German positivist and increasingly for this American legal nobility, the world of law exhausts the formal, objective normative universe. There is no normative ground upon which the legal world can be judged

112. Ibid., 121–23.

as good or bad: law is what is real and law is all that is real. Radbruch warned that in this moral nihilism and resignation could be found a partial explanation for the German legal profession's failure to condemn the totalitarianism of the Nazi state.[113] Our own legal profession, although not faced with a similarly clear-cut moral crisis, at times exhibits a similar moral paralysis and resigned moral relativism.[114]

Romantic Tragedy: Transcendental Jurisprudence and the Tragedian's Jurisprudential Contribution

The tragedian who undertakes the romantic quest is freed from both the lessons of experience and from the habit of moral impotence. A familiar body of classic tragic narrative centers on the dilemma of the citizen subjected to the demands of a legal order that conflict with a higher moral or divine imperative. The romantic tragedian transcends both the contingent constraints of history and the moral stagnation it entails, either through thought, prayer, death, or, ultimately, resurrection. Sophocles' Antigone expressed both her tragic dilemma and its romantic resolution in this passage:

> I did [transgress the law] for such
> Commands came not from Zeus and have no force with me
> nor was it Justice, dweller with
> The god below, who issued them. For they
> Were verily the gods who, for all time
> Established on the earth the very laws
> In strict accord with which I act. Nor are
> Your proclamations of such power that you
> Of mortal birth, can hope to nullify
> Th'unwritten and unerring laws of Heaven,
> For not alone today nor yesterday
> Are these unfailing laws in force. In all
> Past time they lived and to eternity
> Will they endure, nor knoweth anyone

113. See Radbruch, "Legal Philosophy," 78–87, 201–7, 219–26.

114. See, e.g., Stephen J. Adler, "How Much Loyalty Does $22 Million Buy?" *American Lawyer*, July/August 1984, 105–8; Steven Brill, "The Ultimate Insider's Game," *American Lawyer*, May 1984, 1, 81–82.

Where came they into being, nor did I,
Through fear of any mortal's stubborn will
And arrogance, desire to bring upon
Myself a punishment forth from the Gods'
Stern hands for breaking these their laws. Yea true,
I knew full well I must die. Why not,
Tho' you had not proclaimed it and if I
Should die before my time I count it gain
To one who lives as I do in the midst
Of multitudes of woes? Thus it is that
To me at least it is no grief to chance
Upon this fate, but, had I let my own
Dear mother's son in death unburied lie
Most sore distress would then have overwhelmed
My troubled mind but this disturbs me not
Nor causes me to feel one whit of pain.
But if I seem to you to act the part
Of folly, then may I say that the man
Who charges me with folly acts himself
With greater foolishness.[115]

Viewed as narrative, at least a part of the natural law tradition born of tragedy shares the assumptions of this literature. When faced with an immoral state and a tragic dilemma, the modern romantic actor tests the legality or constitutionality of the law through disobedience, to dramatize in order to purge society of the evil. The classically tragic response is quite different, however: the classic tragic hero might disobey the flawed legal system, but she does so through allegiance—obedience—to a higher moral command. Unlike the romantic, the tragedian perceives her illegal conduct not as a freely chosen means of dramatizing and ultimately correcting a flawed legal order, but as the sole moral alternative; for her, there is no truly *human* choice. The tragedian is not engaging in a free political act, thereby affirming the reformed future of the flawed system within which the act occurs. She is engaging in a necessary moral, human act, and thereby affirming a higher morality and her own obedience

115. Sophocles, *Antigone*, trans. Clara Weaver Robinson (Schenectady, N.Y.: Privately printed for Ernest Leffert Robinson, 1958), 24–25.

to it. Tragedy tending toward romance aims us toward the rearticulation of a vision of utopia after having experienced hell. It does not, however, claim to deliver us.

The tragic extremes of our civil-rights and civil-disobedience movements provide us with some modern examples of this sort of tragic heroism. Unlike her romantic counterpart, the tragic civil disobedient has little faith that the disobedient act will ultimately reform or even revolutionize the flawed present system. The tragic disobedient, like the tragic hero, claims instead obedience to a higher order or ideal as her purpose, and freedom from history, pain, suffering, and even death as her method of action.

With the major exceptions of the literature that emerged from the civil-disobedience movement[116] and the briefs written in the Nuremberg trials, however, visions for civilization born of felt conflicts between legal and higher commands have not proven to be an aesthetic sensibility that has sparked the imagination of modern legal theorists. One could reach the curiously false impression from legal literature that the story of our modern legal development has been one of almost uninterrupted convergence of moral and legal orders. This is our loss: we need to understand the utopian visions of those who have suffered at the hands of law while remaining true to a higher ideal. We need to understand, for example, the centrality of the command of love to the utopian jurisprudence of the civil-rights tradition—and how it differs form the eighteenth-century revolutionary's faith in reason. More generally, we need to understand the societies *envisioned* as well as remembered by Holocaust victims and survivors, Vietnam veterans, Hiroshima and Nagasaki survivors, political prisoners, abused family members, and the victims of crime, war, torture, and poverty. The future of community depends not just upon political or even revolutionary action. It also depends upon our imaginative, rational, spiritual, and moral freedom to break free of our present, and to conceive of other ideal worlds.

What we might learn from this overlooked jurisprudential lit-

---

116. See generally Hugo Adam Bedau, ed., *Civil Disobedience: Theory and Practice* (New York: Pegasus, 1969); Edward Allen Kent, ed., *Revolution and the Rule of Law* (Englewood Cliffs, N.J.: Prentice-Hall, 1971). See Robert Houghwout Jackson, "The Nuremberg Case," *The Case against the Nazi War Criminals* (New York: Knopf, 1946), 30–94. For a bibliography of literature about the war crimes tribunals, see John Rodney Lewis, *Uncertain Judgement: A Bibliography of War Crimes Trials* (Santa Barbara, Calif.: ABC-Clio, 1979).

erature is that we must do more than simply decide that we are naturally communitarian or individualistic, selfish or altruistic. We must envision our true, ideal nature, and then prove the viability as well as the beauty of those visions, by living the lives we profess. Only then will we have begun the work of transforming our dreams into reality.

Legal Theory as Narrative: Conclusions

The correlation established in this chapter between jurisprudential traditions and aesthetic myths supports two separate theses. First, and most generally, it demonstrates that our legal theory has an aesthetic dimension that can be separately and meaningfully studied. It is an increasingly common observation that our legal theory is in some important sense "utopian," "visionary," or "aesthetic."[117] We should begin to take this aesthetic dimension of legal theory seriously. Traditional, fictive narration, storytelling, plays a curiously central role in jurisprudence. The stories that theorists such as Holmes, Fuller, and Dworkin tell are not simply ornamental; they are central to—they even constitute—each writer's conception of law. By reading these jurisprudential stories systematically and critically *as stories*, we may achieve a richer understanding of the philosophical arguments those anecdotes are meant to convey. Jurisprudence is part history, part vision, and part method, as is literary narrative. As such it has aesthetic components, including plot, that can and should be understood separately. This chapter has attempted to bring those overtly narrative components of legal theory—plot, characterization, imagery, and mood into the foreground.

Second, and more particularly, the correlation suggests that Northrop Frye's formalistic theory of narrative categories can shed new light on the substantive debates that presently dominate jurisprudential literature. Each of our four jurisprudential traditions expounds a story with a plot closely mirroring Frye's description of

117. See, e.g., Cover, "Nomos and Narrative"; Mark Kelman, "The Past and Future of Legal Scholarship," *Journal of Legal Education* 33 (1983): 432–36; Mark Kelman, "Spitzer and Hoffman on Coase: A Brief Rejoinder," *Southern California Law Review* 53 (1980): 1221. There is simultaneously, and certainly not coincidentally, an increased awareness of the role of aesthetic and narrative in moral theory. See MacIntyre, *After Virtue*, 190–209.

either the comic, tragic, romantic, or ironic myths. Legal theorists, as storytellers, combine narrative method with vision in precisely the way Frye describes. That aesthetic combination of method and vision may account for our most persistent jurisprudential ambiguities. Thus, Frye demonstrates that a narrative romance might reveal either a comic or tragic leaning, as might an ironic narrative, while both tragedy and comedy may tend toward either a romantic or ironic method. As a result, romantic and tragic narratives move through successive phases ranging from comic to tragic extremes, and comedy and tragedy, in turn, each range methodologically from romantic to ironic extremes. The ambiguities in legal theory may be a function of these same tendencies: a natural lawyer combines romantic method with either a liberal or statist vision of the world, whereas the ironist combines realistic method with the same. A liberal combines optimistic vision with either a positivist or natural methodology, whereas the statist combines either methodology with a pessimistic vision.

Three separate inferences regarding the way we read legal theories emerge from our analysis of such theories as narrative. First, if legal theories owe something to our literary imagination, they cannot be fully understood and ought not be read as pure philosophical analysis. Second, if legal theories owe something to our literary imagination, they cannot be properly understood solely as a product of our will. Therefore, legal theories cannot be understood and ought not be read simply as a branch of political rhetoric. Third, because legal theories are in part a product of our literary imagination, they must be read and understood, in part, as art. Each of these inferences will be discussed in turn.

Contributions to Philosophical Analysis

An aesthetic reading of legal theory can sensitize us to similarities and distinctions we could not see by reading jurisprudence solely for its philosophical content. If we are sensitive to the aesthetic dimension of jurisprudence, we can understand better some long-standing jurisprudential debates, which can be viewed, in part, as aesthetic contrasts among competing narrative methods and visions, as well as some debates *within* major jurisprudential traditions, which can be viewed as contrasting aesthetic mixtures of vision and method within major narrative categories.

Such debates not only can be viewed aesthetically, but *should* be. A narrative account of the debate between the natural law and positivist traditions in jurisprudence, for example, reveals why this otherwise analytically sterile debate continues to generate passion and interest. Strictly speaking, the crux of the philosophical conflict between the positivist and natural law traditions is a transparent and comparatively trivial definitional ambiguity as to the meaning of the word *law*. The word can surely have either a *broad* (positivist) meaning or a *narrow* (natural law) meaning. The positivists define law as a sociological fact, in which case bad commands or unjust rules may qualify as law. Alternatively, natural law theorists see law as those rules or commands that meet some specified moral criterion. The word *law* is clearly ambiguous, and the competing definitions could in theory both be tolerated.

But it is *not* the technical, definitional component of the ongoing debate between legal positivism and natural law that keeps it alive. The natural law tradition in jurisprudence is not just a particular way of defining words; it is a manifestation of a romantic literary impulse. Similarly, the legal positivist tradition is a manifestation of the ironic impulse. The compelling differences between natural law and positivism arise because of the deep contrast between the narrative tendencies that romanticize the ideal and those that insist ironically upon the real. The natural lawyer and the positivist are not then just differing over the meaning of the word *law*. They are engaging in contrasting aesthetic projects. The natural lawyer, like the romantic generally, is on a moral quest: he is determined to idealize, often through metaphor, the actual. The positivist is engaged in a different and opposed mission. As an ironist, the positivist is determined to actualize, often through satire, the idealized delusions, illusions, and deceptions of the romantic, and to expose the contingency of our ideas, the particularity of our generalizations, and the historical grounding of our indulgent romanticizations of our world. It is what these theorists are *doing*, not what they are saying, that accounts for the polarization of their positions.

A narrative approach to jurisprudence also helps us see that aesthetic themes, and not philosophical commitments, truly unify the collection of positions within what we call liberalism, positivism, natural law, and statism. The current debate over the nature of liberalism provides the most timely example. Philosophical attempts to identify the essence of liberalism have been peculiarly unavailing. For example, the fashionable Dworkinian identification of liberalism with state neutrality toward competing definitions of the good life fails to account for historical liberals who have advocated a state sponsorship of a well-defined account of the good life, from Mill's and later Dewey's vision of the role of state-sponsored public education in creating a cultured citizenry, to the state-sponsored abolition of poverty envisioned by the liberal advocates of the New Deal and the Great Society.[118] The identification of liberalism with individualism or the free market or communitarianism fails similarly. There does not appear to be a single core of philosophical beliefs unifying liberalism; there are instead a multitude of liberal groups, each with its own core beliefs. This does not mean that liberalism is incoherent, or unsound, or dead, or that it fails. It only suggests that what ties the strands of liberalism together is not a shared philosophy.

A common *aesthetic* thread and narrative outlook unify the diverse positions we call liberalism. As a form of comedy, liberalism exudes an optimistic vision of history, our present culture, and our future. Liberalism is the mode of political narrative that insists upon a comic, communal ending. The liberal's quintessential commitment to and faith in progress reveals his aesthetic insistence upon that ending. Like all comic narrators, liberals portray human nature as profiting from the evolution from restraint to freedom. Liberals whose methods and political commitments differ share this comic, apocalyptic narrative vision, from Ackerman and Dworkin's insistence on principled neutrality, to the New Deal liberals' belief in reasoned reform and progress, to the critical legal scholars' radical insistence on contingent communitarianism. Thus, the philosophical divisions within liberalism become less bewildering when liberalism is viewed as part of the literature of comedy. All comedy ranges from romance

---

118. Dworkin, "Liberalism," 127–28; Mill, "Utilitarianism," 32–42. Even in his later advocacy of governmental restraint, Mill recognized the utility of state enforcement, through testing, of educational objectives. See J. S. Mill, "On Liberty," in *Utilitarianism, Liberty*, 216–19. Dewey's writings on the state and education are collected in John Dewey, *The Middle Works*, 1899–1924, ed. Jo Ann Boydston (Carbondale: Southern Illinois University Press, 1976), and *John Dewey on Education, Selected Writings*, ed. Reginald D. Archambault (Chicago: University of Chicago Press, 1964). See also John Dewey, *Liberalism and Social Action* (New York: G. P. Putnam, 1935).

through irony. Consequently, at one methodological extreme liberals insist on historical fact, while at the other they rely on idealized metaphor. This range does not detract, however, from the unity of the central liberal vision. In all of liberalism as in all of comedy, we progress toward a happy resolution, toward a celebration of life, community, and nature.

A search for the philosophical core of the diverse philosophical positions that fall under the natural law rubric is similarly futile. Saint Thomas Aquinas flatly rejected a facile identification of legal with moral norms.[119] A total association of natural law with objective morality has been disclaimed similarly by Dworkin, who more often identifies natural law with the norms of a cross-generational community.[120] Most if not all modern American natural lawyers reject the equation of natural law with the Blackstonian common law.[121] Again, it does not follow from this diversity that there is no natural law position, or that natural law is dead or incoherent. It simply means that the diverse strands of the natural law tradition are unified more by aesthetic tendencies than by philosophical commitments. The full range of the natural law tradition shares with literary romance the romantic quest for an ideal, an insistence upon a sharp differentiation between good and evil, a methodological reliance upon ahistorical metaphor, and a willingness to derive from the substance of our desires a description of the apocalyptic goal of history.

Legal positivism similarly reveals an aesthetic unity in the face of extreme philosophical disunity. Legal positivists are variously moral objectivists, moral relativists, nihilists, utilitarians, deontologists, and political radicals, liberals, and conservatives. Again, the aesthetic features of legal positivism unify it as a jurisprudential tradition: a search for contingent, historical truth, a concern for history, a reliance upon factual anecdote, and an interest in the less-than-heroic. These shared features are the aesthetic attitudes, not the philosophical commitments, of the legal positivist tradition.

---

119. See Aquinas, *Summa Theological*, Questions 94–96, p. 75–151. Aquinas's modern interpreter, John Finnis, also insists upon the separability of law and morality. See Finnis, *Natural Law*, 23–49.

120. Dworkin, *Taking Rights Seriously*, 160–83.

121. See generally Edgar Bodenheimer, *Jurisprudence: The Philosophy and Method of the Law* (Cambridge: Harvard University Press, 1974), 151–62.

Contributions to Political Discourse

Whether the narrative component in legal theory supplements or masks the theorist's political commitments, as opposed to her philosophical orientation, is a far more difficult question. If legal theory suggests literary categories that in turn ultimately reflect political divisions, the separate study of the aesthetics of legal theory may be a needless detour; if the underlying causes of literary differences are political, one could reveal more efficiently the fundamental divisions of legal thought by moving directly to their political underpinnings.

Frye assumes that though literature, like politics, is a product of our fundamental fears and desires, the literary narrator, unlike the political actor, is relatively autonomous. Our desires and revulsions—the undisplaced myths—motivate both activities, but it is in literature that our desires and fears are realized in *anti*historical dreams. Political theory describes the world as the theorist sees it. For Frye, the literary forum for our desires is thus sharply distinguishable from the historical and the political. Although a part *of* the world, literature is not strictly *about* the world. Knowing the literary component of something is not a way of knowing historical reality. As the formalist insists that legal categories transcend particular cases, Frye insists that literature is ultimately about something other than the momentary, contingent world. Although it evidences our desires and arises from them, ultimately it is about and only responsible to itself (*AC*, 3–29, 350–54).

This formalistic characterization of the relationship of political history and literature is as controversial to modern literary theorists as is legal formalism to modern legal theorists. The modern literary realist is inclined to see narrative literature not as a self-contained metaphor, but as essentially as much a description of the world and our place within it as any historical tract or sociological study. On such a view, there is no meaningful distinction between literary narrative and any nonfictional prose. Thus, Terry Eagleton criticizes Frye's *Anatomy of Criticism* for, among other things, portraying literature as "not a way of knowing reality but a kind of collective utopian dreaming which has gone on throughout history, an expression of those fundamental human desires which have given rise to civilization itself, but which are never fully satisfied there." Eagleton goes on to speculate as to why literature is distinguished from history in Frye's theory:

> Frye's work emphasizes as it does the utopian root of literature because it is marked by a deep fear of the actual social world, a distaste for history itself. In literature, and in literature alone, one can shake off the sordid "externalities" of referential language and discover a spiritual home. . . . Actual history is for Frye bondage and determinism, and literature remains the one place where we can be free. It is worth asking what kind of history we have been living through for this theory to be even remotely convincing. . . . In one sense it is scornfully "anti-humanist," decentring the individual human subject and centring all on the collective literary system itself; in another sense it is the work of a committed Christian humanist (Frye is a clergyman), for whom the dynamic which drives literature and civilization—desire—will finally be fulfilled only in the kingdom of God.[122]

But Eagleton's recapitulation of Frye's vision of literature, intended critically, is actually revealed in the variation that appears in legal theory. Jurisprudence surely evidences a profound "distaste for history" and a "deep fear of the actual social world" and also seems to represent, at least to the theorist, the forum in which we can be free. The persistent use of the narrative hypothetical highlights the legal theorist's antihistorical view of theory. Ackerman's Commander and Dworkin's Hercules are not a "sign" for a Supreme Court justice; Hercules is the romantic hero of a romantic story. Holmes's "bad man" is no more referential than is Hercules. The bad man is not a sign for a pathological criminal, but a figure in Holmes's ironic rendering of legality. The narrative component of jurisprudence, like Frye's description of literature, seems driven by the fundamental human desires that have made civilization possible, but that have never been fully satisfied there and may not be fully realizable there. It seems to share with literature the attempt to articulate both the utopian and the demonic alternatives to history.

122. Terry Eagleton, *Literary Theory: An Introduction* (Minneapolis: University of Minnesota Press, 1983), 93.

Frye's insistence upon the distinctive autonomy and ahistoricity of literature is strengthened, in fact, by the similarity between narrative and jurisprudential categories. The narrative in jurisprudence does serve a peculiarly autonomous function: it uniquely allows the theorist to transcend history through imagination and speculation. The correlation also indicates, of course, that this state of autonomy is not sufficient to bring forth what we have traditionally called narrative literature.[123] The same ahistorical bent, and even the same generic plots, are found in our theoretical writings on the nature of law. We surely can conclude from this correlation that literature, like legal theory, is merely a branch of political rhetoric. But we are equally free to infer that legal theory, like literature, is *not* a product of our political will alone. In that case, an understanding of narrative may add a new dimension to our understanding of the values, both political and nonpolitical, underlying legal theory.

Imaginative Autonomy and Our Moral Experience of Law

Legal theory is a product not only of our philosophical commitments and political will, but also of our narrative imagination. The relatively autonomous world of narrative provides the legal theorist with moral freedom to translate dreams and nightmares into narrative stories of moral choices set in fictive worlds. Reading legal theory as narrative forces us to focus upon our imaginative choices—our responsibility for the worlds we, as theorists, create with words.

Narrative vision, more autonomous than philosophical and political vision, poses choices not open to the empiricist. Similarly, narrative method poses a choice that philosophical and political analysis often lacks. Only in recognizing this role of narrative vision and method can we appreciate the moral significance of our legal theory. The narrative in legal theory, like all narrative, brings us face to face with our moral selves, our moral options, and our capacity for moral action.

The legal theorist's narrative visions, unlike empirical descriptions of reality, do not aim for accuracy. The comic and tragic undisplaced myths that are the core of narrative do not try to describe

123. Eagleton expresses this view. See ibid., 1–16.

the world accurately. We are not compelled to accept or reject an aesthetic vision of human nature that appears in a novel or in a legal theory; we need not accept Dworkin's or Holmes's aesthetic premises any more than we need accept D. H. Lawrence's depiction of human sexuality. Dworkin's apocalyptic, principled legal heaven is not a world we judge by its descriptive accuracy. Although based on a more or less articulable description of human nature, the description is a part of narrative, not fact. Dworkin's Hercules is a romantic hero, not a description of ideal judicial conduct. He is a romanticization of the reasonableness of authority, and his world romanticizes reason itself. The accuracy of Hercules and his world is beside the point: rather, we must ask whether the imaginative vision Dworkin presents is attractive or repulsive, whether it is true not to this world, but to our hopes for the world.

Is Hercules genuinely heroic? Do we find his legal world desirable? Our answers to these questions reveal something about us and the role of law, authority, and reason in our dreams and nightmares. The narrative visions that recur in legal theory lead us to focus upon ourselves and the possibilities we envision for ourselves in a way that strict empiricism does not allow. The narrative vision in legal theory helps us understand our own internal experience of the real world and our idealistic hopes for it. At its best, the descriptive component of the narrative in legal theory can lead us to reexamine our initial experiences of authority, to reassess our early reactions to relationships based on reason and power, and to formulate a wiser, more self-reflective vision of the future moral possibilities of the law.

Similarly, the methodological component of legal theory, read as narrative, reveals a moral choice that a purely analytical reading will often obscure. We are not driven in any sense to choose between romantic and ironic narrative modes. The choice between irony and romance is a free choice between a method of discovery of the actual and a moral quest for the ideal. What choice we make depends not on our philosophical commitments, but on whether we trust the world, whether we have hope for it, whether we find it interesting and are comfortable in it, and which method we find more useful, more compelling, more strategic, and even more fun. The theoretical methods to which we subscribe or with which we feel ourselves in agreement reveal a range of nonintellectual, affective human experiences and autonomous human choices.

Our choice of vision and method in legal theory thus reflects our hopes for the world and our vision of our own role within it. The various protagonists created by legal theorists are not signs for the virtues and dangers of legality, any more than a landscape is a road map. They are not *about* our world—they, like the law itself, are a part *of* our artificial world. Like law itself, they are creations of our desires, fears, and imagination. To the extent that legal theory is narrative, however, it is also art. Therefore we must decide not whether the worlds we envision are true or false, right or wrong. Rather we must decide whether they are attractive or repulsive, beautiful or ugly. Our acceptance or rejection of these aesthetic visions will in turn influence the historical choices we must make. The aesthetic quality of our art, like the quality of our play, deeply affects our lives: our imaginings are not only a part of our present, but a way of determining the limits of our future. This effect can be quite immediate, for although the literary narrator has a detached relation to his hero, we have a pronounced habit of quickly becoming the legal actors we like to imagine.

Of course, not only legal theorists need to be more sensitive to the aesthetic dimension of their thinking on law. Judges, legislators, and lawyers also make methodological and visionary choices, and must refer to their personal histories when formulating a theory of human nature and social interaction upon which to ground their work. However, there is an important difference between the legal theorist and the legal actor: judges, legislators, and lawyers, if acting responsibly, keep the narrative instincts separate from the act of lawmaking, or at least weigh them against other institutional concerns.

Legal theorists, on the contrary, can and should give full rein to their imaginative, utopian instinct. Legal theorists do not make law: they do not decide cases, vote on bills, or undertake the representation of clients and hence the furtherance of those clients' interest. Consequently, they have the freedom that institutional responsibility does not allow; they *are* a step further removed from history than judges or legislators. In lieu of the present world, however, theorists can and must be responsible to the future, imaginable world. They must exercise the freedom that their positions allow; they must acknowledge that legal theory and narrative, unlike politics and law, ultimately are forms of artistic play. We will more fully understand the moral significance of our legal theory once its true nature is acknowledged.

Chapter 9

Narrative, Responsibility, and Death

Stories and Rights

Lawyers are in the business of telling stories and arguing about rights. Sometimes of course these activities overlap: lawyers often tell stories in the course of constructing arguments about rights, and when telling stories, arguments about rights often, if not typically, intrude. Furthermore, various points of legal doctrine themselves demand recourse to stories and the narrative voice. The causation requirement in tort law obviously invites stories: we decide who caused what, basically, by reciting contrasting stories of the injury-causing event, and then decide liability based on, at best, a situated, intuitive judgment of which story seems most compelling.[1] The mitigation stage of a sentencing hearing similarly invites recourse to stories as a means of specifying rights and liabilities.[2] Simply put, stories are a part, and seemingly an indispensable part, of the law with which rights are protected, and as a consequence, storytelling and rights construction inevitably intertwine.

1. For a full discussion of the causation requirement and the impossibility of reducing cause to either fact or law, see Wex S. Malone, "Ruminations on Cause in Fact," *Stanford Law Review* 9 (1956): 60–99. The classic critique of the cause requirement in tort law, and attempt to devise a system of liability that does not employ it, is R. H. Coase, "The Problem of Social Cost," *Journal of Law and Economics* 3 (1960): 1–44. See also Guido Calabresi, *The Costs of Accidents: A Legal and Economic Analysis* (New Haven: Yale University Press, 1970), which defends a theory of tort liability that dispenses with the need to show cause altogether. A defense of the cause requirement, and its use of ordinary, narrative language, appears in Richard Epstein, "A Theory of Strict Liability," *Journal of Legal Studies* 2 (1973): 151–221.

2. F. Lee Bailey and Henry B. Rothblatt, *Fundamentals of Criminal Advocacy*, (Rochester, N.Y.: Lawyers Co-operative Publishing Company, 1974), sec 629; Allen and Rosen, *Criminal Law Advocacy: Criminal Defense Techniques*, (1990), chap. 40.

Nevertheless, stories and rights are discrete tools of the trade, and telling stories and arguing over rights are discrete activities. We know when we are doing one and when we are doing the other. We have a sense, in a torts case, that we are doing something quite different when we lapse into a story about what the farmer did or didn't do to the cowboy, as a means of specifying causation, from what we are doing when we argue about whether farmers and cowboys have rights that might settle the dispute without need of the gap-filling story. Similarly, we have a sense in a criminal case of something very different happening when a defendant's life story is told for the express purpose of mitigating the harshness of a sentence, from what is happening when we argue about whether a right was violated, which might serve as a trigger of his liberty instead. These things feel like different sorts of activities. Minimally, we can say with confidence that storytelling and rights talk require of the lawyer contrasting skills and talents and inspire very different reactions in the lawyer's audience.

But the dual nature of the lawyer's role may signify much more, or at least it has been the burden of a great deal of scholarship over the last ten years or so to claim as much. It may be that the dual nature of the lawyer's business, lawyer as storyteller on the one hand and rights talker on the other, reflects not a seamless web of legal doctrine, practices, and systems that at different points require of the lawyer different skills, but rather a legal system and set of practices that rely on two contrasting mechanisms for resolving social conflicts and for organizing a community against internal divisiveness. Those contrasting mechanisms may in turn rest on contrasting visions of what it means to be a community in the first place. We can certainly imagine communities unlike our own in which one such method is used to the exclusion of the other. Thus, a community might be organized, for example, solely around rights: in such a world, each individual has rights that cannot be invaded by other individuals or by the state without a compelling or overriding justification. When an invasion arguably occurs, either the individuals involved or their agents would have to ascertain what rights are possessed by whom, and what sort of compensation is owed for their violation. Alternatively, a community might be organized exclusively around unifying narratives that specify what roles are to be filled by whom.

When conflict arises, the individuals or their agents would each tell their own story to an arbiter, or elder, who would bear responsibility for weaving their stories back into the fabric of the larger society.

We might plausibly characterize our own legal culture as somewhere in the middle of these extremes. Sometimes we resolve conflicts through arguing about rights, and sometimes we resolve conflicts by employing communal narratives. In very complicated ways, our legal system expects and facilitates the use of both mechanisms, even in the same case. We might, then, characterize the work of lawyers as furthering, as well as reflecting, each of these forms of conflict resolution and, implicitly, each of the underlying visions of society on which that form rests. When lawyers resolve conflicts by telling stories, they contribute to the creation of one sort of community, and when they resolve conflicts by arguing about rights, they contribute to the creation of a community organized in that very different fashion.

Over the last decade, by virtue of a range of interlocking intellectual currents, a broad normative question has been raised about the moral value of rights talk on the one hand, and storytelling on the other, as competing ways of organizing both society and the conflicts to which social living gives rise. An implicit question about the moral value of the lawyer's role has followed. The question is this: Are there any overriding moral differences between storytelling and rights construction, such that one form of resolving social conflict is inherently better than the other? Is the form of society presupposed and furthered by rights talk morally superior or morally inferior to the form of society presupposed by stories and narrative? Is it the case, for example, that the entire Western, democratic, largely liberal apparatus of political, legal, and human individual rights is, intrinsically, the most moral way to organize social conflicts? If so, does it follow that when lawyers (and others) argue about rights, solely by virtue of that fact alone, that they are engaging in an intrinsically moral activity? Or, alternatively, is it the case that storytelling is a better way of organizing society and storytelling a better way of resolving disputes than that of a rights regime? And, if so, does it follow that legal storytelling brings out the best of what lawyers have to offer? Does the impulse to resolve conflicts by telling stories rest on a superior conception of human community, and the impulse to resolve the same conflicts by arguing about rights rest on a different and inferior conception? Do rights serve one set of moral goals and stories serve a lesser set?

Two very different accounts of the relative value of stories and storytelling on the one hand, and rights and rights talk on the other, have been articulated in the legal literature. One romanticizes rights and argument at the expense of storytelling, and the other romanticizes storytelling at the expense of rights. The first such account, and undoubtedly the dominant view in this culture, is that rights express a superior and more mature conception of human community, and hence, that rights construction is an intrinsically moral human enterprise.[3] Rights express our respect for others and our willingness to accord them equal dignity, even when their conception of the good life, their religious beliefs, their private lives, and their pleasures and dreams are drastically different from our own.[4] They express our desire to have, ideally, a perfectly inclusive community: all individuals have rights, not just those who are most like us, of the same race, sex, tribe, or clan, or those with whom we can readily empathize, or those with whom we can readily identify. The work of society, and hence of law, is to understand what rights we have. But whatever those rights may be, they must be shared by all members of the human community, and not just a select subgroup. Rights express our acknowledgment of the entitlements that accrue and ought to accrue solely by virtue of the individual's humanity. Therefore, as we expand and perfect our regime of rights—to include, as rights holders, women, ex-slaves, children, animals, and to include as rights more and more spheres of life—we morally improve both our community and our individual selves. We broaden and deepen our sense of humanity and expand exponentially our potential for social interaction, stimulation, transcendence, and growth.

On this view, stories are a viable, but decidedly inferior, mechanism for ordering social relations, and storytelling a decidedly less noble enterprise when undertaken for explicitly moral or social pur-

3. I take Ronald Dworkin's account of the liberal rights tradition as its most powerful justification and accurate representation. See R. M. Dworkin, *Taking Rights Seriously* (Cambridge: Harvard University Press, 1978), 131–206. See also Bruce Ackerman, *Social Justice in the Liberal State* (New Haven: Yale University Press, 1980).

4. See generally R. M. Dworkin, "Liberalism," in *A Matter of Principle* (Cambridge: Harvard University Press, 1985); and Ackerman, *Social Justice*, 10–20.

poses. When we lapse into storytelling as a means of resolving conflict, we do so because we have failed to perfect an ideally all-inclusive regime of rights. We tell stories in the causation stage of a tort case or the mitigation phase of a criminal trial because we simply haven't yet discovered an acceptable means of specifying cause or criminality in the more precise and more just language of rights.[5] Or, even worse, we tell stories to give vent to our childlike longing for a lost patriarchal society, and a familial means of resolving disputes within it.[6] Stories are at best gap fillers, then, and at worst a hangover from a less mature societal era. They are the remnants of a qadilike legal culture and carry the attendant risks: stories bind the community not in a shared and noble fate, but in a xenophobic and repressive disdain for outsiders, internal critics, and nonconformists of all political, religious, and cultural stripes.[7]

They not only fail to guard against, but they positively invite, the risks of nonobjectivity: they resolve disputes, to the extent that they do, by appealing to our unconscious prejudices, superstitions, sentiment, and weakness.[8] They assign roles and obligations in a hierarchical way that intrudes upon the rights, choices, and freedoms of individuals.[9] On this view, then, when lawyers argue about rights they are obviously engaging in moral work of a very high order indeed. Regardless of the position taken or the outcome of the dispute,

5. See Calabresi, *Costs of Accidents*, 293–300; and Coase, "Problem of Social Cost," 27–28. In Walton v. Arizona, 110 S. Ct. 3047, 3061–62 (1990) (Scalia, J., concurring in part and concurring in the judgment) Scalia makes a similar argument regarding the mitigation phase of a capital sentencing hearing. In Scalia's view, the open-ended discretion of the jury to hear and weigh the defendant's story stands in contradiction to the constitutional mandate for certainty and predictability in the death-sentencing field.

6. Cf. Henry Summer Maine, *Ancient Law* (London: J. M. Dent and Sons, 1917) (as societies mature, they move away from a legal system that assigns responsibilities according to fixed status, and toward a system that assigns responsibility according to "contract," or voluntarily assumed duties).

7. This point is well made in Toni M. Massaro, "Empathy, Legal Storytelling, and the Rule of Law: New Words, Old Wounds?" *Michigan Law Review* 87 (1989): 2099–127; Mark G. Yudof, "Tea at the Palaz of Hoon: The Human Voice in Legal Rules," *Texas Law Review* 66 (1988): 589, 602–21.

8. Massaro, "Empathy," 2113; and Yudof, "Voices," 594–95. A similar point has been argued by critical-race theorists, in response to the critique of rights put forward by critical legal theorists. See, e.g., Kimberle Williams Crenshaw, "Race, Reform, and Retrenchment: Transformation and Legitimation in Anti-discrimination Law," *Harvard Law Review* 100 (1988): 1331–87.

9. Cf. Maine, *Ancient Law*.

the very activity is itself profoundly moral work. Every argument, every piece of rights talk, reaffirms the community's commitment to respect each individual and her rights. Rights talk engages its participants and audience in the work of creating a world in which rights are not just taken seriously[10] but are constructed or discovered in an open, dialogic, rational, legal forum, designed not only to protect the dignity of each individual, but also to generate and nurture in each citizen the mutual respect for others on which that dignity is dependent.[11]

The dissident, but at least arguably ascendent, view in the legal community is that rights and rights talk rest on a decidedly inferior, and even impoverished, understanding of the human community and of the best ways to resolve conflict within it, and storytelling, by contrast, presupposes and facilitates a morally richer form of social organization. According to legal theorists variously associated with the law-and-literature movement,[12] the critical legal studies movement,[13] feminist legal theory,[14] critical race

10. See Dworkin, *Taking Rights Seriously*, 184–205. See also Ackerman, *Social Justice*, 349–78.

11. This has been a central contention of the modern liberal republicans. See, e.g., Frank Michelman, "Law's Republic," *Yale Law Journal* 97 (1988): 1493–1537; and Cass R. Sunstein, "Beyond the Republican Revival," *Yale Law Journal* 97 (1988): 1539–90.

12. See James Boyd White, *Justice as Translation: An Essay in Cultural and Legal Criticism* (Chicago: Univrsity of Chicago Press, 1990); James Boyd White, "What Can a Lawyer Learn from Literature?" review of Richard A. Posner, *Law and Literature: A Misunderstood Relation Harvard Law Review* 102 (1989): 2014–47; Gerald P. Lopez, "Lay Lawyering," *UCLA Law Review* 32 (1984): 1–60; Kim Lane Scheppele, "Telling Stories," *Michigan Law Review* 87 (1989): 2073–98; Symposium on "Law and Literature," *Mercer Law Review* 39 (1988): 739–935; Symposium: "Law and Literature," *Texas Law Review* 60 (1982): 373–586; "Pedagogy of Narrative: A Symposium," *Journal of Legal Education* 40 (1990): 1–250; and chap. 5 in this volume.

13. The seminal pieces are Peter Gabel, "The Phenomenology of Rights-Consciousness and the Pact of the Withdrawn Selves," *Texas Law Review* 62 (1984): 1563–99; Mark Tushnet, "An Essay on Rights," *Texas Law Review* 62 (1984): 1363–1403; Duncan Kennedy, "Form and Substance in Private Law Adjudication," *Harvard Law Review* 89 (1976): 1685–1778.

14. See, e.g., Judith Resnik, "On the Bias: Feminist Reconsideration of the Aspirations for Our Judges," *Southern California Law Review* 61 (1986): 1877–1944; Carrie Menkel-Meadow, "Feminist Legal Theory, Critical Legal Studies, and Legal Education or 'The Fem-Crits Go to Law School,'" *Journal of Legal Education* 38 (1988): 61–86; Carrie Menkel-Meadow, "Portia in a Different Voice: Speculations on a Warner's Lawyering Process," *Berkeley Women's Law Journal* 1 (1985): 39–63; Lynne N. Henderson, "Legality and Empathy," *Michigan Law Review* 85 (1987): 1574–2653; Robin West, "Jurisprudence and Gender," *University of Chicago Law Review* 55 (1988):

theory,[15] and in a different way, conservative and communitarian theoretical perspectives,[16] stories and storytelling bind us together in unique and morally salutary ways. When we tell stories, we not only convey information, but we share a piece of history; we expand not only our knowledge of what happened, of what someone did, but also of why and how they did it, of how it felt, why it seemed necessary, how it fit into a worldview.[17] Stories expand our knowledge not only of objective history, but also of what is unaccessible, the subjective life of the other. We learn what it is to walk in another's shoes, to experience another's pain, to anticipate another's pleasures, and by so learning we enlarge our own individual humanity and our society's sense of inclusion. Legal arguments about rights, at least in our liberal-legal culture, by contrast, are often intended to divide us, and to shield us from, rather than sensitize us to, the demands of others.[18] Therefore, when lawyers engage in storytelling, they are participating, however fleetingly, in a superior form of social organization that presupposes a morally superior conception of human community than that presupposed by rights talk. Stories, not rights talk, enable us to break down barriers between persons from radically different backgrounds, to reclaim and honor the traditions or our past, to empathize with others, and to actually build upon, rather than simply rest upon, the bonds of community. It is this enterprise, then, that should be and to some extent is at the heart of the lawyer's role.[19]

Against this set of claims, rights theorists have begun to offer a

1–72; Martha Minow, "Justice Engendered," *Harvard Law Review* 101 (1987): 10–95.

15. See Richard Delgado, "Storytelling for Oppositionists and Others: A Plea for Narrative," *Michigan Law Review* 87 (1989): 2411–41; Mari Matsuda, "Public Response to Racist Speech: Considering the Victim's Story," *Michigan Law Review* 87 (1989): 2320–81; Patricia Williams, "The Obliging Shell: An Informal Essay on Formal Equal Opportunity," *Michigan Law Review* 87 (1989): 2128–51; Derrick Bell, *And We Are Not Saved: The Elusive Quest for Racial Justice* (New York: Basic Books, 1987).

16. The now classic treatment is Alasdair C. MacIntyre, *After Virtue: A Study in Moral Theory*, 2d ed. (Notre Dame, Ind.: University of Notre Dame Press, 1984). For a similar argument from a legal conservative, see Anthony T. Kronman, "Precedent and Tradition," *Yale Law Journal* 99 (1990): 1029–68; Anthony T. Kronman, "Living in the Law," *University of Chicago Law Review* 54 (1987): 835–76.

17. See Delgado, "A Plea for Narrative," 2414–15; and Matsuda, "Considering the Victim's Story," 2322–23.

18. See Gabel, "Phenomenology of Right-Consciousness," 1; Kennedy, "Form and Substance," 1699–1700.

19. This argument is powerfully made in Julius G. Getman, "Voices," *Texas Law Review* 66 (1988): 577–88.

response. The individual, not the community, is the prime moral datum of a decent society, the rights theorist argues, and the romanticization of the community indulged by literary, conservative, and progressive theorists, albeit for very different reasons, dangerously loses sight of that essential fact.[20] The community is not necessarily nurturant, benevolent, tolerant, or friendly, and if it is, law is not necessary to regulate relations within it. Rather, communities can be suffocating, oppressive, dictatorial, authoritarian, xenophobic, and conformist. The purpose of law is to protect the individual against the suffocating homogeneity of an oppressive community, the occasionally violent, sometimes unjustifiable, and often untenable demands of a potentially dictatorial state, the paternalistic and meddlesome expectations of family, parents, or school, or, more simply, the prying, suspicious eyes of the too-nearby neighbor. A community so restrained is likely to be morally superior—more tolerant, more nurturant, less intrusive, and more caring—to a community unrestrained. It is, accordingly, rights talk, precisely because it rests upon and creates barriers between the individual and the other, that presupposes and facilitates a morally justifiable vision of community, social organization, and resolution of social conflict.

In the rest of this chapter I will make two interrelated suggestions. First, I want to make the broadly conciliatory suggestion that both rights talk and storytelling are clearly necessary to moral decision making, and that both rights and stories are necessary to a society sufficiently integrated to call itself a community, but sufficiently diffuse so as to be nonoppressive. A regime of rights that is unsupported and uncomplemented by narratives that explain the source of those rights does indeed give rise to an excessively legalistic and alienating community, while a society bound by stories and unresponsive to claims of individual right does risk excessive authoritarianism in the name of communitarian necessity or harmony. Second, and more specifically, I will argue that one difference, among many others, between storytelling on the one hand and rights talk on the other, at least in this culture, is that we typically or often tell stories when we want to either assign or deny responsibility for some event, and we talk about rights when we want to assert the irrelevance of responsibility. Both the examples given at the outset of this chapter are

20. See, e.g., Yudof, "Voices," 591; and Massaro, "Empathy," 2121–23.

examples of this general claim: the causation element of a tort claim is the element that ultimately assigns responsibility, and it typically invites a story as the means of doing so, and the mitigation phase of a sentencing trial is the means by which moral responsibility for an action is minimized, and again typically proceeds by way of narration of the defendant's life story.

If this is right, then whatever may be the merits of a rights-based regime, one of the dangers of a society that relies too heavily upon rights and insufficiently on narrative, is that it may be dangerously inattentive to the very real need to assign and then acknowledge both individual and societal responsibility for the consequences of actions. Literary, race, feminist, and critical legal theorists are then right to be wary of a glorification of rights that totally eschews stories and denigrates the narrative voice. Resistance to stories masks (or evidences) a deeper, and undeniably serious, antipathy: a society that disdains stories as a means of organizing society and resolving conflict is almost assuredly resistant, and dangerously so, to the burdens, claims, and demands of social responsibility. Conversely, however, a regime that revels in stories and storytelling at the expense of rights runs the opposite risk: it almost undoubtedly assigns and relies upon responsibility in spheres of life in which responsibility ought to be irrelevant. As a result, it will often, and in the name of responsibility, unduly constrain the very freedom without which responsibility of any sort cannot possibly exist, much less thrive.

Rather than argue directly for either the general or the specific claim, I will offer instead one illustration, drawn from the death penalty and habeas corpus cases of the Supreme Court's 1990 term.[21] The phenomenon I want to examine is the following: the conservative majority's opinions in each of these cases rely heavily, if not explicitly, on the powerful rhetorical force of narrative as a means of assigning

21. The Supreme Court in the 1990 term confirmed nearly every death penalty case it heard. See Sawyer v. Smith, 110 S. Ct. 2822 (1990); Saffle v. Parks, 110 S. Ct. 1257 (1990); Boyde v. California, 110 S. Ct. 1190 (1990); Clemons v. Mississippi, 110 S. Ct. 1441 (1990); Blystone v. Pennsylvania, 110 S. Ct. 1078 (1990): Whitmore v. Arkansas, 110 S. Ct. 1717 (1990); Walton v. Arizona, 110 S. Ct. 3047 (1990). The Court drastically restricted the scope of habeas corpus review, directing the federal courts to accord almost total deference to determinations of constitutionality made by state judges. See Sawyer v. Smith, 110 S. Ct. 2822 (1990); Saffle v. Parks, 110 S. Ct. 1257 (1990), and Butler v. McKellar, 110 S. Ct. 1212 (1990). I have discussed this in detail in Robin West, "Taking Freedom Seriously," *Harvard Law Review* 104 (1990): 43–106.

responsibility for the violent crime irrevocably and entirely to the individual defendant.[22] In each case the majority retells the facts of the underlying crime, and by doing so pushes the reader to embrace its ultimate conclusion that the defendant and only the defendant must bear responsibility for these crimes. The dissents, in stark contrast, rely heavily and explicitly on the force of rights and eschew the narrative voice entirely. The defendants' rights have been violated, and it is the Court's duty to remedy those violations. Responsibility for the crime is utterly irrelevant. Thus, the majority uses the narrative voice to convey its subtextual message of individual responsibility, and the dissenters use rights talk—and narrative silence—to convey their subtextual message that individual responsibility is irrelevant. Uncoincidentally, I will argue, the dissents construct a world in which rights trump all, and responsibility—individual or otherwise—matters not at all, while the majority creates a world in which responsibility is all and rights all but disappear.

Both outcomes, both methods, and both visions of community, I suggest, are untenable. The majority opinions suffer from their steadfast refusal to accord individual rights their due, and the consequence really is, as the dissents argue, that the freedom of all of us, not just the lives or liberties of these defendants, has been significantly restrained. The dissents suffer from their equally steadfast refusal to consider the cases before them in terms of responsibility, either societal or individual, for the horrendous misery incurred by victims and perpetrators of violent crime. The consequence is that the dissents fail to address either the subtextual message of the narrative voice in the conservatives' opinion—that the individual, and the individual alone, is responsible for these crimes—or the human reality that demands that some such message be supplied—the need, in these cases compelling, to assign responsibility for acts that in their brutality are almost impossible to fathom.

The Cases

In a series of cases in the 1990 term, the Supreme Court narrowed drastically the scope of habeas corpus relief accorded unconstitu-

22. See, e.g., Sawyer, 110 S.Ct. 2825; Saffles, 110 S.Ct. 1259; Clemons, 110 S.Ct. 1444–45; Boyde, 110 S.Ct. 1494.

tionally detained or excluded citizens, broadened the states' power to narrow the scope of the jury's discretion to hear evidence that might mitigate a criminal defendant's blameworthiness and, hence, the sentence, upheld a trial judge's instruction to jurors not to be moved by their sympathy for the defendant and hence impose a lenient sentence and let stand a death sentence, imposed on the heels of a prosecutorial argument to the jury that had falsely suggested that the jury's verdict would be only advisory.[23] By so doing, the Court broadened considerably the states' power to put to death criminal defendants charged with capital crimes. Each of these cases prompted an eloquent dissent from the liberal minority, decrying the majority's abrupt and (it should be noted) activist abridgment of the writ of habeas corpus, their cavalier disregard of the constitutional rights of defendants, and their mangling of the relevant precedential authority.[24] I have addressed elsewhere[25] and will not revisit here the merits of the majority and dissenting opinions in each of these cases. What I propose to examine instead is the contrasting rhetoric of the majority and dissenting opinions, and in particular, this phenomenon: in spite of the irrelevance, legally, of the facts of the underlying crime, the majority decisions upholding these death penalties all begin in the narrative voice with a recounting of the story of the crime. The liberal dissenters, just as uniformly, eschew the narrative voice entirely, and give no account of, narrative or otherwise, and generally make no reference to, the underlying crime. Why this difference, and what is its effect on the reader? What do we learn from the stories, all legally irrelevant, told by the conservative majority? What do we learn from the dissents' narrative silence?

Let me begin with the majority decisions. In virtually every death case decided in the 1990 term, the conservative majority opinion begins in the narrative voice, recounting the story of the victim's

23. See Sawyer v. Smith, 110 S.Ct, 2822 (1990); Saffle v. Parks, 110 S.Ct. 1257 (1990); Butler v. McKellar, 110 S.Ct. 1212 (1990); Clemons v. Mississippi, 110 S.Ct. 1441 (1990) (holding that an appellate court may reweigh aggravating and mitigating circumstances and affirm a death sentence after an improper sentencing procedure below has been struck down); Blystone v. Pennsylvania, 110 S.Ct. 1078 (1990) (upholding Pennsylvania's death-sentencing scheme, even though it requires the death penalty if the jury finds one aggravating circumstance and no mitigating circumstance); Saffle v. Parks, 110 S.Ct. 1257 (1990); Sayer v. Smith, 110 S.Ct. 2822 (1990).

24. See, e.g., Sawyer, 110 S.Ct. 2833–41; Saffle, 110 S.Ct. 1264–74; and Butler, 110 S.Ct. 1218–27.

25. West, "Taking Freedom Seriously."

death. What we learn from these stories is that the murders in these cases, without exception, are grisly, macabre, and seemingly inexplicable acts of violence—these are, after all, capital crimes. First, as told by the majority, the defendants themselves have no apparent sense of the magnitude of their action. They personify the lack of regard for human life that constitutes the requisite criminality to sustain a conviction for a capital crime. For example, in *Sawyer v. Smith*, Justice Kennedy explains:

> For reasons that are not clear, petitioner and Lane struck Atwood repeatedly with their fists and dragged her by the hair into the bathroom. There they stripped the victim naked, literally kicked her into the bathtub, and subjected her to scalding, dunkings and additional beatings. Petitioner left Lane to guard the victim, and apparently to rape her, while petitioner went to the kitchen to boil water to scald her. Petitioner kicked Atwood in the chest, causing her head to strike the tub or a windowwell and rendering her unconscious. The pair then dragged Atwood in to the living room, where they continued to beat and kick her. Petitioner poured lighter fluid on the unconscious victim, particularly her torso and genital area, and set the lighter fluid afire. He told Lane that he had done this to show "just how cruel he could be." There were further brutalities we do not recount. Atwood later died of her injuries.[26]

The victims, in each of these accounts, are drawn with enough specificity that the reader quickly but powerfully identifies with the victim's essential, fleeting, and senselessly snuffed humanity. In *Clemons v. Mississippi*, for example, the victim, lying in his own blood after being fatally shot in the course of delivering a pizza, lifts his head for a second, as the defendant runs back to his car, and then dies:

> When the pizza delivery vehicle arrived . . . Clemons . . . entered the vehicle [with a shotgun] and ordered the driver, Arthur Shorter, to get out of the car. Shorter was told to take any money he had out of his pockets, which he did. Clemons then told Shorter to lie down, took a bag of money and some pizza from

26. 110 S.Ct. 2822, 2825 (1990).

> the delivery vehicle, and was about to return to the car where Calvin was sitting when Hay asked if Shorter had seen Clemons's face. When Clemons answered in the affirmative, Hey told him he had to kill Shorter. Shorter begged for his life but Clemons shot him and got into the car with Hey and Calvin. As they drove away, Calvin looked back and saw Shorter raise his head once. Shorter died shortly thereafter.[27]

The striking, horrifying, and unifying feature of these murders, as narrated by the majority, is that they are both essentially chance encounters between strangers, in which what is casually exchanged happens to be death. They could just as well have been, the reader senses, casual encounters for the exchange of sex, money, goods, conversations, a joke, or an insult. The radical disjunction, or discontinuity, between the immeasurably great value of what is being destroyed—a young life, with its hopes, dreams, and possibilities; someone's lover, child, parent, friend, or neighbor who may have had, possibly, a great talent for happiness, or love, or societal service, or art, or simple decency—and the minuscule, trivial, "perceived gain" that prompted the murder—the desire to avoid apprehension for a banal, stupidly planned, insignificant robbery, the urge to indulge a taste for sexually sadistic pleasure, the pointless need to show a useless or worse sort of mastery over women, or sometimes, a simple malevolent whimsy[28]—leaves in the reader, I submit, a palpable, profound, and almost physical need to reestablish sense and meaning in the universe. These murders, as retold in these decisions, are deeply and existentially disturbing. They are, in every sense of the phrase, postmodern murders: they strip the natural world of its hierarchy of values—life, love, nurture, work, care, play, sorrow, grief—and they do so for no reason, not even to satisfy the misguided pseudo-Nietzschean desire of a Loeb or Leopold to effectuate precisely that deconstruction. They are meaningless murders.

The reader of these cases rebels against this violent deconstruction of life's meaning, no less than Arthur Shorter, the victim mentioned above, rebelled against the destruction of his life by briefly lifting his head, before succumbing to death. These stories are dis-

27. 110 S. Ct. 1441–45 (1990).
28. See, e.g., ibid; Sayer v. Smith, 110 S.Ct. 2822 (1990).

turbing, I think, because they give rise to a simple primal fear that our collective attempt to reassert meaning and value in a world deconstructed by random violence, needless starvation, willful cruelty, and blindness to human suffering, will be as fleeting and unsuccessful as this victim's momentary and pitiful attempt to grasp and hold onto his young life; to not let it go—not yet. The reader is swamped by a physical as well as psychic need not to succumb, not be drawn, not be sucked under, not to be seduced by the meaninglessness of these murders, into the falsely sophisticated, David Lynchian belief in the meaninglessness of the particular lives ended—the life of a pizza delivery boy, a car mechanic, a waiter, a date—and then to the nihilist conclusion of the meaninglessness of life itself. It is, I suggest, the body as well as the heart, or soul, or mind, that refuses to acquiesce in the assault on life and meaning.

Why are these narratives in these cases? They are not relevant, by any stretch of the notion of relevance, to any configuration of the legal issues raised on appeal. I am not sure why they're in there. But this much, I think, is clear: the narratives in these cases have the effect, whether or not intended, of pushing the reader to assign personal responsibility for the murder and its consequences, including the arrest, trial, and its outcome—imposition of the death penalty—squarely and irrevocably on the defendant. The purpose of including these narratives is not simply to convey information: here's what the defendant did. That, to repeat, is irrelevant, and the justices certainly know that. Rather, these narratives create a palpable need to reassert responsibility and human agency for a momentous act and momentous deprivation, so that we can again feel in control of destiny. They create a need to assign responsibility, not just liability and not just guilt. The defendant's ultimate responsibility for the murder is, in a nutshell, essential to the coherence of these stories as human stories, and the coherence of these stories is essential to the meaningfulness of our lives. Against the imperative of the defendant's individual responsibility, the curtailment of his right to a jury that has heard all mitigating evidence and proper instructions, and that has not been tainted by impermissible prosecutorial arguments, pales in significance. Indeed, that curtailment even seems both necessary and desirable. The narrative in the conservative opinions ultimately validates the assignation of responsibility for the death to the defendant, and by so doing reestablishes, momentarily, order and meaning in a violently deconstructed world. Curtailment of rights emerges as a small but necessary price to pay.

After the recitation of the narrative, in each of these cases the conservative majority then proceeded to uphold the death penalty and, as noted above, in the course of so doing narrowed considerably the scope of the constitutional rights of these defendants and the rest of us to life and liberty. But against the backdrop of the defendant's responsibility for the victim's death, and the reestablishment of meaning that assignation of responsibility accomplishes, this narrowing of rights seems insignificant, oddly irrelevant, certainly unobjectionable, and perhaps even desirable. It is hard to care, in short, about prosecutorial misconduct, or erroneous jury instructions, or unduly narrow evidentiary rulings after digesting the import of these deaths. What matters is that the defendant be held responsible. The defendant's responsibility for his crime seems to be all that protects us against the fragility of both meaning and biological life.

What is at least equally striking in these cases is the complete absence of narrative and the narrative voice in the dissenting opinions of the Court's remaining liberals. The liberal dissenters in these death cases ignore in its entirety the history that landed the defendant in the boat he's in. The dissenters argue, not narrate, and they argue about rights, not responsibility. What the majority has done in each case, according to the dissents, is truncate individual rights to life and liberty, protected by the writ of habeas corpus and enumerated in the Bill of Rights. Responsibility for the crime from the perspective of the liberal dissenters, is decidedly not the issue. Rights protect the individual against the community's need for coherence, for order, for meaning, for assignation of role and responsibility, for assertion and reassertion of the natural order.[29] Rights ensure us peace to create chaos, disorder, randomness, change, from which we might fashion a new order. They guarantee a realm of freedom from the social need to conserve the meanings of the past, so that new meanings may emerge. Rights must exit, should exist, even in these cases, precisely because not in spite of the fact that they frustrate our need to reestablish, through the assignation of responsibility, order and meaning onto a disrupted world. The lack of narrative in the dissenting opinions in the death cases sends an unequivocal message: responsibility

29. See Dworkin, "Liberalism," 181–204; Dworkin, *Taking Rights Seriously*, 240–65.

for the crime is irrelevant. It is irrelevant, of course, doctrinally. Responsibility is also irrelevant, however, to the ideal inherent in the regime of rights itself.[30] Rights ensure freedom, and freedom is freedom from—freedom from assigned order, designated ties, bonds of community, interdependence, and mutual need.

What I want to suggest here is that both of these worlds, and both of these styles of opinion writing, are deeply dissatisfying. The majority opinions' dismissal of rights and disregard of rights talk is, of course, doctrinally alarming. The blatant disregard of rights evidenced by the current majority also, however, reflects and perpetuates a pervasive fear not just of these particular criminal defendants, but of the individual more broadly construed: of his appetites, his desires, his ambitions and drives. It reflects a feeling of certain doom, a certitude that we are not to be trusted. The use of narrative in the majority's decisions fills a very human, even physical, need for order and meaning, but their dismantling of rights frustrates an equally compelling but less visible set of needs, for spontaneity, change, diversification, growth, and transcendence. By attending obsessively to our deep, instinctual urge to acknowledge the value of biological human life by assigning ultimate responsibility for its trivialization through casual homicide, the conservatives on the Court have responded to a very real need to honor and value life, but by dismantling and trivializing rights, they have refused to honor that which renders life of value. For it is surely, at least in part, rights—compulsively reduced by the Court, in various opinions, to "interests," to matters of convenience and levels of intrusion, and grounded, the Court now says, not in moral principles but in positive rules[31]—that facilitate the spontaneity of love, capacity for relationships, possibilities of friendship, potential for happiness, and opportunity for fulfillment and self-development in work that make life of such great

30. See Dworkin, "Do We Have a Right to Pornography?" in *A Matter of Principle*, 335.

31. See, e.g., Hodgson v. Minnesota, 110 S.Ct. 2926, 2970–71 (1990) (state may "burden" individual's interest in reproductive freedom by requiring notification of both biological parents, if judicial bypass provided as alternative); Cruzan v. Director, Mo. Dep't. of Health, 110 S. Ct. 2841, 2851–52, 2856–57 (1990) (competent persons have a "liberty interest" in refusing unwanted medical treatment); Michigan Dep't of State Police v. Sitz, 110 S.Ct. 2481, 2486–88 (1990) (holding that a state has the power to stop motorists at traffic checkpoints without probable cause in order to stem the tide of drunk driving, in large part because the level of intrusion is minimal); Butler v. McKellar, 110 S. Ct. 1212 (1990).

value. Rights are obviously not sufficient, but they are necessary to life's value.

The dissenting opinions also depict a deeply unsatisfying world, but for very different and I think more complicated reasons. I do not mean to argue and do not believe that the failure of these dissents resides in their refusal to "hold the defendant accountable" for his crime. Nor are the dissenters oblivious to all issues of responsibility; they are acutely aware, for example, of the narrowing of judicial responsibility for constitutional law and error effectuated by the majority opinions in the habeas corpus cases.[32] What is missing from the dissents is any sort of narrative, or counternarrative, that could respond to the need to assign responsibility for criminality itself, whether to the defendant, society, or history. There is no narrative account given, individualist or otherwise, of responsibility for the murder that "caused" in some sense the sentence, or for the defendant's life circumstances that "caused" in some sense the murder, or for our social world that "caused" in some sense the defendant's circumstances. The effect is a peculiar and disorienting disjunction between the legal issue on which the cases turn—the jury's duty and entitlement to hear and consider all aspects of the defendant's life history that might, in the jury's mind, mitigate the crime and hence the harshness of the sentence, and the defendant's correlative right to a jury so informed—and what is learned about the defendant's circumstances or the social world, from either the majority or the dissent, which is absolutely nothing. The result is that while the dissenters go to lengths to decry the virtual abandonment of the strong rights tradition of the Warren era, they respond to the subtext of the majority's decisions—the assignation, through narrative, of responsibility for the crime to the defendant, and to the defendant exclusively—with complete silence.

What are the consequences of this narrative silence in the dissenters' decisions? I think there are three, all of which are adverse to the dissenters' overriding liberal commitments to mercy and compassion in the sentencing process, as well as to liberty and life. First, consider the effect of this narrative silence on the thoughtful, conscientious reader of these cases, open to but undecided about the legal issues and the rights under consideration. Such a reader will

32. See Butler v. McKellar, 1218–19; Saffle v. Parks, 110 S.Ct. at 1265; and Sawyer v. Smith, 110 S.Ct. 2833–34.

read the narrative of the murder as told by the conservative majority and respond with a basic horror to the defendant's act, and to the loss of life for which he is apparently responsible. The reader then turns to the dissent, and, if she is convinced by the legal argument, will respond with a righteous anger to the deprivation of rights committed by the Court, and for which it is responsible. But it is hard to live with both of these responses simultaneously—an almost biological horror at senseless killing, and righteous anger at the deprivation of rights affected by the Court's holdings. It may not be unduly speculative to suppose that many readers will come away from these cases with their first response—the horrified reaction to senseless killing, intact, and at some level, even if convinced by the dissenters' legal arguments, care just a little less about the curtailed rights of the defendant. They come to take those rights, so to speak, just a little less seriously.

Second, by neglecting or refusing to propose a counternarrative of responsibility for criminality, the dissenters in these cases make credible in a particularly poignant and damaging way the charge that liberalism's definitive focus on rights comes at the cost of human community, connection, and responsibility. The refusal to speak to responsibility at all—coupled, as it is, with the absence of any narrative voice—unambiguously conveys the message that a world of rights is one in which fortune, death, accident, fate, privilege, and power are randomly distributed; in which no one causes anything; in which we are shielded by rights from our responsibilities and ties to each other, to our past, to the future, and to the consequences of our actions.

Third, and to my mind of greatest importance, by eschewing both the narrative voice and themes of responsibility, the liberals neglect an opportunity to construct an alternative understanding of societal responsibility for criminality that might challenge the unbridled individualism of the narrative account provided by the conservative majority. Without some such narrative of shared responsibility for violent crime, the freedoms protected by the rights defended by the liberals seem simply unjustified. By neglecting the hard work of proposing a narrative of shared responsibility for violent crime, the liberals underscore, rather than challenge, the public tendency to view these defendants, and not just their acts, as inexplicably alien, horrendous, and inhuman—and to view their lives as therefore expendable. By neglecting the narrative voice and themes of responsibility, the dissenters, undoubtedly contrary to both their professed and actual ends, further alienate, by further mystifying, the criminal defendant charged with a capital crime. The defendant for unexplained and (the impression remains) inexplicable reasons has committed an indescribably inhuman crime. By their silence, the liberals underscore rather than challenge the tendency to view the defendant as well as the act as inhuman, and thus to discharge him from the human community. The lack of an articulated narrative of shared responsibility for his criminality ultimately has the utterly predictable consequence of validating our desire to deny not only our shared responsibility for the defendant's violence, but our responsibility for the defendant's fate as well. The liberal's narrative silence validates our societal self-delusion that the capital defendant's fate is not inextricably linked, through chains of causation, responsibility, commonality, and community, with our own.

Let me conclude programmatically. In death penalty cases, the conservative majority should indeed attend much more carefully than it has to rights of life and liberty, and to arguments defending them. I suspect that to make such a suggestion is to whistle in the wind. I also want to urge, however, that liberals on and off the Court should attend much more carefully than they do to themes of responsibility as well as rights. When they do so, they should embrace the narrative voice that is the natural and perhaps inevitable means by which responsibility is ascribed. We need to learn from the liberal dissents not just that criminal defendants have a right to a jury that has heard their life story, we need to hear the life story. We need to understand what happened and why. We need to hear about the event that caused the arrest, about the life circumstances that caused and arguably mitigates the criminality of the event, and the social realities that engendered, facilitated, or permitted the life circumstances. We need to learn once again to recognize these people as human, as like us. We need that gap of empathic understanding closed. We need to be given a stake in their lives, and in the communities from which they come. We need to be made responsible. By focusing solely on endangered rights, the dissenters not only shield the defendant from responsibility, but more importantly shield and delimit the responsibility of the law-abiding community for the violent criminality in our midst as well.

Why should the liberal dissenters take on this work? They should do so, I submit, not in order to mitigate the crime, or lessen the responsibility of the criminal, but rather because the victims of crime deserve it, the communities that fear crime need it, and the intractable problem of violent crime demands it. Let me explore these points through an analogy. In the film *Born on the Fourth of July*, Ron Kovic, the film's protagonist, while in battle in Vietnam kills, in some sense accidentally, several Vietnamese women—including a young mother and an elderly grandmother—and in the confusion that follows kills one of the soldiers in his own command. Upon realizing what he has done, Kovic is momentarily paralyzed with horror and uncertainty: he can't take his eyes from the dying women, and he desperately wants to try to save the life of a hysterically crying but apparently unharmed baby, who will most certainly die if simply left alone. To shock him into moving, Kovic's commanding officer yells at him to get out of the hamlet, and in the course of so doing supplies a narrative account of responsibility for the civilians' deaths; "Get out! It's not your fault! They got in the fucking way!"[33]

Kovic survives the battle and returns home, where he quickly learns that he simply cannot live with the narrative ascription of responsibility for the civilian deaths given by his commander. The remainder of the film then traces the course of healing on which Kovic embarks, not only from the deaths he has caused, but from the violently disingenuous narrative of victim responsibility that those killings had spontaneously elicited from his commanding officer. The first stage of that healing is his belated acknowledgment, after bouts of drunkenness, flashbacks, post-traumatic stress, and breakdown, of the deep inadequacy of that account. The second stage is Kovic's eventual decision to own his deed—to assume personal responsibility for these deaths. Thus, at what is clearly a turning point in the film and in his own life, he seeks out the parents of the dead soldier and tells them the true story of their son's death—that he had accidentally killed him in the confusion following the "accidental" killing of civilians.

But this narrative too proves inadequate. The final stage of healing, and the final third of the film, is Kovic's participation in the incredibly difficult societal labor of articulating and then

33. *Born on the Fourth of July* (Universal City Studios, 1989).

acknowledging a different, harder, truer, narrative of responsibility for these war crimes. Those crimes were indeed the acts of particular individuals—of Private Kovic, of Lieutenant Calley, of Captain Medina. But responsibility for Vietnamese war crimes ran beyond the particular soldiers who pulled the trigger or the particular officers who gave the command, as it was the burden of that film, to its everlasting credit, to show. Kovic, Calley, and Medina were themselves products of a culture that glorifies war, militarism, and violent hatred of women, of the weak, and of the foreign. Surely, it would diminish the responsibility of Calley, Medina, or Kovic for the deaths of Vietnamese women and children not one bit if we could socially acknowledge, own, and act on the criminality of our culture, and the violence heaped upon Southeast Asia and its citizens in pursuit of those criminal ends. Similarly, it would diminish the responsibility of Sawyer, Saffle, and Butler, the defendants in three of the Court's criminal cases in the 1990 term, not one bit for us to acknowledge, own, and act on our responsibility for having created a culture that ignores the needs and tramples on the aspirations of huge numbers of its citizens, that glorifies even while it criminalizes and punishes acts of violence, that checks only ambiguously the feelings of hatred, social antipathy, and fear of the other that often facilitate the spread of violent crime. The liberal dissenters might help us begin to accept the fact of our complicity in this violence, and hence spark an ethical commitment on our part to do something to stem the tide, by showing, through narrative when necessary, the extent of our responsibility, no less than it insists, through argument, on the scope and depth of our dangerously threatened rights.